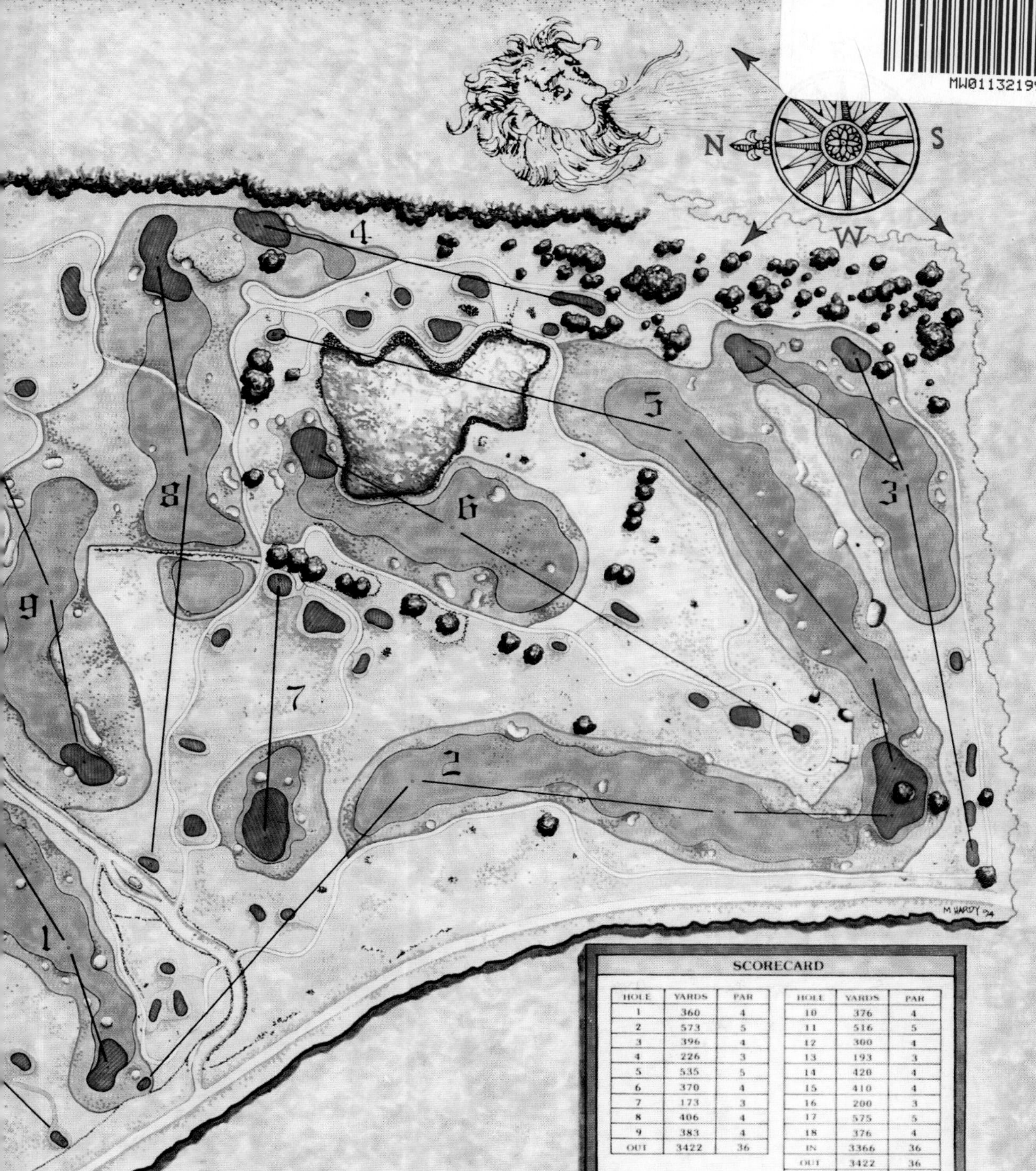

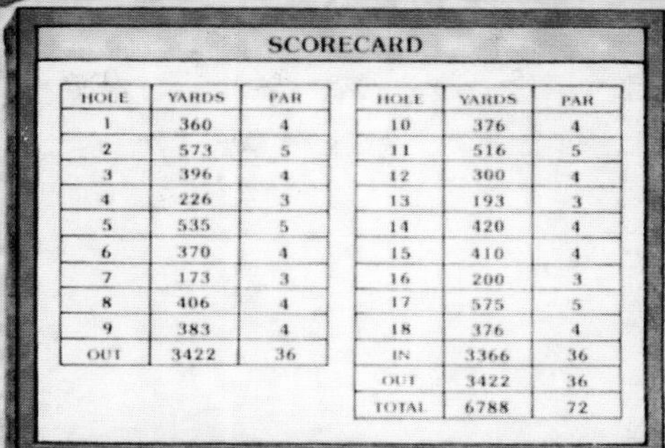

SCORECARD

HOLE	YARDS	PAR
1	360	4
2	573	5
3	396	4
4	226	3
5	535	5
6	370	4
7	173	3
8	406	4
9	383	4
OUT	3422	36

HOLE	YARDS	PAR
10	376	4
11	516	5
12	300	4
13	193	3
14	420	4
15	410	4
16	200	3
17	575	5
18	376	4
IN	3366	36
OUT	3422	36
TOTAL	6788	72

Course Architect: Michael J. Hurdzan

NTBRUSH

CALEDON TOWNSHIP, ONTARIO

GOLF COURSE ARCHITECTURE

Design, Construction & Restoration

Dr. Michael J. Hurdzan

GOLF COURSE ARCHITECTURE

Sleeping Bear Press
121 South Main St.
P.O. Box 20
Chelsea, MI 48118

Printed in Canada

10 9 8 7 6 5 4 3

Library of Congress CIP Data on File
ISBN 1-886947-01-5

Michael Hurdzan (b. 1943) is one of America's most respected golf course designers. A past president of the American Society of Golf Course Architects, he holds a Ph.D. in environmental plant physiology studies from the University of Vermont. His firm, based in Columbus, Ohio, has designed over 150 new courses in North America and internationally, and has remodeled dozens of other layouts throughout the United States. A frequent speaker at turfgrass, golf, and land planning symposia, he is the author of the widely circulated monograph, *Evolution of the Modern Green,* and is acknowledged as an innovator in design techniques for lowering construction costs and improving maintainability of golf courses. He is a noted authority on the environmental impacts of golf courses, where at Harvard School of Design he teaches a two-day summer seminar on that topic. He has contributed to books on the subject, and had his Widow's Walk course selected as the first national environmental demonstration project for golf course development.

Dr. Hurdzan is also Colonel Hurdzan, who recently retired from the United States Army Special Forces Reserve program. He spent 23 years in command of Special Forces (Green Beret), Infantry, and Psychological Operations units, where he became an acknowledged expert and instructor in survival techniques and guerrilla warfare. His idea of excitement used to be parachuting onto a pitch black drop zone, with 90 pounds of combat gear, to run a clandestine operation. Now his hobby is just racing sports cars.

DEDICATION

This book is dedicated to my deceased father, Michael Gaylord Hurdzan. He, as an immigrant coal miner's son, started to caddy at age 10 to help his family survive the Great Depression. He recognized early that golf was perhaps the only ticket he had to escape the poverty and misery that trapped people in a life in the West Virginia coal camps. He had only an eighth grade education, but he mastered the game of golf and the art of handling people and recognizing opportunity and seizing it. Golf was the tool he used to break through seemingly impenetrable barriers, and all he ever asked for was a chance to prove himself. He was able, with simple skills, to provide my mother Mary, sister Kathy, and me with a comfortable but modest middle class lifestyle that also was full of golf.

My Dad lived by simple rules: know—and never ever forget—your friends, and your enemies; hard work can overcome any adversity; and never trust a person who will cheat at golf. He always played the ball down and putted out on every hole, and he expected you to do the same. He had a competitive killer instinct that was scary, but he was a shy, humble man who could be a gracious runner-up—although that didn't happen much.

My Dad never experienced the golf courses of Great Britain, nor did he ever see two of my greatest creations: Devil's Pulpit and Paintbrush. Had he had that chance, I know he would have been as passionate about them as I am. I carry his spirit with me so he now sees golf courses through my eyes, feels them beneath my feet, and experiences them through my clubs.

My father left a golf legacy that he shares with perhaps thousands, or tens of thousands, of other men of golf over the past 400 to 500 years. It isn't measured by tournament victories, money earnings, or competitive records. Instead, it is a bloodline of sons and daughters who carry on their fathers' passion for golf, by somehow earning an honest living through golf. Many are second generation, some are third, and a few families are four or more generations deep in the traditions and service to golf that have made it the greatest game on earth. Be they caddies or greenkeepers, professionals or superintendents, writers or publishers, club or ball makers, golf course architects or builders, merchants or manufacturers, and many others not named, throughout them runs a sense of duty and pride that is eternal. My work and this book are part of my Dad's legacy.

Perhaps no man ever loved golf or his son more than my Dad, but I am trying, and if I am successful, I am sure he will happily and graciously accept being runner-up.

Table of Contents

ACKNOWLEDGMENTS

There are many people who have inspired me and taught me during my years as a golf course architect, foremost of which was Jack Kidwell.

At age 13, I went to work for Jack as a greenkeeper on his family-operated nine-hole public golf course, and as a field hand when his golf course design activities took him to the project sites. He allowed me to tag along with him everywhere for the last 40 years because I honestly believe he saw a passion in me for golf courses that matched his own, so he freely gave of his time, knowledge, trust, and encouragement. He accepted me in as a full and equal partner in 1970, and taught me the practical and textbook methods of designing and building a golf course. Those foundations, plus the saintly way he lived, shaped my life in untold ways, and are the true sources for any achievement I might enjoy. This book shares just a small part of what that master architect taught.

Nearly of equal value is the safety net provided by my family, which allowed me to set seemingly unobtainable goals and gave me the confidence to relentlessly pursue them. My Mom and Dad, who were both obsessive and skilled golfers, instilled in me a love for the game equal to theirs, but sadly not their prowess. It wasn't in the genes, for my son Christopher has all of my skills, plus the talent of his grandparents, so the epicenter of our family continues to be golf. But perhaps it is to a non-golfer that I owe the most, for my dear wife Linda has taught me the fine art of balancing personal and professional interests to produce the most satisfying and complete existence possible. With Linda's unflagging support and insightful counsel (and nagging at times), I measure my disappointment in minutes, and my happiness in decades. This book is a product of all of those specific folks, and the legions of friends, acquaintances, clients, employees, and colleagues who have brightened and influenced my life.

Sincere thanks is owed to many people who helped me finally get this book published. Among them are my ASGCA colleagues and proofreaders, including Geoffrey Cornish, Robert Muir Graves, Roger Rulewich, Dick Phelps, Alice Dye, and Bill Amick. No publisher was interested in the text until Joe O'Brien of GCSAA heard of it, read it, and passed it on to Dr. Gary Wiren and Gary Grigg, CGCS, who confirmed Joe's opinion that it must be published. The GCSAA board's support of the project in conjunction with Sleeping Bear Press is recognized. As a result, profits generated by sales of this book will go back to GCSAA for a scholarship fund. Lastly, associates in my firm, Dana Fry, David Whelchel, Bill Kerman, Scott Kinslow, P.J. Barton, and Bob Grossi, shared my duties and responsibilities among themselves to give me the time and freedom to complete this work.

A very special recognition is owed to five good friends and accomplished communicators: Ron Whitten, Architectural Editor for *Golf Digest,* for helping me take almost 600 pages of raw text and cut it in half; Brad Klein, Architectural Editor for *Golf Week* and freelance writer, for further refining and organizing text and chapters; *Golf Digest* Senior Editor Jerry Tarde read the raw text and gave me the incentive to get it published; David Shedloski, media columnist for *Golf Week* and freelance writer, assisted me with the King's English; finally, Mark Hardy, a former employee of Tom Fazio and mine who is now with Rick Smith, is the golf artist extraordinaire who is responsible for turning my rough illustrations into works of art.

Introduction

Few realms of sport induce as much reverie as the world of golf courses. These are, after all, playfields of infinite variety. The only thing that these playfields all share is the hole 4¼ inches in diameter. Everything else is up for grabs: appearance, length, width, elevation, and severity of slope. Moreover, the natural settings—the given terrain into which the holes fit—vary markedly from one site to the next. There are world-class courses on seaside linksland, on parkland, and on meadowland, as well as in deserts or in dramatic mountains.

Moreover, there are a great number of fine courses that anyone can play. One need not be a professional golfer to enjoy a round at St. Andrews or Pebble Beach. Once on such courses, players can measure themselves against the game's memorable players and golf shots. Regardless of how well they play, golfers are able to partake of the game's history and traditions.

The recurring hope of being able to play such courses creates inspiration during winter months or on rainy weekends. Small wonder that lists of best courses abound: top 100, the best in the state, best resort layouts, and so on.

As part of the widespread fascination with golf courses,golfers have expressed curiosity about the processes by which raw land is transformed into inspirational golf ground. Players of all abilities are legendary for their ruminations about best holes and memorable courses, and their opinions about features of their home course that are worthy—or in need of a few sticks of dynamite. Indeed, it has often been said of golfers that as a breed they are all amateur course architects. One need only spend time with an energetic green chairman at a private club to appreciate how valid this statement is.

But as people quickly discover when they are lucky enough to have input in any aspect of golf course design (or redesign), the reality of the enterprise is far more complex than the lubricated conversation at the 19th hole. There is a tremendous amount to be learned about the trade of golf course design and the techniques professional architects draw upon in building courses. A mastery of these skills enables golfers to speak

Figure 1. 1920s cigarette cards depicting different styles of golf courses.

and act more knowledgeably, and perhaps even play better. Such skills enable a project to be outstanding, rather than mediocre or incompetent. Indeed, a full understanding of the tasks involved allows us not only to appreciate the achievements of golf architecture for their own sake, but also to become more complete golfers, with a fuller understanding of the game we love to play. Learning the elements of sound course design might even help golfers improve their games by enabling them to properly read golf courses during a round and to appreciate the subtleties of strategy and contouring that present themselves on various shots.

The main focus of *Golf Course Architecture: Design, Construction, & Restoration,* however, is to educate those with an avocational or professional interest in the craft of contemporary golf course architecture. It explores the techniques by which new golf courses are planned, budgeted, built, and maintained. The golf course superintendent is an integral link between the architect and the golfer, for it is often the golf course playing conditions that determine how well the golfer likes the design.

Much of the popular writing about golf course design today is merely laudatory, the stuff of public relations people and not of real architectural aficionados. Much the same could be said for the recent spate of picture books—those glossy, full-color volumes that sit on coffee tables. They may cater to the public tastes for impressive photo opportunities, but they tell us nothing about the creative processes through which a mundane patch of turf becomes a well-manicured, creatively shaped golf site.

This golf course book, by contrast, is a little more old-fashioned, in the sense that it is largely educational in purpose. It is an attempt to demonstrate step-by-step what it takes to create a golf course. As such, it is the only comprehensive account in print explaining what is involved in designing and building golf courses. To that end, it reviews contemporary standards for planning, drawing, constructing, and growing-in the golf courses. Along the way, it goes into great detail. And necessarily so. After all, in the fields of civil engineering, landscape architecture, agronomy, and hydrology, details are everything. The book establishes the theoretical foundations of course architecture and then illustrates how the two-dimensional plans on paper are to be transformed into actual three-dimensional landforms. In most cases, I have used my own work, not because it ranks with the game's greatest, but because it is the work I know best, and there is no more helpful way to teach than to draw upon personal experience and repertoire.

To be sure, substantial literature already exists concerning golf course design. For nearly a century now, players, journalists, and golf architects have been weighing in with their thoughts on what makes great—and not so great—golf courses. Bernard Darwin's *The Golf Courses of the British Isles* (1910) is as much travel literature as architectural analysis. Three-quarters of Charles Blair Macdonald's *Scotland's Gift: Golf* (1928) is a self-serving autobiography, but the one-quarter of it displaying the insights of the man who did, after all, invent the term "golf course architect," makes the hours spent reading it more than worthwhile.

Perhaps the three most influential texts are all themselves the products of architects who helped transform the field during its much heralded heyday in the 1920s, the so-called Golden Age of golf course architecture. Here the foundational works to be consulted are Robert Hunter's *The Links* (1926), Dr. Alister MacKenzie's *Golf Architecture* (1920), and George Thomas' *Course Architecture in America* (1927).

A good measure of how treasured these books are is that antiquarian bookshops are besieged by orders for them, and that original editions now fetch resale prices in the thousands of dollars. But a more important measure is that the insights contained between their covers have withstood the test of time.

But the principles of sound design must also be implemented into working practice, and it is here that these classic texts leave something to be desired. The world has changed since these seminal texts first appeared. The techniques and practices governing sound course design are far more refined, the equipment far more sophisticated, the regulatory climate far more demanding, and the expectations about conditioning far more exacting than anything that prevailed dur-

Figure 2

ing the age of the classical master designers. In short, since the advent of sound strategic thinking about course design, the manner by which basic principles are to be implemented has undergone nothing short of a revolution in technique. As impressive and consistent as the achievements of the game's master architects were, certain developments in thinking have evolved in ways that require the most refined professional attention.

The classic writings were silent, for instance, on the differential placement of tees. No regard was given to women players, senior golfers, or players of different skill levels. Nor was much given to economic considerations. These writings were also products of their times in terms of the things not addressed, because to address such contemporary topics as wetlands, environmental permitting, soils testing, massive earthmoving, irrigation, subsurface irrigation, and contour planting was inconceivable until the last 20 to 30 years. This is not to fault these writings, but merely to suggest that such classic works, powerful in their lasting vision, cannot serve as sufficient guides to the immense complexities of golf course development in the late twentieth century. Indeed, it is a sad commentary on the fate of the classic genius that many of the game's architectural visionaries would probably have great trouble practicing today for lack of the necessary training and skills that are now standard for the profession. There is much interest of late in golf course architecture. For years it was virtually ignored; indeed, the texts named above never sold well and were out of print for years before being recently reissued. Why, then, the recent surge of interest in the field?

Several sources of renewal suggest themselves. Among them are the attempts by golf publications to promote courses—and also themselves—by running periodical compilations of various categories of "bests." Perhaps, as well, the disappointment of so much recent ultramodern course design has led golfers to look back to an era in which sound classic design values were accepted as standard practice. Surely the ready accessibility of international flight has brought such venerable courses as St. Andrews, Royal Dornoch, Ballybunion, and Lahinch within reach—and vacation budget—of vast numbers of golfers. The USGA might also be credited with a certain share of responsibility (in the good sense) when, for example, it took the chance of bringing the U.S. Open back to Shinnecock Hills Country Club on the far eastern end of Long Island in 1986, and again in 1995. When the Open returned to The Country Club, in Brookline, Massachusetts, in 1988, Rees Jones' masterfully sensitive restoration showed the golf world that getting in touch with the past offered a sound guide to the future. Compared to much of the work being poured out by modern architects during the boom years of the time, these vintage courses impressed the public and tournament players alike, as sound, thoughtful, and subtly

Figure 3a. 1890s photograph of Hell Bunker, St. Andrews.

Figure 3b. Donald Ross at the 17th hole, "The Witch," at Royal Dornoch.

Figure 4. Shinnecock Hills.

beautiful design values that seemingly had been forgotten for a generation or more.

One other source of renewal must be credited, and it is one that provides hope to authors when they sit and pen their books: the publication of *The Golf Course* in 1981 by Geoffrey Cornish and Ron Whitten surely did more than any single event to remind readers and golfers of the treasure represented by their courses. Herbert Warren Wind had single-handedly carried the literary torch for sound design in two generations of golf articles published in *The New Yorker*. But Cornish and Whitten's text, recently reissued as *Architects of Golf*, was the singular work which forever solidified the place of the architect as a key contributor to the game of golf. In creating a popular audience for course design, the book also spawned professional interest in the specifics of the craft. The pages that follow, then, can best be understood as providing the practical substance without which the regard for golf courses remains merely romantic. It is my hope that in exploring closely how golf courses are built, the reader will be able to convert his or her fascination into a state-of-the-art education.

Part I

Theory

I

What is Golf Course Architecture?

Let's begin with a question or two: "What is a golf course, and what is golf course architecture?"

Basically, a golf course is a spatial arrangement of holes on a tract of land with clearly designated starting points called tees and specific finishing points of four and one-quarter inch holes cut in the ground. Any facility that meets these minimum standards can be called a golf course, whether it is a miniature one made of cement, wood, and carpeting, or a well-groomed natural one of grass, trees, and water.

Evolution of the Golf Course

Golf course design, in simple terms, is the arrangement of these starting and ending points. If, in the process of arranging these points, the landscape is not modified or changed, then the golf course is merely "laid out" (see figure 5). If the terrain is modified or changed, then the course is "built." If the building of a golf course follows a preconceived plan, then the course is "designed." The set of principles, rules, laws, style, experience, education, and imagination

Figure 5. In Scotland before 1800, the earliest golf courses were "laid out" on the common or public ground near the sea.

Figure 6. Early golf course routings had crossing holes, but as more people played the course, the danger of crossing holes was recognized and eliminated.

that guides perceptions relative to the design of the golf course is golf course architecture. In other words, golf course architecture is the theory and planning required to modify terrain and soil to accommodate the game of golf.

However, important distinctions must be made if we are to study intelligently the history, scope, and requirements of the discipline of golf course architecture.

For its first 400 to 600 years, golf was played mostly on linksland exactly as it was found, with no thought given to modifying the ground. In earliest forms, some golf holes were miles long and were played in random directions across the links (see figure 6) with one or two wooden clubs and a ball made of boxwood. When more people wished to use this common ground, it became necessary to establish some limits and rules for its use. This requirement meant that corridors had to be established, like lanes on a highway, for groups of golfers to follow. This arrangement ultimately resulted in outward and inward nines. Next came the designation of particular areas with natural turf cover that permitted the permanent installation of the target holes. These became "greens." Since selection of the greens was done by popular opinion or agreement, golf course design per se was really not yet practiced. In the early rules of the eighteenth century, for instance, the tee shot for the next hole had to be played from within one club length of the previous putting hole (see figure 7). As more golfers used the golfing grounds, the area immediately adjacent to the hole became worn. Play slowed because a group could not pitch on until the one ahead had teed off. Such developments, unanticipated in the earliest rules of the game, led to the creation of the professions of course maintenance and design. First, it was decided to assist nature in healing the increasing amount of wear to the green by removing the teeing ground from the vicinity of the

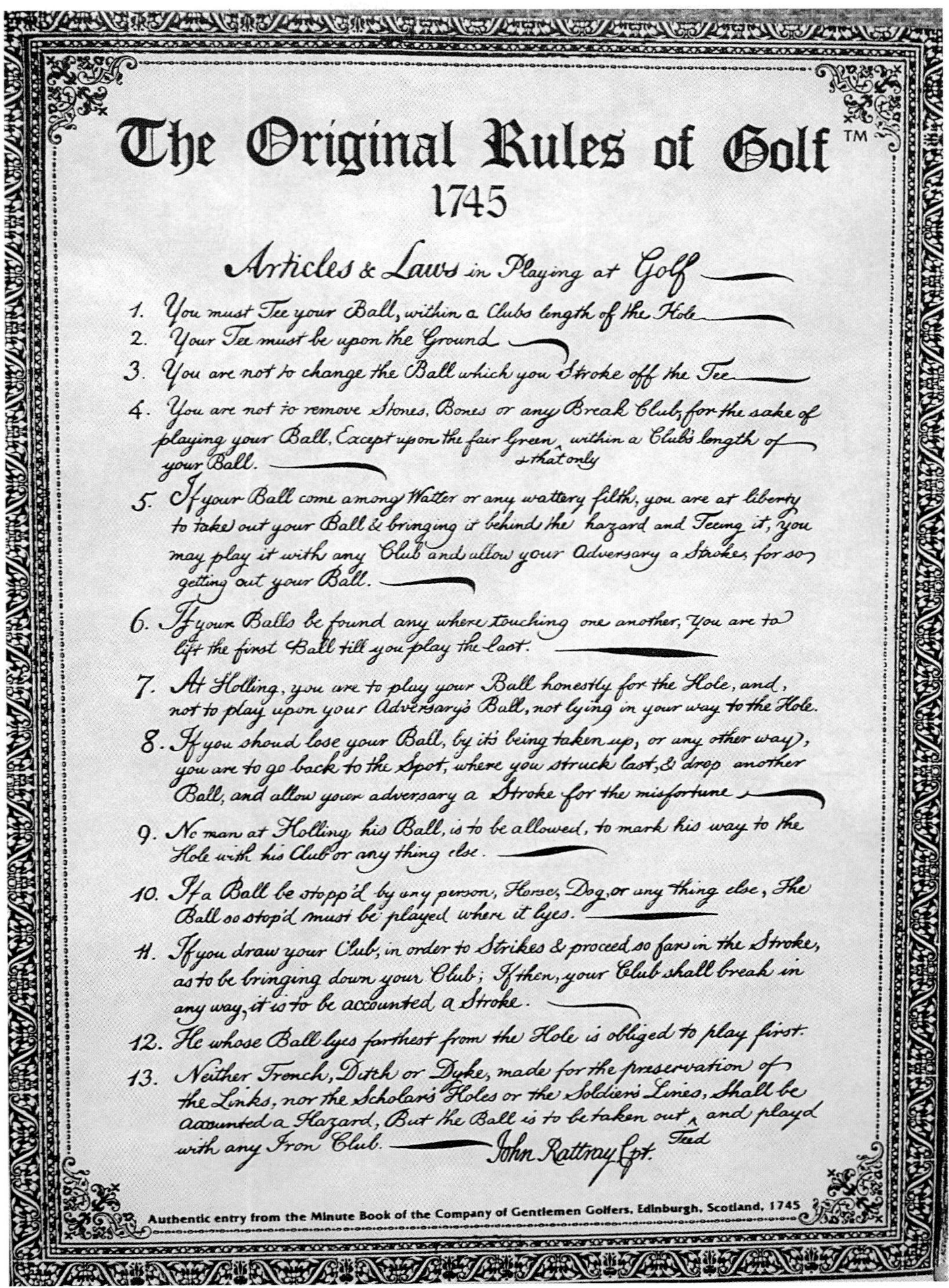

The Original Rules of Golf ™
1745

Articles & Laws in Playing at Golf

1. You must Tee your Ball, within a Clubs length of the Hole
2. Your Tee must be upon the Ground
3. You are not to change the Ball which you Stroke off the Tee
4. You are not to remove Stones, Bones or any Break Club, for the sake of playing your Ball, Except upon the fair Green, & that only within a Club's length of your Ball.
5. If your Ball come among Watter or any wattery filth, you are at liberty to take out your Ball & bringing it behind the hazard and Teeing it, you may play it with any Club and allow your Adversary a Stroke, for so getting out your Ball.
6. If your Balls be found any where touching one another, You are to lift the first Ball till you play the last.
7. At Holling, you are to play your Ball honestly for the Hole, and, not to play upon your Adversary's Ball, not lying in your way to the Hole.
8. If you shoud lose your Ball, by it's being taken up, or any other way), you are to go back to the Spot, where you struck last, & drop another Ball, and allow your adversary a Stroke for the misfortune.
9. No man at Holling his Ball, is to be allowed, to mark his way to the Hole with his Club or any thing else.
10. If a Ball be stopp'd by any person, Horse, Dog, or any thing else, The Ball so stop'd must be played where it lyes.
11. If you draw your Club, in order to Strikes & proceed so far in the Stroke, as to be bringing down your Club; If then, your Club shall break in any way, it is to be accounted a Stroke.
12. He whose Ball lyes farthest from the Hole is obliged to play first.
13. Neither Trench, Ditch or Dyke, made for the preservation of the Links, nor the Scholar's Holes or the Soldier's Lines, Shall be accounted a Hazard, But the Ball is to be taken out, Teed and play'd with any Iron Club. — John Rattray Cpt.

Authentic entry from the Minute Book of the Company of Gentlemen Golfers, Edinburgh, Scotland, 1745

Figure 7. Rule #1 stated that golfers were required to tee off within one club length of the previous putting hole.

previous green. Soon, men were hired to care for the greens, and they often decided where to relocate the tees. No one knows who was the first golfer to study this situation and make a conscious decision about the placement of a golf feature. Whoever it was, he was the first person ever to design a golf hole. Starting from this time, and on until the middle of the late nineteenth century, planners, usually professional golfers, simply laid out golf courses with little or no actual construction taking place. These golfers would study the land, find the best greens sites, mentally catalog or map their locations, and then develop and stake a routing plan of holes that best utilized the natural features. This was golf design at its most basic level, though not yet golf course architecture in the true sense.

A layout or routing plan of a golf course is like a floor plan of a building (see figure 8). The floor plan shows the relative relationship of the dining room, bathrooms, kitchen, and bedrooms. Similarly, a routing plan shows the relative relationship of golf features to one another. The floor plan does not show the structural details necessary for construction, such as the foundation, walls, pipes, wire, ducts, and structural frame. Likewise, a routing plan does not show surface and subsurface drainage patterns and details, irrigation, details of greens, tees, ponds, bunkers, and planting details. Almost anyone can draw a floor plan of a building, but they would not be called a building architect. Almost anyone can draw a routing plan for a golf course, but they should not be called a golf course architect. A golf course architect is one who has the technical planning processes to modify a site to maximize its golfing features, so that the completed site is fun and safe for the people who use it, and so that it accommodates reasonably priced, long-term maintenance of the finished golf course. What counts as "reasonably priced," however, will depend upon the needs and pockets of the facility owner. This means, as we shall later see in some detail, that while there are basic principles for designing and maintaining a golf course, the parameters of acceptability and tolerance will often be established by economic forces that limit the architect.

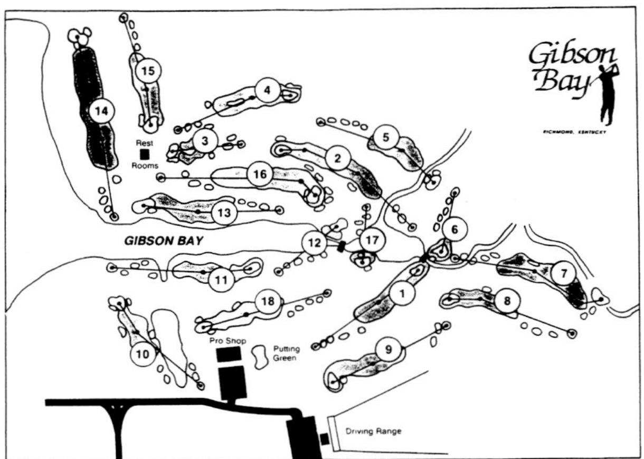

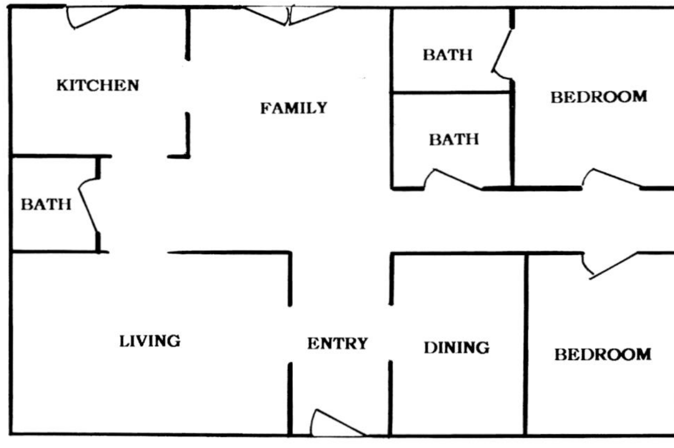

Figure 8. The routing plan of a golf course and a floor plan of a house show only spatial relationships, not design details.

Evolution of Design

Three categories of golf design concepts have been popularized in writings since the 1920s. They are commonly referred to as penal, heroic, and strategic philosophies of design. A fourth category has existed in America since the post-war golf course building boom of the 1950s—freeway golf. An understanding of these four basic concepts is essential to appreciating the theory of golf course design.

In its infancy and up to the middle 1800s, golf was played on the land exactly as it was found, with the most desirable areas being on sandy linksland, which offered rolling terrain, hazards of open sand, and fine grasses (see figure 9). As the need for more golf courses increased, linksland was not often available, so less desirable ground was used. Often, to give inland areas the look and character of linksland, humps and hollows and sand-filled hazards were built. Since no green fees were charged, there were no means to derive income from the play of golf to repay construction costs. The thrifty Scots built golf courses as inexpensively and as basically as possible. This meant a minimum amount of earthmoving was done, for not only were there no funds for construction, but also there was no earthmoving equipment. Horse or mule teams with a slip scoop worked alongside men with shovels and wheelbarrows to move whatever earth required shaping. The men who directed the construction of these first courses were often golf professionals of accomplished playing ability. These men felt that the greatest evil in golf was the topped shot.

Until the beginning of the twentieth century, golf balls were difficult to get airborne. The old feather-stuffed "feathery" golf ball, used until well into the nineteenth century, was notoriously difficult for players to get airborne. But the "feathery" ball would run along the hard dry ground nearly as far as a shot properly played through the air. To penalize such inelegantly struck shots, the early architects built steep-sided, unnatural-looking elevated earthworks placed directly across the line of play (see figure 10). This was penal design in the purest sense, in that all but the most perfect shot would be punished. This philosophy of design was prevalent until well past the turn of the century (see figure 11), and may have accounted for the immediate popularity of the gutta-percha ball in the 1850s, which was more lively than a feathery, and the 1902 introduction of the wound ball, which outflew the gutty, and thus allowed ordinary golf shots to clear hazards placed for featheries. But rather than changing design philosophies, golf course designers of the period continued to endorse the principles of penal design and simply adjusted hazard placements to allow for the gutty ball.

Figure 9. This painting, called the "First International Foursome," by Allen Stewart, shows how golf was played with the feathery ball on the Leith Links in 1682.

Figure 10. Early "built" golf courses had very crude earthworks as hazards.

Figure 11. One of the first published aerial views of an American golf course shows the penal bunkers and mounds.

Course designers gradually recognized the artificiality of these man-made features and their unfairness to all but the most expert of golfers.

In recent years, a number of well-publicized designers have made fabulous reputations as creative designers by simply camouflaging penal design. Whenever you see a course with greens ringed with sand, water, or tall grasses, and greens too flat or small to receive the shot played to them, suspect penal design (see figure 12). When the only approach to the landing area or green is blocked by a mandatory carry across a hazard, it is penal design. This is not to say that all penal holes are bad. In fact, some of them are quite extraordinary (see figure 12b). But if more than four or five holes on a course are of the penal concept, then the course as a whole must be considered penal and becomes virtually unplayable for the vast majority of golfers. Of course, not all penal courses are bad; some are well done. But such courses win little favor when compared to true strategic courses such as St. Andrews, Augusta National, and Cypress Point.

Evolution of the Golf Course Architect

Penal style designers, notably the accomplished amateur player Charles Blair Macdonald (1856–1939), delighted in copying great holes instead of creating new ones. Among his favorite Scottish holes for emulation in the United States were: the Redan, the 15th at North Berwick (see figure 13); the Road Hole, the 17th at St. Andrews; the Postage Stamp, the 8th at Troon; and the Cardinal, the 3rd at Prestwick. But it is difficult, if not impossible, to copy a great hole, since subtle changes in the terrain or the natural setting totally alter the feel of the hole. Regardless of the talent of these designers and builders, they simply could not replicate the original charm or character of famous holes. They could only create inferior facsimiles of legendary earthworks. Yet in attempting these copies and by paying homage to classical seaside holes, they contributed to an attitude among golfers that true golf could only be played on linksland, and that inland golf was a poor substitute.

As the need for more golf courses developed in Great Britain, Europe, and America, golf course design emerged as a profession populated not just by accomplished golfers, but also by intelligent men who were sensitive to the look of the landscape and the abilities of the average golfer. These thinking designers began to go against fashion and decried the penal design concepts. In a desire to retain their distinct advantage over less skilled players, golf professionals defended penal courses. But a new breed of designer, led by British native H.S. Colt (1869–1951), began to modify penal concepts by moving the hazards away from the direct line of play to provide some relief for the less accomplished golfer (see figure 14). There were still as many hazards on these new courses, but instead of penalizing the topped shot—which was less frequent with the then popular solid gutta-percha ("gutty") ball or emerging wound rubber ball called a "Haskell"—hazards now penalized the sliced and hooked shots. This design concept gained quick acceptance, for it made golf more fun for the average golfer, who at least had a chance to play the holes "up the middle" without having to carry various minefields. Moreover, strategic design enabled more players to enjoy the game without having to hit expert shots each time. Strategic design was thus grudgingly accepted by golf professionals, who were beginning to realize financial benefits from the growing legions of golfers.

Evolution of Design Philosophy

The Old Course at St. Andrews has long been judged to produce the best of golf, in part because it is acknowledged as the incubator of the game. But its influence upon design derives not from its historical antiquity, but rather from the basic and enduring soundness of its design principles. During the last decade of the nineteenth century and into the first decade of the twentieth, The Old Course was analyzed continually by intelligent and articulate men who studied golf course design with as much detail and method as one would devote to any emerging science (see figure 16). With the number of great minds devoted to the study of The Old Course, it was only a matter of time before the alluring

Figure 12b. A crude example of a penal-designed golf green. There is no option but to play a perfect approach shot or be penalized.

Figure 12a. The 15th hole at Cypress Point—a well-camouflaged example of penal design, where less than perfect play is penalized.

Figure 13a.

Perhaps the most copied hole in golf: the 15th or Redan Hole at North Berwick, Scotland (a) and C.B. Macdonald's copy of it at National Golf Links, Southampton, Long Island, New York (b).

Figure 13b.

Figure 14. By the late 1800s, the strategic school of design, led by H.S. Colt, was moving hazards away from the direct line of play.

qualities that made golf at St. Andrews so special were isolated and understood and a new philosophy of design formulated. The strategic principles of its design were codified as a result of these studies.

The essence of strategic design is that nearly every hole offers alternative routes to the green, with hazards of differing severity requiring golfers consciously to decide at the tee a route to the target that best suits their game. At St. Andrews, golfers were and are required to think strategically, to execute shots that best balance risk and reward, and to play a match against an opponent who is doing the same. Many early golf books refer to the members of a renowned foursome at St. Andrews, each attacking the hole from a different direction, each suited to their individual skills, with all of them achieving success along their distinctive line of play (see figure 17).

This is still possible. St. Andrews remains the premier match play course of the world, a layout where a player who is down has the option of gaining holes by taking greater risks than his opponent. This is the epitome of strategic golf—optional routes to a hole, with each route having its own characteristic collage of risks and rewards.

Once the principles were understood, the next problem was to build such golf holes on featureless land at a moderate cost. Golf architects who espoused strategic design mentally cut away the flesh and sinew of St. Andrews until they had only the skeleton to study. From these skeletal remains they saw that the true essence of strategic design was offset angles of play. Hazards were placed so that players who chose a landing area that flirts boldly with hazards were rewarded with an easier shot on the next stroke over the player who chose not to risk the hazard. If the green on a particular hole was best approached from the left side of a fairway, then a fairway hazard would be built on the left side to balance reward with risk. The golfer who played boldly and safely to the left side was rewarded by having a better angle of approach to the green than the golfer who chose to play to the right of the hazard. Thus, strategic design in its best form rewards the good shot-maker without penalizing the less accomplished, and allows each to maximize the best parts of his game while minimizing the importance of his weaknesses. If a golfer does not drive the ball well, he may choose to play wide of hazards on his drive and rely on the sureness and strength of his iron play to make him competitive.

Over time there also has developed a compromise between the strictly penal design philosophy and the less punitive philosophy advanced by advocates of strategic hazards philosophy. This compromise was called "heroic design." Its idea was to present a penal hazard but give each golfer a chance to carry as much of the hazard as

Figure 15a & b. The golf ball evolved through various materials, starting with boxwood (pre-1400), followed by the feathery, which was replaced by the gutty in the 1850s, and climaxing with the wound rubber band Haskell ball in early 1900s. That evolution continues today as the search for a better playing, longer flying, more durable ball goes on.

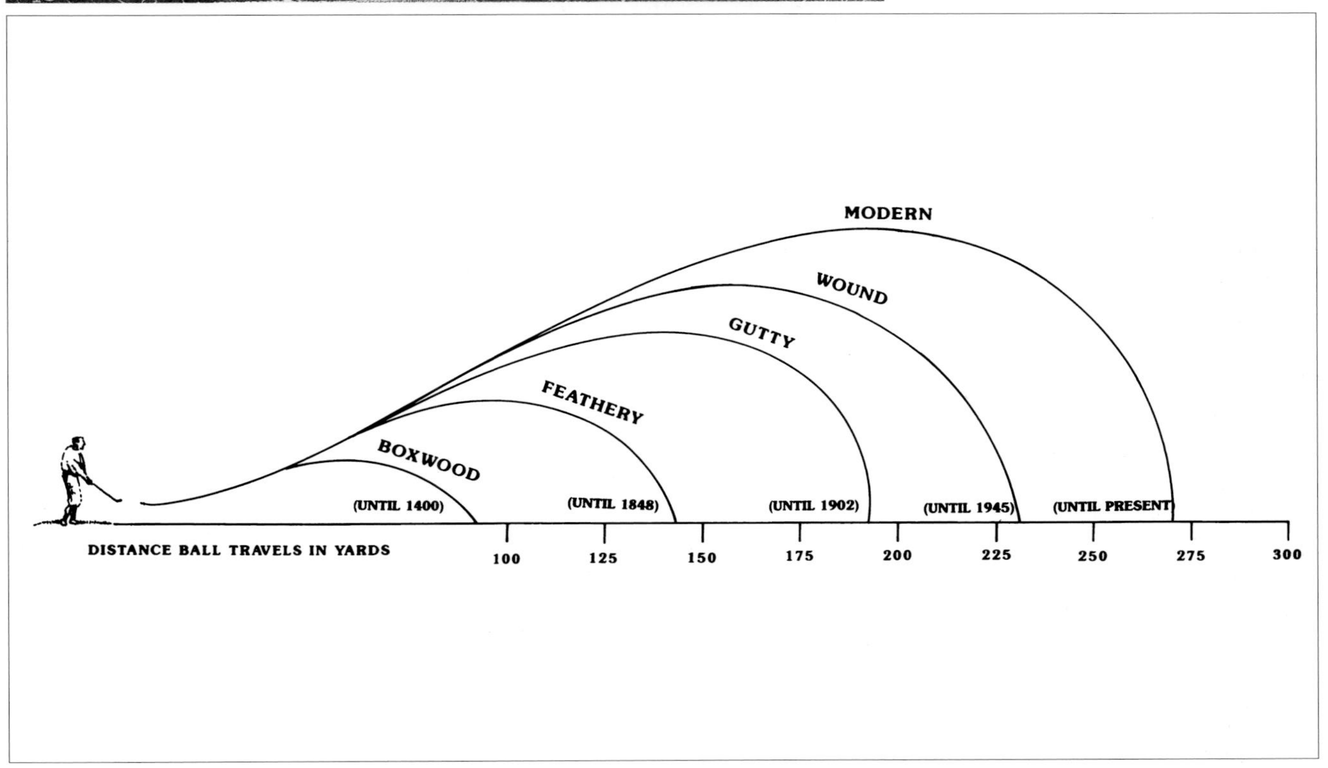

Circa	Material	Distance Driven
(Until 1400)	Boxwood	90 Yards
(Until 1848)	Feathery	140 Yards
(Until 1902)	Gutty	190 Yards
(Until 1945)	Wound	230 Yards
(Until Present)	Modern	270+ Yards

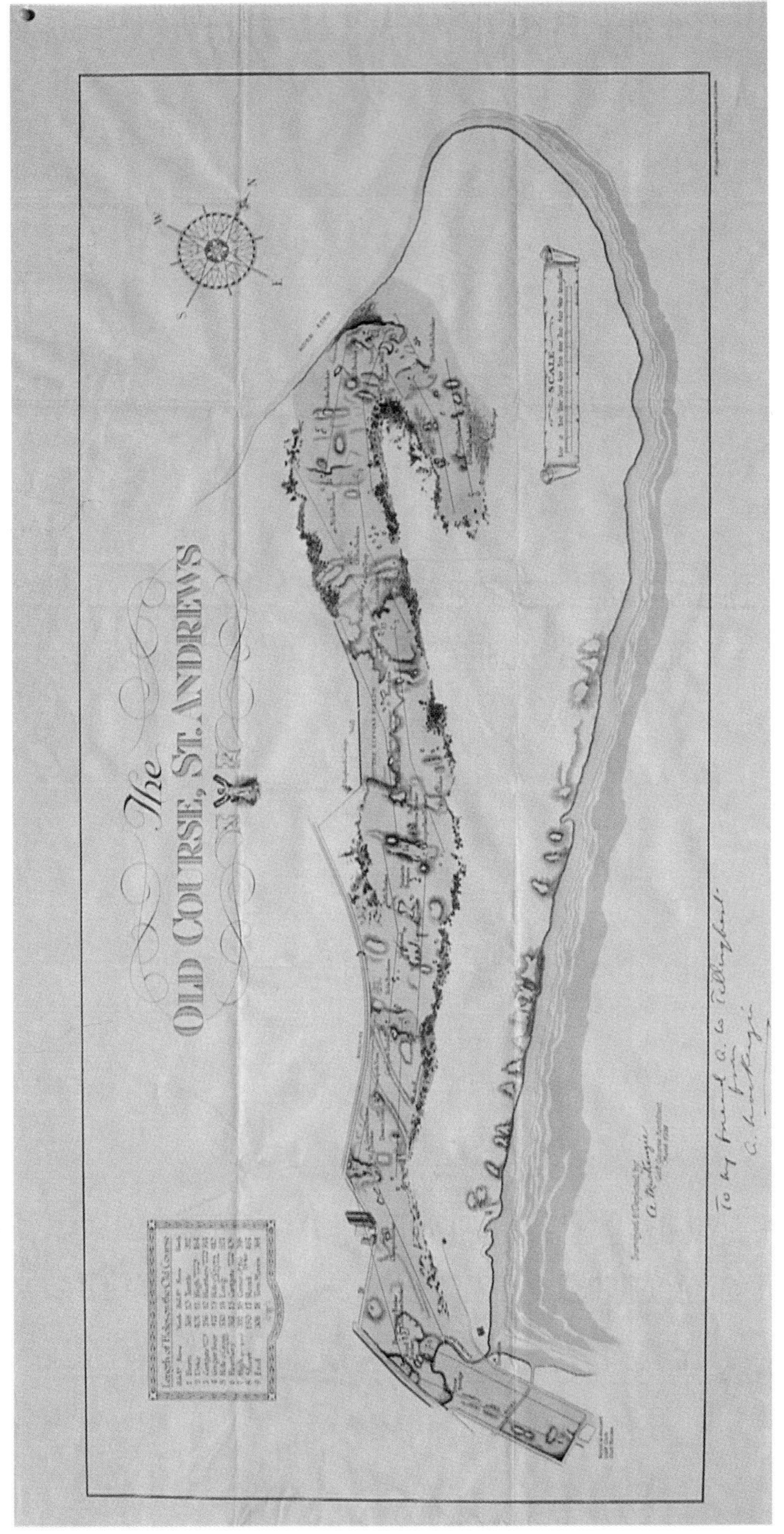

Figure 16. Golf course architect Dr. Alister MacKenzie carefully studied and mapped the Old Course at St. Andrews to better understand its timeless architectural features. This copy of MacKenzie's map was a gift from him to another famous designer, A.W. Tillinghast.

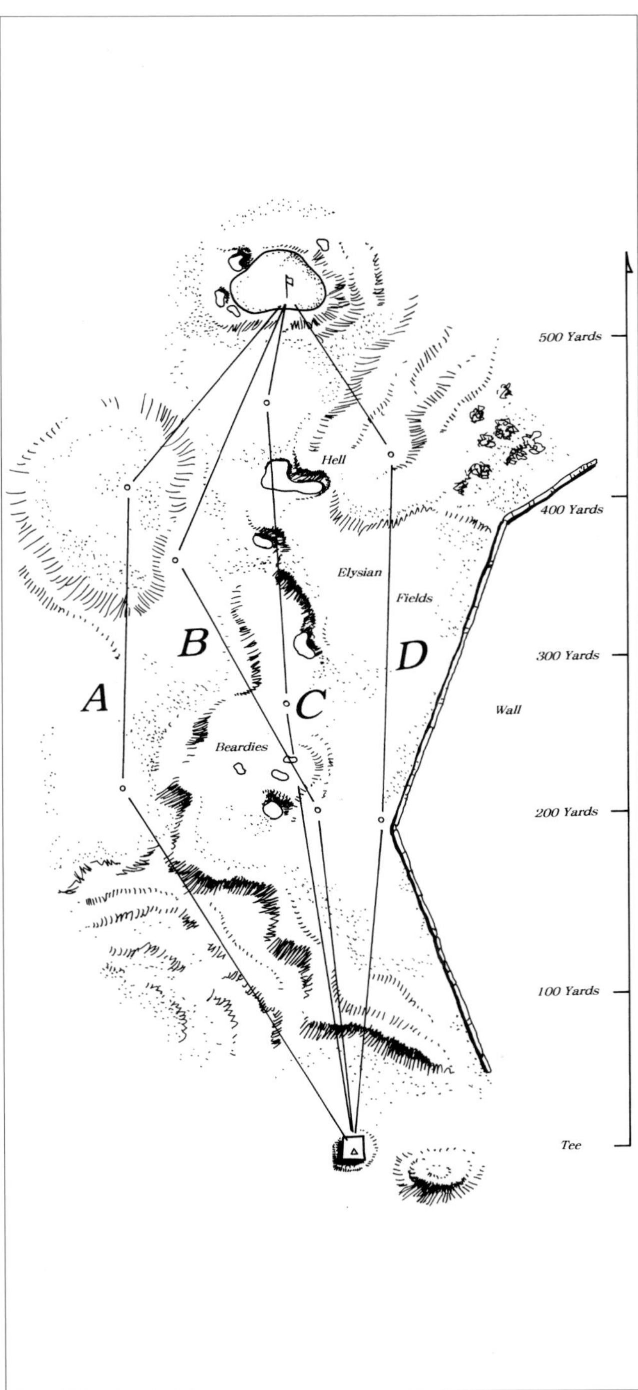

Figure 17. The 14th hole of the Old Course at St. Andrews is often used to show how four golfers of different skills can play the strategy best suited for their respective games. At the 1995 British Open, Hell Bunker claimed another famous victim, as Jack Nicklaus took four shots to get out.

he wanted to, as exemplified by the 18th hole at Pebble Beach. In good heroic design, the more that was risked the greater the reward. The timid player could completely avoid the hazard but have a much longer shot to the green. The strong daring player, meanwhile, could fly the main portion of the hazard and be rewarded with a simple unobstructed second shot (see figure 18).

On the surface this design philosophy seemed fair, for it provided the golfer with a choice. This accounts for its overwhelming praise and popularity. But still it benefitted the strongest player the most, effectively exaggerating the difference between average and superior golfers. Moreover, heroic holes became repetitious and lacked the challenge, satisfaction, and elusiveness of the old links courses such as St. Andrews.

In the years after World War II, there also developed a distinctive approach to golf design, in large measure to accommodate the growing throngs of people who began taking up the game. Indeed, America became populated (some might say "overpopulated") with a fourth category of golf course design—freeway golf. Freeway golf evokes images of flat paved areas lacking in surface expression, and clearly defined straight and parallel edges extending from point "A" to point "B" to encourage high speed and efficient movement, with all distractions placed to the sides of the main right-of-way (see figure 19). Freeway golf is further characterized by tees that take on the geometry of squares or rectangles properly aimed down the freeway, and round greens at the terminus flanked by symmetrically oval, expressionless bunkers. At its most dogmatic, a freeway golf course has fairways mowed in straight line patterns and trees lined up in straight rows along the fairway, much like guardrails or guideposts. Instead of mileage markers, bushes, trees, rocks, or steel monuments are placed at intervals to tell how far it is to the destination. The intent of freeway design is to move golfers through this maze of straight lines in the most expedient manner possible, not allowing them freedom of choice on how to play the hole and severely penalizing those who deviate to the sides of the fairway. Since no thought is required to play the course, the only methods to separate

Figure 18a. Classic heroic holes include C.B. Macdonald's 5th hole at Mid Ocean (above), or the 18th hole at Pebble Beach. In both cases the golfer is invited to "bite off as much of the hazard as he can chew."

Chris John

Figure 18b. The 6th hole at Eagle's Landing in Ocean City, Maryland is nearly identical to Mid Ocean's 5th, except for Mid Ocean's hilltop tee.

Figure 19. After World War II, many golf courses took on a "freeway" look, with parallel fairway edges, geometric forms, and straight-line patterns of trees, bunkers, and mounds.

the skills of players are to add length and provide tricky putting surfaces. Everything is maintained in the most uniform manner possible to give it a universal look and feel. This kind of golf course is best suited for medal play, for it tests only the ability of the golfer to consistently and mechanically execute the golf stroke while following the one correct line to the green.

It is true that some freeway golf courses are nicely camouflaged with large flowing earthwork, dramatic hazards, and railroad ties or rock walls. But underneath this artificial facade lies the dead weight of cement. Such golf courses are lifeless, providing a venue for the game without any semblance of its soul. Unfortunately, such facilities are attractive to owners because of their suitability for high-volume, daily fee play. The result is that a majority of golfers experience the game on courses with little or no architectural value beyond their serving as an occasion for hitting a succession of golf shots.

It may be useful to examine how freeway golf became so prevalent in America. After World War II, golf again became a game of the common people, and after the Korean War it grew at such a rapid rate that there were not enough experienced architects around to fill the demand (see figure 20). As a result, when the demand for new golf courses soared in the late 1940s and early 1950s, we began to repeat the cycle that had occurred one hundred years earlier. Experienced golfers or golf professionals were enlisted to lay out courses using minimum budgets and they made them look like what they thought a golf course should look like. The earthwork was crude and often the design was penal or, even worse, the hazards were moved clear out of the way or totally eliminated to speed up play and to facilitate mechanized maintenance tech-

Facilities & Courses/U.S.

Facility Growth (1931–94)

Year	Daily fee Facilities	Municipal Facilities	Private Facilities	Total Facilities
1931	700	543	4,448	5,691
1934	1,006	566	4,158	5,725
1937	1.070	637	3,489	5,196
1939	1,199	699	3,405	5,303
1941	1,210	711	3,288	5,209
1946	1,076	723	3,018	4,817
1949	1,108	750	3,068	4,926
1952	1,246	751	3,029	5,026
1955	1,534	877	2,807	5,218
1958	1,904	855	2,986	5,754
1961	2,363	912	3,348	6,623
1964	3,114	1,015	3,764	7,893
1967	3,960	1,210	4,166	9,336
1970	4,248	1,321	4,619	10,188
1973	4,710	1,466	4,720	10,896
1976	5,121	1,650	4,791	11,562
1979	5,340	1,778	4,848	11,966
1982	5,494	1,848	4,798	12,140
1985	5,573	1,912	4,861	12,346
1988	5,748	1.937	4,897	12,582
1991	6,272	2,046	4,686	13,004
1994	7,126	2,190	4,367	13,683

NGF Golf Reference and Media Guide / 1995–96 Edition

Figure 20. Golf has grown at a fairly steady rate since World War II.

niques. One typical design innovation, for instance, was building greenside bunkers just far enough away from putting surfaces as to allow room in between for a tractor-pulled, five- to nine-gang mower to pass (20 to 30 feet) (see figure 21).

Since golf was no longer a game of the wealthy, and there were so many brand new golfers who had no frame of reference about golf or golf courses, they accepted anything that had functioning tees and greens as a golf course. In time these golfers internalized that golf courses were supposed to have rectangular tees, straight fairways, round greens, and flat oval bunkers. This new wave of golfers was happy with anything green, and their contentment perpetuated more golf courses just like the ones they had learned the game upon. The experienced and more discriminating golf architects were so busy they had no time to protest this proliferation of crude methods or primitive philosophies. In fact, many were pressured to forego artistic designs and to yield to the cookie-cutter approach merely to satisfy market demand for their services. This was a prosperous time for golf course architects, for there were many clients, bundles of money, and tons of sophisticated earthmoving equipment available, with no end in sight.

Figure 21. After World War II, labor-saving devices such as 9-gang mowers became popular. Many golf courses of the late 40s, 50s, and 60s were designed to accommodate them, which contributed to the evolution of the "freeway" style golf courses.

Evolution of Golf Course Architecture as a Profession

Regrettably, the state of the art was not advancing, for there was little creativity expressed during this time, the exceptions being Robert Trent Jones, Sr., and Dick Wilson, who were quite innovative. However, most of the new golf course architects who entered the profession during this boom time were not studied in golf course design, so they copied what they saw until they gained enough experience to dare to break from the established pattern. The greatest deviation came, in true cyclical fashion, with the rekindled popularity of heroic-type holes, free-form tees, sprawling greens, and jigsaw puzzle–shaped sand traps. As golfers and golf architects gained experience and sophistication, there began a slow movement away from the formalist geometry of the postwar era. This innovative trend continued until the early 1970s, when the oil embargo of 1973 caused a rapid decline in the building rate of golf courses.

The newly competitive golf design market actually had a salutary effect on architectural standards because it drove out many less talented designers, whose only claim to fame in bullish times had been their ability to deliver work quickly and inexpensively. Their work now had a tougher time holding up under the pressures of the design business. Many ended up abandoning the field to a nucleus of men who had acquired experience in the field and were slowly advancing the concepts of design along lines first championed in the pre-Depression era by visionaries such as Colt, C.H. Alison (1882–1952), Alister MacKenzie (1870–1934), A.W. Tillinghast (1874–1942), Donald Ross (1872–1948), and Stanley Thompson (1894–1952). The unproclaimed leaders of this long road back were Geoffrey Cornish (b. 1914), Robert Bruce Harris (1896-1976), James G. Harrison (1900–1995), Robert Trent Jones, Sr. (b. 1906), Bruce Mathews (b. 1904), C.E. "Robbie" Robinson (1907–1990), Howard Watson (1907–1992), Dick Wilson (1904–1965), and William Gordon (1893–1973). Perhaps the most dynamic of the "new" golf course architects of the 1950s was Larry Packard (b. 1912), who not only was a gifted land sculptor who pioneered the "free-form" look of our craft, but also moved the American Society of Golf Course Architects from a social organization to a highly regarded professional institution.

Only in the last two decades has there been a trend to reexamine design theory and to try to resurrect the spirit of St. Andrews, and with it, strategic design. But the process has been slow for three general reasons. First, it takes more land to build a strategic hole than to build a penal or freeway type, and land is expensive. Second, most of the golf market, especially in the public sector, expects to see and play freeway golf; designs that make golfers think tended, at least until recently, to meet with initial resistance, since such designs were more complicated, and somewhat more expensive to play, than run-of-the-mill daily fee layouts. Finally, few modern golf architects understand the subtle nuances of strategic design, and thus couldn't skillfully apply them. But today, the beauty and natural-looking complexity of such strategic courses have been meeting with far more acceptance (see figure 22). It is therefore hoped that a better understanding of golf architecture by all golfers can serve as a further catalyst to revive the principles of strategic design. The goal, after all, in producing such courses, is to balance equity with aesthetics to reward the good player without hurting the poor player, while making the course pleasing to the eye.

It must also be said, partially in response to the monotonous quality of freeway golf design, that penal course design also made something of a comeback in an attempt recently to make golf courses more interesting. With architects searching for a way to toughen up courses for the most advanced players, penal design attracted those who saw "degree of difficulty" as a criterion of sound design (see figure 23). Moreover, such designs proved visually stimulating, regardless of their playability on the ground. This presented real estate developers with an alluring theme to secure a market niche for their particular golf course property. The signature hole was born!

To reiterate, penal design is that body of golf course planning that dictates a particular shot

Figure 22. Golf course architects of the 1990s are mastering not only the nuances of strategic design, as their predecessors did in the 1920s, but also technological advances in construction that are making golf courses into art forms.

value, offers few or no alternative shot choices, and penalizes all imperfect play. In its most primitive form, it is seen as mounds, water, or bunkers placed in the direct line of play. Many accomplished golfers revere penal courses, for these golfers enjoy the risks of a bayonet-type assault of a course, hoping that lady luck will make them the victor. But victories in golf should be decided by fairly testing the player's ability to execute all types of shots under all types of conditions, and not by mere gimmickry in design. If a high winning score for a tournament is to be the leading indicator of the greatness of a course, then I can offer a formula for producing the greatest course in the world. Make every hole its maximum allowable length, make the greens very small, have them pitch away from the line of play or crown them, let the greens get very hard and dry, place a profusion of deep hazards very near these greens, let the rough grow four to six inches long, and place as many obstacles in the driving area as possible. Then hope for strong winds on the tournament days and offer a huge purse for those who survive. When the finest players in the world cannot break eighty, this course will be touted by golf magazines and fans as the number one challenge in the world. If anyone dares to say the course is unfair, then tell them that life is unfair and that if their game is not up to the challenge they should simply stay home. It is regrettable that score has become a standard for the ingenuity of a golf course; this is an insensitive indicator. Golf should be a recreation and a pastime, not solely a competitive game. The tail is wagging the dog when the competitive side of golf dominates the recreational value of golf. The sooner we cease revering and perpetrating camouflaged penal designed courses and return to

Figure 23. Some penal design elements can be skillfully and artistically presented to make golf holes "look hard, but play easy," such as the 4th hole at Naples National.

strategic principle, the greater will be the enjoyment, participation, and growth of golf.

The architectural spirit of St. Andrews is that golf is a game matching skill and strength to strategy. At St. Andrews, there is no one correct line to the hole, but multiple lines, with hazards balancing risk and reward. That's an ideal every golf architect should strive to attain, and the kind of golf course every player should demand.

2

Basic Criteria

No matter which design concept is used, the end result of any golf course design is supposed to be one that is enjoyable, relaxing, and a fair test of shot-making ability (see figure 24). But these rather subjective criteria are largely dependent upon the condition of a course and the skill level of the golfer, and therefore are not useful or meaningful to a golf course architect. Instead, architects use criteria that are more objective in nature and are less emotionally generated. These criteria, listed in their order of importance, are:

1) Safety (to golfers and to adjacent land users)
2) Flexibility (variation in length to accommodate all abilities)
3) Shot value (variety in required shots, lengths, and targets)
4) Fairness (severity of hazards and placement in order to offer risks and rewards)
5) Progression (sequence of holes and their associated shot values)
6) Flow (the overall movement of golfer traffic)

Doug Ball

Figure 24. The golf course should take on ethereal qualities, but also remain a fun place to play golf.

7) Balance (equality in distribution of par, shot values, and progression)
8) Maintenance cost (long-term problems, long-term costs, problems or limitations, cost-benefit ratios)
9) Construction planning (projected total cost, problems or limitations, cost-benefit ratios)
10) Aesthetics (the look, feel, impression of the golf course)
11) Tournament qualities (match vs. medal play, accessibility for galleries)

This list is akin to the activity chart of elements used in chemistry. The criterion that is higher on the list takes precedence when conflicting with a criterion (or element) below it. In general, the most important criterion for a golf course, the one that should take precedence over all others, is safety. This concern should be both to the golfer and maintenance staff using the course and any person or property adjacent to the course. The next six criteria deal with making a golf course as pleasant and pleasurable to the golfer as possible, and presenting the golfer with a fair challenge. These six considerations should take precedence over the long-term maintenance factors. Long-term maintenance, since it is a never ending process, should be more important than construction considerations, which are a one-time cost. Then come the purely aesthetic considerations, which, while not meant to be minimized, must be sacrificed before any criterion above it. Lastly comes tournament qualities of a course, for at best, only one or two weeks will be devoted to tournament play. The remainder of the year the course must properly serve those golfers who routinely play it and foot the bill. Because each of these is an important element, more explanation of each is necessary.

Safety

As previously mentioned, safety is by far the most important single consideration on a golf course. Golf is a rather passive recreation and its participants should not play the game in fear of being hit or of hitting someone with an errant shot. Sadly, people have been hit by golf balls and as a result have lost sight in one eye, lost teeth, had bones broken, or even been in danger of losing their life. Sometimes these accidents are a result of negligence on the part of the golfers, but other times it is because the golf course was improperly designed. Having occasionally watched people hit the ball between their own legs, or shank one 90° off line, or slice a ball two hundred yards off the target line, we all realize that no golf course can be made totally safe. Of course, no home, highway, or office building can be made totally safe either. But proper design that respects common playing patterns can markedly reduce the probability of a serious accident.

There are no golf course design standards, so each golf course architect must prudently set his own guidelines for safety based upon the foreseeability of where and how golfers hit their shots. In the event of an accident, designers may have to defend their personal guidelines in a court of law, and perhaps against the views of another expert witness. What follows are the author's personal guidelines (see figure 25).

The most obvious safety measure involves the right side of a hole, since most beginning and casual golfers slice shots off the tee. An architect can reduce danger in slice impact areas by staggering tees so that players on each hole won't slice into the same area. If impact areas cannot be physically separated, then safety buffers, such as bunkers, rough, trees, ponds, or non-turf vegetation can be used. A safety buffer can be anything that will discourage the golfer from swinging away instead of controlling the shot, or anything that stops the mishit ball in flight or on the roll. Some years ago the author did some fairly extensive study of where golfers hit the ball in relation to their aiming point and apparent line of play. Although unpublished and not statistically validated, the data indicated that 92% of golf shots fall within 15 degrees either side of their apparent line of play to a specific aiming point. This observation can be used as a planning rule of thumb which is modified depending upon topography, vegetation, wind direction, altitude, length of shot, etc.

Another method to provide safety is to offset

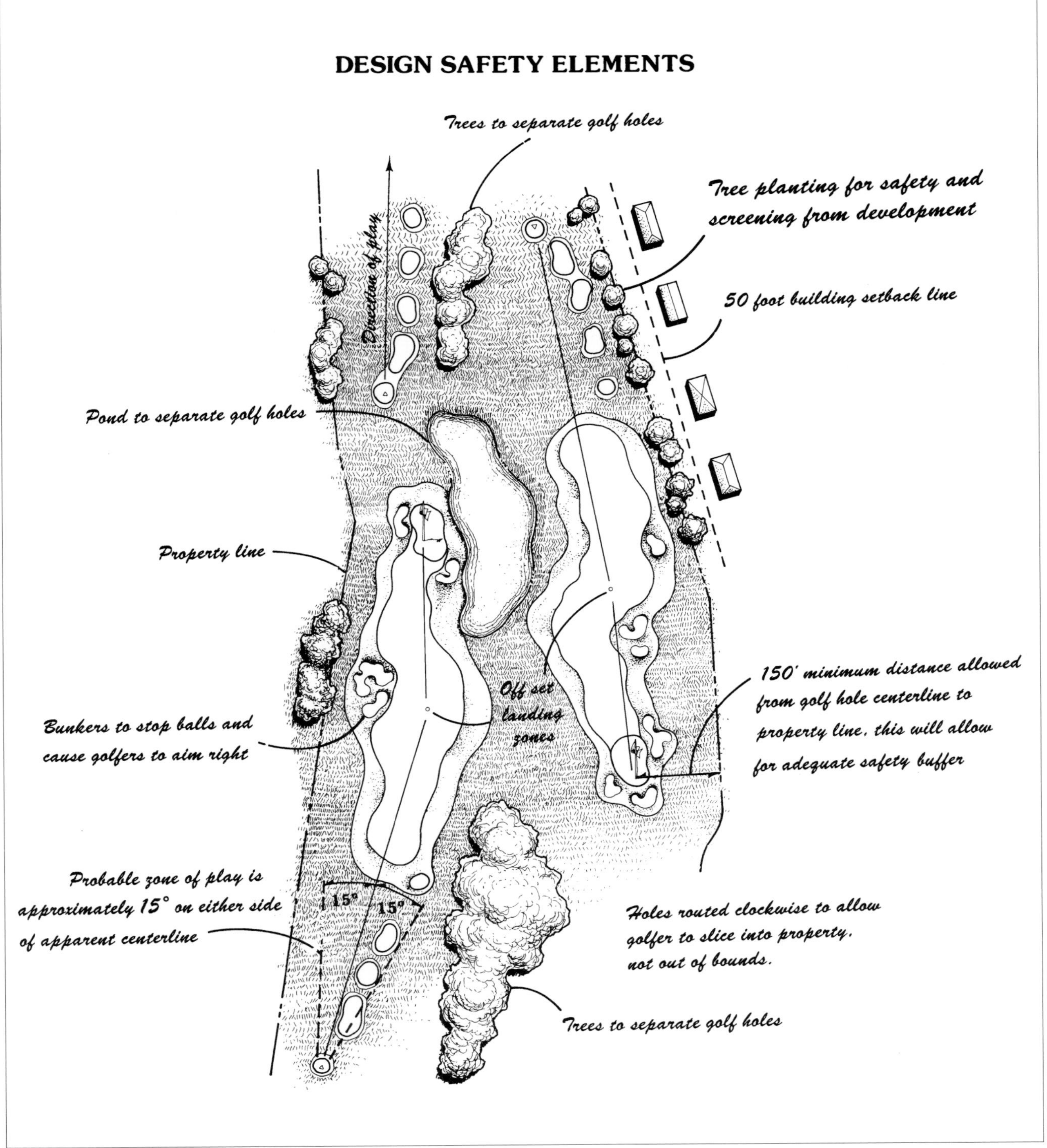

Figure 25. Hurdzan design guidelines can be used as a starting point, and adjusted based on the topography, vegetation, altitude, prevailing winds, adjacent land uses, and anticipated play level of each specific site and project.

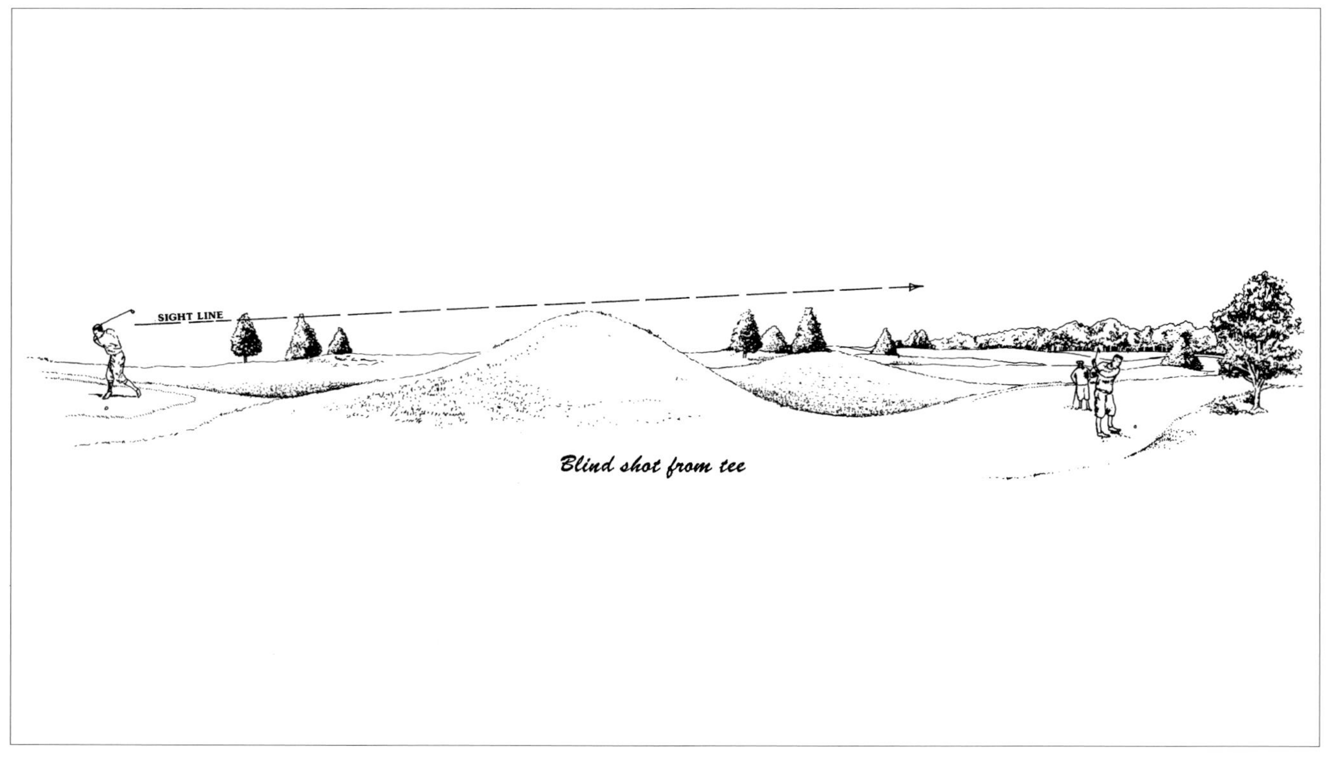

Figure 26. Blind shots on golf courses can be mitigated or eliminated in several ways.

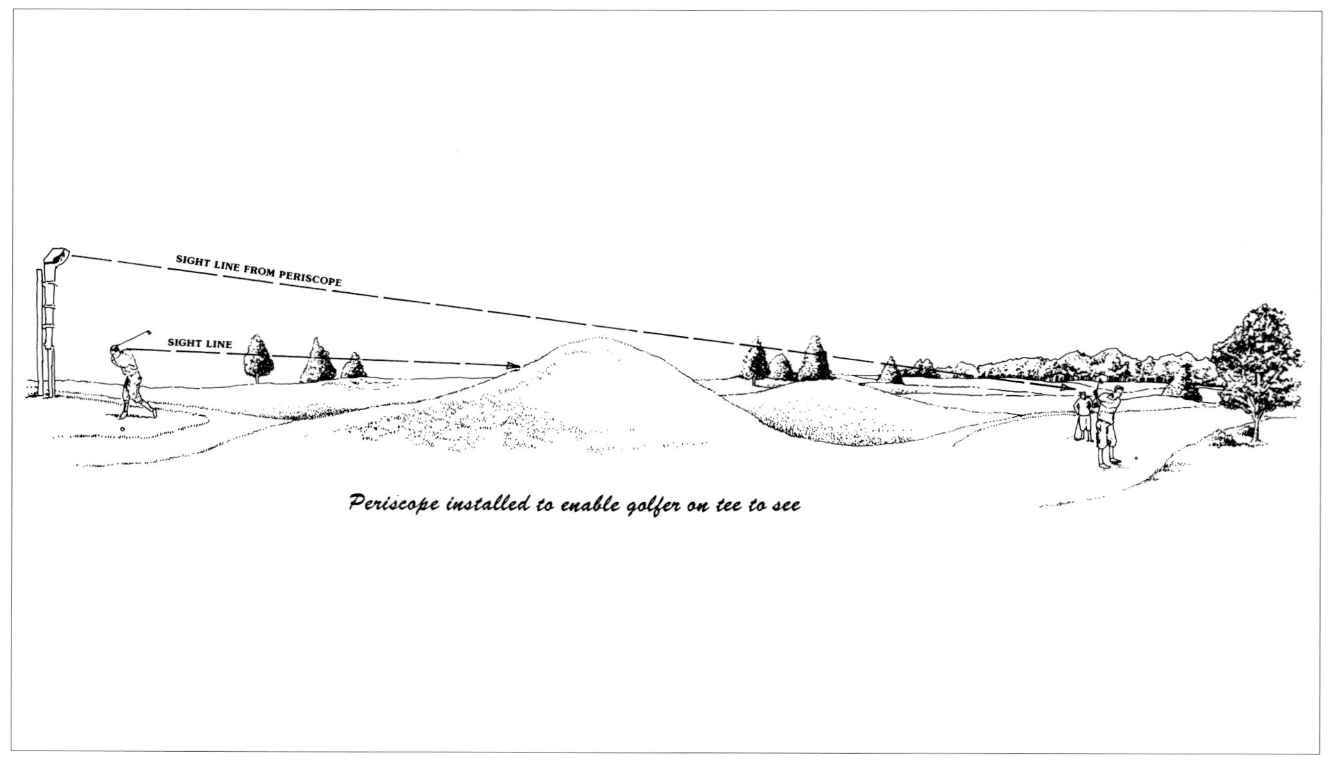

Tees elevated & mound partially lowered to unmask blind shot

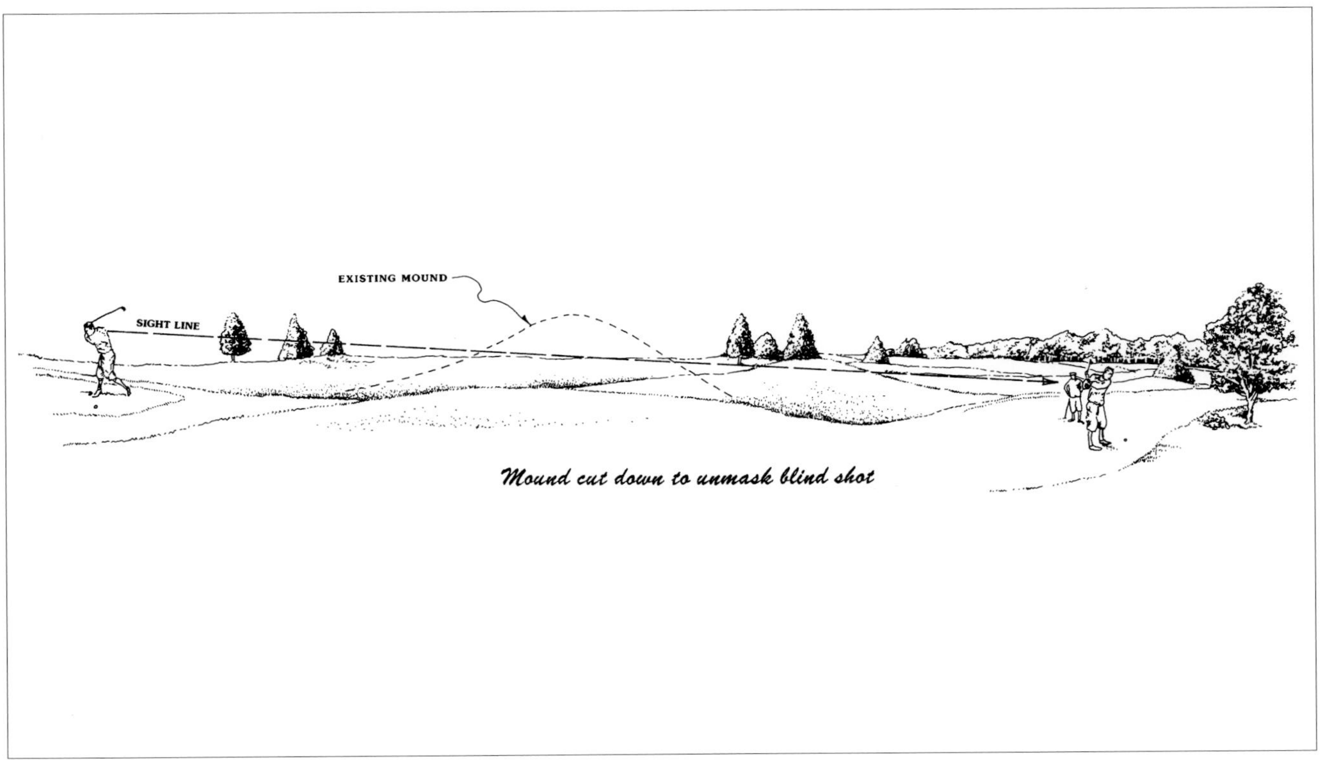

Mound cut down to unmask blind shot

the play angles at the tee so that the golfer is forced to set up to hit away from a danger zone. This means placing tees for the poorest golfers closest to the danger zone so they are hitting away from it, not toward it. Experience has shown that it is easiest to control errant shots nearest the tee, when the ball is at a low elevation and has not gone a great distance. Near the tee, wild shots can be controlled by mounds, closely planted trees, dense bushes, or artificial barriers. Barriers such as fences are the least desirable method, for most often they are linear and unsightly. But no matter how ugly, if fences are needed they must be used; aesthetics must always bow to safety. Properly built artificial barriers can be made somewhat attractive by using climbing vines and flowers.

Another situation that cannot easily be tolerated on a golf course is when common play areas are blind to golf shots that may land there. These blind impact areas occur when golfers cannot be seen by the group behind them or by players on an adjacent hole who might hit the ball to the area. This condition is most common on hilly ground, where the horizon line of a ridge or hill is very near the tee. Blind shots are quite common on links or links-type courses, for that is the nature and charm of these sites. However, golfers who play these courses must exercise extreme courtesy and caution to avoid accidents.

There are four solutions to blind impact areas (see figure 26). The optimal solution is to unmask the blind spot by excavating the horizon line down or making a saddle cut, so that the golfers in the danger zone can be seen. Often this is not possible because the offending ridge is underlaid with rock that is too costly to remove. The next best solution is to raise the tee to such an elevation that the line of sight is moved above the horizon line. This solution is not always workable, for it might require such a high tee that it would be too costly to build and maintain. The third solution is the use of a periscope or mirror atop a pole, either of which raises the line of sight up very high without elevating the golfer at all. If properly constructed, painted, and located, periscopes can be made to blend so well with the background that they are unobtrusive. There is also something to be said for their novelty effect, as long as they are not used more than a few times on any site. The last solution is perhaps the most commonly used, but has many shortcomings. It is the warning device, usually a bell that the group ahead rings to signal the group behind that the impact area is safe. The problem is, many forget to use the bell or the group behind does not hear it. Bells should be avoided, if possible, for the burden should be placed on the group behind to maintain a safe interval, not on the group ahead.

Other areas of safety that should be considered by the golf architect include pathways, steep slopes, stair design, bridges, high cliffs, aging trees, dangerous wildlife, banks, slopes of water hazards, and poisonous plants. In all instances, warnings in the form of signs or written statements should be given to each golfer. Where possible, unsafe conditions should be corrected. If correction is not possible, then fences, markers or guards should be used to remind the golfer of the danger. Nothing is more important than safety.

Frequently the golf course architect can lessen unsafe conditions by his routing of the golf course. One method is to try to keep out-of-bounds limits to the hook side, since fewer golfers hook and thus fewer neighbors will be endangered by errant shots. On rolling ground, a golf course architect can route his course so that slices will bounce into a slope instead of run down one. A good rule of thumb for a safe routing is to have the right side of the impact area higher than the left side (see figure 27). If the ground is flat, mounds should be located and built to control the slice. Of course, the impact area of sliced shots must still be conducive to finding the ball and playing the next stroke, so if possible a good design philosophy is to cut the golf hole down into the ground so the sideslopes create containment. Mounds create rejection of golf balls that bounce off their far sides, thus moving the golfer further off line. If mounds are to be used to create containment, they should be placed outside the 15° angle of probable play, as done at Cook's Creek in Circleville, Ohio (see figure 28).

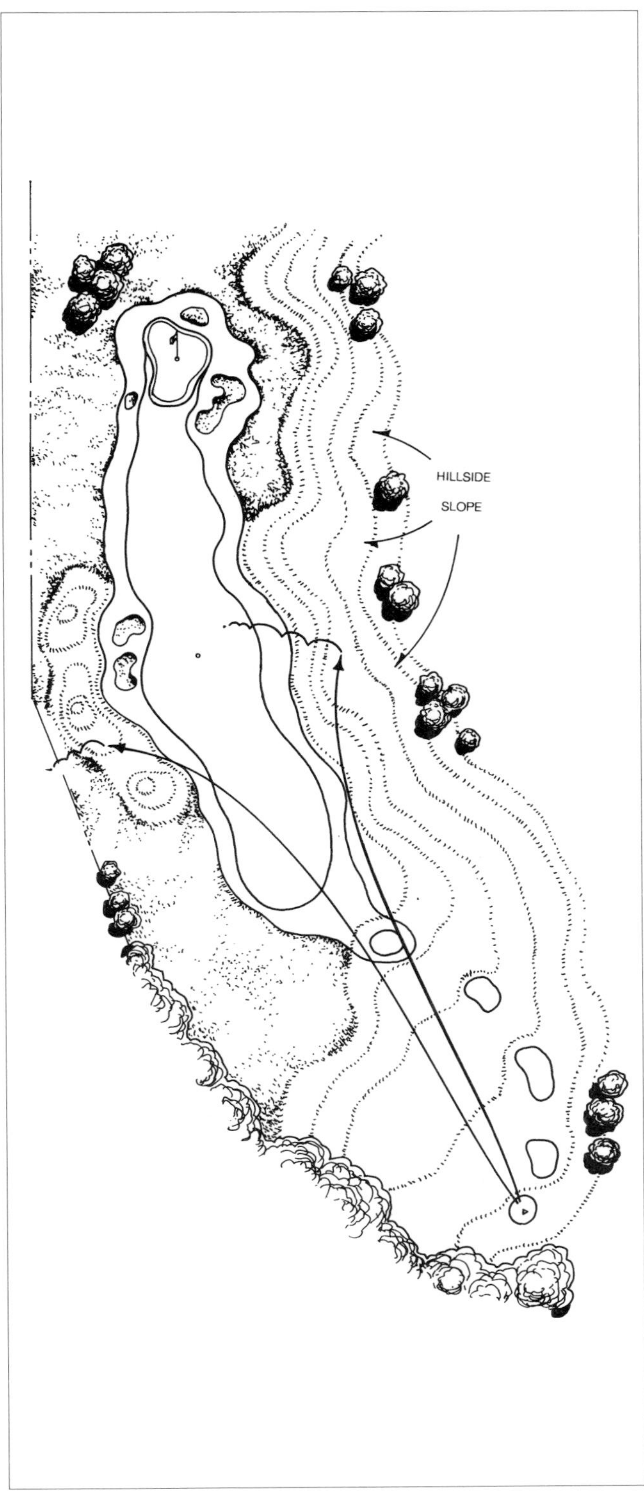

Figure 27. Containment golf holes should slice into hillsides, and mounds that reject balls to worse fates should be avoided.

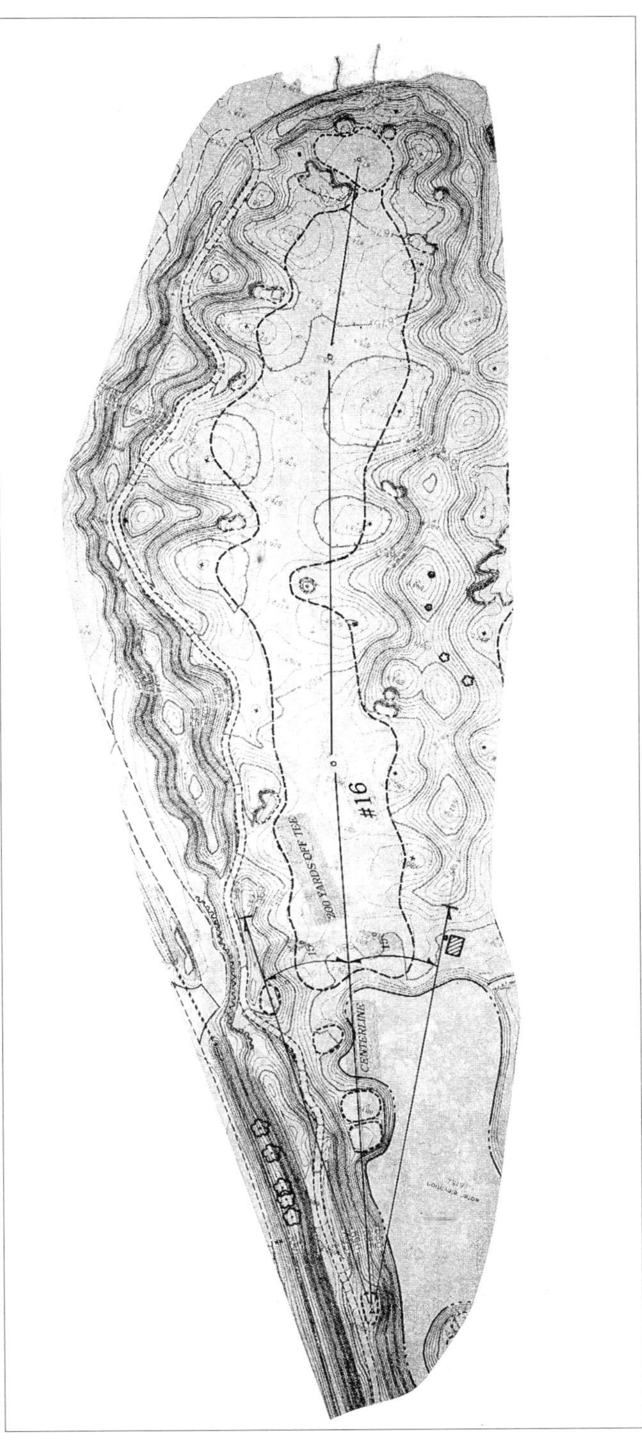

Figure 28. Containment mounding outside the 15° angle either side of centerline will not compound the golfer's problems on errant shots. Being left with a blind shot over these mounds is not likely at Cook's Creek.

Flexibility

The next criterion a golf course architect may use to evaluate a golf course is its flexibility in length to accommodate the abilities of all golfers. This really can only be achieved by multiple tee markers and multiple tees. The best indicator of flexibility is to consult the scorecard if it shows the yardage from multiple markers. Distances on golf courses are normally measured from the center of the tee down the center of the play line to the center of the green. Since the ball travels most of that distance in the air, it is air distance that is measured, not ground distance. If there is close to 2,000 yards difference between the front and back markers, and this total difference is reasonably distributed among all holes, then the course has good flexibility. If flexibility is lacking, then decisions should be made to construct either more front tees, or back tees, or both.

Figure 22 shows an example of good flexibility using five sets of tees, each of which is located at selected positions from the prime landing zone for each of five general classes of golfers. Pro tees are normally located 270 yards from the prime landing area, scratch men's tees at 240, the average golfer's tee at 210, the better female and senior men usually at 175 yards out, and novice and super senior tees at 140 yards to the landing zone. Research by the National Golf Foundation indicates the average male golfer can hit a drive 199 yards of carry and roll, while the average female hits it only 131 yards. Few experienced observers of average golfers would dispute these distances. Allowances for high altitude should be made as well, and a rule of thumb is 10% greater distances at 5,000 feet above sea level.

Shot Value

Shot value is another criterion utilized in analyzing a golf course. Shot value is a largely misunderstood concept. It is meant to describe the value of a required golf shot as related to its difficulty or allowable margin of error. It is dependent upon the length of the shot, the size of the target, the severity of influencing hazards, and the ground from which it is executed. It represents an attempt to quantify the physical qualities of a golf shot so each can be compared to other golf shots. A good method is to refer to a table published by the USGA in their course rating handbook on target areas that can be hit by scratch and average golfers 66% of the time (see figure 30). An architect can use this table to adjust the size of target areas on greens or fairway landing areas to allow golfers a 66% statistically probable chance of success.

For example, the longer the golf shot, the more exaggerated the flight of the ball will be in response to a mishit. A 4-iron shot will deviate further off line than will a 7-iron shot, even though in both instances the ball had the same sidespin imparted to it. So, if the same impact area is used for both clubs, there will be less margin of error permitted for the 4-iron shot and therefore it has a higher shot value (see figure 31). But if the impact area for a 4-iron is much larger than that for a 7-iron, then their shot values may be the same. Similarly, the shot value for two shots of equal length to target areas of equal size can be different if one must be played from a slope and the other from flat terrain, or one from a fairway and the other from longer grass. Shot value describes the allowable margin of error for any given shot depending upon its length, target area, and terrain.

There is no empirical method to measure shot value except to estimate it by the intuitive process accumulated by experience. Shot value is an illusive measure, for a change in the wind direction or speed can force a reevaluation of all shots. But for purposes of this discussion, and in the mind of the golf architect, shot value is determined by assuming a constant prevailing wind direction and speed. Variance is allowed for holes that run into, down, or across the prevailing wind, but there is little point in trying to factor in fluctuations such as seasonal conditions.

While shot value in the singular sense refers to the difficulty of a particular golf shot, collectively it refers to the variety of golf shots required on one course. Although confusing, this dual concept permits comparison of one hole with another as to the difficulty of the required

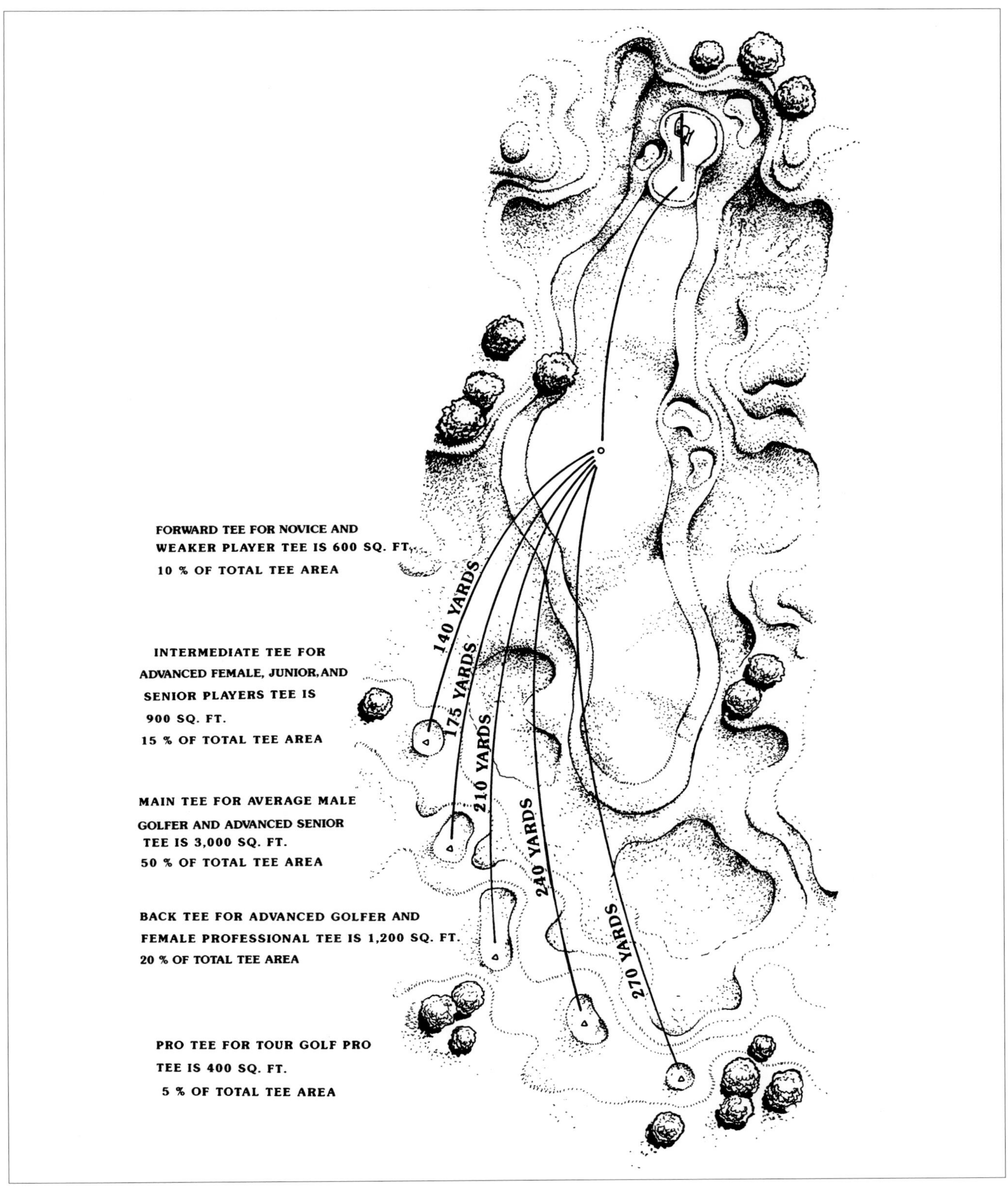

Figure 29. Five sets of tees are commonly used to match skills and numbers of golfers in each category.

Accuracy Table
(All Distances in Yards)

Length of Shot	Scratch Golfer Width	Scratch Golfer Depth	Bogey Golfer Width	Bogey Golfer Depth
	Dimensions of Expected Landing Area			
70	9	13	14	17
80	10	14	15	18
90	11	14	16	19
100	11	14	16	20
110	12	15	17	21
120	12	15	17	22
130	13	15	18	23
140	14	16	19	24
150	15	16	20	25
160	17	17	22	27
170	18	17	24	28
180	20	18	26	30
190	23	18	29	34
200	26	19	33	37
210	29	19	—	—
220	32	20	—	—
230	35	20	—	—
240	38	20	—	—
250	41	21	—	—

Figure 30. The USGA Course Rating Manual Uses this Table to Determine 66% Accuracy of Scratch & Bogey Golfers

shots, and comparison of one golf course to another as to the variety of required shots.

In essence this is what handicapping of holes and Slope Rating[1] of golf courses is all about. The basis of the United States Golf Association's slope course rating system is a determination of collective shot values in order to assess the overall difficulty of a course. A golf course architect, on the other hand, is interested in what factors make a course difficult so he can provide a wider variety of factors. The ultimate goal of any golf architect is to design the perfect test of golf—one that would have such a variety of holes and shot values that every club in the bag and every conceivable type of golf shot would be presented. Ideally, the course should be so diversified in its required shots that it is the best all-around golfer who would win a competition on it rather than someone with a hot putter or uncanny driving ability (see figure 32).

Fairness

The next criterion that a golf course architect uses is fairness—the type and severity of hazards and variety of alternative approaches to each hole. Fairness can be judged for an entire hole, for a particular hazard, or for a particular feature or a combination of all of them. If enough holes on a course are judged unfair to most players, then one must conclude that the golf course is unfair. A golf hole is deemed unfair if there is but one route to the hole, which must carry a severe hazard, and the required shot is beyond the ability of most golfers. The most common instance of an unfair feature is a forced water carry over 175 yards. Another is the use of deep traps with soft sand located so far from the green that they are beyond the range of most sand blast shots. One last example is a green so fast and steep that a golfer may barely touch the ball and yet watch the putt roll off the green. Overall, fairness is a subjective judgment of risk and rewards formulated within the assumed abilities of all golfers intended to use the facility. Generally, the more options of approach that are presented to the golfer, the fairer the hole will be.

Progression

Progression, the fifth evaluation criterion, is a term describing the sequence of holes and their associated shot values. The great Canadian golf course architect, Stanley Thompson, devised a chart to graphically show the shot value for each

[1]The Slope System is a refinement of the USGA Handicap System. It adjusts a player's handicap for the difficulty of the course he plays. Slope Ratings range from 55 to 155, with 113 being the average. Assume your handicap is established on a course with a 113 slope rating. When you play a course with a Slope Rating higher than 113, your Course Handicap will be higher than your USGA Handicap Index. When you play a course with a Slope Rating lower than 113, your Course Handicap will be lower than your Handicap Index.

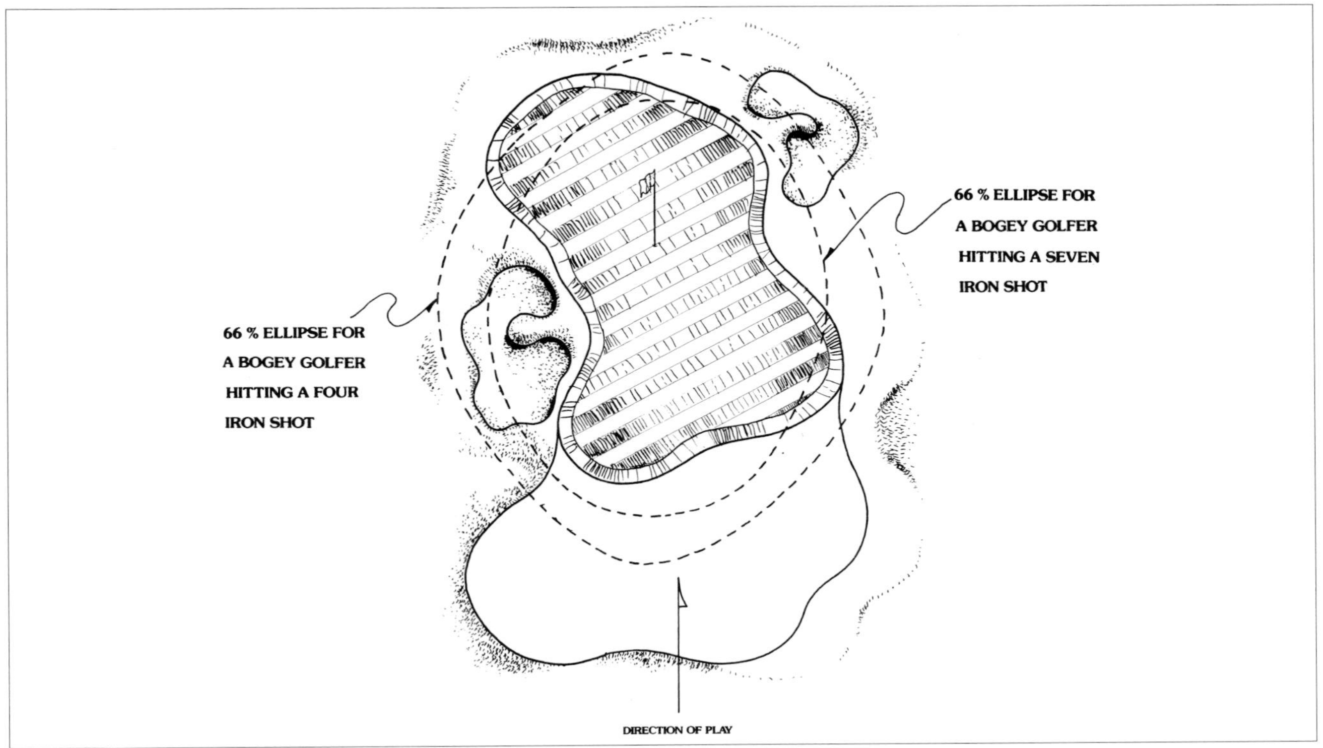

Figure 31. Applying the USGA table for 66% accuracy of a bogey golfer can help the golf course architect set hazards in relation to the club played for the approach shot.

hole as well as their progression based upon length (see figure 33a & b). Although not as sensitive to hazards and playing conditions as the slope system, Thompson's chart visually illustrates the variety of shots required by a particular golf course. It is helpful in evaluating various routing plans, as well as in understanding the nuances of a universally heralded course.

A sensitive golf course architect will plan a course design to provide progressively higher shot values as the round proceeds, since it takes most golfers a few holes to loosen up. It is desirable for a golf course to start slowly with gentle shot values and to become progressively more demanding, culminating in a climax on holes 7, 8, and 9, then starting slowly again at number 10, and then to reach a feverish climax on holes 16, 17, and 18. Ideally, the final three holes should be a par 3, 4, and 5, though not necessarily in that order. An ideal progression matches the test to the readiness of the golfer about to take the test.

In addition, since match play produces the most exciting brand of golf, this ideal progression gives a player a chance to rally on the last three or four holes if he is willing to take additional risks, and puts pressure on the player ahead in the match. An example of a classic finish is the 17th at St. Andrews Old Course, the difficult Road Hole, followed by the 18th, which is an unassuming par 4 that is easily reachable in two (and that can occasionally be reached on the drive, if wind conditions are right), combining both risks and rewards. Many matches have come to those holes dead even or one down, and many times a match was won or lost by aggres-

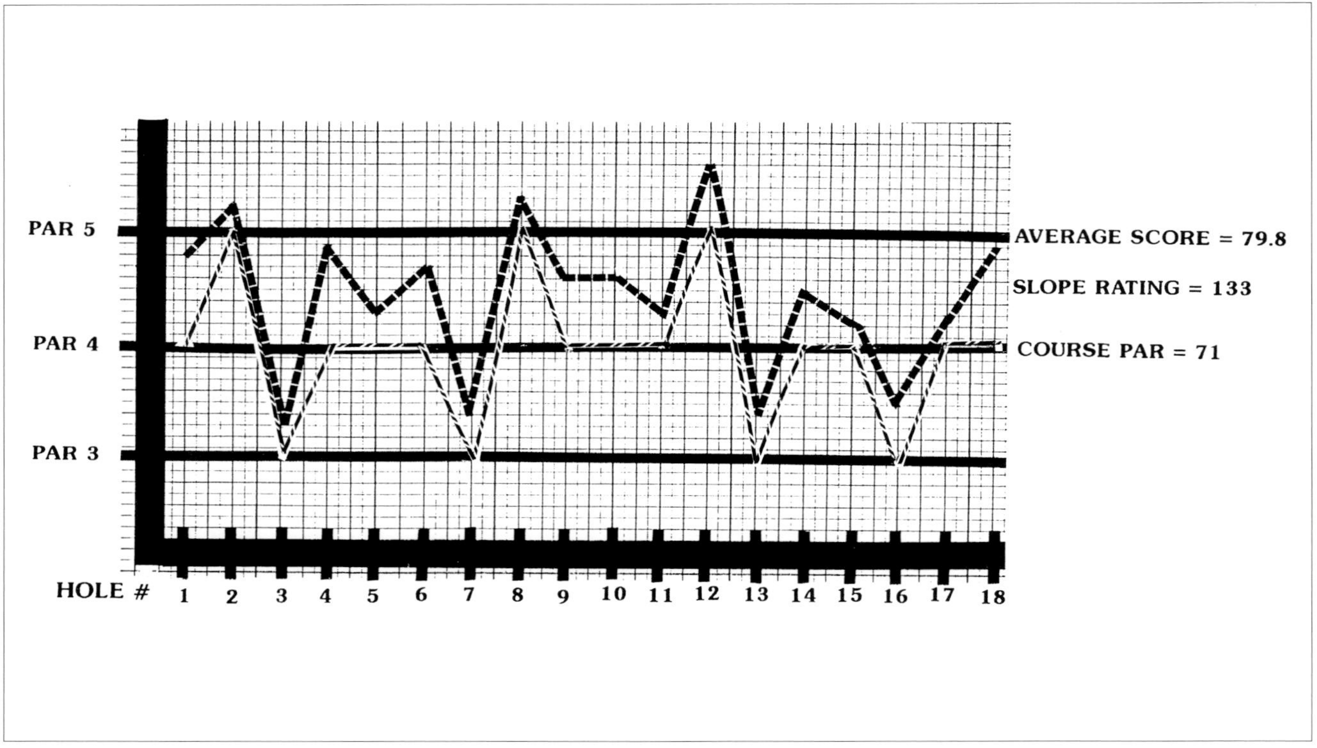

Figure 32. How average scores of 100 U.S. Amateur qualifiers can be graphed for each hole to evaluate fairness, progression and flow of a golf course, as well as to validate the slope rating for each hole. Golf course was Hickory Hills Country Club, Grove City, Ohio and this was for the 1993 local qualifier.

sive or timid play. They are holes whose greatness owes much to their relative position in the progression of the round. They demonstrate that progression in the routing of golf holes is analogous to the increasing crescendos of music that culminate in a triumphant finale.

A version of this culminating rhythm animates the Devil's Pulpit Golf Course north of Toronto, Canada. A round there brings the golfer through an emotional ringer of shifting tensions in terms of terrain, length of hole, and severity of featuring. The opening hole at Devil's Pulpit is a dramatic downhill par 5 offering a vast array of strategic options (see figure 34). The hole is awesome in its scale and boldness, yet deceptively easy to play. Subsequent holes then begin gradually to accelerate in intensity, and the back nine reprises the rhythm, though at a decidedly more feverish pitch. The last four holes were designed to reward bold and aggressive play, starting with the very difficult drive at the 15th hole (see figure 35). At sixteen, a par 3 across a lake, the green offers the whole gamut of pin placements from low key to sheer terror. Seventeen is a difficult uphill par 4. Then eighteen completes the cycle by enabling the golfer to go for broke at a reachable par 5 if the fairway cross bunkers can be carried from the tee, and the bowl-shaped green reached in a second bold stroke.

Flow

The next characteristic of a golf course that the golf course architect evaluates is flow, or the movement of golfers around the routing. One of the greatest objections to the game of golf is the time needed to complete a round. Ideally, a four-hour round seems an acceptable expenditure of time to most people, but much beyond that and the pace of the course is so slow that many golfers lose concentration, play worse, and enjoy the round less. Moreover, a golf course proprietor has a stake in making sure that players can get around in reasonable time. Therefore it is incumbent upon a golf architect to ensure that the golf course has a continuous and moderately paced flow. With golf carts a seemingly indispensable part of North American golf, allowances for traffic flow and car paths figure heavily in golf course design.

Golf course maintenance may be the single most important moderator of flow, because conditions such as deep rough, slick greens, or shaggy hazard banks can needlessly slow play. Therefore, proper design must recognize the current state of maintenance programming, which means a close working relationship between the golf course superintendent and the architect during all design and construction phases. However, there are some usual precautions that a golf architect can take to encourage brisk play. He can try to start the round with fast-playing holes like medium-length par 5's, followed by moderately paced holes like shorter-length par 4's, and leave slow playing holes like long par 3's to the middle or end of each nine. Of course, sometimes site conditions do not afford a golf architect the luxury of pacing the course, and then he must put holes where they fit, occasionally even starting or ending with a par 3. But even in this situation he can control flow somewhat by reducing the difficulty of individual holes. In general, the fewer the hazards on a hole and the shorter the hole relative to par, the faster it will play.

As stated before, the average, male, right-handed golfer hits a driver about 200 yards carry and roll, and the shot is usually off line to the right. Therefore, in placing hazards to keep play at a brisk pace, one should usually try to keep right side hazards either small, or removed as far from the fairway centerline as possible, or beyond the range of the average player. This is especially true of water hazards or the occasional out-of-bounds. Likewise we ensure that underbrush or debris is removed from the rough area so errant shots are easy to find and play. This holds true for hazards such as grassy hollows or sand bunkers, which should usually be built shallow and flat to simplify the second shot. Often such hazards speed up play by keeping errant shots from going into far worse peril or farther off line.

Another design consideration for speeding up play is to avoid left to right slopes in the fairway landing area for average golfers, and make the fairways as wide as possible by minimizing the rough area. Fairways can also be molded through earthmoving and shaping to be flat, convex, or concave. This author prefers concave or "containment" fairways to keep most balls in the fairway and out of the rough. This not only speeds up play but also makes golf much more enjoyable. The key to fast play is make it easy for the golfer to find his ball and be left with a second shot that he is comfortable playing.

Balance

An item related to both flexibility and shot value, but of much less importance in our list of criteria, is balance. When a golf course architect speaks of design balance he is usually referring to the equality or distribution of par, shot values, and golf course length. Since most golf courses are made up of two nine-hole loops, the idea is to split the golf course into two equal parts as measured by par and yardage. The reasons for this custom are not entirely clear. Doubtless, some of it can be attributed to the classic links at St. Andrews, where the progression of par on the "inward" nine mirrors that of the nine holes "outward." In more contemporary parlance, the idea of balance also derives from the fact that nearly half of all golf played on an eighteen-hole course is of only nine holes, so it would seem desirable to provide these nine-hole golfers with their share of the challenges. It also hinges on the fact that many golfers are required to begin play on the back nine, especially during time of heavy play. If the nines are balanced, a much smoother crossover can be made from one nine to the other than if one nine plays considerably faster (or slower) than the other. In

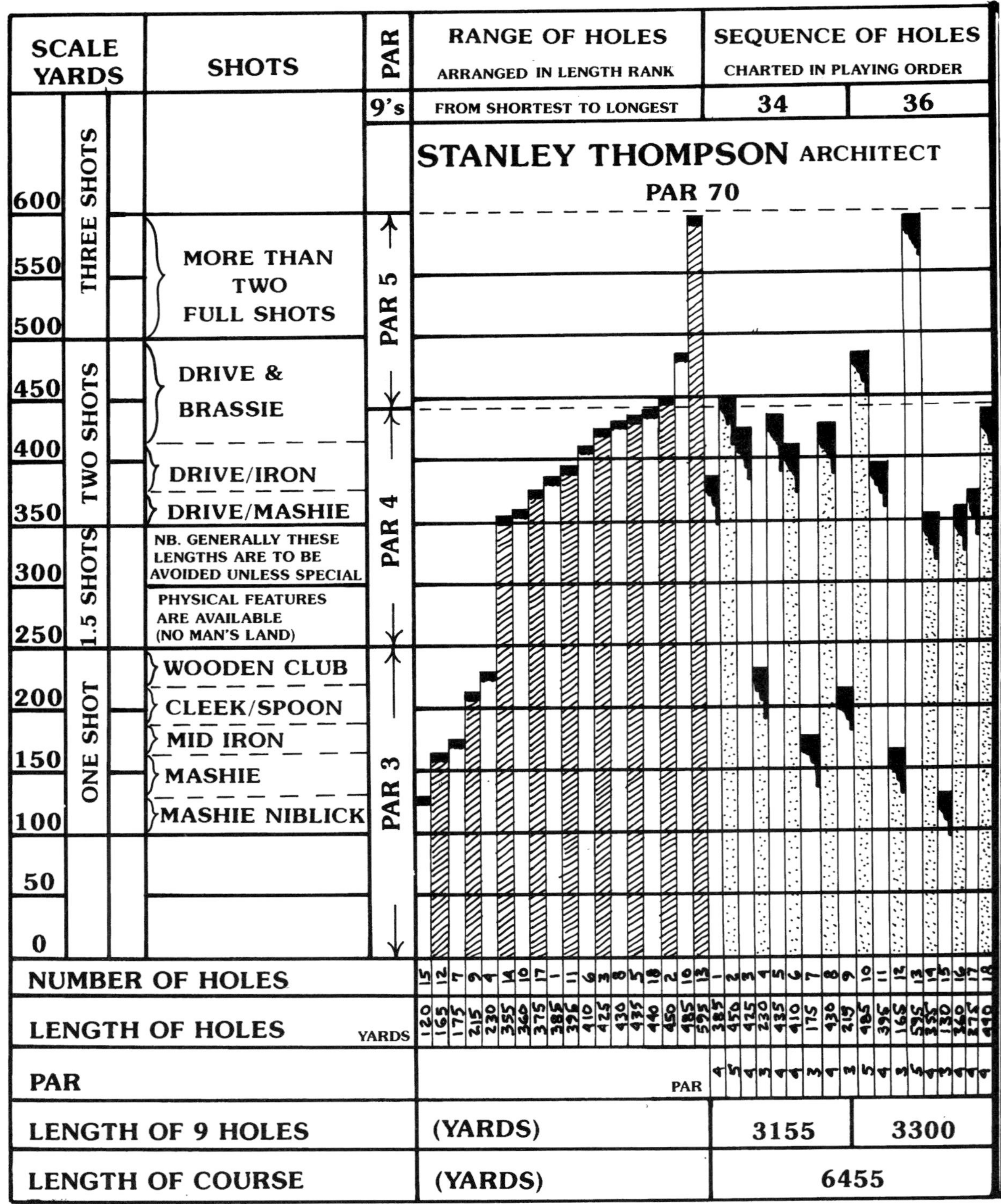

Figure 33. On the left is a bar graph system used by Stanley Thompson to analyze his routing plan for progression, fairness, shot value, and flow. I graphed out Devil's Pulpit Golf Course, but using modern clubs and distances, for the same reason.

SEQUENCE OF HOLES CHARTED IN PLAYING ORDER		RANGE OF HOLES ARRANGED IN LENGTH RANK	PAR	SHOTS	SCALE YARDS
36	36	FROM SHORTEST TO LONGEST	9's		

MICHAEL HURDZAN ARCHITECT
PAR 72

PAR	SHOTS		SCALE YARDS
			600
PAR 5	MORE THAN TWO FULL SHOTS	THREE SHOTS	550
			500
PAR 4	DRIVE/LONG IRON	TWO SHOTS	450
			400
	DRIVE/SHORT IRON		
	DRIVE/WEDGE		350
	NB. GENERALLY THESE LENGTHS ARE TO BE AVOIDED UNLESS SPECIAL PHYSICAL FEATURES. ARE AVAILABLE (NO MAN'S LAND)	1.5 SHOTS	300
			250
PAR 3	THREE IRON	ONE SHOT	200
	FOUR IRON		
	FIVE IRON		
	SIX IRON		150
	SEVEN IRON		
	EIGHT IRON		
	NINE IRON		100
	PITCHING WEDGE		
	SAND WEDGE		50
			0

Sequence of holes (charted in playing order):

NUMBER OF HOLES	1	2	3	4	5	6	7	8	9	10	11	12	13	14	15	16	17	18
LENGTH OF HOLES (YARDS)	478	364	182	445	396	415	132	485	406	413	459	423	512	425	438	230	456	503
PAR	5	4	3	4	4	4	3	5	4	4	4	4	5	4	4	3	4	4

Range of holes (arranged in length rank from shortest to longest):

NUMBER OF HOLES	7	3	16	2	5	9	10	6	12	14	15	4	17	11	1	8	18	13
LENGTH OF HOLES (YARDS)	132	182	230	364	396	406	413	415	423	425	438	445	456	459	478	485	503	512

3303	3859	(YARDS)	LENGTH OF 9 HOLES
7162		(YARDS)	LENGTH OF COURSE

Figure 34. The first hole at Devil's Pulpit is played to the left of spruce tree by average golfers, just to the right of it by scratch players, and to the right fairway by the experts. It is risk and reward at its best.

any case, it has been traditional to keep the course balanced.

The reader is referred back to Stanley Thompson's bar graphs (see again figure 33), to note that he used the right side of his chart to graph the golf holes in order of their sequence. This allowed him to see not only the balance of the golf course, but also the variety of shot values and their progression and make judgments about possible flow patterns. This simple graph is an important tool in evaluating a golf course.

All the criteria discussed so far have dealt with the playability of the golf course for the average golfer. Since it is the customer or member who pays for the course, he or she should be the first concern. The customer must be made to feel that golf is worth the time and money spent on it.

Long-Term Maintenance

Following the golfer in importance is long-term maintenance. Here, too, we find a balance between the quality of the product and the cost of that product to the customer. Every effort should be made to reduce costs yet achieve a quality high enough to attract customers. A good analogy is the automobile industry. Most people would agree that the best car in the world is the Rolls Royce. Yet there are very few Rolls Royces on the road because few people can afford its ultra-high, ultra-expensive quality. Most people are content to drive a lesser-quality, affordably priced garden variety auto. The same can be said of golf courses. Most would agree that Pebble Beach is among the best in the world, but with green fee in excess of $225 per round, few can afford such quality on a steady basis. Therefore,

Figure 35. The final four holes at Devil's Pulpit can be played aggressively along the yellow line of play, or conservatively along the orange one.

the management team of any golf course must identify the desired level of quality for which its customers will be willing to pay, and must avoid exceeding that level.

Much of the cost of routine maintenance is a function of the golf course design. It cannot be overemphasized that a golf architect needs to design features that are compatible with projected long-term budgets. To do this a golf course architect must be thoroughly familiar with maintenance procedures, the efficiency and limitations of maintenance equipment, the unit cost of maintenance for each feature, and the factors that complicate long-term maintenance. The counsel of a golf course superintendent is always advised and valued. Even with this knowledge, the designer must sometimes make compromises between easy maintenance, the golfers' best interests, and the construction budget. For example, because the single most important item on a golf course is drainage, golf course architects must place great emphasis on it. Most concentrate on subsurface drainage, prescribing plastic tile with some gravel backfill at a cost of about $4.00 per foot when installed by a golf course contractor. To tile drain all of the fairways of an 18-hole golf course would take about 125,000 feet of tile, or $500,000 just for tile. In some situations this may be a necessary expenditure, but in most instances construction budgets do not provide for such an expensive proposition. So the golf architect must compromise and install tile only where it is clearly needed, provide good surface drainage in the other areas, and leave it to a golf superintendent to install additional tile as funds become available from golf course profits. The preferred method is surface drainage of at least 2%, supplemented with subsurface drainage of tile or pipes.

Construction Planning

It is in the construction planning phase that such decisions are made. During this phase, the golf architect continually confers with the golf course superintendent to assess cost-to-benefit ratios for almost every detail of the course, especially on maintenance issues (see figure 36). Together they know generally what the client wishes to spend and the unit cost of construction and maintenance, and they are aware of site problems and their solution costs. Therefore, they can evaluate any and all design features to obtain maximum benefit for the time and money invested. If, in evaluating a design, the designer finds it would go well beyond the construction maintenance budget, the client should be presented with these cost-benefit ratios in order to decide whether to allocate the extra maintenance money or have the golf architect change the design. In any course design, there is a point where it is false economy to reduce costs further or alter a design. The client should be made aware in writing of that limit. This way the choices made purely to cut costs won't later reflect back unkindly upon the skills or reputation of the golf architect or golf course superintendent.

Aesthetics

Another criterion the golf architect uses when evaluating a golf course is its overall aesthetic value. Lately the author has come to believe that to the North American golfer aesthetics are important—perhaps the most important part of a golf course—although cosmetics have little to do with the actual playing of golf. The 1980s saw heavy emphasis placed upon "the look" of the course in order to gain widespread recognition through dramatic photographs, often at the expense of playability of the course. But the courses that looked the best were usually regarded as the most desirable, and hence established a fashion trend in golf courses. However, many golf course architects place less emphasis on visual qualities of their contemporary works, and strive for a more classic look and playability, where cosmetics can be added or supplemented at a later time. This, for instance, is what was done at the 9th hole at Devil's Pulpit, where a

Figure 36. The relationship between aesthetic presentation and ongoing maintenance cannot be separated, and the golf course superintendent can advise both the designer and the owner about those issues.

Doug Ball

Figure 37. The 9th hole at Devil's Pulpit was designed to have "the look," where golf and nature blend together in an intense but aesthetically pleasing way.

split rail fence was able to be incorporated (see figure 37). It endows the bunkering and sculpted greenside lake with a more classical rather than a high-tech look. A complete golf course is not only a sound, fair, and fun test of shot-making, but also is rich in the visual qualities that make it memorable.

Tournament Qualities

Lastly, a golf course is evaluated by the golf course architect for its potential to host a tournament. In doing this, he is concerned with both the overall test of golf that the course will present and its provisions for galleries. As a test of golf, the course should normally stretch to at least 6,800 yards for a men's tournament and 6,000 yards for a ladies' event, have relatively small but good landing areas, provide at least four competitive pin positions on each green, and have a large practice area. If the main purpose of building the course is to provide a tournament site, then it should be analyzed from the perspective of the tournament. The same is true of the design and construction of individual golf features, which will be expected to have a different form because they are serving a different function—that of tournament golf instead of recreational golf.

It is helpful in the initial design stage if the golf architect knows whether the tournament event will be match or medal play, because the hazards can be located differently on a match play course than on a medal play one. On a match play course, the closing holes should afford multiple routes offering different risks and rewards, with at least one route of extreme proportions. This allows the trailing player to go for broke and risk everything. In medal play, where players are not eliminated, but rather awarded

Figure 38. The closing hole of the golf course should be filled with drama to provide a fitting climax to a great round of golf. The short par 4 18th hole at Glenmaura National can play to one of two greens separated by a creek.

places, only golfers with a last chance to win would take such high risks, so better use can be made of the land and hazards (see figure 38). The finishing holes on a medal play course provide the most drama if they are designed to encourage some risk to make up strokes and force the leader to play somewhat aggressively, but not to the extreme that a match play course might.

On a project currently being co-designed for the City of Palm Desert, California, by the author and John Cook, PGA Tour Player, gallery considerations include sufficient all-weather parking, separation between holes for spectators, control gates, bridges of proper size, fairway crossings, scoreboard locations, spectator seating (be they mounds or grandstands), restroom and refreshment locations, service roads, first-aid stations, waste control, television camera locations, wire routes, and of course, spectator safety. British Open courses are temporarily outfitted in this manner from head to toe, transforming bleak seaside outposts into modern venues with complete spectator amenities. If a course is expected to host a large tournament annually, then many of these considerations can be taken into account during the initial design and be made a permanent part of the course to the point that the camera towers are placed before final shaping of the golf hole(s), and then based upon how the camera "sees" the hole, the final shapes can be adjusted to maximize the television appeal.

As a veteran international and PGA Tour Player, John also provides invaluable experience and insights into the playing characteristics of the golf course, from a total tournament perspective. His concerns center on not only the shot value, progression, and sequence of holes, but also their visual or illusionary qualities, the strategic decision-making and intimidation factor of each shot, and how competitors relate spatially with spectators. We discuss the entire experience for competitors from where and how they arrive, their club accommodations and amenities, warm-up or practice facilities, flow on and through the golf course as well as press and V.I.P. areas, interview rooms, and locker room necessities. Designing for tournament golf requires a holistic design experience.

So much for the theoretical basis of evaluation that a golf course architect uses when analyzing a golf course routing plan. By using the criteria detailed above, he studies that plan to reduce conflicts, increase variety, control costs, and maximize the golfing value on a parcel of land. By establishing priorities of consideration, the architect ensures the soundness of the total plan. This is not to say that these priorities are without compromise. On the contrary, most golf courses are a series of compromises. But all things being equal, each criterion higher on the list should be given preference over those beneath it.

3

HAZARDS

In 1913, Aleck Bauer wrote a book called, *Hazards: The Essential Elements in a Golf Course Without Which the Game Would Be Tame and Uninteresting.* That succinctly describes the necessary but elusive ingredient that makes golf so interesting, refreshing, and even addictive. Imagine a golf course that was perfectly flat, with no hazards or tall vegetation—the sort of place that might be found on a turf-covered dry lake bed, say, the Bonneville Salt Flat Links. The golf course would exist in only two dimensions: length and width. This two-dimensional course would be totally uninteresting, for every hole would be virtually the same except for variations in length. There would be no hazards such as trees, bushes, sand traps, water hazards, or uneven lies. Every shot would play the same and the ball would roll identically and true with every stroke. The place would be so flat that one could imagine seeing the curvature of the earth on every horizon. Sound like a nice course?

Of course not. But the exercise illustrates that what endows a golf course with expression, with personality and soul, is the third dimension. And the altering of this third dimension gives golf course architecture its distinctive identity as an art form. In amalgamating these two thoughts—that golf is made interesting by hazards and that hazards are products of the third dimension—we arrive at a corollary postulate: with the exception of putting, the majority of golf is played in the air. The ball is struck from the ground, but it moves through the air, through the third dimension (see figure 39).

Lastly, we need to appreciate that the purpose

Figure 39. A golf course with only the dimensions of length and width, lacking the critical dimension of height, is boring to look at and to play. Believe it or not, this land is home to one of Southern England's famous old golf courses.

of a hazard is to make playing a golf shot from within its boundaries more difficult than a shot not played from within the area of the hazard. Therefore, hazards are features or situations that complicate the golf shot and are to be avoided if possible. The consequences of being in the hazard should mentally intimidate the golfer, albeit to different intensities. The rules of golf more technically define hazards and play within them, but for purposes of discussion we will use the term hazard as described below.

In a general sense, a hazard takes the form of any physical feature that makes the playing of a golf shot more difficult. Some examples, in order of the increasing severity of their effect on the average golfer's shot-making ability, are:

1) long grass
2) non-turf vegetation
3) slopes
4) mounds
5) depressions
6) grass traps
7) sand traps (bunkers)
8) rocks, boulders, and stone
9) man-made structures
10) trees
11) water

Natural features—such as wind, sun, temperature, humidity and altitude—may be just as effective in complicating shot-making, but these factors are beyond human control, and may change rapidly. These factors, along with such fleeting annoyances as divots, spike marks and footprints, fall into the broad group of situations or factors beyond control called "rub-of-the-green." Our concern, however, is not with the accidents of golf, but with those realms that can be reasonably anticipated. Golf may be a game of luck, but when it comes to course architecture, everything is by design.

Let us then examine those architectural devices that can be exploited, engineered, or built as part of the golf course planning process (see figure 40a & b).

A good starting point is the observation that the severity of each hazard depends on the extent the third dimension is altered, the type of hazard, and where the hazard is placed. For instance, it is generally acknowledged that a deep bunker filled with fine soft sand and requiring a blasted shot is more severe than a shallow trap of firm sand that allows the ball to be pitched or putted from it. Likewise, if the deep trap is located very near the green, it is considered less severe than if the same trap were placed 200 yards from the green. The penal school of design would accept all hazards being as severe as possible no matter their location. Strategic design, however, would seek to make the penalty match the crime—or in the case of golf, the errant shot.

Severity, then, is a function of structure, location, and the allowable margin of error of the shot to be played from the hazard. For each type of hazard there is a wide range of severity, and it is the intended degree of severity that must be manipulated and matched to balance the risk with the reward of the design intent. In addition, the existence and nature of hazards should be known to the golfer so that he can evaluate their severity and then consciously choose to either play a shot that is safe or one that risks the hazard's penal qualities. (Penal design philosophies find nothing wrong with blind hazards.) The measures of a truly fair hazard in strategic design are its visibility to a golfer, its difficulty in proportion to the error that caused the ball to land in it, and its balance of the risk to the reward.

Not all hazards affect all players in the same manner. The beginner or less accomplished golfer who is still trying to learn the fundamentals of the game will find any hazard difficult because he does not have the knowledge or the expertise to extricate himself. Therefore, hazards should be placed with respect to the play patterns of these golfers so they can learn and enjoy the game unencumbered by too many hazards. These players are entitled to their share of the spice of golf, but not so excessively as to discourage their finishing or returning to the game. On the other hand, if the purpose of the hazard is to intimidate and test the best of players, then it must be severe. Perhaps this is why most tour professionals tend to endorse penal design and severe hazards. They sometimes seem to have forgotten there are other levels of players besides those who regularly challenge par.

Lastly, not all hazards are meant to exact a

Figure 40a. The 17th hole at Devil's Paintbrush demonstrates how many types of hazards can combine to produce a great golf hole.

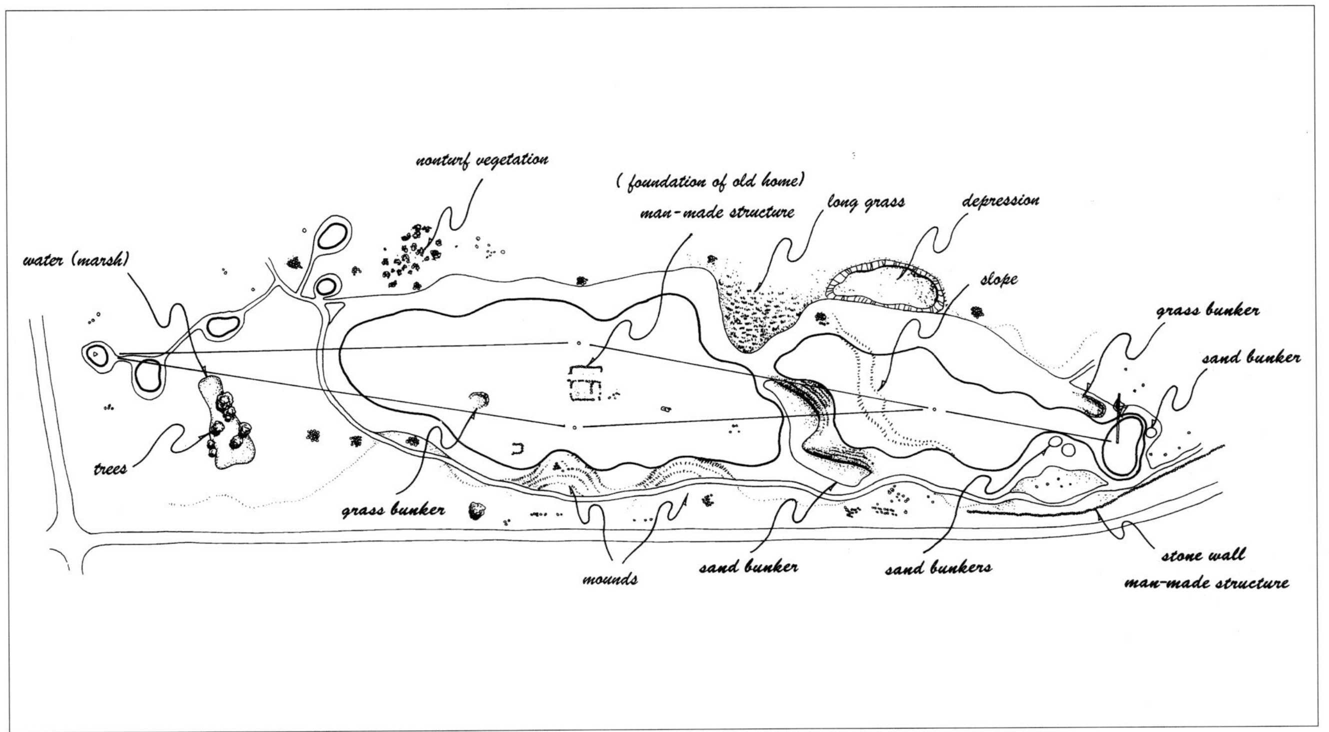

Figure 40b. This hole shows the composite of all hazards and architectural devices that a golf course designer has to work with.

penalty. A hazard can also exist to provide definition to a hole, to act as a safety buffer between congested areas, to serve as an aesthetic feature, or simply to prevent balls from landing in an area of greater jeopardy. If the feature only does one of these things, the hazard has some justification for its existence. If it does more than one task, all the better.

Long Grass

The least severe hazard is "rough"—or any turfgrass that has been allowed to grow to a height that makes the golf shot more difficult. It is generally accepted that fairway grasses maintained at a height of 1/2 inch or less to 3/4 of an inch support the ball in a way that permits the most direct contact between club and ball, without interference by the turf. In other words, on close cropped grass, there is no physical feature to obstruct the golf swing, and there is a wide margin of error to produce an acceptable golf shot. However, as the turf is permitted to grow longer, the ball will have a tendency to settle down into the grass blades instead of being supported cleanly on top of them (see figure 41). When the ball does settle into the leaves, it is more difficult to get good club-to-ball contact because the grass blades get between them. The result is that the grass blades cushion the force of the blow, making it difficult to advance the ball. If the player is strong enough, or lucky enough, to get the ball airborne, it tends to have less backspin, and thus will fly perhaps a lesser distance than normal without much bite, in a manner that is more difficult to control. These shots are called "flyers" or "floaters." Long grass can hinder the golf swing by catching the club head on the backswing to throw off the golfer's timing, or it may slow down the club on the downswing, thus greatly reducing the force of the club before it gets to the ball. Ultimately, of course, the higher the grass, the greater these effects are, until finally it reaches a point where no golfer can hit the ball.

Rough is a hazard whose severity can be manipulated by changing the height of cut to establish strategy and to balance risk with rewards. On any course, the selected impact areas main-

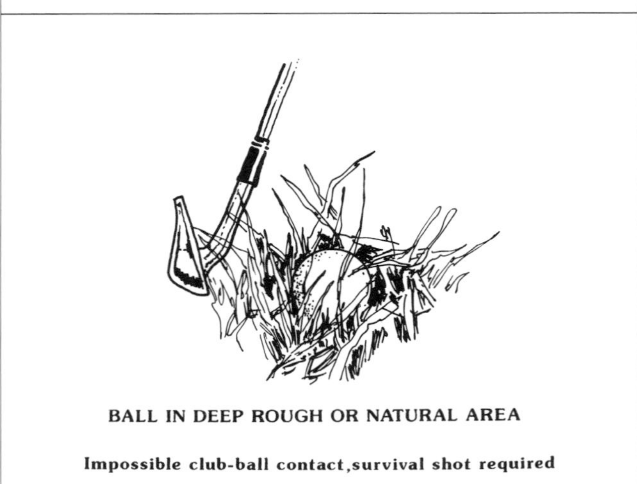

Figure 41. The maintained height of grass determines its degree of penalty.

tained at optimal playing height are the fairways, while the longer grass areas, commonly called rough, are used to define peripheral playing areas and to penalize a shot that misses the preferred landing zones. The degree to which rough should penalize a golfer should be proportionate to how far the ball misses the fairway. It does not seem reasonable that a ball missing a fairway by only a few inches should be penalized as harshly as one that misses by 20 yards.

It is this concern in strategic design to create fair hazards that has led many golf course superintendents to cut an intermediate or so-called "friendly" rough. If deep rough is cut at 2 1/2 inches or more, then a strip of friendly rough about 15 to 20 feet wide alongside a fairway may be kept at 1 1/2 inches. Having two or three heights of rough cut is practical, for it adds only a few more dollars to the overall maintenance budget, yet creates a more interesting and equitable test of golf than "all or nothing maintenance," which equally condemns all who veer even minimally from the intended path.

Most golf architects who endorse strategic design principles use rough sparingly. This is because the early linksland courses, especially St. Andrews, had little or no rough as we know it today. Animals that grazed such linksland were indiscriminate about where they ate, so there was no clear-cut definition between fairway and rough. In fact, rough extending from tee to green along both sides of the fairway was purely a product of the introduction of mowing machines, not of golf course architects. In the heyday of strategic design, almost no rough was planned. That's still the case at a few select courses, such as Augusta National or one of the author's newest designs—Naples National Golf Club in Florida—where there is no rough at all (see figure 42). While closely mown fairways provide distinct demarcation with rough, all too often fairways are cut in unnatural straight lines, imparting an alien, linear, freeway look. In the past few years, however, many golf course superintendents, in reaction to the predominance of the straight lines on their courses, have adopted contour mowing patterns that provide flowing natural lines between fairway and rough.

Contour mowing offers a chance to use the hazard of rough to reintroduce strategy into a golf course. But contour mowing does not simply mean mowing some curves along the edge of fairways. Contour patterns must be in response to the topography and existing golf features and, most importantly, to the playing patterns of all golfers (see figure 43). Therefore, a contour mowing pattern should provide for the widest fairway at the anticipated landing areas at 175 yards and 220 yards out from the white or middle tees. The narrower fairway landing zones should occur at less than 60 yards from the front tees. Contour

Bill Kozma Photography

Figure 42. Naples National has no rough—only tees, greens, fairways, bunkers, water, sand scrub, and pine straw. Total turf area is about 45 acres.

Figure 43. Contour mowing—as on the 16th hole at Lassing Pointe in Burlington, Kentucky—creates wide landing zones where needed, reduces total fairway area, and accents design intent.

mowing patterns should similarly respect the second, third, and fourth impact areas as well for each group of golfers. A good rule of thumb is to make the fairway widest where most average golfers hit it, but require the longest player (who is more often than not the most accomplished) to face the narrower driving or impact areas, so that if he chooses to hit it long he must also hit it with control. Since the severity of the hazard of rough is largely a function of mowing height, the reward can be easily matched to the risk.

This discussion of rough assumes that the same kind of grass covers an entire course. When golf was played on native turf, before our modern sophistication in plant breeding and selection, a golf course was indeed covered with the same basic turf mixture, if by no other process than the ecology of natural selection. However, it has now become common to plant different varieties of turfgrass on different parts of the course. Tees and greens receive the fine bladed, best adapted varieties of turf types, usually bent grass or Bermuda grass. Fairways are usually planted with somewhat less sophisticated cultivars or are less intensely maintained than tees and greens. Fairways are normally mowed less often and at a higher mowing height than tees and greens. They are also watered less, and are given less fertilizer, pesticides, topdressing, and aeration treatment compared to tees and greens. Similarly, roughs are given even less intensive maintenance than fairways. They are often unwatered and planted to less sophisticated turf varieties, and by definition are mowed higher. Since rough is a hazard, the condition of the rough is an area of little concern. But since hazards are one of the "spices" of the course, perhaps more concern should be given to roughs. Deep rough can be particularly severe when fairways are narrow. A course whose reputation rests solely on impossible rough conditions and narrow fairways is not only boring to play, but may also lack enough spice to leave sweet-tasting memories. Consider, for instance, the conditions found at most U.S. Opens, especially those played at Olympic in 1955, or Oakmont in 1983, or Shinnecock in 1986 and 1995.

Golf course architects well-versed in agronomics know that different types of turf grasses have different habits of growth and different physical structure (morphology)(see figure 44). It is also known that some grasses, such as Bahias, fescues, and buffalo grass, are more difficult to play from than Bermuda, bent, or bluegrasses. Therefore, instead of planting all roughs uniformly with the same grass variety, certain species should be planted in selected locations. At an impact area that consistently offers the best angle of approach, a reward for hitting it can easily be balanced with a risk of an adjacent rough planted in some special, hard-to-play-out-

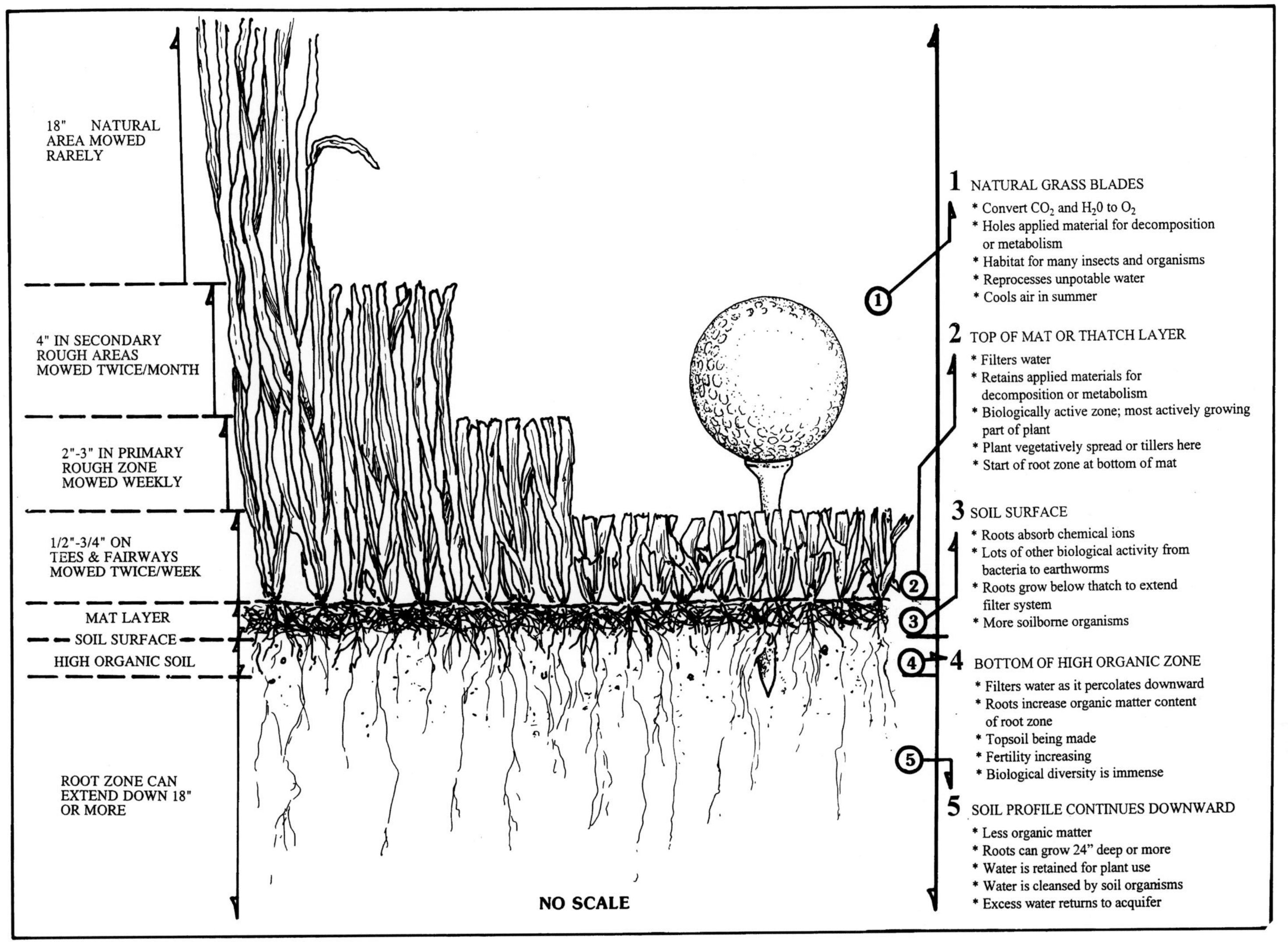
18" NATURAL AREA MOWED RARELY
4" IN SECONDARY ROUGH AREAS MOWED TWICE/MONTH
2"-3" IN PRIMARY ROUGH ZONE MOWED WEEKLY
1/2"-3/4" ON TEES & FAIRWAYS MOWED TWICE/WEEK
MAT LAYER
SOIL SURFACE
HIGH ORGANIC SOIL
ROOT ZONE CAN EXTEND DOWN 18" OR MORE
NO SCALE
1 NATURAL GRASS BLADES
* Convert CO_2 and H_20 to O_2
* Holes applied material for decomposition or metabolism
* Habitat for many insects and organisms
* Reprocesses unpotable water
* Cools air in summer
2 TOP OF MAT OR THATCH LAYER
* Filters water
* Retains applied materials for decomposition or metabolism
* Biologically active zone; most actively growing part of plant
* Plant vegetatively spread or tillers here
* Start of root zone at bottom of mat
3 SOIL SURFACE
* Roots absorb chemical ions
* Lots of other biological activity from bacteria to earthworms
* Roots grow below thatch to extend filter system
* More soilborne organisms
4 BOTTOM OF HIGH ORGANIC ZONE
* Filters water as it percolates downward
* Roots increase organic matter content of root zone
* Topsoil being made
* Fertility increasing
* Biological diversity is immense
5 SOIL PROFILE CONTINUES DOWNWARD
* Less organic matter
* Roots can grow 24" deep or more
* Water is retained for plant use
* Water is cleansed by soil organisms
* Excess water returns to acquifer
1
2
3
4
5

Figure 44.

of grass. This offers more diversity of challenge and can also add a change in color and texture to the landscape. The uniform use of planted grasses results from the same mentality of mass production that gave us freeway golf courses. Sadly, even golf architects with the knowledge and skill to use with sensitivity different grasses in different locations have often ignored their use. All too often designers are so busy that it's much easier simply to specify one rough seed mix for all rough areas than to take the time to patiently select several grass types, or talk with a knowledgeable superintendent about the options. Less skilled designers who were pressed into service by the burgeoning demand for golf courses simply followed the "one-mix" method of the others. This may be changing, as the major seed suppliers are now employing grassing experts to work with golf course architects to more intelligently select turfgrass types and cultivars (see figure 45).

Non-Turf Vegetation

Another type of hazard related to roughs is areas planted or populated with non-turf vegetation. These areas are beyond the limits of the rough, out of expected play patterns, and are characterized by plants that receive little or no maintenance and are native to the site. The most common examples are the heaths and heathers and gorse of Great Britain, the ice plants of the Pacific coastline, the reeds and grasses of coastal wetlands, the prairie grasses of the plains, the sand and scrub of pine forests or barrens, and the leaves and pine needles of forests. These plants or plant debris are usually low growing compared to accompanying bushes, shrubs, and trees, and if you can find your ball among them, it is normally possible to play it out. The severity of this type of hazard, and its effect on the golf shot played from it, again can be controlled by the golf course designer. One such material is pine needles or pine straw, which is easy to find a ball in and play from, which is why it was used so extensively at Naples National (see figure 46). However, native unmowed grass can grow 18 inches high and then often the intent of the ensuing shot is simply to get the ball back into play. Such recovery shots often involve more luck than skill. Non-turf vegetative hazards have so little flexibility in their degree of severity that great care and thought must be given to their location and dis-

Figure 45. Grasses of different colors, textures, and heights make the golf course interesting to play, visually stimulating, and ecologically friendly. This is Annbriar Golf Club in Waterloo, Illinois, where bent grass, zoysia, tall fescue, hard fescue, and native grasses blend together.

Figure 46. Pine straw is an excellent substitute for turfgrass roughs at Naples National.

tribution. A golf shot played from non-turf vegetation is often unrewarding and adds little to enjoyment of the game. This is often simply a survival shot.

Slopes

Slopes and undulations are hazards that do add to the enjoyment of the game. Bernard Darwin wrote that "undulation is the soul of the golf course." More precisely, it may be the extent and abruptness of the third dimension as it departs from the flat or level that provides "the soul of the course." Slopes exert two effects on play: they change the relationship of the ball to the golfer's stance and swing, and they also cause a moving ball to change direction and speed.

In its gentle form, a slope is not very intimidating. Although most golfers strike the ball best on level lies, it takes only small swing or stance adjustments to compensate for a mild slope. But as the slope becomes steeper, its effect becomes more dramatic. It can affect a player's balance and alter his swing plane, thus complicating his ability to properly play a controlled shot from the slope. The steeper the slope, the more penalizing it becomes.

The three standard methods for describing a slope are as a percentage, a ratio of length to height, or an angle of degrees. For example, the same slope can be described as a 20% slope, a 5:1 slope, or an angle of 11° 19′ (see figure 47a).

For this discussion we will use the ratio method, for it is much easier to visualize one foot of rise in five feet of length than it is an 11° 19′ angle or a 20% rise. As a matter of reference, some common rule of thumb limits for slopes are respected.

Knowing these slope activity limits, a golf architect can plan his use of slopes to best suit his design intentions. For instance, if natural slopes are steeper than 2.5:1 (40%) and they cannot be

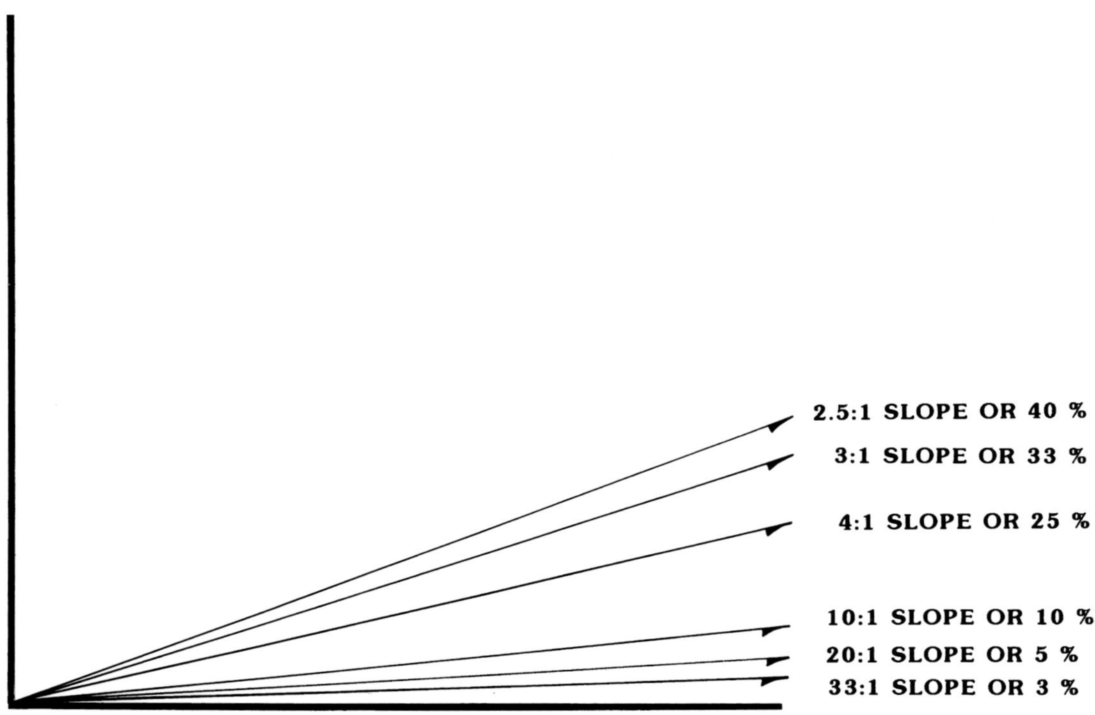

Figure 47a. Slopes can be expressed in various ways, and define limits for golf activities.

Slope	*Percentage*	*Limit of Activity*
2.5:1	40%	maximum that can be mowed with specialized riding mower
3:1	33%	maximum that can be mowed with riding mower
4:1	25%	maximum used for banks of greens and tees
10:1	10%	maximum for walking golfers over short distance (100 yards)
20:1	5%	maximum for walking golfers over long distance
33:1	3%	maximum overall putting surface slope to keep ball in control on Bermuda grass or ryegrass
50:1	2%	minimum to make water surface drain over turf and maximum overall putting surface slope to keep ball in control on bent grass putting green
100:1	1%	minimum overall putting surface slope to surface drain
200:1	0.5%	minimum fall for corrugated drain tile lines
1000:1	0.01%	minimum fall for smooth-walled pipe

Figure 47b.

softened by earthmoving, then these areas will require hand maintenance and will be costly to be kept in a playable condition. Therefore an architect will attempt to route the golf course so these areas can be left as minimum maintenance areas. Conversely, if the land has less than a 50:1 slope to it (2%), this land will not surface drain and presumably will be swampy after receiving water unless the slope is steepened or subsurface drainage is provided. Most other slopes are to be found between these two extremes and can be considered acceptable golfing ground. On very flat ground the use of long flowing mounds in fairways and roughs provides very suitable hazards. Severity can be balanced with reward by simply adjusting the steepness of the slopes. On very hilly ground, the reverse is true. Instead of providing slopes as hazards, the golf architect creates level impact areas as rewards for properly played shots. Usually, when working on hilly ground, the creation of level areas requires steepening adjacent slopes, and most often, the larger the level area created, the steeper the side slopes will be. (Most golf courses in Japan are on harsh terrain, which accounts for why they all look so similar, having either narrow landing zones or steep side slopes or both.) Thus a skillful golf architect can nicely balance reward with proportionate risk by adjusting slopes.

On greens, the use of slopes narrows the margin of error, not by affecting a golfer's balance but by complicating the roll of the ball both onto and upon a putting surface. This complication takes two forms. It causes the rolling ball to depart from a straight path by following a contour (see figure 48a & b). This is called "break." The complications introduced by slopes on and around putting greens include influencing the speed of a rolling golf ball, making it roll faster or slower as compared to a ball struck with the same force on a level surface. Thus the margin

Figure 48a. In his 1920 book, Golf Architecture, Dr. Alister MacKenzie used this green, the 18th at Sitwell Park, as a good example of undulation in putting surface which gave "a wide choice of places for the hole . . ."

Figure 48b. When greens putted "slow," more slope could be designed into the putting surface.

of error in a putt is a direct function of a slope as it affects both speed and break.

With modern, close-cutting mowing equipment, cutting heights of 1/8 inch or less, and improved fine-bladed turfgrasses, it is possible to make a green too fast for the slope of the green, so that after the ball leaves the putter it continues to pick up speed until it rolls off the green. When that happens putting becomes pure luck, and not a fair test of skill. It has been found by experience that a 2% (on bent grass) or 3% (on Bermuda) slope is about the maximum overall slope on a green that still permits a golfer to control the ball. This is not to say that no portion of the green should exceed 2% or 3%. Rather, the overall pitch of the entire green should be less than 2% or 3%. In fact, uniformly sloping greens are boring. It is the change in pitch over short distances that makes putting interesting.

The watchword on green slopes is control. The overall speed of the green must be matched to the overall slope of the green so the golfer can control the ball and exhibit his skill. The master architects of the past realized the necessity of matching speed with slope and designed accordingly. So when one finds old greens with a 7% or 8% slope, it is a reflection of the less sophisticated grasses and mowers of that time that produced slower greens, not of an architect's desire to punish a golfer (see figure 49a & b). Unfortunately, succeeding green committees and greenkeepers may thoughtlessly apply modern technology to produce fast greens on the designer's older form and unwittingly create an unfair situation. A classic example is the conversion of highly undulating—but grainy—Bermuda grass greens to closely cropped bent grass. Suddenly, the same green slopes seem unfair because the ball rolls so much quicker.

The lower limit of slope on a golf green is 2% on Bermuda grass and 1.5% on bent grass—the minimum that still accommodates surface drainage of water. This does not mean that portions of the green cannot be dead level; rather, it means that in order to facilitate optimal plant growth, excess surface water from rains and irrigation must be removed by percolating through the soil profile, instead of surface draining to green surrounds. To do this requires a complete understanding of the dynamics of water movement in sandy soils, so fast internal drainage is provided. Thus the various methods of green construction must be analyzed and the one that best supports the long-term maintenance should be selected (see figure 50).

Knowing these general limits, a golf course architect can extend his system of risk and rewards through the use of slopes on the greens. Unless a green is devoid of structural features, there must be an integration of other hazards with slopes of the putting surface. For example, if a portion of the green is to be protected with sand bunkers, then that portion of the green may be less sloped than a portion not protected. The design intent is that the golfer who wishes to risk the sand should be rewarded with an easier putt than the player who chooses to play safe, away from the bunker (see figure 51).

There are, by the way, multiple tools available to the sensitive and skilled golf architect. Thus far we have examined only two types of hazards—vegetation and slopes—both of which offer degrees of severity within themselves. Consider, then, how much more difficult a golf hazard can be as a combination of elements, say a steep slope covered by long grass. Now the required golf shot is more difficult by both individual factors. This sort of a synergistic effect, where the total effect is greater than the sum of its parts, may be even more penalizing depending upon its location within the golf hole. It is not a golf architect's duty to make a golf hole difficult, but rather to make each hole a fair test of golf, each one a balance of risk and rewards.

Mounds

Another type of hazard related to slope is mounds. Mounds differ from slopes in that they appear to change direction and steepness more quickly and are usually placed solely as a hazard. Mounds usually have abrupt slopes of less than 10:1, and have defined edges along most of their entire circumference at the base. Slopes, on the other hand, blend harmoniously into adjacent contours, and have few or no defined edges.

The purposes of mounds are to affect the bound and roll of a ball that strikes them, to make shots played from them more difficult by disturbing the golfer's balance, to alter a golfer's swing plane, and to obscure a target. The use of mounds to affect bounce and roll of a golf ball becomes more important the closer one gets to the cup. Mounding within a putting surface greatly complicates reading and interpreting the speed and break of a putt. When several mounds are used within the putting surface, however, putting can become an overly dominant part of a round, and thus distract attention from the (lack of) soundness of the golf course in its entirety.

As for mounds that surround a putting surface but are not a part of it, the closer to a green a mound is, the lower may be its profile and yet the greater will be its influence. For example, a small mound only 2 to 3 feet high with 6:1 or 8:1 outslopes placed directly in front of the green can be a fair separator of golf shots (see figure 52). Shots landing short of the green that may otherwise run up onto the putting surface will tend to stop short because of the upslope of the mound. Shots just barely landing over the little mound may strike the mound's downslope and run well past their desired resting spot. In both cases, these shots were penalized, but penalized fairly. Conversely, a shot played precisely to the intended impact area and avoiding the small ridge is properly rewarded by finishing on the green within easy range of the cup. This concept of strategy was used to set the shot values on the 11th hole at Cook's Creek outside Columbus, Ohio, a 300-yard par 4. During the design of this hole, John Cook and the author decided this form of hazard was perfectly suited for this hole (see figure 53a & b).

This example assumes the preferred target was a spot on the green, which is the normal case with approach shots on courses with modern irrigation. However, decades ago (before the American fetish for soft, lush green conditions) it was not possible to fire a ball at a flagstick as indiscriminately as most golfers do now. Instead, because of dry conditions, a ball would bounce and roll for great distances, so allowances had to be made for the ground game as a vital part of all approach shots. The pitch-and-run shot was a more valued weapon in a golfer's arsenal. Today, a thoughtful golf architect may depart from the American norm and require on a particular hole that the proper shot to a green land short and run onto the surface. By using mounds or slopes (or both) short of a green to affect the bounce and roll of a ball, or by building a reverse slope into a green to deny a lofted pitch shot, the architect can reward the player who recognizes the required pitch-and-run shot and properly executes it. It was just such a design feature that made the Redan hole—the 15th at North Berwick—so famous (see again figure 13). The Redan was first reproduced by C.B. Macdonald as the fourth hole at his National Golf Links of America in the early 1900s, and has been copied on many other occasions by talented designers such as Seth Raynor (1874–1926), A.W. Tillinghast (1874–1942) and Robert Trent Jones (b. 1906), and virtually every other major architect.

Mounds and slopes are of value in fairway im-

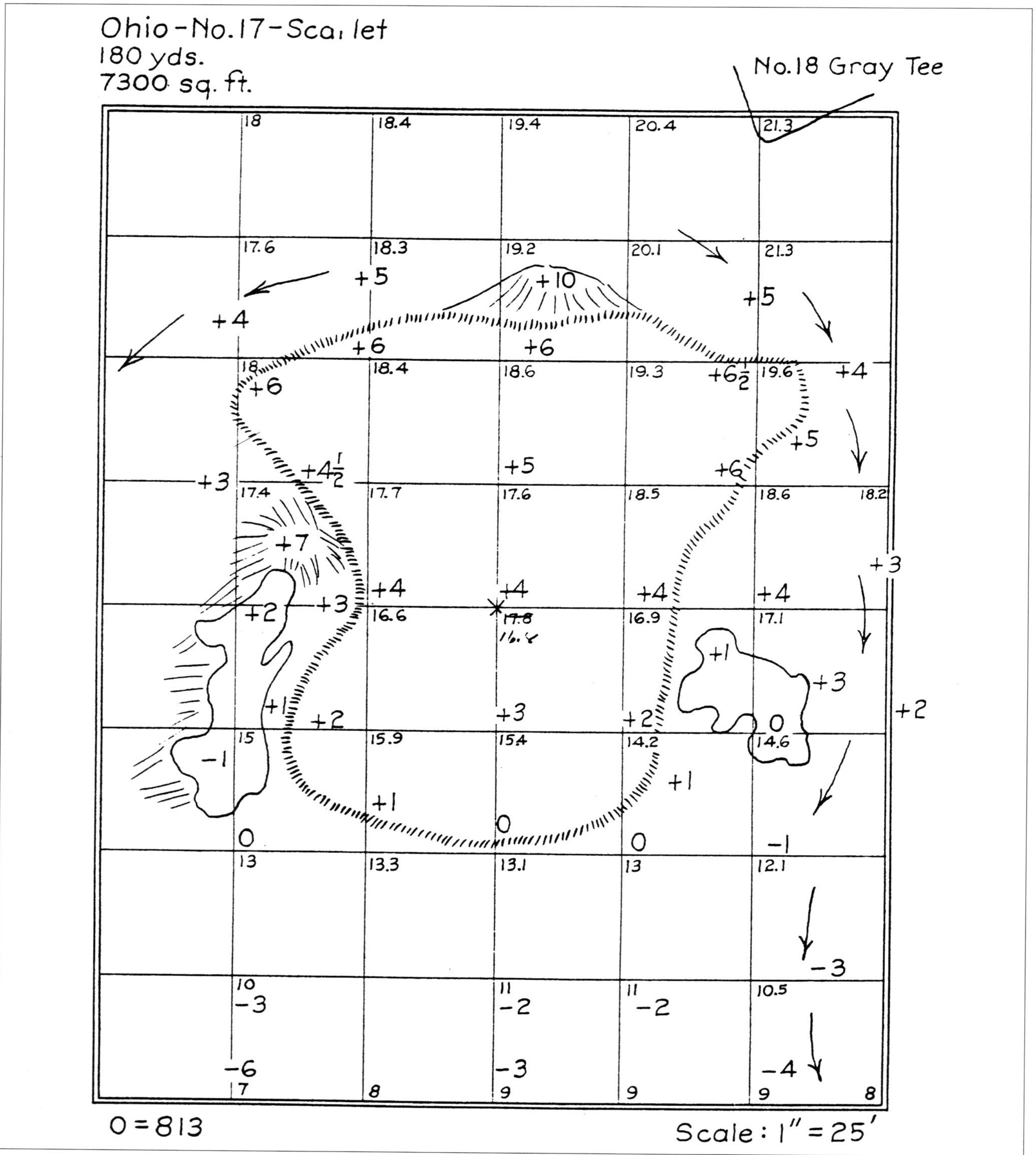

Figure 49a. The 17th green at Ohio State University's Scarlet Course, before (a & b) and after (c) it was rebuilt to soften slopes from 6% to 3%.

Figure 49b.

Figure 49c.

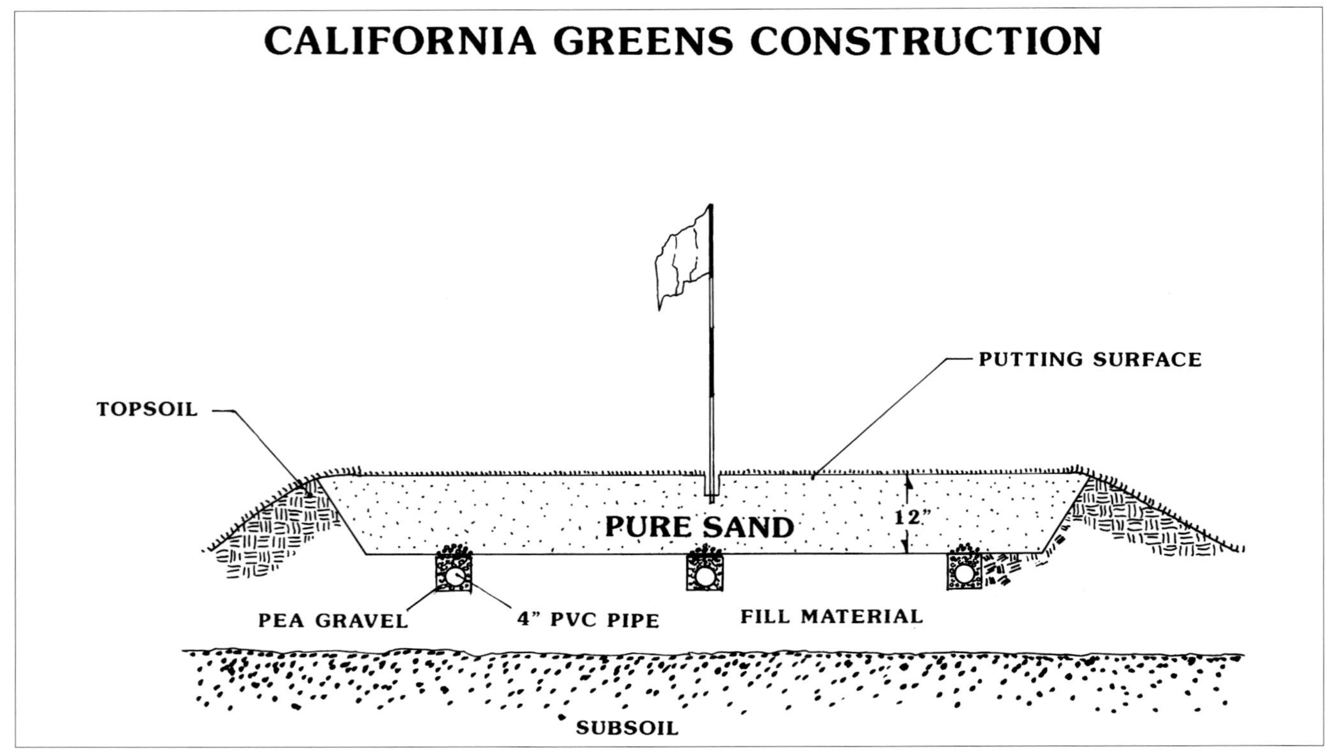
CALIFORNIA GREENS CONSTRUCTION
PUTTING SURFACE
TOPSOIL
PURE SAND
12"
PEA GRAVEL
4" PVC PIPE
FILL MATERIAL
SUBSOIL

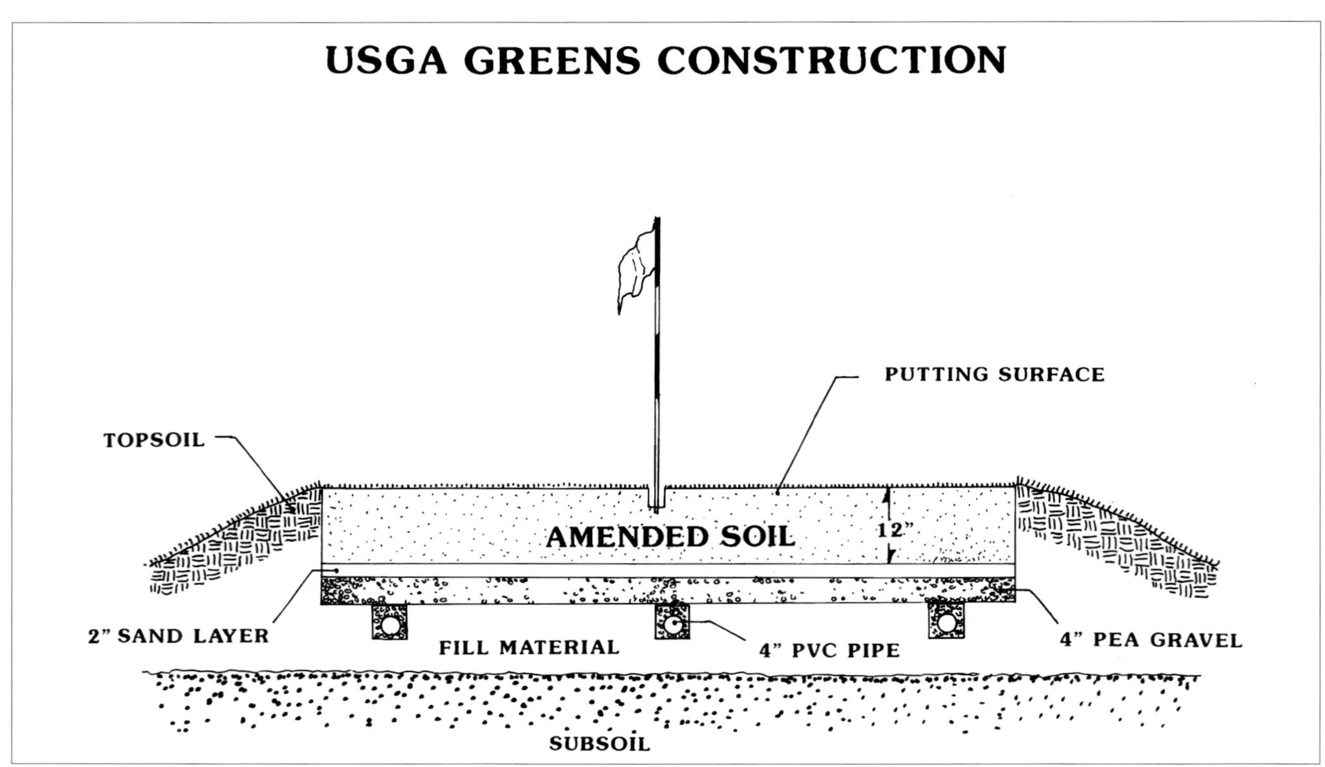
USGA GREENS CONSTRUCTION
PUTTING SURFACE
TOPSOIL
AMENDED SOIL
12"
2" SAND LAYER
FILL MATERIAL
4" PVC PIPE
4" PEA GRAVEL
SUBSOIL

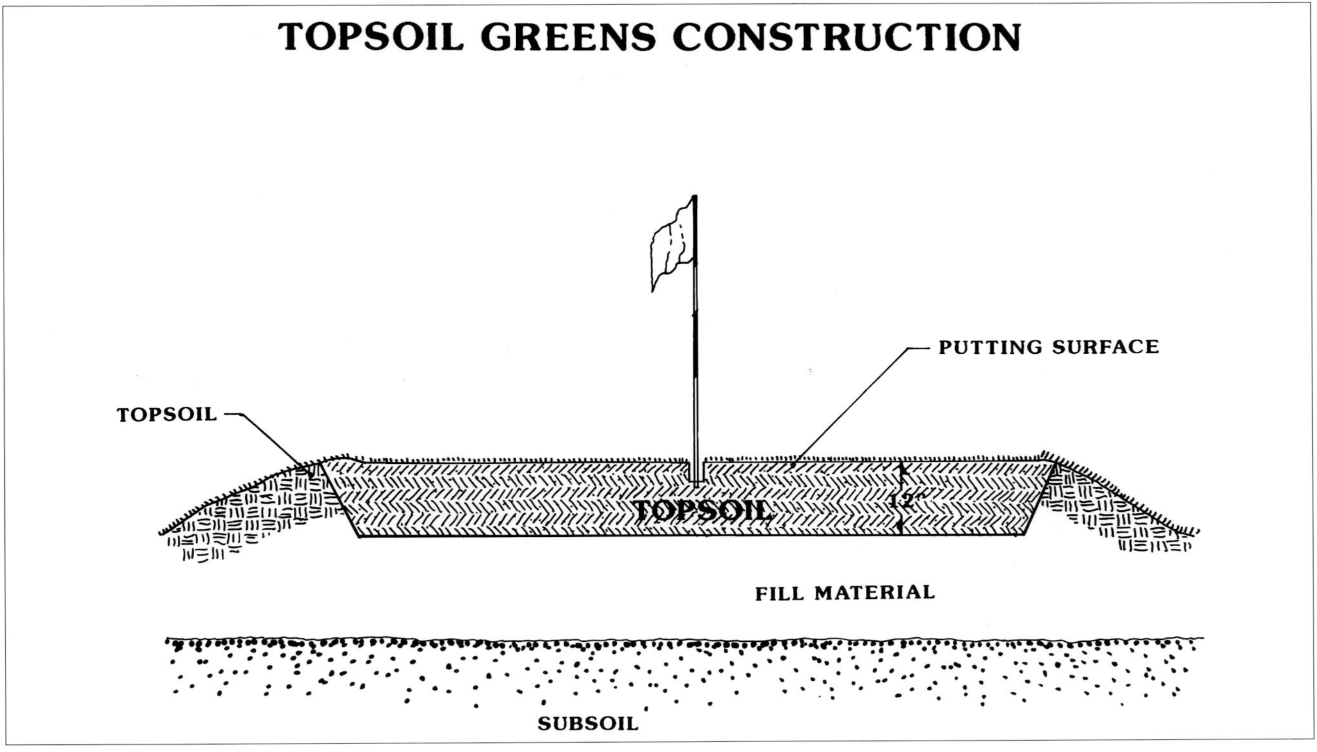

Figure 50. The three most common methods of interior green construction. Each has its own advantages and disadvantages, so no one method is correct for all golf course projects.

Figure 51. Notice how most of the green approach is open to receive any shot, while hole locations behind bunkers demand very precise play. This is the second hole at Naples National, a long par 5.

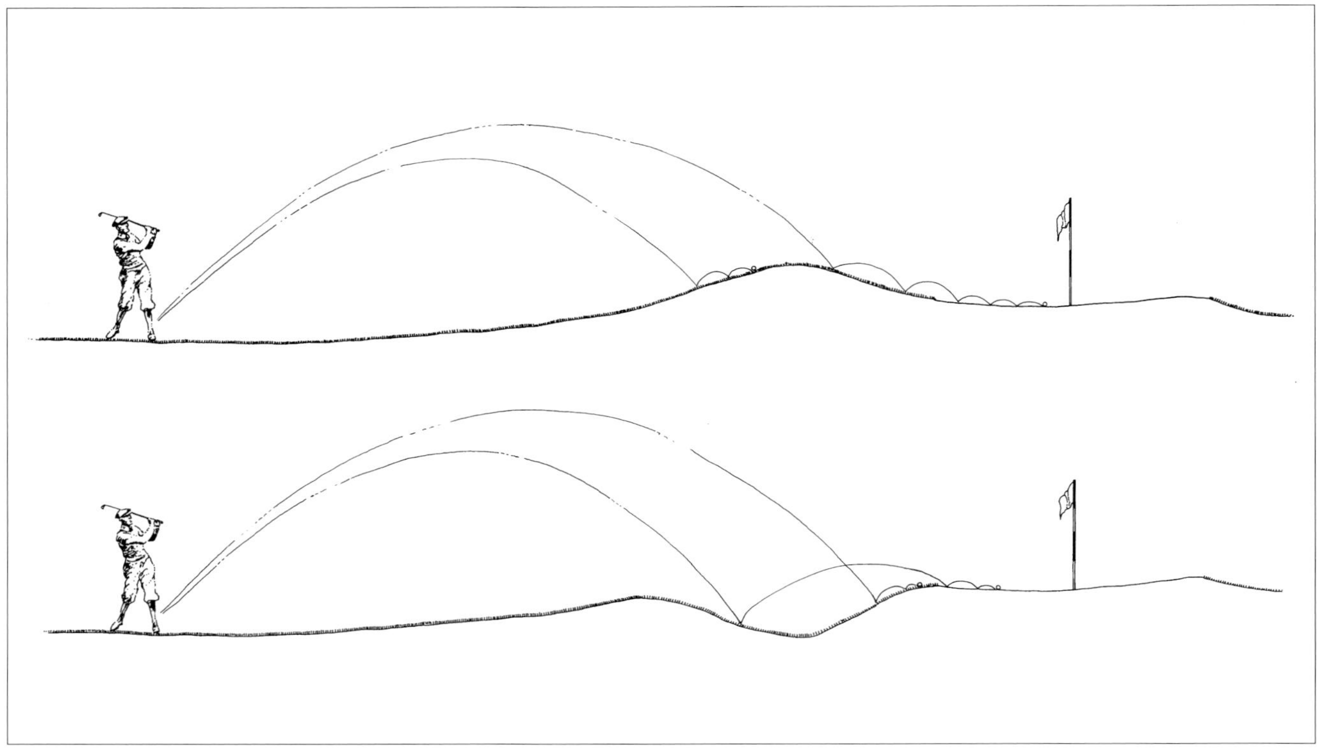

Figure 52. Mounds and depressions in front of greens result in distinct differences in shots of similar length depending on whether the ball lands on an upslope or downslope.

pact areas, too (see figure 54). If an architect's intent is to build some strategy into his fairways by rewarding a properly placed tee shot with a longer run as compared to an imperfectly struck drive, it can be accomplished by building a large mound or slope in the landing area so that a ball landing on the downslope will run a longer distance than one hitting the center of the fairway. To accentuate the effect of this feature, the backside of the mound and fairway beyond can be kept dryer than other parts of the fairway. This architectural device was used on the 8th hole at Devil's Paintbrush in Caledon, Ontario (an Irish links-type course), where it added another dimension to an otherwise routine drive (see figure 55).

A mound as a hazard can often dictate a choice of clubs to a player if he wishes to clear it. On tee shots and long iron approaches, or in windy areas, high mounds can be devastating hazards, for they require the golfer to put the ball up into the wind at least high enough to clear the mounds, but a shot that fails to clear them is severely punished by the awkward shot that must be played next. Several holes featuring such mounds are found in Scotland and England on holes at Gleneagles, Muirfield, Prestwick, Royal St. Georges, Lahinch, and one of the author's best creations, Devil's Paintbrush. Such hazards are best suited to harshly undulating terrain or mountainous terrain, especially where wind is a factor.

One last function of a mound is to obscure a golfer's view of the intended target. Golfers are deeply concerned about where their ball comes to rest, fearing that if they can't see it they're likely to lose it. Golfers also get upset if they strike a ball well and have it end up in a less than perfect position. By toying with such emotions and by building features into the holes that are likely to elicit subtle responses from players, a golf course architect can create illusions that

Figure 53a. At the 11th hole at Cook's Creek in Circleville, Ohio, John Cook, PGA Tour Pro, and I designed a driveable par 4 of 300 yards from the pro tees, but added a small ridge in front of the green to reward only the perfectly placed drive.

Figure 53b. John, his sister Cathy, Dana Fry—who was my lead designer of Cook's Creek—and I discuss design details.

Figure 54. Mounds and slopes in fairways occurred naturally on the linksland, and hence became a natural part of golf. As golf moved inland, often mounds were created with crude earthmoving equipment as hazards, but today most fairway undulation is done to control surface drainage water.

Doug Ball

Figure 55. Being designed in an Irish links style, Devil's Paintbrush gave me many opportunities to build a landing zone that was kept drier, and hence made drives longer. At the 8th hole, one only needs to clear a historic stone wall to gain an extra 20 to 40 yards on the drive.

test, and often shatter, the player's concentration. A mound or ridge that reveals only a portion of a particular golf hole often causes a golfer to look up, tighten up, or flinch during a golf swing.

The ultimate example of mounds obscuring a view are blind golf holes. Most architects today do not personally like blind golf holes, and generally such holes should be avoided. But occasionally a blind hole serves as an appropriate test of a golfer's ability to assess the proper shot and then to execute it without benefit of visual information. A variant of the blind shot that may, if deployed sparingly, find acceptance, is intentionally to design the back portion of the tee so that the front portion of the tee blocks the view of the target area, thus challenging scratch golfers a bit more. Some of the most revered courses in the world—Muirfield, Prestwick, Lahinch, and Royal Troon, to name a few—have totally blind shots, and these holes have produced some memorable shots in golf, mainly because they delay gratification and increase anticipation (see figure 56). A golf shot that appears to be perfectly struck but requires a minute or two before the final result is observed is a golf shot that won't soon be forgotten. (This technique of "hiding" is most natural, appropriate, and accepted on European-type linksland golf courses. However, this technique was used quite liberally at Devil's Paintbrush because of its Irish links style (see figure 57).

Depressions and Grass Traps

Closely related to the mound hazard, yet antithetical in appearance, is the depression. A depression can range from something as slight as a

Figure 56. "The Dell" is the name of the par 3 156-yard 6th hole at Lahinch. This is a blind tee shot to a green set between four huge mounds. A white rock indicates the correct line of play for that day's hole location, but to play too boldly leaves a difficult chip shot.

swale on a putting surface to something as dramatic as a deep chasm (see figure 58). Obviously, on greens the purpose of the depression is the same as that of mounds and slopes: to cause a ball to break away from the intended path or to change speeds. However, outside the boundaries of a green, the differences between depressions and mounds are more pronounced. Most depressions that come into the line of play present an upslope on its green side and a downslope toward the tee side, which is the opposite of a mound. This may at first seem a small difference, but consider the effect this may have on a golf ball. Using the earlier example of a small mound in front of the green, now substitute a small depression of equal dimension in place of the mound. In that circumstance, a ball landing well short of the green strikes the downslope of the depression instead of the upslope of the mound, and may well run up on the green instead of stopping short. From the same approach area, a ball struck more firmly now strikes the upslope of the depression and stops short, rather than bouncing down the mound and onto the green. Note how this seems to penalize the better struck shot, but only if airborne approach shots are considered better than bounce and run shots.

What a depression provides is yet another tool with which to plan strategy in a design. The skilled architect may design one hole with a depression before a green in order to reward the shot that lands on the downslope or the depression. Another hole may feature a mound in front of a green so that a high approach will have the advantage. The ideal landing area need not always be close to the hole. In fact, it is such variety within a hole or among holes on a golf course that makes the game interesting.

Depressions, for purposes of this discussion, are hazards. If a ball comes to rest on the downslope of the depression, it calls for a much more difficult chip shot than a shot on an upslope. A depression can also make the distance to the hole appear to be visually shorter than it actually is, especially if the depression or swale is directly in front of the green. This compounds the problem of club selection for the golfer. There are numerous courses where a golf architect has constructed swales to conduct surface water away from the front of the green, and in the process made the green seem one or two club lengths closer. This illusion is particularly strong when the swale is broad and has gentle sideslopes.

Discussion of depressions leads directly to the next type of hazard—grass traps and sand traps, or bunkers. Their names define the difference between them. While both are depressions, one is grass covered while the other has a sand surface. Both normally are bordered by

Figure 57. The 14th hole at Devil's Paintbrush is a blind second shot, played over a guide rock, to a green that looks like it would have been at home in the 1800s.

Figure 58. Grassy hollows and mounds around greens make golf interesting and challenging.

turf cut at fairway or rough height. The only distinction between a simple depression and a grass trap is that there is usually longer turf growing in the latter. To mow the turf in a grass trap at the same height as other turf areas around it converts it into a depression. The severity of most depressions depends solely upon their slope and depth, but a grass trap derives its severity not only from those two elements but also from the influence of long grass within its confines. Once again, a golf architect can adjust the risk of the hazard against the reward it protects. The same principle of hazard placement applies as before. A recovery shot from a grass trap should be kept within the realm of fairness by carefully considering its location and degree of difficulty.

Bunkers

Sand traps, or bunkers, as they are officially known, should respect the same principles in degree of difficulty of the recovery shot and location balanced against the reward (see figure 59). A sand trap or bunker is considered a slightly more intimidating hazard than grass traps because the footing is less firm in sand, the club cannot be grounded, the depth of sand varies, and the lie one confronts is often a matter of luck. To average golfers, sand traps present a greater threat than grass traps. Conversely, professional golfers would rather play from sand than long grass because they can achieve better ball contact and thus better control of the ball's spin. Sand bunkers should be distinguished from native sand or waste areas which are unmaintained and in which the golfer is permitted to ground his club. It is a very subtle difference, indeed, but if it is raked, it is a bunker, and if not, it is a waste area.

Although there are no rules regarding severity and placement of bunkers, in general the sensitive golf course architect will try to make traps farther from the green less severe than ones close to the green (see figure 60a–f). This is done by giving fairway bunkers gently sloping sand surfaces with no high mounded areas in the direct line to the hole. The closer traps are placed to the green, the more severe they usually are.

The construction of a bunker can be mitigated to exact a penalty of as little as 1/10 of a shot for a flat, firm bunker without a lip that can be putted out onto the green, to as much as one full shot caused by a deep, steep-walled bunker where the only relief is to play the ball back toward the tee and not forward toward the green.

A green and surrounding hazards should not be considered separate entities, but rather a single functioning unit. Together they comprise what is known as the green complex. The putting surface should be large and gentle enough to allow for some margin of error for a recovery shot to it.

Like grass traps, sand traps derive much of their personality from the texture of the covering surface. There is a vast difference in playability between two otherwise similar traps if one is filled with fine and rounded sand and the other with coarse or angular sand. In general, the finer the sand and the more rounded the individual particles, the more difficult it is to play from. Finer sand usually produces more buried lies, looser footing, and more difficulty in transferring club head force to the ball.

Because most golfers expect perfectly consistent playing conditions, golf architects rarely prescribe a variety of sand types on the same golf course. But such an idea would prove interesting and would add a new dimension, requiring more mental calculation to determine what type of sand is present and how to play the best shot from it. In fact, it might be interesting for designers to expand their repertoire of trap materials to include sawdust, pine needles, or other such natural materials indigenous to the immediate area or region. Notice the pictures of Naples National Golf Club where jungle areas were cleared of underbrush and covered with pine straw (see figure 61).

Bunkers are not strictly used as hazards, for they can serve any one of five major functions (see figure 62):

1) strategy—defines shot values
2) retaining—keeps balls from worse fates
3) safety—stops errant shots
4) directional—defines play direction
5) aesthetic—just plain looks good

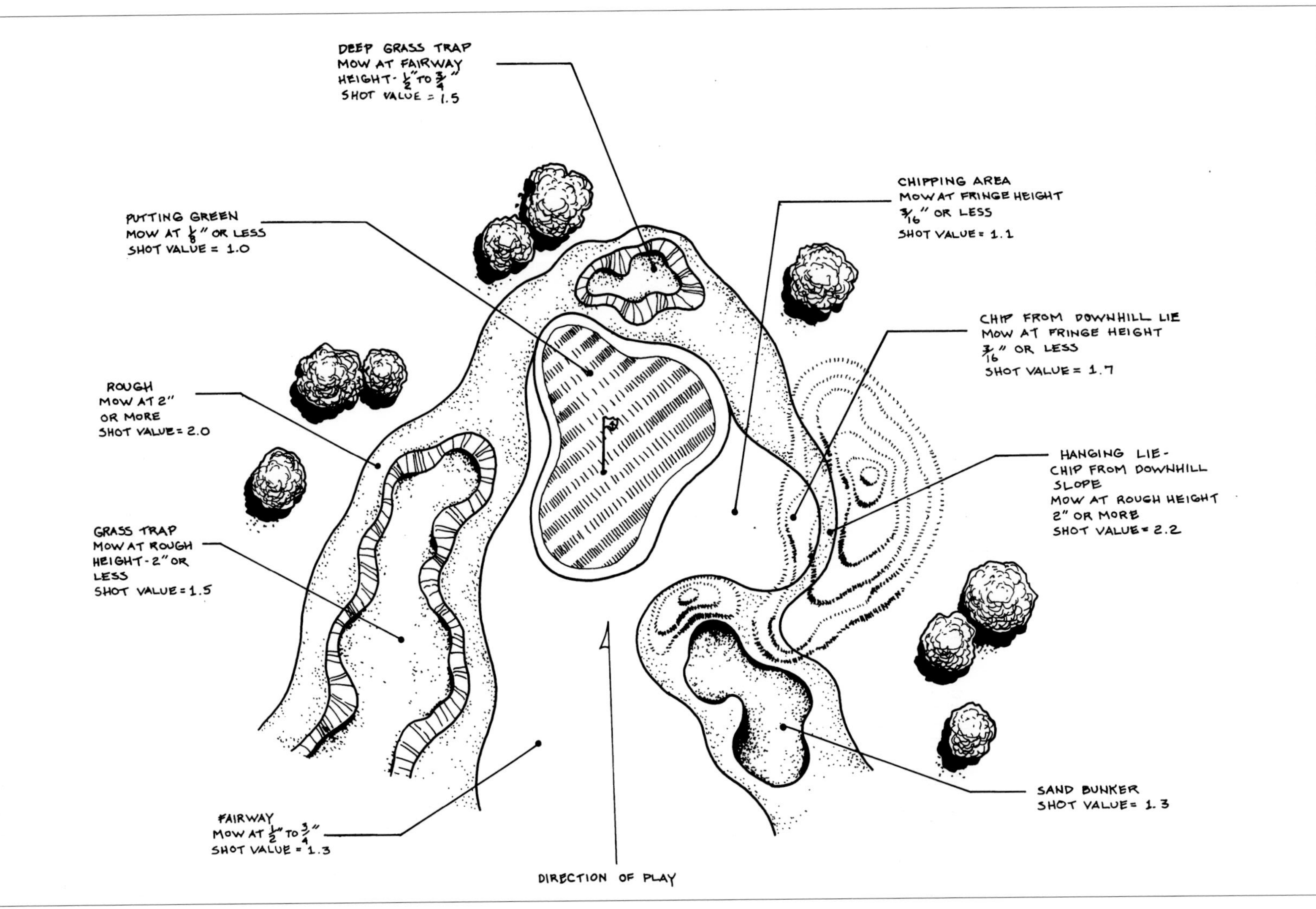

Figure 59. Assuming that the putting green has a shot value of 1.0, the golf course architect can assign shot values to approaches around the green. This permits the designer to match the penalty to the crime.

FAIRWAY BUNKER
OFTEN QUITE LARGE
USUALLY SHALLOW IF LONG DISTANCE TO GREEN
EASY TO PLAY OUT TOWARD GREEN
VISIBLE FROM TEE
PENALTY VALUE IS ONE QUARTER OF A SHOT

APPROACH BUNKER
OFTEN MEDIUM SIZE
USUALLY MODERATELY DEEP
VERY VISIBLE
REQUIRES SKILLFUL SAND PLAY
PENALTY VALUE IS ONE HALF OF A SHOT

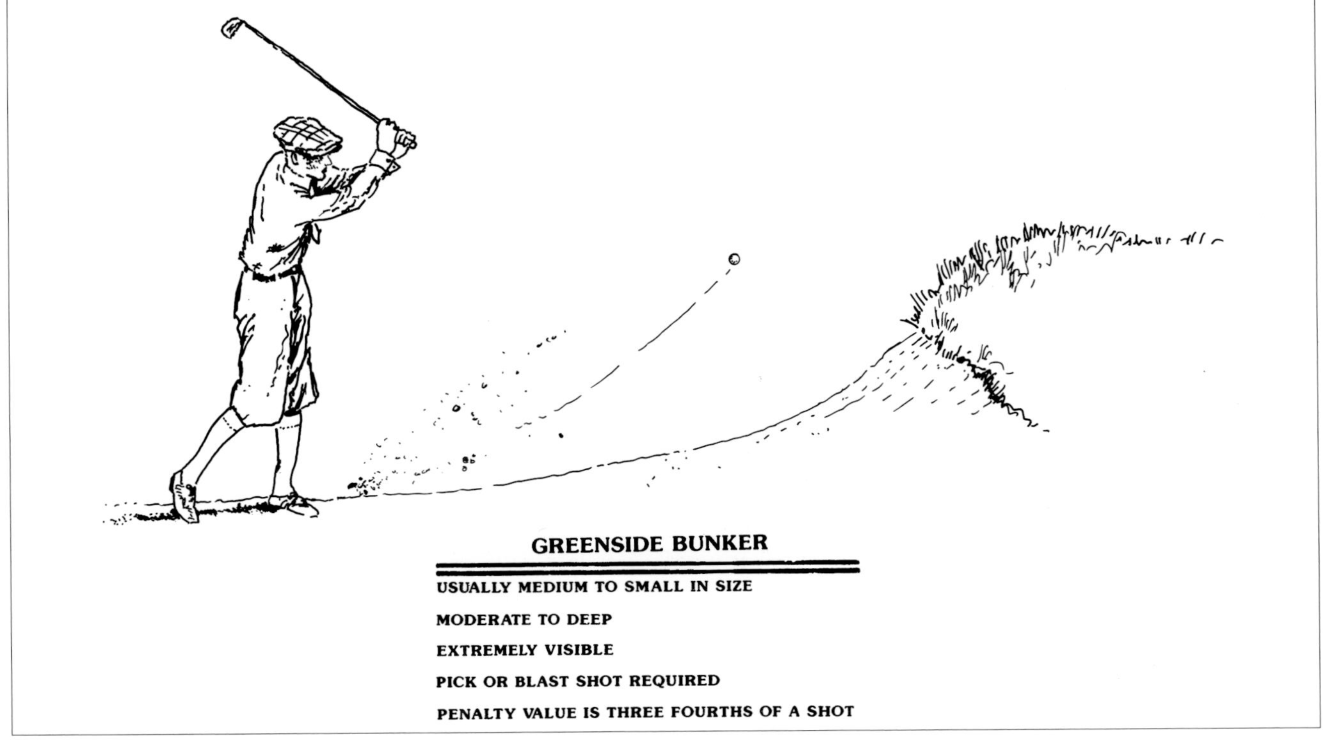

Figure 60a. The golf course architect can control the penalty inflicted by the bunker, or shot value, by the design of the bunker. In general, fairway bunkers are made less harsh than greenside ones, but to avoid repetition, key bunkers are often made harsh no matter their location.

Figure 60b. A shallow greenside bunker.

Doug Ball

Doug Ball

Figure 60c. A deeper greenside bunker.

Doug Ball

Figure 60d. A very deep greenside bunker—but notice the ball.

Dana Fry

Figure 60e. A shallow fairway bunker.

Doug Ball

Figure 60f. The 13-foot-high sod wall bunker at the 17th at Devil's Paintbrush resembles, but dwarfs, the Hell Bunker on the Old Course at St. Andrews. In fact, this may be the largest sod wall bunker in the world. Notice the city of Toronto in the background 35 miles away.

Figure 61. Pine straw is a natural alternative to turfgrass at Naples National.

If a bunker serves any one of those purposes, it should have the proper form that best serves that purpose. This is an art unto itself that the master architects learned through keen observation and trial and error. The best designer not only has a sense of how to perfectly place the bunker, but also knows what scale and slope it has to be to communicate to the golfer as well as serve its intended function. To my mind, Dr. Alister MacKenzie and Stanley Thompson were the best, and one only needs to play Pasatiempo, Cypress Point, or Banff Springs to be convinced (see figure 63).

Mention of naturally occurring material assumes that if a material is native to a golf course site it can be considered as part of the course and be used as a fair hazard. Incorporating a wider range of elements gives us more courses with local flavor or personality, such as crushed seashells or coral for sand. In addition, thoughtful use of these elements in the golf course ties the course into its surroundings, so that one senses a more authentic harmony between the natural, undeveloped land and the necessary artificiality of the course within it.

Rocks, Boulders, and Stones

Even rocks, boulders, stones, and gravel can be used as hazards. They tend to act in a similar way, causing a random deflection of a ball that strikes them. The amount of deflection is the same for all rocks larger than golf ball size, but as rocks are graded down in size to gravel, the deflection is less. In many areas of the world, particularly in mountainous regions, it is not uncommon to find a golf hole playing along rock walls perhaps hundreds of feet high. This is not only attractive but necessary, for the cost to drill and blast rock can be as much as thirty times more expensive than to move an equivalent volume of soil. Therefore the golf architect is forced by budget constraints to move as little rock as is necessary to make the hole playable. Playing along or between sheer rock walls is an interesting and unique situation, particularly if a golfer's lifestyle provides little opportunity to experience the strength, scope, and grandeur of mountainous terrain. At Glenmaura National in Scranton, Pennsylvania, the entire 12th and 17th holes were created by drilling and blasting (see figure 64). High rock walls are an extreme use of

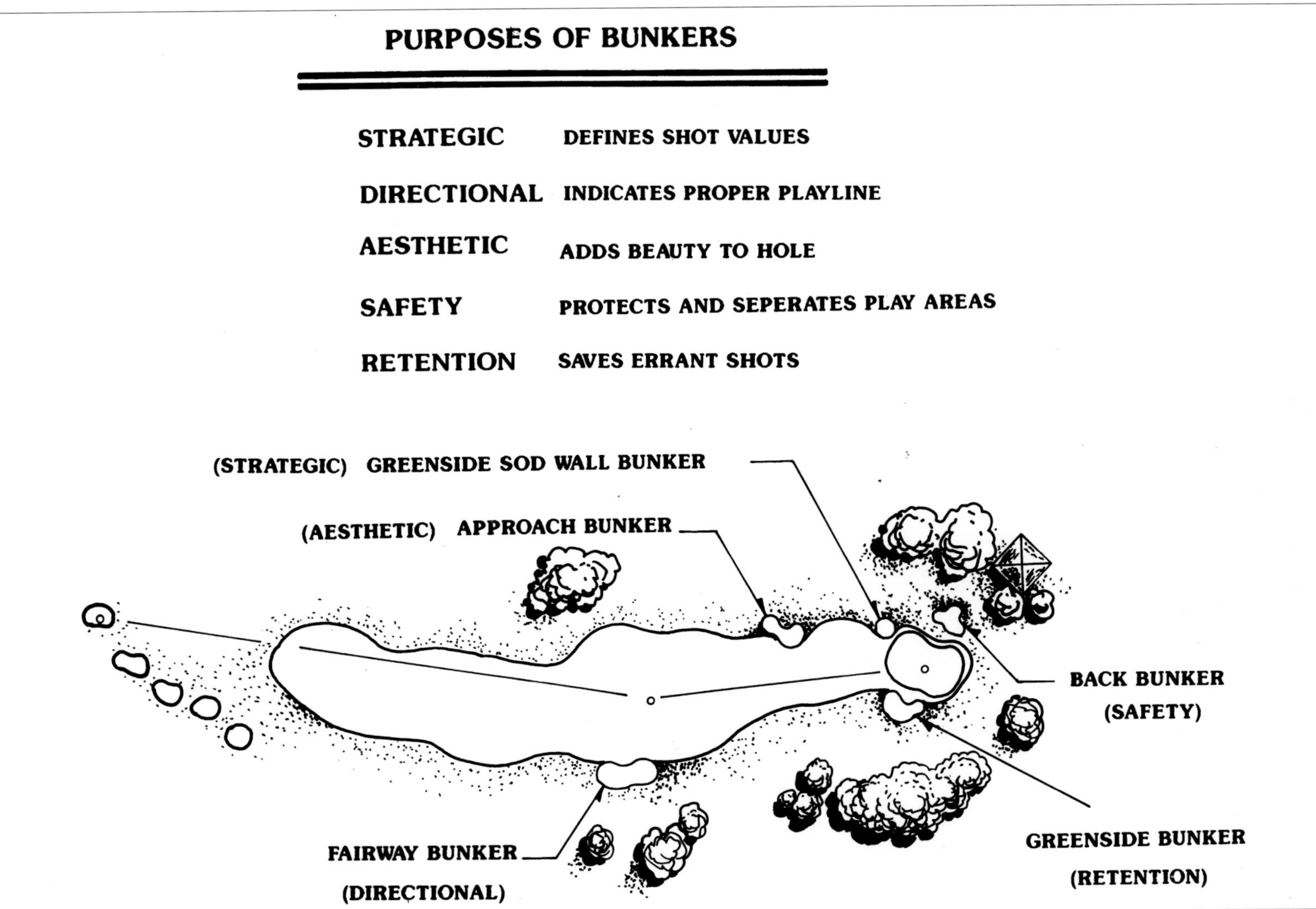

Figure 62. Bunkers can serve any of five distinct functions, depending upon what the designer wants them to do.

Figure 63. Dr. Alister MacKenzie was a master of the art of bunkering. As an example, notice how, on the 9th hole at Cypress Point (a 291-yard par 4), the bunkers start with a crisp edge next to the playing surface and then make a transition to the natural, and all the color, texture, and heights are in perfect balance.

Figure 64. Drilling and blasting of 100,000 cubic yards of rock ledge was the only way to transform the Scranton, Pennsylvania mountainside into Glenmaura National. The entire 12th hole was blasted out. Notice the high wall on the right side. Some members have talked about adding a rope ladder.

Rolling Greens Photo

rock, but if done properly they can become a very natural part of the course. Rocks are used to a lesser degree as an occasional backdrop or infrequent outcropping. At Westwood Plateau, above the city of Vancouver, British Columbia, the 12th and 13th holes owe much of their personality to the rock walls left from blasting in green sites (see figure 65). In these forms rocks are not really considered hazards in the purest sense, but rather obstructions to golf course building that are concessions to the dominance of nature.

However, rocks can be used as hazards in certain situations. The effect of rocks as hazards in most instances is to cause the random bounce of the ball and not to complicate the playing of a golf stroke. Of course, if a ball comes to rest among the rocks, the next shot will certainly be complicated, but this should not be the main objective of rocks as a hazard. That is too capricious to be fair. A good example of the proper use of rocks is the 18th hole at Pebble Beach (see figure 66). If one is unsuccessful in trying to make a heroic carry of a corner of the beach on the drive, or if he hooks his tee shot, he might well end up among the huge shelf of rocks that form the jagged shoreline. This is a fair hazard, for there is adequate fairway to the right of the beach, the rocks are natural to the site, and no player is forced to play anywhere near them.

On the other hand, a traditional use of rocks is a stone wall or rocky ridge existing in the direct line to the hole. This was common on golf courses before the early 1900s and has become popular again in recent times, where rocks have been incorporated in designs for penal purposes, such as at Naples National and Devil's Paintbrush. One contemporary golf architect known for his unorthodox use of materials placed 4-foot-high boulders in the middle of a sand trap. Not only do those rocks look out of place, they also place a golfer in double jeopardy of not only facing a sand shot, but also being blocked from shooting directly at the putting surface.

The use of naturally occurring rock formations that are thoughtfully integrated into the golf course add charm, color, and character to the landscape. But since little can be done to adjust the severity of rock hazards, their incorporation in a golf hole must be handled intelligently if they are to be fair components of a test of golf skills. At Glenmaura National Country Club in Scranton, Pennsylvania, much of the course was carved out of the granite mountainside, flanked by existing and beautiful tree-punctuated ridges, or routed to expose golfers to massive rock formations. At the 8th hole in particular the hole was designed to give the golfer the option of playing over or around an old stone quarry. The effect is not only dramatic but also unforgettable (see figure 67a & b).

Man-Made Structures

Another type of hazard with an influence on golf similar to rock is man-made structures. Although the effect of structures can be to block the line of approach to a target, in most instances such structures are an incidental rather than an integral part of a golf hole. The most renowned man-made structures affecting play on a hole were the old black sheds along the right side of the 17th on the Old Course at St. Andrews. If one chose to do so, the sheds could be carried from the tee, dramatically shortening the approach to the green. The reward carried with it a big risk, however, for if one failed to drive over the sheds, he would either be out of bounds or blocked from all but a lateral shot out to the fairway. The sheds, a natural and dramatic alteration of the third dimension, were not built as a hazard. They just happened to be there, and added a uniqueness to the hole. Sad to say, the old black sheds were demolished years ago, and in their place is a tall fence approximating the silhouette of the sheds, which carries neither the charm nor the drama of the old sheds. Now new "sheds" have been built by the Old Course Hotel which are almost as good as the originals (see figure 68).

Another man-made structure on the same hole (in fact, the one for which the hole is named) is the paved road immediately behind the green. This road is but a thin path literally just a few feet beyond a shelf-like green that is angled diagonally and runs from front right to back left. There is no margin of error on the far side of the putting surface, so that even an ap-

Henebry Photography

Figure 65. The entire par 3 12th hole at Westwood Plateau was blasted out of a granite mountainside. Trees were topped for sight line, while stumps were left for environmental purposes.

Figure 66. The 18th hole at Pebble Beach uses a rock seashore to form a classic heroic-design par 5.

Figure 67a. Previous coal mining had left a quarry, which I incorporated into the design of the 8th hole at Glenmaura National.

Figure 67b. When rock ledge was encountered during the construction of EagleSticks in Zanesville, Ohio, and no money was budgeted for its removal, it was made into a design feature on the 9th hole.

proach shot hit precisely in the correct direction can fade just enough from left to right to find itself on the famed road—or worse yet, beyond the road, nestled beside another man-made feature, a stone wall. This combination of road and wall cost Tom Watson his bid for his sixth British Open title in 1984, when he could only manage a bogey after his approach shot was too long, while eventual winner Seve Ballesteros cinched the title by making par. The recovery shot from the road is a unique and difficult shot. Yet while this man-made structure is intimidating, the hole is still memorable and exciting, and fair because the challenges are all clear to see. The sheds, road, and wall themselves would not have gained recognition had it not been for the type of green that naturally existed there. The second shot to this 461-yard par 4 is invariably a long one, and the green is protected in front by a rather small but severe sand trap called the Road Bunker. Only the best of approach shots will hold the green. It takes a delicate chip from the road to hold the green coming back without rolling into the Road Bunker. It was the fortuitous combination of man-made structures of different proportions along with a perfectly sited combination of green and bunker that together have made the Road Hole at St. Andrews one of the most famous in all of golf.

Figure 68. My 13-year-old son Christopher at the 17th hole on the Old Course at St. Andrews. The caddy shifted his aim to play over the word "Old," Chris hit it well, and was in perfect position on the fairway.

The lesson of the Road Hole is that if the golf course architect finds the right situation, the use of structures as hazards is not only acceptable but also can produce some fascinating golf. However, if structures are improperly placed and are not of the correct proportions, they can be too penalizing and appear as gimmickry, and a golf course is better off without them. For these reasons the author felt blessed while designing Devil's Paintbrush's 17th hole to have century-old man-made structures of stone foundations and an animal water trough made of concrete in what was a perfectly positioned driving zone area (see figure 69). Consequently, the fairway was made 100 yards wide but divided into three distinct landing areas by the ruins. The second shot on this hole must carry another man-made structure—a 12-foot-high sod wall bunker—and the third plays to a small green that slopes off toward a stone wall that was constructed on the property line.

Wooden bulkheads, be they made of railroad ties, posts, or planks, fall into the category of man-made structures. This type of structure is usually built close to the line of play and thus carries with it the possibility of a ball glancing off it and striking a golfer. Care should be taken when building railroad tie features (especially in sand traps) to build the wall with an angle of repose that permits an imperfect shot to ricochet harmlessly away from the golfer. A good example is the semicircular, wood-faced "bounce" bunker on the 3rd hole at Hillcrest Country Club, Batesville, Indiana, or the much larger example on many holes at Devil's Paintbrush (see figure 70). This bounce bunker was

Figure 69. The foundation ruins of an old farmhouse and barns were preserved and made an important part of the 17th hole at Devil's Paintbrush. Local rules allow for a one-shot penalty drop rather than risk more strokes.

Doug Ball

Figure 70. The concept of using wooden walls to shore up bunkers dates back to the middle 1800s in the United Kingdom. In Canada at Devil's Paintbrush these walls serve the same functional purpose, as well as giving color and texture to the landform.

Figure 71. Royal County Down, Ireland

built so that a golf ball striking it would bounce in no predictable way. Yet there is no danger of a ball bouncing back at a golfer because of the gentle angle at which the boards rest.

This discussion of hazards began with the least intimidating, most naturally occurring hazard, and has progressed through to the most intimidating, penal, and unnatural ones known to golf. Within this flexible spectrum and within each type of hazard a latitude of severity exists so that an architect can match risk to reward. But the final two types of hazards to be discussed, while very natural and as normal to a golf course as the others, are practically inflexible. Little can be done to adjust their penalizing effects, and thus great care and thought must be given to their placement. These hazards are trees and water.

Trees

Let us first consider trees. In early Scottish writings about golf courses and their construction, trees were decried as being unfair and having no place on a golf course whatsoever. This was a natural sentiment for linksland players, where the tallest growing plants were 4- to 5-foot gorse bushes (see figure 71). Surely the first time a linksland player was exposed to the agony of properly striking a shot only to have it bound off of a tree or two, he cried "foul!" Then when he could not easily extricate his ball from this maze, he no doubt cried "double foul!" (This probably resulted in a double bogey, or worse yet, one of the game's first known "others.") Indeed, some early writings called trees "sand traps in the sky."

But the need for golf courses near population centers forced the introduction of inland golf, and with it trees were unavoidable. Trees on golf courses gradually became accepted in Great Britain, especially when they were properly cleared away to provide adequate playing area. As trees on golf courses became normal, so did their encroachment into the playing area, until we finally had the embryonic stages of freeway golf design: a narrow corridor cut through a forest of trees. Today, trees are considered an essential part of most golf courses, for they have a pristine grandeur and a feeling of sylvan sanctity that is most compatible with the relaxed mood of golf. A golf course without trees in the modern American concept of golf is an anomaly and can only be justified if environmental conditions prevent growing trees (see figure 72).

Henebry Photography

Figure 72. Trees have become an obsession, if not a requirement, on most North American golf courses. The par 3 6th hole at Westwood Plateau in Vancouver, British Columbia owes much of its character to 90-year-old hemlock trees.

The use of trees on some courses is a necessary part of the course, for they serve several purposes. They define golf holes. They make good safety and noise buffers. Trees also provide a welcome change in color, texture, and height to the landscape. For golfers, trees provide shade. Aesthetically they enhance the visual image of a golf course by casting shadows whose length and intensity are at constant variance. Trees also support wildlife, thereby tying golf closer to nature. They reduce surface evaporation and serve as sources of oxygen production, a service much needed in urban and suburban areas. Finally, they affect the strategy of play by causing diverse wind patterns, thereby making golfers think.

Although trees increase the maintenance costs of a course, most golfers agree they are worth the price. But one must not forget that trees are perhaps the most unforgiving and unavoidable hazard on the golf course, so their locations must be well-planned. Since golf is basically an aerial game, the third dimension of height can exaggerate the severity of a hazard. Trees are the most dramatic occupants of the third dimension, so it should be intuitive that it can be very easy to make a golf hole or an entire golf course unfair through the indiscriminate use of trees. Much lip service is paid by well-meaning green committees about preserving the golf architect's intent on a golf course. These same people then plant trees capriciously throughout a course and destroy the original design concepts, often in the name of "beautification." But if a golf course is characterized by poor planning and lacks good shot values and well-designed golf features, the wholesale planting of trees might at best cosmetically compensate for the drabness of the basic design. But if the golf course was done by a competent golf architect, then trees should only serve to frame the work rather than to crowd the canvas. Much of the indiscriminate planting of trees is the result of a committee being unable to imagine what the trees will be like at maturity. Many clubs embarking on tree-planting programs have the best of intentions, but they innocently and simplistically believe there is nothing to planting a few trees and see no reason to have a professionally prepared plan.

It is not just golfers who ignore the penalizing

effects of trees. There are many well-known golf course architects who lack an understanding of trees on golf courses, and as a result subconsciously endorse a very penal concept of design.

Having established both the beneficial and sinister role of trees in golf, let us examine some guidelines for their application. First, impact areas on treed holes should be large enough to allow for a normal margin of error for the shot played to it. In general, for driving areas in fairways, this margin is about 40 yards from dripline (the outside edge of the tree canopy) to dripline. For shorter shots the dripline-to-dripline distance may be reduced commensurate with the length of shot, but it should rarely ever be less than 20 yards. In some instances, particularly if specimen trees of exceptional quality are threatened, the golf feature should be adjusted to provide a fair opening. As a last resort, an architect may forego fairness on such a hole, but it had better be for the sake of a magnificent, one-of-a-kind specimen (see figure 73, Blackthorn Oak). Trees near greens present special problems. Not only do they make maintenance of the green more difficult because of the shade and reduced air effects, but also they often reduce the opening to the green of a high-trajectory pitch shot. The smaller the opening, the less margin for error a golfer has. Hence, a tree near a green might deprive the green of its strategic character. The use of trees near greens can be very penal if the hole is of adequate length and has otherwise well-conceived golf features. If the hole is exceptionally short, the use of a guardian tree is more likely justified and shown by the example of the 6th hole at Naples National, a par 3 of only 124 yards (see figure 74). However, the use of trees in the middle of normal-sized tees, fairways, sand traps, or greens is usually offered merely as a gimmick, particularly if it forces the golfer to play some freak shot to overcome the tree's presence. On the other hand, a specimen tree—or a stand of specimen trees—can be used to split a double wide fairway, such as at the 10th hole at Devil's Pulpit in Caledon, Ontario (see figure 75a) or the 11th hole at Willowbend on Cape Cod (see figure 75b & c) .

Another problem with the use of trees on a golf course is providing for a fair chance to recover from within a treed area. This is most easily done by keeping a distance between tree trunks at 22 to 28 feet. Such a dispersion of trees

Figure 73. When a golf course architect is lucky enough to have a 300-plus-year-old oak tree, like at Blackthorn in South Bend, Indiana, he builds the golf hole around it.

Figure 74. When a par 3 is only 124 yards long, like the 6th hole at Naples National, having a "sand trap in the sky" (tree) makes the hole challenging, fun, and memorable.

Figure 75a. The tree in the 10th fairway at Devil's Pulpit is testimony to the owners' (Chris Haney and Scott Abbott) insistence, the members' patience, and the god of lightning's sense of humor. I argued against keeping the tree, but now it has become the hole's signature.

Figure 75b. These pine trees in the 11th fairway at Willowbend on Cape Cod make golfers decide how close to the right they will dare to go. The trees add a heroic element to the penal style of the drive and approach which must carry over two cranberry bogs. Therefore this hole is both heroic and penal.

Figure 75c. The view from the prime landing spot onto the green on #11 at Willowbend Cape Cod, Massachusetts.

Figure 76a. The relationship between various types of trees (height vs. density) and their closeness of planting to the golf hole is shown. Although this example is for northern latitude trees, the same principles of selection and placement apply in all situations.

permits growth of turfgrass under them, and still allows large-scale mechanized maintenance equipment to move in and around the trees. The remaining trees should have lower limbs removed up to a height of 8 to 10 feet so one can easily move about under the trees, even on a tractor seat. This also allows light and air to reach the turf. Another consideration is that the golfer should be able to find his ball quickly and play it out, and that is why pine straw is a good substitute for turf under trees.

If possible, a wide variety of trees should be maintained and planted, not only to add visual diversity to the landscape but also as good insurance against a pestilence that may kill one particular type and leave the course treeless. The failure to do this has cost many clubs dearly. The popularity of the American elm on North American golf courses made many fine clubs vulnerable to the continent-wide blight that wiped out these trees by the early 1960s. Other diseases and insects are slowly ravaging other types of trees with similar but less dramatic effect than the loss of the American elms.

Trees aren't entirely inflexible as hazards. There is some variation in the height of growth, density of canopy, and the overall limb structure of trees (see figure 76). Selection of the proper characteristics is often determined by the intended function of the tree. For example, some coniferous trees, such as spruce, tend to have dense compact foliage that makes them well-suited as safety and noise buffers, hole dividers, and year-round accents. Their pyramidal shapes do not severely limit aerial spaces as they grow taller, so they are well-suited for positions near greens or in narrowly confined locations. Other trees, such as locust, are rather airy with thin foliage and give only light shade to the turf below.

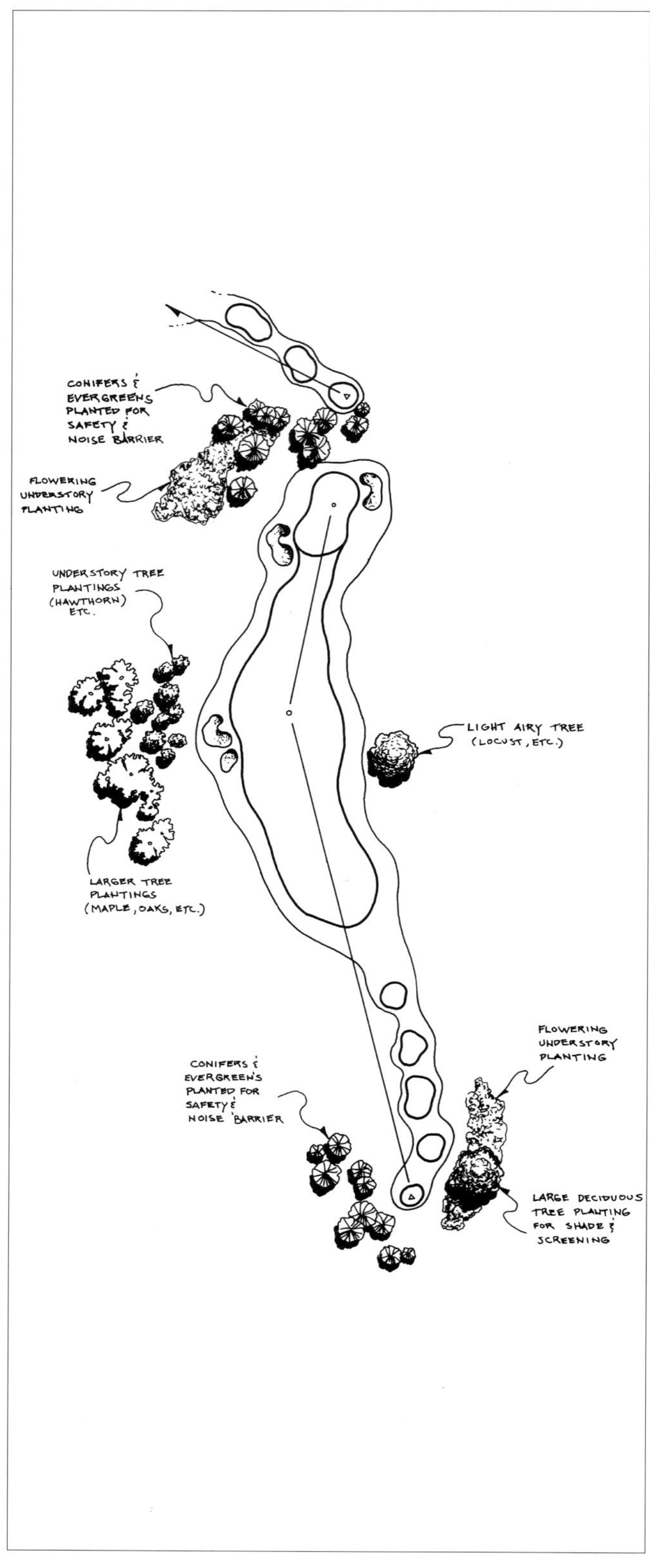

Figure 76b.

But they add a lacy feel to the third dimension and permit a reasonably good chance of a ball passing through the canopy. This type of tree is well-suited for the inside corner of doglegs or in modest rough along shorter holes. Trees that reach massive size, such as oaks, will become towering barriers to golf balls and should be used near tees, adjacent to wide play areas, or where a dramatic accent is needed. The intelligent use of trees requires an understanding of the nature of the golf shot to be affected and the growth habit of the tree and how it will blend into the surrounding native vegetation.

Not all trees on a golf course exist for strategic purposes. In fact, the preponderance of trees and shrubs serve a decorative purpose and thus should be located as far from anticipated play areas as possible. Flowering trees planted along the perimeter usually appear as a colorful backdrop if planted some distance beyond play areas. Decorative plantings observed from a distance also permit a mixture and harmony of colors that can be accented with other plants. The same plantings located near to play are seen as individual elements and not as a composition. The epitome of sensitive and thoughtful use of decorative plants on a golf course is surely Augusta National. The serious student of golf course landscaping should examine that course as the ideal model. Selection of all plant material should be based upon improved cultivars or varieties of plants that are able to better resist pests or stressful environments. Care should be taken, however, not to plant trees that are out of character with surrounding or natural vegetation. We must never lose sight of the fact that we are framing a golf hole and not starting an arboretum.

Water

The other unforgiving hazard commonly found on a golf course is water. Water is the most penal hazard of all, for its severity cannot be adjusted and there is rarely a chance for recovery. Since it exacts such a harsh penalty with little recourse, the location and use of water hazards must be carefully planned.

Water hazards have a valid place on the golf course because they add an element of do-or-die

Dana Fry

Figure 77. Looking from behind the 16th green at Cook's Creek, and realizing that nearly every hilltop is a tee, it is easy to understand how the hole can play from 228 yards down to 90 yards and be enjoyable for all golfers.

risk that places a high reward for a well-executed shot. But if a design concept that incorporates water is to be strategic, alternate provisions must be made for the timid or less accomplished golfer. One method is to leave an alternative route around the water hazard of at least half the width of a fairway. Another is to ensure that the poorest golfer is exposed to the shortest carry over the hazard, while the best player has to contend with the longest carry. This is most often accomplished by varying the surface configuration of the water hazard and using multiple tees. For example, a par 3 hole might play 180 yards from the championship tees across 150 yards of water, while from the front tee the hole may only play 100 yards over 20 yards of water (see figure 77).

Because most beginners and less accomplished golfers tend to slice the ball, placing the water hazard on the hook side will usually protect them from hitting the water while intimidating better players who usually tend to hit right to left.

Where possible, banks of water hazards should be sloped so as to discourage a ball from being drawn down into the drink. For this reason, many skillful golf architects plan depressions or bunkers at the edge of water hazards to try to deflect or stop a ball from trickling into the water (see figure 78).

The most critical feature of a water hazard is its spatial relationship to the normal playing patterns of golfers. Water hazards located directly in front of the tee affect only the poorest of golfers and therefore should be of narrow dimension and intended to serve a purely aesthetic purpose. As the location of the water hazard is moved down the fairway away from the tee, the closer it can move into the landing zone, for the further out it is, the less it affects the poorer

Chris John

Figure 78. Some bunkers are designed to retain errant shots from far worse fates. The small flat bunker to the right of the green on the 12th hole at Eagle's Landing, Ocean City, Maryland is a retaining bunker.

The use of the highly penal hazard of water provides a balance of risk and reward that is strategic golf at its best. The water holes at Augusta National present a case study of strategic design, reflecting the creative genius of Dr. Alister MacKenzie and of other golf architects who modified his original work. When John Cook and the author were designing John's semiprivate golf course near Columbus, Ohio, John suggested using the design concept of the 13th at Augusta National on the 10th hole. Although the creek had to be created (appropriately called Cook's Creek, for the family), the hole is an exciting par 5 that rivals the original (see figure 79).

player. According to PGA Tour statistics, the average length of the drive for the best players is 270 yards. So it's not unconscionable to use a water hazard to create the smallest impact area at a distance of 270 yards or more from the championship tee, while allowing generous-sized landing areas immediately to the front and back of this distance for the average player. A golf course architect can adjust his risk and reward values simply by adjusting the location of the hazard. In a truly effective use of water, the risk factor should seem in balance with the reward, so that most golfers will debate the risk and reward question. A good example of this concept is the use of Rae's Creek on the 465-yard par 5 13th hole at Augusta National. After playing an average-length drive of 270 yards, a pro golfer must evaluate whether to play short of the 20-foot-wide creek that meanders along the front of the green, or risk going for the green where a mishit shot may cost him precious strokes. The creek is perfectly situated to pose this dilemma. If it were located just a few yards to the right or left, the decision would be much easier.

Water also serves many useful purposes on the golf course. Aside from strategic uses, water is an excellent safety buffer. It can be a reservoir that promotes diverse aquatic wildlife, enhances a course's aesthetics, and perhaps provides a source of irrigation. In the construction phase, water hazards often provide badly needed fill material with which to raise fairways and build tees, greens, bunkers, and mounds, or as sediment ponds to protect surface water. Water is more prevalent on modern golf courses because we now have sophisticated and powerful earth-moving equipment with which to construct water hazards. But with this plethora of equipment architects must be even more cognizant of the severe impact of water on golf, or modern-day designs will slip back into purely penal concepts.

Other Hazards

There are some other types of hazards that are the essential elements of which Aleck Bauer wrote. However, such limits are imposed on the

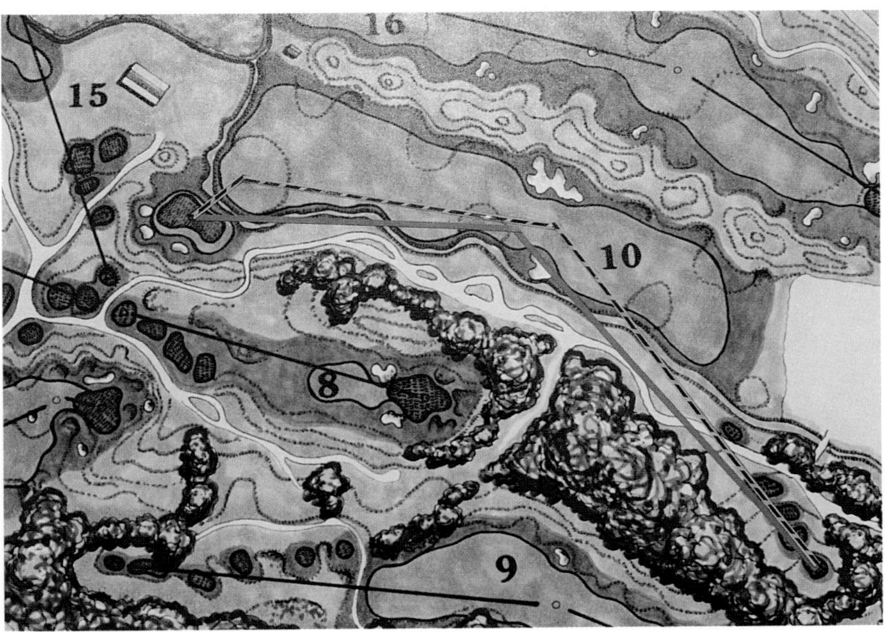

Figure 79a. This drawing shows how the 10th hole at Cook's Creek can be aggressively attacked (orange line) or conservatively played (yellow and black line). The design inspiration was John Cook's admiration of the 13th hole at Augusta National.

Figure 79b. Looking from a perfectly placed drive on the 10th hole at Cook's Creek, with a chance to reach the par 5 green in two. The Creek and landform were artificially made from a flat cornfield.

golf course architect by the site and are not really hazards that can be used or abandoned depending upon an architect's imagination. One that comes to mind is out-of-bounds. Out-of-bounds hazards are as real and severe as water, but can be minimized by skilled routing of the course. If a site is of such a size or shape that out-of-bounds near play areas are unavoidable, then the same principles apply for "O.B.'s" as for water hazards. If possible, out-of-bounds should be on the hook side, its effects mitigated by mounds, traps, or trees, and angles of play directed away from the boundaries. Of course, since out-of-bounds exacts such a severe penalty (of stroke and distance), it is possible for the strategically minded designer to set up some interesting risk and reward situations using them.

Other uncontrollable site factors that can be hazards are power lines, concrete floodways, and access roadways. Less common but worthy of mentioning are features such as historic structures, well pumps (oil, gas, and water), Indian mounds, burial grounds, ancient rights-of-way, and required engineering structures.

Hazards are the spice in the broth of golf that makes it distinctive, interesting, memorable, and subjective. What makes a good golf course great is how hazards are presented and how they communicate with and enchant the golfer.

4

Form and Function of Green Complexes

In biology there is a body of evolutionary thought, first codified by Charles Darwin, called natural selection. Paraphrased, that theory contends that those biological entities that can best adapt to a given environment will thrive and those unable to adapt will perish. This is popularly known as "survival of the fittest."

Form Follows Function

In architecture there is a similar body of practical thought that says the form that an object takes must be a reflection of the function it is designed to serve. This is commonly called the axiom of "form follows function." With golf courses, we are dealing with organic entities that must adapt to both environmental stresses and practical demands. Golf courses must take the form that best suits their intended function. Therefore, individual features of a golf course are products of form and function designed to be adaptable to environmental stresses.

Natural selection recognizes the slow evolution of species in response to changing environmental pressures or stresses. As living organisms are pushed to their physiological limits, some will be able to survive as a result of some small genetic deviation, and those survivors who perpetuate this deviation in their offspring will give rise to a slightly new organism. Living organisms that cannot cope with physiological and environmental stresses will die.

A golf green is a living complex of plants, all possessing the same basic genetic information and thus nearly a monoculture of turfgrass plants. Golf greens are constantly subjected to environmental stresses and may be unable to naturally withstand the wear and abuse placed on them (see figure 80). Given enough time, perhaps through natural selection, there may emerge a plant that can successfully cope with

Figure 80. Golf greens can exist in stressful environments if they are properly built and managed, as at Del Safari Golf Course in Palm Desert.

these stresses given to a golf green. (One would speculate that one strain of annual bluegrass, *Poa annua*, may eventually emerge as the fittest.) But golf architects need not wait for the natural selection process of turfgrass, for man has learned to manipulate the environment to reduce environmental stress on plants. This manipulation is called agriculture, and on golf courses it is called turfgrass management or agronomy. If golf courses are to remain covered by a tightly knit sward of grasses, man must control environmental stresses placed on these plants. Much of this environmental control can be incorporated into a design, or at the very least can be aided by use of proper design parameters.

The concept of form follows function means that there is always a form, of a given size, shape, and material, that will best fulfill the practical requirements of every function. If the function of a door is to permit controlled passage of objects through a solid wall, then the form it will take will be the result of practical considerations of its function. If the object is a small dog, the door will assume a smaller form than if the object is an elephant. Likewise, the choice of building materials for the door will be compatible to the practical intended use of the door. A waterproof cloth is fine for a dog door, but steel bars are necessary for the elephant. The designer of the door must know and understand what function the door will serve before he can design one that most practically fulfills all its requirements.

Marrying turfgrass management to the concept of form following function, it can be concluded that golf features must be designed not only to serve their golfing function, but also to provide improved growing conditions for easy maintenance. Truly good golf course architects do not ignore agronomics when designing a golf feature. To design for agronomic improvements requires an intimate knowledge of golf course maintenance as much as of the game of golf itself. That's why the profession of golf course architecture cannot be taught in a single college curriculum. It is a multidisciplinary subject requiring as much plant science as engineering or architecture, as well as an understanding of the game of golf.

Determining Slope and Size

Let's examine how the most heavily used features on a golf course—the putting surfaces—are planned with both function and maintenance in mind. We begin by defining the functions of a green, which is to provide a plant-covered surface around the hole suitable for the smooth roll of a putted golf ball. The form a green takes to satisfy this function must be level enough for putting, usually not more than 33:1 (3%) slopes or less than 100:1 (1%) slopes. Since the rules of golf suggest that the hole should be at least 15 feet from the edge of the green, a green with a single cup setting would have a 15-foot radius and a total size of 706.5 square feet. ($A = \pi r^2$, $A = 3.14(15)^2$, $A = 706.5$.). So, ignoring for the moment the agronomics involved with a green, the form of a green with just a single pin placement is a circle, 706 square feet in area, with smooth slopes of less than 33:1 but greater than 100:1 covered by closely mowed plant cover.

However, when the agronomics are considered, the form becomes more complex. First, there are only a limited number of turf-type plants that can be continuously mowed at a short height of cut, so part of the form must be a turf variety that is best adapted to the environmental conditions of the site. To maintain the health of this turf, one must provide a good root medium that has a proper balance of water, air, soil particles, and nutrients. This media must be well-drained and must resist compaction to maintain this balance. Experience and research have taught us that one of the best root media is sand (of medium to fine particle sizes), perhaps mixed with a percentage of organic matter, underlain with tile, and with surface drainage of at least a 100:1 (1%) slope, with the average across the green of at least 1.5% slope.

But if a green with only one cup setting gets very much use, the turf will sustain much physical damage and have little chance to heal. That's why hole locations are changed daily on every green of most golf courses. As we provide for additional cup settings, we are changing the functional parameters of the green. Hence the form of the green must change accordingly. On a heavily played golf course, experience has shown that the most seriously injured turf is a 10-foot circle around the cup, and it will take about two weeks, or 14 daily cup changes, for the injured turf completely to heal before we can use this spot once again for a hole placement. The damaged area for each hole location is 314 square feet, $(A = \pi r^2)$ $A = 3.14 \times (10)^2 = 314)$. If every green needs at least 14 cup setting areas, the minimum size of any green should be 4,400 square feet (314 square feet × 14 cupsets = 4,396 square feet). This is not the total size of a green, but rather this is the minimum area of the green that would be suitable for 14 hole placements (see figure 81).

Any green having its entire surface available for cup settings is nothing more than a flat patch of smooth grass, with little or no character or strategy built into it. If a golf architect is to provide surface expression of a green, including areas not necessarily suited to pin placements, then these areas must be in addition to cupset areas. So the form of the green will change accordingly. Using an additional 1,000 to 2,000 square feet of putting surface for artistic purposes extends the size of the green on a heavily played golf course to 5,400 to 6,400 square feet.

The overall theory of greens design should examine the soil physics involved with the rootzone material, the proper use of tile drainage, surface drainage, soil chemistry, and routine maintenance practices. There are four commonly used methods of subsurface green construction. They are:

1) simplified construction using naturally occurring soils or sand with no tile drainage
2) the improved method, which uses tile drainage under sand organic matter mix
3) the California method, which uses pure sand underlain with tile drainage
4) the USGA method of green construction, based on the theory of layering different sized materials and allowing the forces of gravity and capillary action to maintain an optimal moisture level in the rootzone

Discussion of these various methods can be found in other texts or in a booklet by this author called *The Evolution of the Modern Green,* which is available from the American Society of Golf Course Architects and the Golf Course Superintendents Association of America. There are advantages and disadvantages to each method, so a golf course architect must thoroughly understand the particular theory and its cost if he is to choose the proper method. When designing a green, the limitations of the chosen method cannot be ignored nor even minimized if the green is to cope successfully with environmental stresses.

Although we've mentioned slope, surface drainage, and tile drainage, we've not been specific about their influence on the form of a green. Assume that a green is to be built on a perfectly flat site and will have 6,000 square feet of putting surface (100 feet deep and 60 feet wide). In order to properly surface drain this green, the minimum slope to this green must be 100:1, a 1-foot pitch in 100 feet, and the maximum is around 33:1, or 3 feet of pitch in 100 feet. So the highest part of this putting surface must be at least 1 foot above grade to obtain surface drainage and could be 3 feet at the extreme. We've previously said that green banks should feature at least 4:1 outslopes to accommodate maintenance equipment and access by golfers. So now add the 1 to 3 foot dimension of height and outslopes to the previously discussed list of form considerations. We also know that tile drainage must have at least 200:1 fall to work effectively. If the land is very flat between the green and the tile exhaust point and the distance is long, then the drainage tile must either be placed very deep in the ground or the green will have to be raised another foot or two to obtain the necessary fall in the tile line.

Thus far, all formal considerations have been governed by agronomy and have not included consideration of any strategy or shot values determined by any mounds or bunkers. When mounds and bunkers are made a part of green structure, then further changes in form must occur. For example, suppose that a golf architect wishes to add a simple 20-foot-diameter oval bunker to the front of the green. The form of the sand trap by itself is a result of the function that the architect wishes it to serve. This would include size, depth, and shape. Considering maintenance, the golf architect knows that if the trap

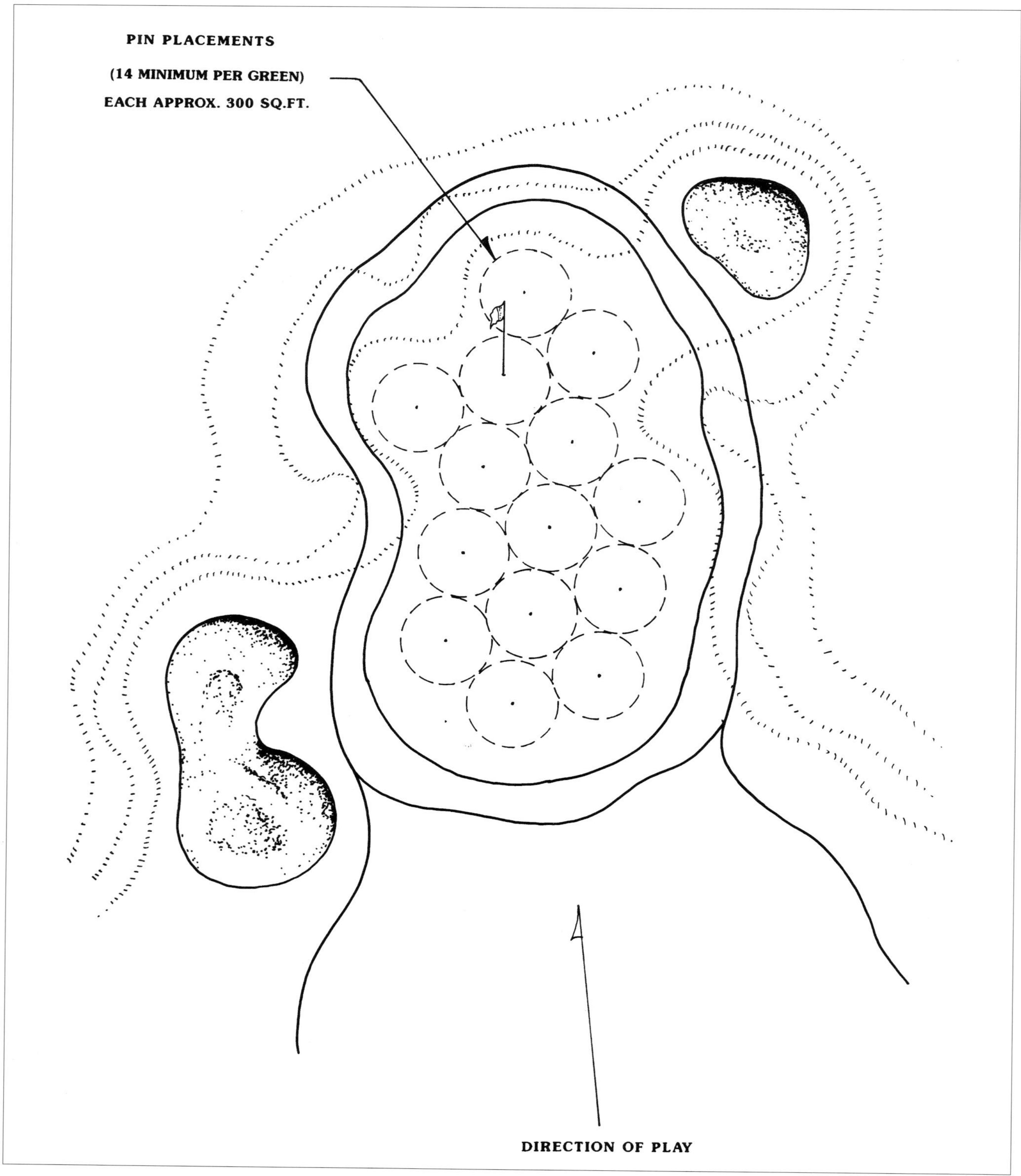

Figure 81. A modern green of about 6,000 square feet should yield at least 14 hole locations to spread out wear, and allow the putting surface to recover before being used again.

Grand Valley State University

The Meadows Golf Course at Grand Valley is distinguished by simple but elegant green settings.

is to be tile drained, then the elevation of the bottom of the tile will dictate the depth of the bunker.

On a perfectly flat site, this means that the front edge of the trap must be raised above grade at least 6 inches to avoid becoming a water pocket. Further, if the golf architect wants the face of the sand trap to be visible to approaching golfers, the sand face should be at least 3 feet above grade. Since the back of the trap is above grade, it has an outslope that should be maintainable with a riding mower, so the slope must be at least 3:1. The form of the trap to this point is that the front edge is 6 inches above grade, the back of the trap is 3 feet above grade, and the trap has a 20-foot oval shape with a 3:1 outslope. When the green and sand trap are integrated into one complex, their forms must also be integrated (see figure 82). Often there is a whole new set of agronomic or maintenance considerations that must be respected in such cases. An architect must decide how close the bunker should be to the putting surface. If the green is to be mowed with only a walking greens mower, which can turn around in only 3 or 4 feet of space, the bunker can be as close as 3 feet from the putting surface and still allow for greens mowing. If a labor-saving triplex riding greens mower is to be used, then 8 to 10 feet is needed for this larger machine to make a turn, and the trap must be located farther from the edge to accommodate it. It is also desirable when constructing a bunker to surface drain water away from the sand to prevent sand erosion, for that would cause too many plugged lies in bunkers, as well as requiring extra maintenance. To direct surface water away from surrounding bunkers, the edges of the sand trap bordering the green must be higher than the green so surface water from the edge of the trap drains away from it and

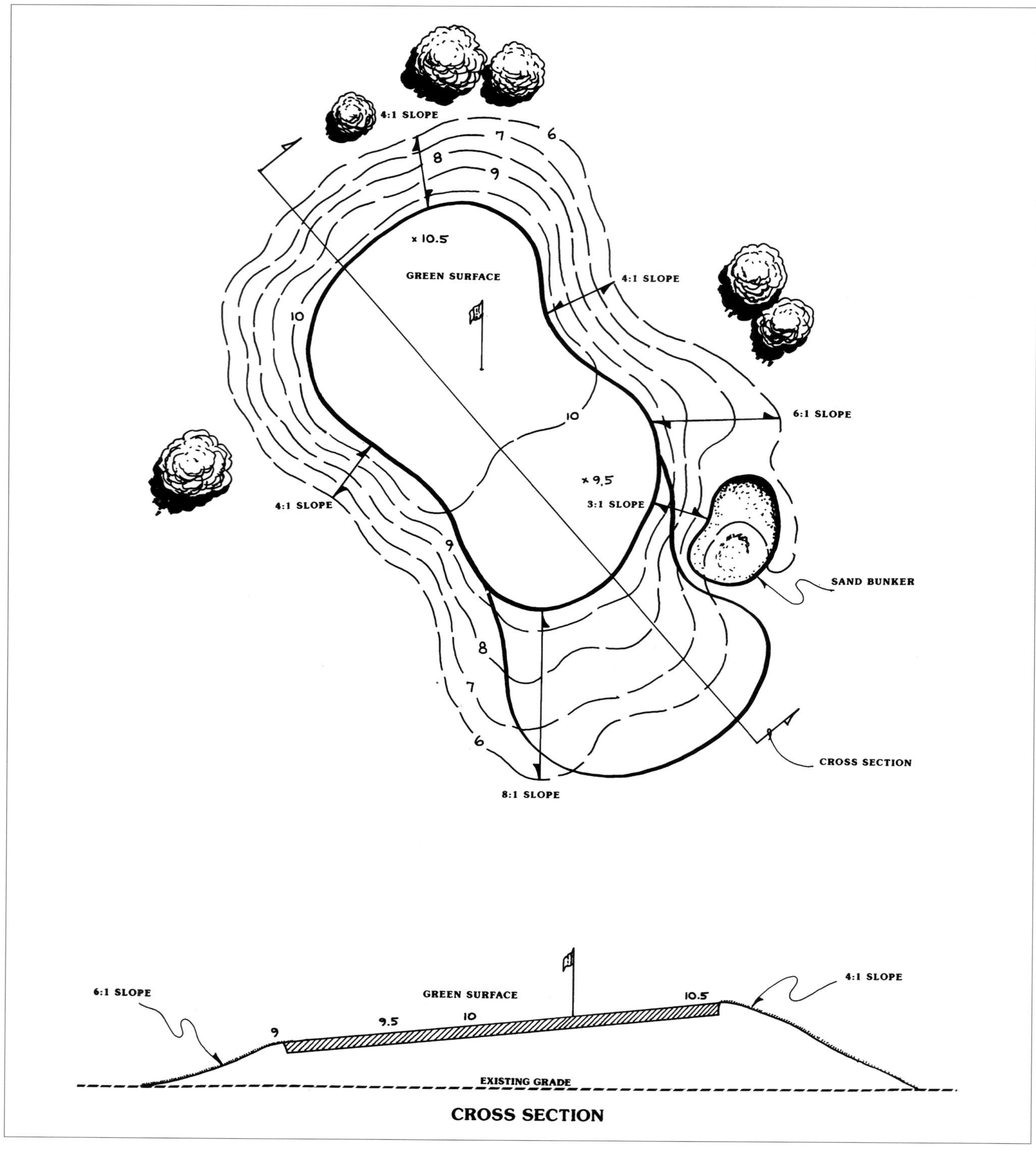

Figure 82. This green meets the minimum "form" necessary to perform its intended "function" of providing a well-drained, healthy putting turf. Although many greens are built that disregard these principles, the skill of the golf course superintendent must be relied upon to overcome excessive stress to the turf. Size and slope are key design criteria.

toward the green. Lastly, the designers may consider the long-term effect that the sand blasted from the bunker will have upon the green. Accumulations of such sand can be avoided by placing the bunker further from the putting surface.

Figure 83. A well-designed golf green at Annbriar Golf Course in Waterloo, Illinois that respects the principles of size and slope. The rootzone is the California system; notice how the surface water on and around the green is controlled and directed into grassy hollows.

Now the form of the green-bunker complex is as follows: the green has about 6,000 square feet of putting surface, with a growing medium of sand and perhaps organic matter, underlain with tile drainage, planted to an environmentally adapted turfgrass, raised at least 1 to 3 feet above grade, with 4:1 outslopes, having one 20-foot oval sand trap, located 8 to 10 feet from the putting surface, its front edge raised 6 inches above grade and its back edge raised 3 feet above grade, with 3:1 outslopes, directing surface water away from the bunker, and with tile drainage under the trap. This is a well-designed green complex. The forms are following the functions they must serve (see figure 83).

Strategy in Green Design

In the above examples, no consideration was given to golfing factors such as length of approach shot, possible traffic patterns, surrounding natural and artificial golf features (trees, water, out-of-bounds, other golf holes), any of which would change the form and function of the green. The best golf course architects are sensitive to all of those influences, and when they respect the axiom of form following function and sound agronomic principles, their architecture will endure many stresses and last many trouble-free years. While one design criterion for a green is to provide optimal growing conditions for its plant cover, another criterion deals with golfing aspects of greens.

The old cliche, "large greens for long approach shots, small greens for short approaches," is just that, an old cliche. While it is perfectly logical that one should provide an impact area on the green of sufficient size and slope to receive the shot played to it, such dogma ignores agronomic parameters as well as the fact that a modern green can contain numerous impact or target areas. A golf architect can build strategy into a putting surface by manipulating the contours of the green to provide several distinct landing areas, each of which may demand a distinctly different type of approach shot (see figure 84). Since most golfers are happy just to hit a green and are not overly concerned about strategic landing areas, a golf architect may design 75% of a green to provide ordinary hole locations accessible via routine approach shots. But the remaining 25% of the green would be reserved for competitive hole place-

Figure 84. To go for right-side pin position at the 16th hole at TPC Jacksonville Stadium Course means taking lots of risks. So Pete Dye complicated the putt of the conservative middle-of-the-green player with a small ridgeline. Also notice the left rear target area defined by the small ridgeline flowing away from the left pot bunker. Nice job, Pete.

ments that demand special shot-making (see figure 85). This is done by the use of sand traps, or external or internal mounds and slopes, or by adjusting the size of the landing area on the putting surface. Obviously, competitive hole locations cannot be effectively designed on round, oval, or square greens. The green must be free-form in shape and well-integrated with many strategic hazards. By using free-form greens, a golf architect can also more easily blend the green into the site or take advantage of special natural features near the green. On some special sites, like Glenmaura National, there was a natural waterfall behind the 18th green site with a nicely flowing stream toward the fairway. The committee and this author could not decide which side the green should go on, so we built them both. Now the target area on this medium-short par 4 is defined by the creek (see figure 86).

A golf architect's first task is to examine a green site and mentally tabulate its topographical features, surrounding drainage patterns, existing vegetation, and special features. Having done this, and with knowledge of the size of the green he must build, he will consider the length of shot that will be played to the green, the trajectory of that shot, and the area from which the approach shot will be played. He will also consider prevailing winds, angles and tracks of the sun, and probable traffic patterns for pedestrians and golf carts from the fairway to the green and from the green to the next tee. With those factors in mind, he will start to draw a mental image of the best green for that site.

Since the process of mentally designing a

Figure 85. Sometimes hazards are even used in greens, to define target areas, especially on large or double greens.

Rolling Greens Photo

Figure 86. The 18th hole at Glenmaura National in Moosic, Pennsylvania has two greens, one on each side of a small stream. This is a fun way to conclude an exciting round of golf.

green is in large part intuitive, it might be helpful to describe a golf architect's thought process to demonstrate how every square foot of the green is carefully planned and is not a product of some ethereal inspiration.

For purposes of simplicity, assume the site I've selected for this particular green is perfectly flat and devoid of natural features, except for a hillside as a backdrop (see figures 87a–g). First, I consider the type of shot being played to the green by the average golfer. If the approach shot is relatively short with a high trajectory, the landing areas within the green can be smaller, and with less slope, than if the approach shot is a long iron shot. If the approach shot is a fairway wood, then the landing or area may be as large as for a long iron but with less slope since the incoming ball from a fairway wood has a higher trajectory and will be less likely to roll than a long iron shot. The object is to provide a landing or target area that is proportionate in size to the margin of error of the shot being played to it. In my example the distance from the fairway driving zone to the green is only 120 yards. I now enlarge the 1″ = 50′ blob I drew on the routing plan for a green to a scale of 1″ = 20′ (see figure 87c).

Next I consider what the normal line of play to the green is. Usually, that's down the middle of the fairway. However, if for some reason I suspect the line of play will be from some other angle, I'll make adjustments in the position of the green so that it opens up best, and is most accessible, to the expected line of play. This is an important way to establish the strategy of the hole by favoring one angle of approach over another through hole location. Then I try to determine what will be the expected traffic pattern of golfers, carts, and maintenance equipment to the green. I do not want to funnel people into a narrow path that would quickly wear out.

Once I know the expected line of play, the pri-

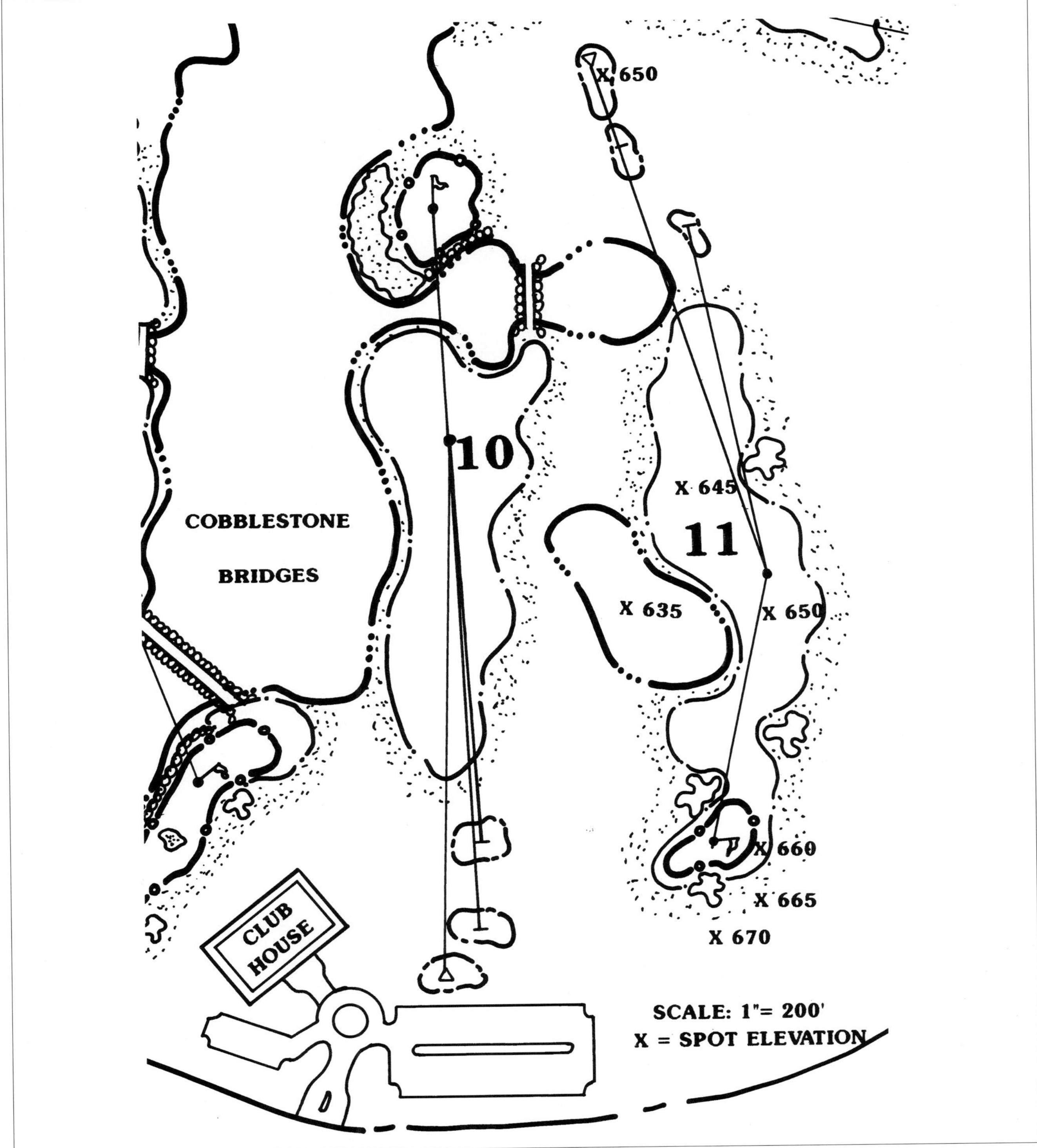

Figure 87a. Initial routing at a scale of 1″ = 200′ shows the 11th hole with simple shapes —tee at the top of a small hill, fairway in the valley, and green at the base of a small hill. The next step is to assess how the hole will be played, then properly shape, size, grade, drain, and develop strategy at a scale of 1″ = 50′.

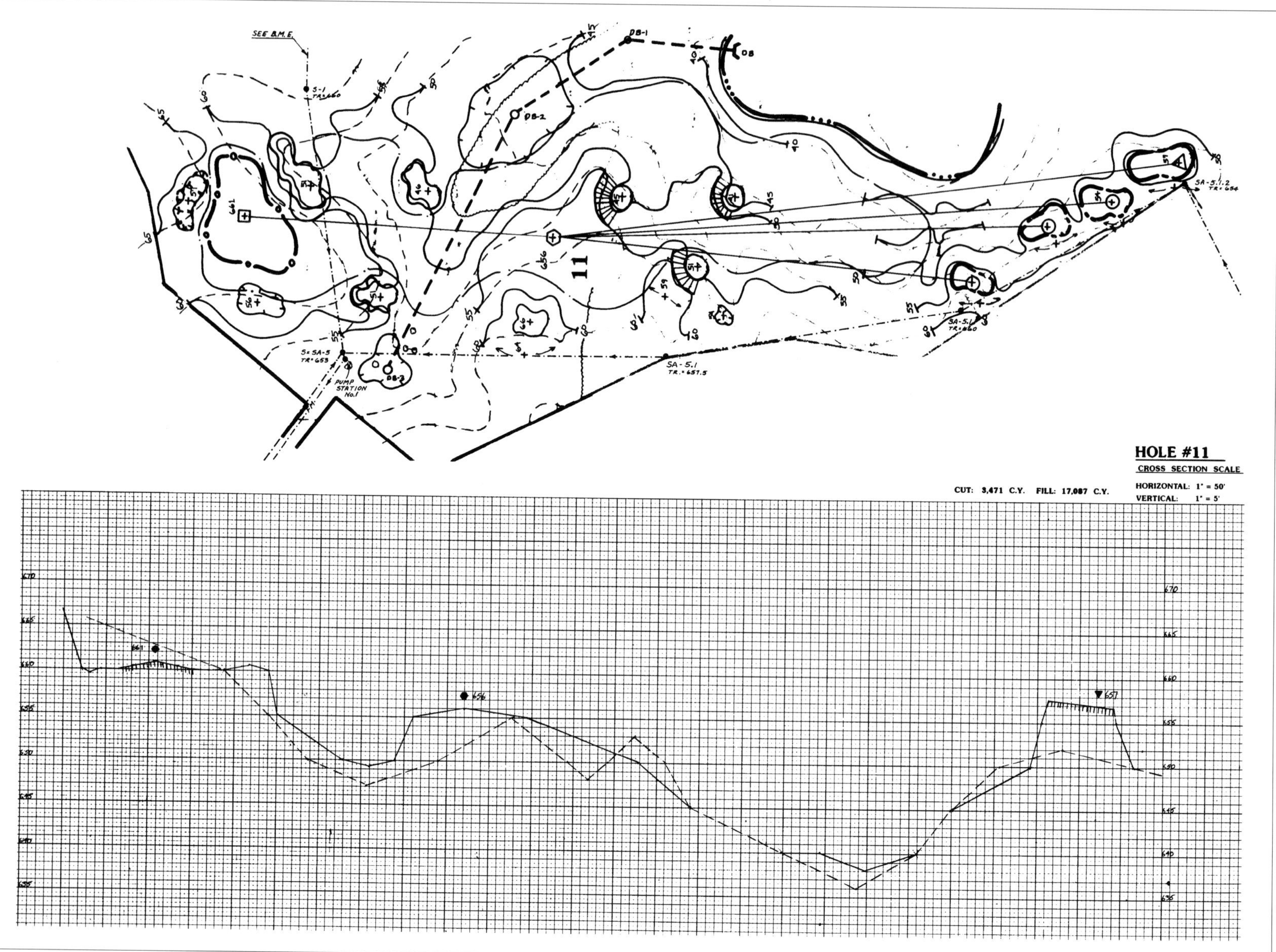

Figure 87b. The 11th hole is designed and graded at a scale of 1" = 50', before green, tees, and bunkers are designed at a scale of 1" = 20'.

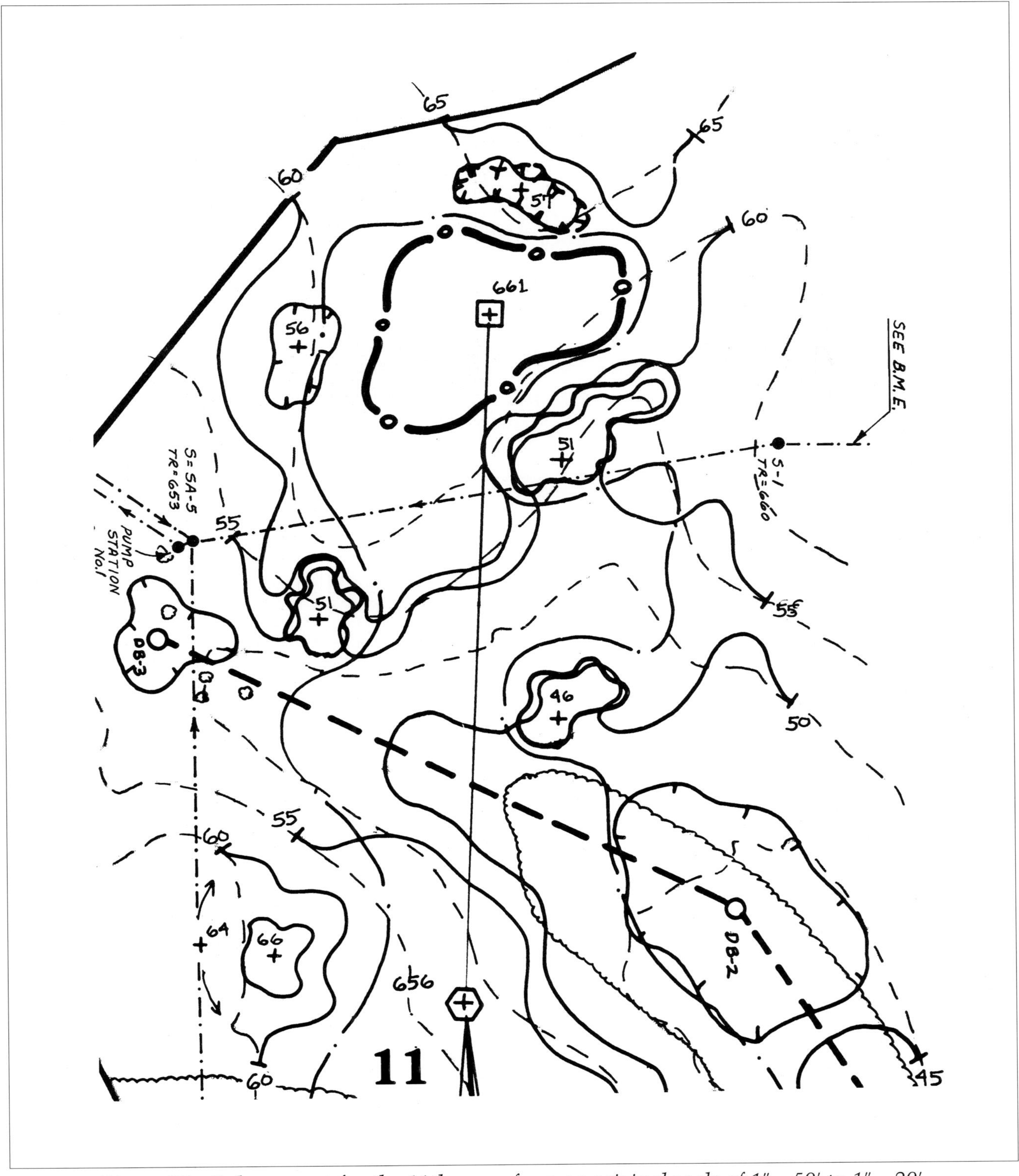

Figure 87c. Enlargement for the 11th green from an original scale of 1″ = 50′ to 1″ = 20′. Detailed design of the green can now begin.

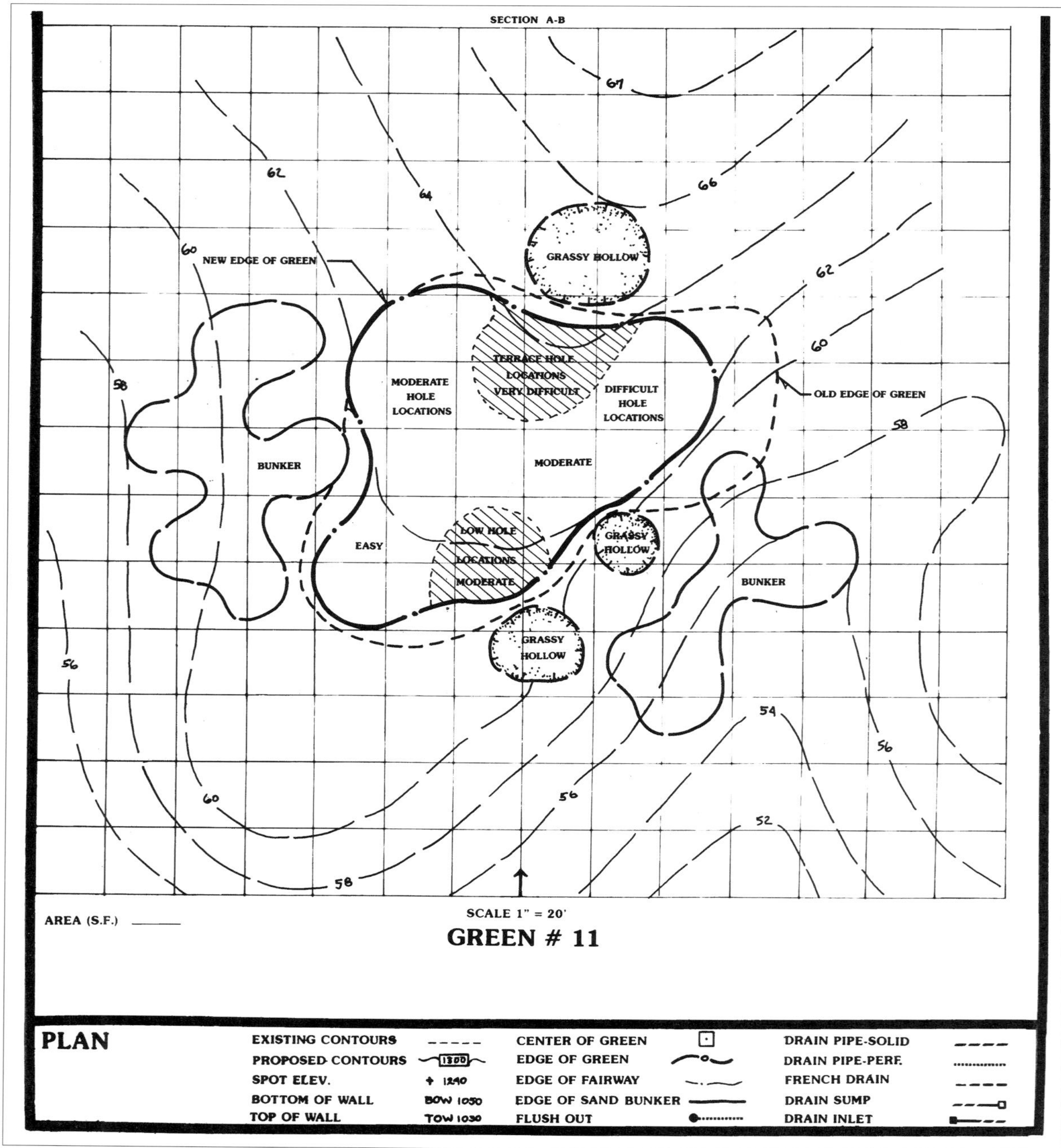

Figure 87d. The enlarged green site is added to a standard grid plan sheet, along with the topography, then revisions are made to the green size and shape, along with some preliminary strategy decisions about possible hole locations and hazards.

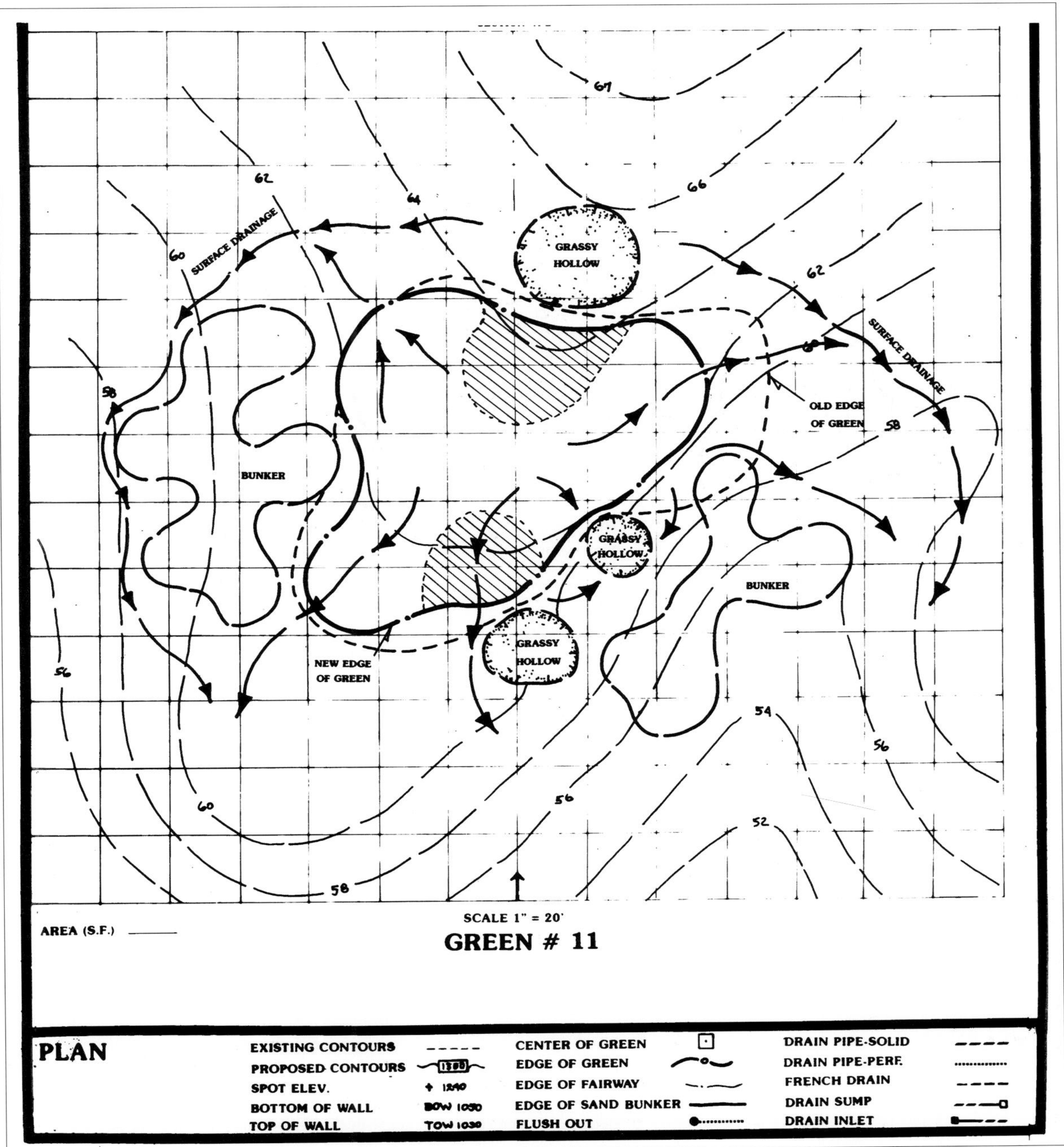

Figure 87e. The surface drainage of the green and its surroundings are shown at first as arrows, and later as proposed 2-foot contour grading changes.

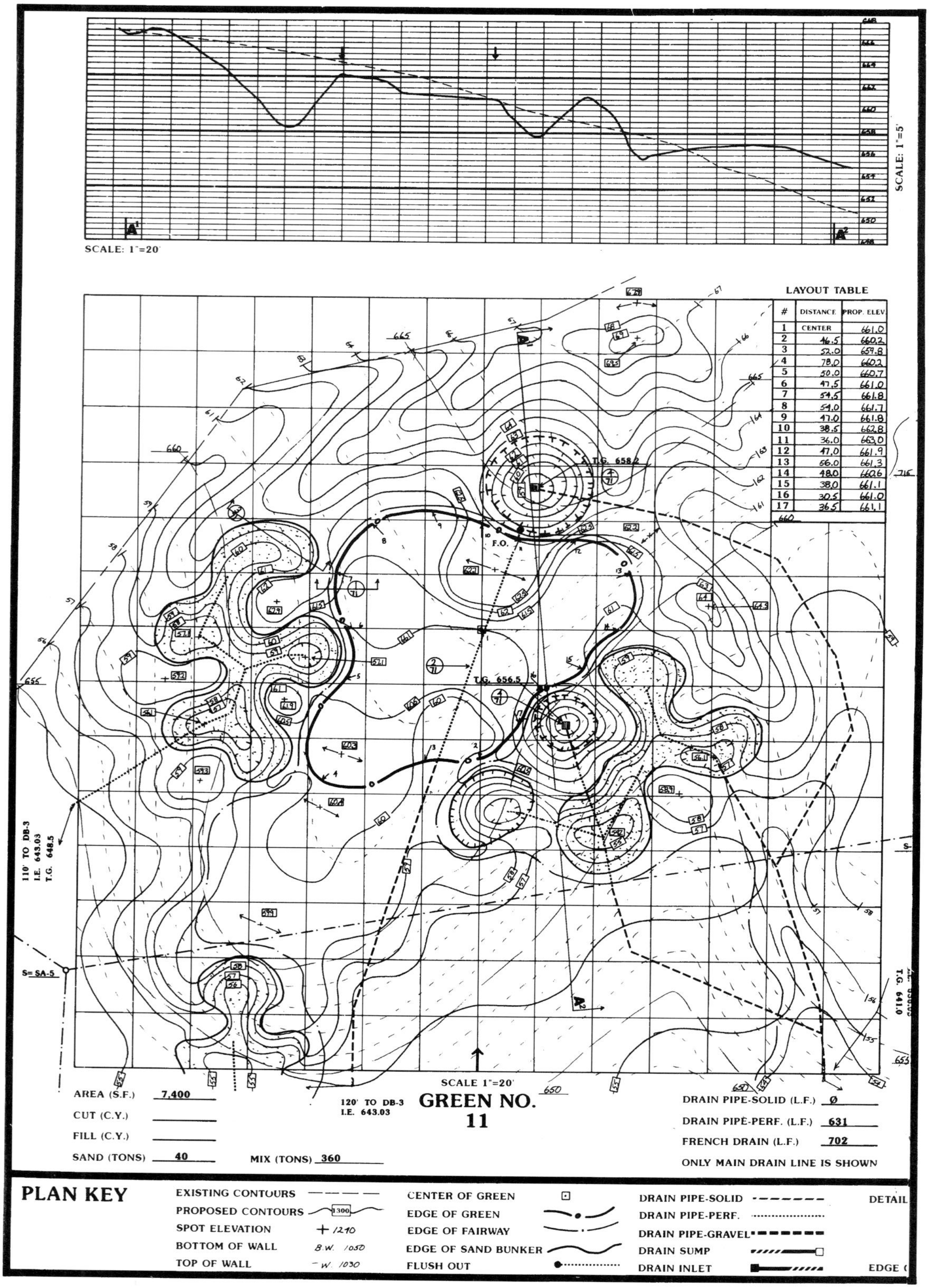

SCALE: 1"=5'

SCALE: 1"=20'

LAYOUT TABLE

#	DISTANCE	PROP. ELEV.
1	CENTER	661.0
2	46.5	660.2
3	52.0	659.8
4	78.0	660.2
5	50.0	660.7
6	47.5	661.0
7	54.5	661.8
8	54.0	661.7
9	47.0	661.8
10	38.5	662.8
11	36.0	663.0
12	47.0	661.9
13	56.0	661.3
14	48.0	660.6
15	38.0	661.1
16	30.5	661.0
17	36.5	661.1

T.G. 658.2

F.O.

T.G. 656.5

110' TO DB-3
I.E. 643.03
T.G. 648.5

S=SA-5

SCALE 1"=20'

120' TO DB-3
I.E. 643.03

GREEN NO. 11

AREA (S.F.) 7,400

CUT (C.Y.)

FILL (C.Y.)

SAND (TONS) 40

MIX (TONS) 360

DRAIN PIPE-SOLID (L.F.) Ø

DRAIN PIPE-PERF. (L.F.) 631

FRENCH DRAIN (L.F.) 702

ONLY MAIN DRAIN LINE IS SHOWN

PLAN KEY

EXISTING CONTOURS

PROPOSED CONTOURS 1300

SPOT ELEVATION + 1210

BOTTOM OF WALL B.W. 1050

TOP OF WALL T.W. 1030

CENTER OF GREEN

EDGE OF GREEN

EDGE OF FAIRWAY

EDGE OF SAND BUNKER

FLUSH OUT

DRAIN PIPE-SOLID

DRAIN PIPE-PERF.

DRAIN PIPE-GRAVEL

DRAIN SUMP

DRAIN INLET

DETAIL

EDGE (

Figure 87f. A detailed green plan, from which a contractor can estimate, schedule, and build the entire green complex.

Figure 87g. The completed 11th green at Cobblestone Creek, Victor, New York.

mary opening to the green, the type of landing areas needed, and the probable traffic patterns and agronomic considerations, I'll start to make design decisions about the green. Since the green site is perfectly flat, I may wish to raise the green to give it visual definition, as well to develop surface drainage and fall in the tile system. Since the green site is at the base of a hill, it may not need definition and can be built closer to the ground as long as I provide for drainage. But in the case at hand, the green will be raised to give it some backdrop and depth definition. I would probably shape in ridgelines coming out from the hill and flowing through, into, or around the putting surface. Into or between these ridges I could place bunkers or grassy hollows. Grassy hollows are preferred because they can be used to capture and retain surface runoff from the hillside above until the tile drainage gets rid of it. So I measure the 1″ = 20′ enlargement and find the green has about 10,000 square feet and I want a big green—including collars—of about 7,000 square feet, so I build in small target areas with space-wasting ridgelines. Using a scale or ruler, I will give the green the possible shape and size I think will best suit this hole and site.

Whenever possible, I try to surface drain the green in three or four different directions so that all of the surface water doesn't run to one area (especially the front of the green) or onto other traffic areas that would become too wet and increase localized compaction. Since the putting surface is going to surface drain in different directions, there will be several small slopes within the green instead of just one large front-to-back or side-to-side pitch. By knowing the effect these small slopes will have on putting, I can plan strategy. I now transfer my revised 1″ = 20′ enlargement to a green detail sheet where I will add topography and start adding design details necessary for construction (see figure 87d).

Since the goal of strategic design is to reward

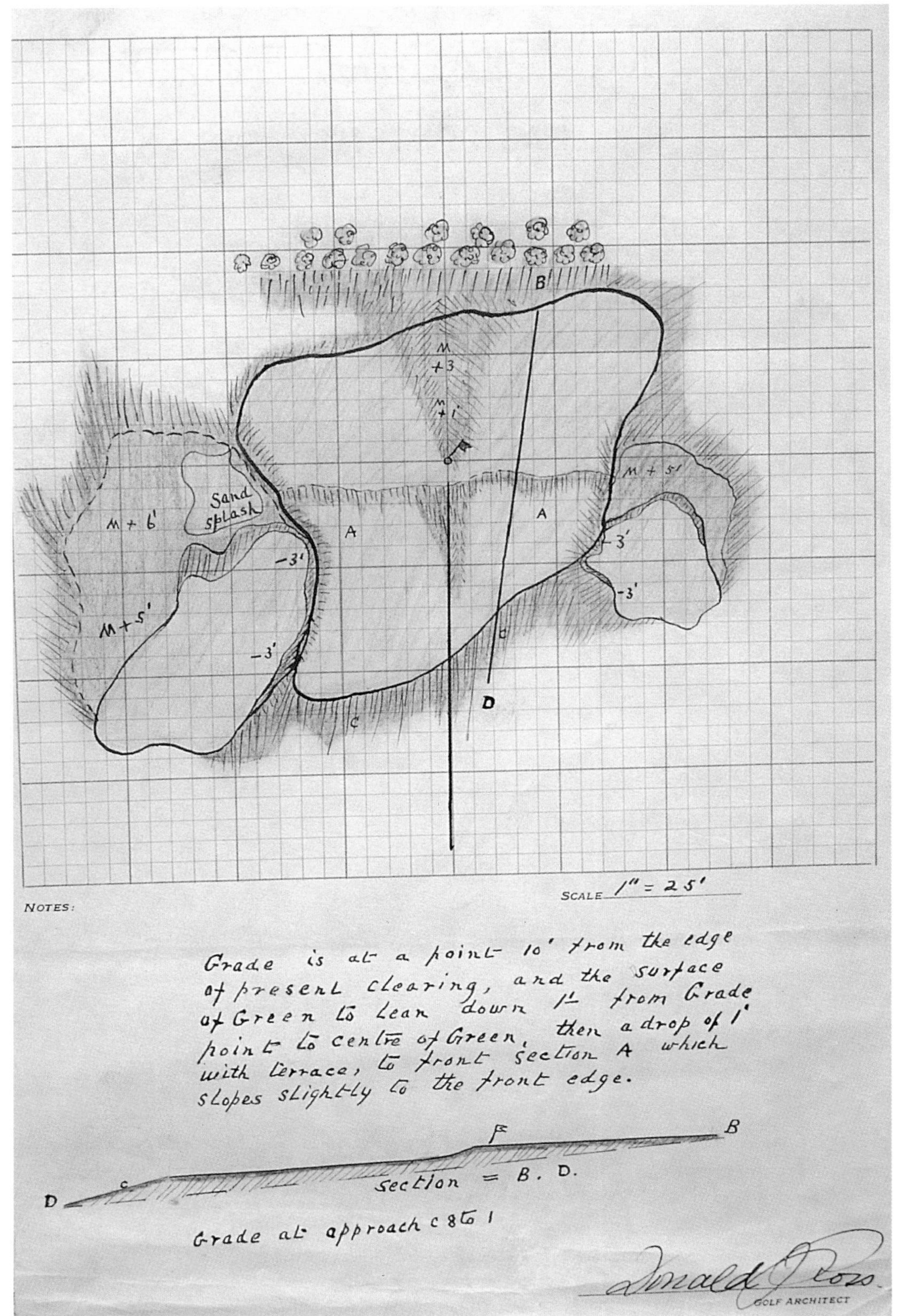
B
M +3
M +1
M + 5'
Sand splash
M + 6'
A
A
-3'
-3'
-3'
-3'
M + 5'
C
C
D
SCALE 1" = 25'
NOTES:
Grade is at a point 10' from the edge
of present clearing, and the surface
of Green to lean down 1' from Grade
point to centre of Green, then a drop of 1'
with terrace, to front section A which
slopes slightly to the front edge.
B
D
C
Section = B. D.
Grade at approach c 8 to 1
Donald J Ross
GOLF ARCHITECT

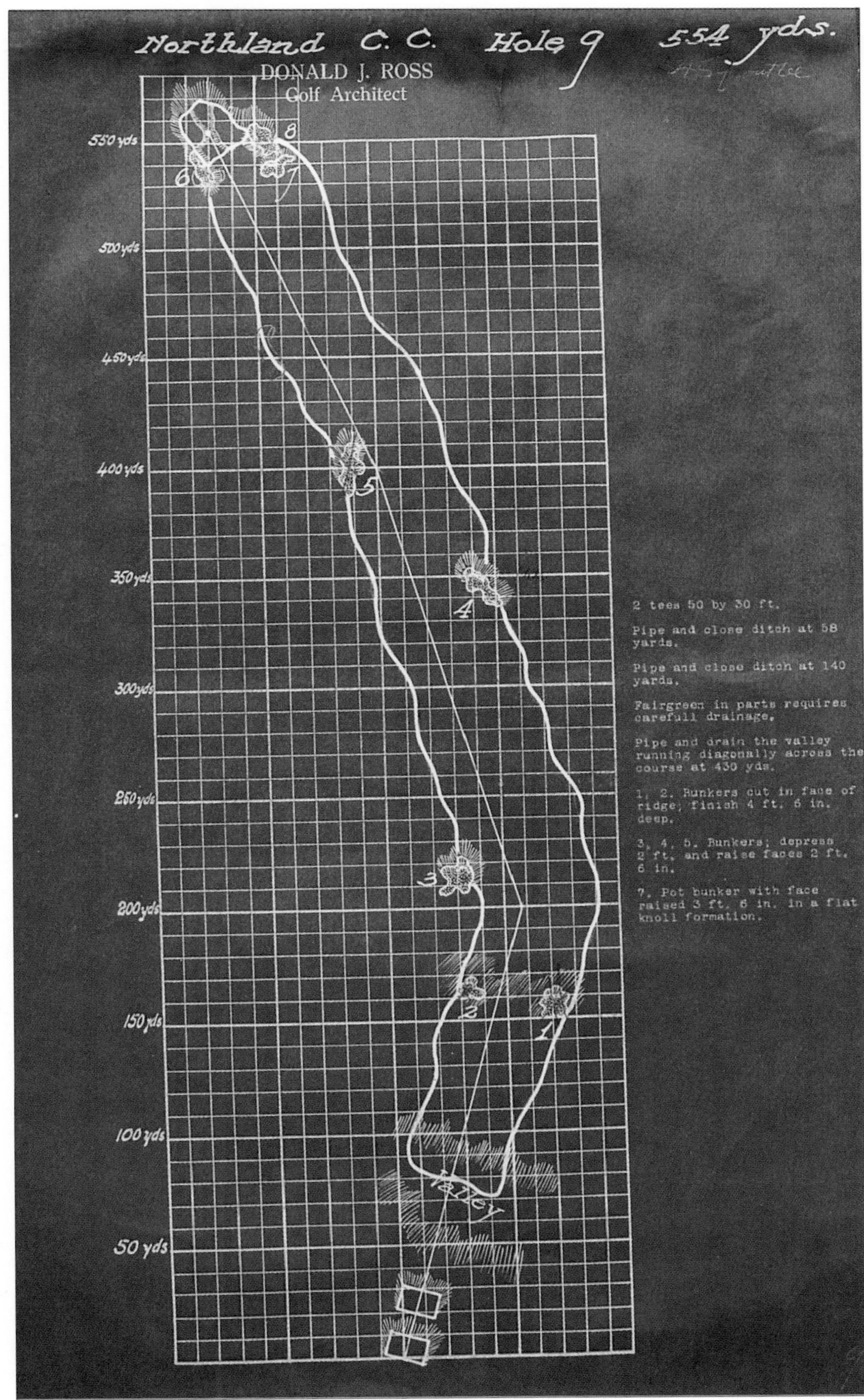

Figure 88. Donald Ross used drawings to convey his design intent, which is what allowed him to be so prolific. Hand-colored and signed Ross drawings are quite rare.

the good player without unduly penalizing the poor player, I'll plan small, strategic hole positions on about 25% of the green that require a golfer to execute a near perfect shot if the ball is to stop near the hole. To determine the appropriate size for any given target area within a green I refer to a table published by the USGA as part of their course rating handbook for Slope Rating teams. I use this guide to determine approximate target size and adjust it up or down depending upon other design criteria. These hole locations are still accessible to the less bold player who plays to an open or unguarded portion of the green, but his putt may be longer and more complicated. Since eight and nine irons and a wedge would be played to the green at Cobblestone Creek, I set up very difficult hole locations on a terrace at the back middle, easy positions in the front and middle, and moderately difficult ones in right middle and left rear (see figure 87e).

To protect these competitive hole positions, I'll employ hazards of such severity as to balance the reward with the risk. If the approach shot to the green is only a wedge, then I'll not only make the landing area within the green smaller, like on a terrace or a slight depression, but I will also protect it with severe hazards, such as deep sand traps, grassy hollows, or water. If the approach requires a long iron, I'd instead favor shallow sand traps, mounds, or grasstraps. For proper protection of a competitive hole placement, I might make one hazard more severe than the other, such as mixing bunkers and grassy hollows, to force the golfer to decide whether there is an advantage to missing it long, short, left, or right. Since one purpose of any hazard is to intimidate the golfer mentally and disturb his concentration, whenever the golfer starts to question club selection or doubt his ability to make the required shot, the hazard has been effective. In all of these situations, I try to remember that hazards are like spices: a careful balancing and blending of them produces the most satisfactory and memorable results.

In summary, I arrived at my intended design for a green by carefully analyzing the specific function of the green with regard to approach shots; by establishing the primary line(s) of play; by providing most of the green with easy but interesting hole positions and approaches; by selecting a few competitive hole locations and protecting them with suitable hazards; by providing for wide traffic corridors; and by molding all of that into an integrated unit that respects agronomic considerations.

If a conflict arises between the most interesting green (from a golfing standpoint) and the best application of agronomic principles, then I must resolve that conflict by deciding what is in the best interest of the owner, or what is consistent with the budget. To my way of thinking, it is better to sacrifice a unique design than to indulge in a personal fancy and have the project go beyond reasonable costs. Besides, it's part of the challenge of the profession to take a poor site on a low construction budget and still create a pleasurable golf course.

The final step in designing the green is to add the details necessary for the contractor to build it. This includes proposed contour lines, spot elevations, surface drainage indicators, tile lines and catch basins, quantities and areas of work to be done, layout information, and any other pertinent information (see figure 87f and g).

This process has gotten a bit more technical over the years, but it was started by Donald Ross, Colt, MacKenzie, Alison, Raynor, and others back almost 100 years ago (see figure 88).

5

From Tee to Fairway

Many golfers may be surprised at the amount of time and thought involved in designing tees and fairways, and as with greens the guiding concept is form follows function.

Next to a green, the most-used feature on the golf course is the tee. The concept of tees has changed over the years. Centuries ago, one had to tee off within one club length of the preceding putting cup (see figure 7). Eventually a physical separation of tee and green occurred, and tees became small level areas more often than not of dirt devoid of grass due to the intensive use they received. Some older golfers today still talk of the "tee box," a reference to that period before the wooden golf tee was invented when a box of moist sand was provided adjacent to the teeing ground so each golfer could tee up his ball on a mound of sand (see figure 89a & b). With the advent of the wooden golf tee, grass-covered teeing grounds became more popular, and it was found that to keep good turf on them required lots of tee space to permit the turf to recover from wear. It also became popular to use more than one set of markers on a tee to give the golf course more flexibility in length. As multiple markers became more popular, so did large linear tees and finally free-form multiple-level tees that allow the strategic-minded golf architect to vary both the length of a hole and the line of play to the target.

Form Follows Function

Since functions of the tee have evolved and changed over the years, its form is now different, too. While the basic function of a tee has always been to provide a level surface and firm footing from which to hit a tee shot, modern tees are now expected to measure up to greens in terms of turf quality and height of cut. So while flexibility—a golfing consideration—plays a large part in the form of modern tees, most tee func-

Figure 89a. The term "tee box" originally meant a wooden box containing moist sand with which to tee the golf ball. This 1907 ad shows a tee box with the sand and water necessary for making a sand mound tee. As wooden tees became popular such tee boxes disappeared.

Figure 89b. A 1917 Golf Illustrated *picture of Banff Springs Golf Course. Note the tee box of moist sand for teeing the ball, and the horse carriage.*

tions revolve around agronomic concerns. Even golfers who care nothing for good design and do not control the ball well enough to worry about strategy still insist on well-manicured greens and tees. To golfers, maintenance may well be more important than design.

Determining Tee Size

The form of the modern tee is a reflection of its maintenance requirements. A rule of thumb used to determine the proper size of teeing area for each hole says that a wood-shot hole should have 150 square feet of tee surface for each 1,000 rounds of golf played on it per year. If the course only plays 20,000 rounds per year, as is normal for midwestern country clubs, then wood-shot tees should be a minimum of 3,000 square feet (150 × 20). For public courses that average 40,000 rounds per year, the tee area should be 6,000 square feet. On iron-shot holes, the rule of thumb is 200 square feet per 1,000 rounds per year. Thus, on a public course booking 40,000 rounds a year, the iron-shot hole tees should approach 8,000 square feet.

These rules of thumb assume topsoil is used as the growing medium for the turf covering the tees. Research has shown that soilless mixes such as the sand/organic matter used for greens provide more optimal growing conditions than topsoil, so less time is needed for the turf to heal itself when grown on these mixes. Knowing this, a golf course architect can often partially compensate for smaller tees by providing an improved rootzone for turfgrass grown on the tees. However, rootzone mixes are expensive and add to the total construction costs, so one must carefully evaluate the cost-benefit ratio of their use.

Determining Tee Slopes and Locations

Since tees will receive intensive maintenance, they must be receptive to normal labor-saving equipment (see figure 90). This doesn't mean gang mowers, but it may mean triplex mowers or walk-behind single-unit mowers such as those used on greens or for trimming. Tee banks must be at least 3:1 slopes, with traffic areas of 4:1 for walking golfers, and egress must be provided to all tee surfaces for normal maintenance equipment. Since tees must provide firm footing and

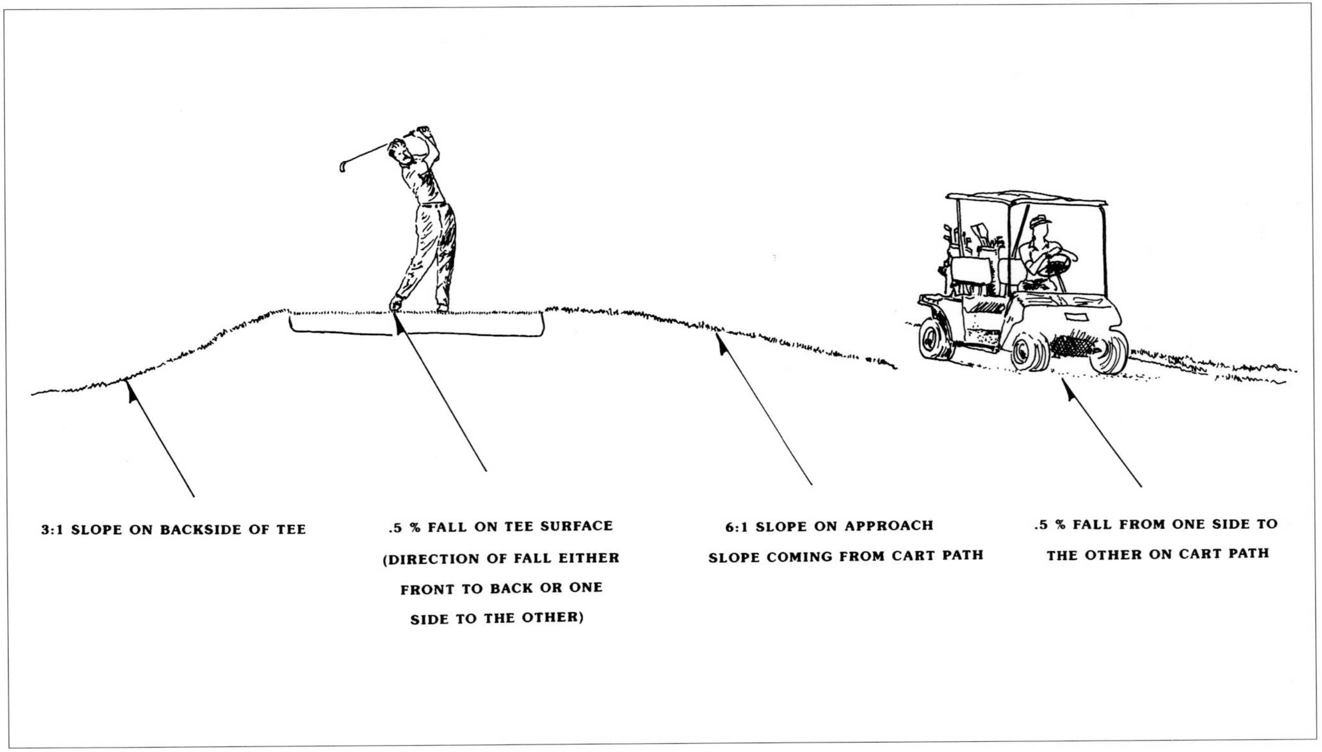

Figure 90. General guidelines in sloping tees.

be basically level yet drain surface water well, tees are usually raised above ground, are slightly crowned or, if the surface is large enough, very gently, almost imperceptibly pitched (1%). The only real options in tee design available to a golf course architect are the proportioning of the required tee surface, and tee placement. The most common proportioning of the tee surface is to provide 50% to 60% of the total for the average golfer—the commonly called middle tee(s). Then, depending upon the anticipated usage the course will get from beginners, juniors, ladies, and seniors, about 25% to 35% of the tee should be frontal teeing ground, and the remainder should be for back or championship tees. As we have already discussed in Chapter 2, different classes of players hit the ball, on average, very different distances. This has a significant impact on how we place our tees. In general, we know that professional men golfers drive the ball about 270 yards; skilled male amateurs hit it 240; average men and the very best women golfers drive the ball about 210 yards; the good lady golfer and the senior citizen hit the drive about 175 yards; and the average female golfer and novice hit a driver about 140 yards (see figure 29). If a common impact area on the fairway is to be used by all of these golfers, the placement of their respective tees must coincide with their abilities. So each set of tees is separated by about 35 yards. This assumes all of the tees are in a line and use the same path of play, and hence face the same golfing situations in the tee shot landing area with the same margins of error.

Although this system is common and has some merit, it may not make the best use of the terrain, natural features, or golfing elements. Many times a far more exciting golf hole can be made by changing the angle of play to a landing area by offsetting a tee. Thoughtful golfers know,

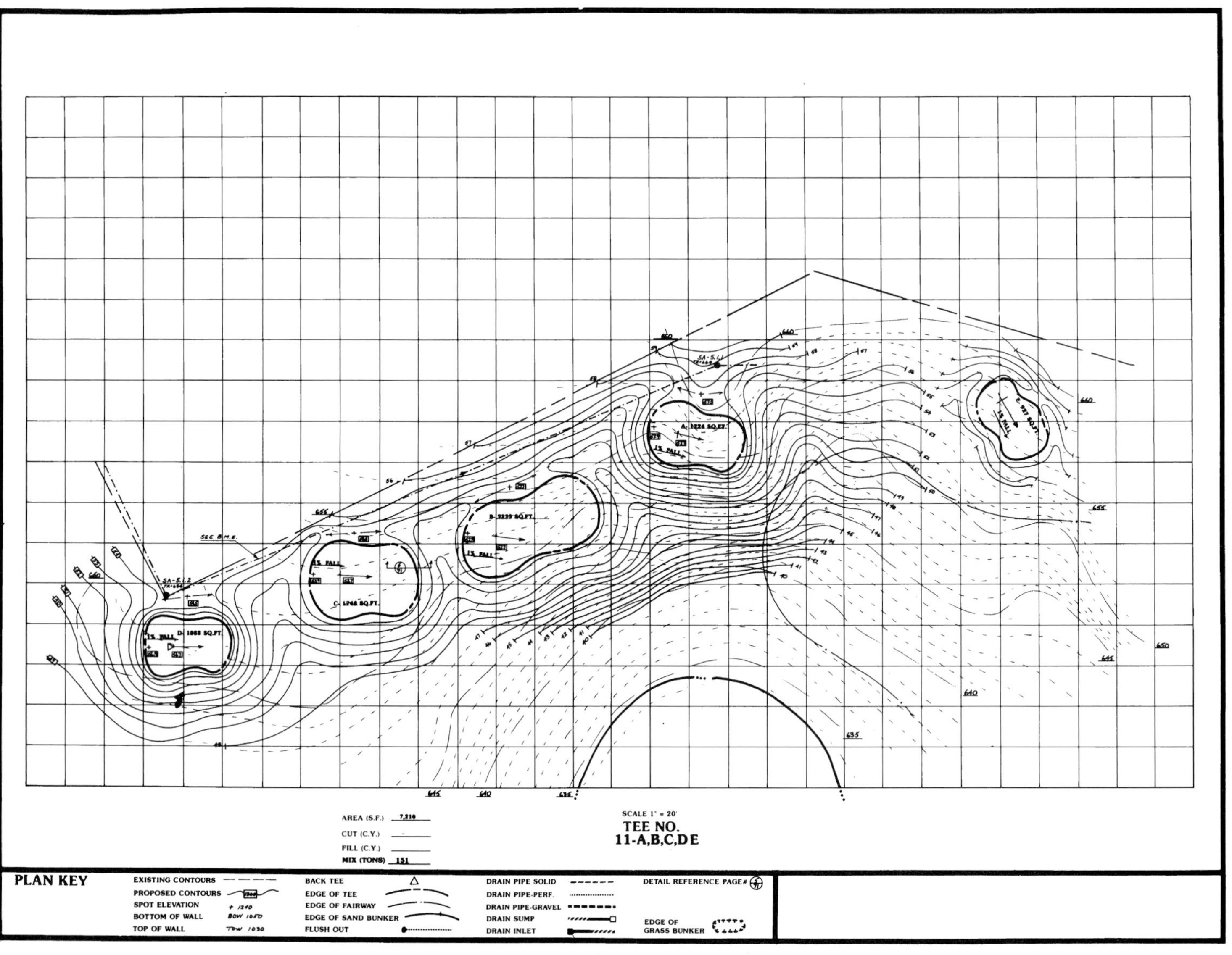

Figure 91. A detailed plan, or working drawing, for the construction of a 5-tee complex.

for instance, that when there is lateral trouble, the safest play is to line up on the side of the hazard and play away from it. This creates more margin of error and affords a better angle away from trouble. But if a hazard runs down the left side of the hole, the unthinking golfer will tee up as far to the right as possible, believing he is getting away from the hazard, when in actuality he is putting that hazard more into play. The thinking golfer, on the other hand, will tee up as close to the left side as possible and hit away from the hazard. Using this principle, a golf course architect can manipulate probable impact areas by laterally offsetting the line of play from each tee. Naturally, in strategic planning the most difficult angle of play will be faced from the back tee and the easiest from the front tee. On a hole with a left side hazard, I would probably place the front tee as far left as practical, and the back tee as far right as fairly fits into the design. On the 11th hole at Cobblestone Creek that is precisely how the tees were designed and how detailed plans were prepared to allow the contractor to bid and build the work (see figure 91)

A golf course architect usually tries to adjust the height of his tees to permit a clear view of the intended impact area. He does this for visibility, both so any group of golfers ahead can be seen and so a player can enjoy watching a well-played shot roll to a stop. However, for the back tee, a golf course architect may choose to locate a tee at such an elevation as to only provide for safety, making the group ahead visible just from the waist up. By doing this, the back tee player cannot clearly see the entire impact area or any surrounding hazard, and may start to doubt the situation, his club selection, or himself. Another technique used to disquiet the back tee golfer is to misorient the tee so that the golfer feels the tee is pointing in a wrong direction. A classic example is the back tee on the par 3 6th hole at Oakmont, which directs the golfer well to the right of the green, and requires that he overcome this by adjusting toward the most terrifying part of the green. Many skilled golfers have been fooled by this subtle shift in alignment.

The other tool that the golf course architect can employ at the tee is the use of low mounds that are integrated within the tee but not actually part of the playing surface. These mounds tend to intimidate golfers, who fear that a thinly struck or low shot may be deflected or stopped by them. Most golfers have no conception of how high a ball is when it is only a short distance from the clubhead. In most instances, it is much higher than one thinks, but since we have all hit low shots, any obstruction causes concern. In some situations, a small mound tight alongside a tee can add additional excitement to a hole. The same can be said of the skillful use of other three-dimensional objects such as trees, bushes, grasses, or rocks, but care must be taken not to overuse these elements. In the same way, high mounds or objects near a tee can act as safety buffers to stop misstruck shots that might otherwise cause damage. Conversely, thinly struck shots may ricochet off tee markers, ball washers and benches, rocks, or other obstructions placed in the line of play. These safety considerations should not be ignored by golf course management.

Tees offer an opportunity for a golf course architect to apply whatever landscaping skill he might have in endowing the tee with a distinctive look (see figure 92). Tees are natural places to use wood or stone walls, exotic showy plants, unusual landforms, and even man-made structures, such as wooden post fences—keeping safety of golfers in mind.

Fairway Form and Function

The form of fairways also follows their functions. Fairways are characterized by uniform, closely mowed turf of a height of 1/2 to 3/4 inch. Such maintenance practices require that fairways be level enough to take close mowing without scalping the turf, be well-drained to handle rainfall and irrigation, and be smooth enough to allow golfers to ride in golf carts at high speeds in comfort. In order to serve these functions, fairways are finish-graded with a land-leveler, scarifiers, and floats, or other fine grading equipment to produce a very smooth playing surface. The value of well-drained easy-to-mow fairways is indisputable, but the result is that many times the land must be worked and shaped

Figure 92. One of the distinctive features is the landscaping around the tee at EagleSticks, Zanesville, Ohio.

Figure 93. A 1917 ad for a fairway mower that specifies it can be ". . . quickly detached from the tractor and changed to a horse drawn type if desired."

Figure 94. The integration of fairways and roughs at the Meadows Course at Grand Valley State University is a return to the classic look of the 1920s.

in ways that our predecessors would never have imagined. The pleasantness of having the golf ball cleanly perched on a well-drained, verdant, uniform fairway turf has come to be expected, and is perhaps not as appreciated now as in the past. In the early days of golf, it was a rub of the green if one was fortuitously blessed with a good lie or cursed with a bad lie (see figure 93). It was part of the charm of the older courses that a fairway's functions were loosely defined and their form unmodified to permit the natural charm of the ground to remain.

Today, however, it is common to strip every bit of topsoil from a golf course and shape with bulldozers the entire parcel of land to include tees, greens, fairways, rough, and even out-of-play areas. At first this may seem an extravagance, and at times it is, but generally the goal of this site shaping is a matter of changing the form to fit the function of drainage. As previously discussed, for the golf course superintendent to properly manage and provide the playing conditions that golfers expect, he must have a well-drained growing medium. Although costly, it is easy to justify using special soil or blends on tees and greens. However, to use modified soils on fairways and/or roughs would cost tens of millions of dollars. Therefore, the golf course architect chooses the most reasonable alternative, which is to control surface water drainage patterns through shaping.

Some good rules of thumb are never to drain water across or down the middle of a fairway, never let it drain more than 50 yards to reach a catch basin or tile inlet, and have at least 2% slope toward the tile inlet where northern grasses are used, and 3% slope in southern turf areas. The resulting landform is a series of humps and hollows, methodically spaced to control water movement. In areas of significant precipitation, this has meant the end of the level fairway of yesteryear, in exchange for the advantage of a functional drainage system. Form and function can never be separated.

Another evolution in fairways is their integration with roughs. In the past, fairways were called fairgreens, which was a more descriptive term. Fairgreens connotes landing areas containing managed turf to afford good lies en route to the putting surface (see figure 94). Those areas were irregularly shaped, and usually of sufficient size to permit some margin of error in shot-mak-

Figure 95. A freshly sodded fairway and rough at St. Albans Country Club, St. Albans, Missouri. Note the tractor, to get some scale of this fairway that was fully shaped and piped for drainage. Remaining areas will be planted to fine fescues that make a transition into native grasses.

ing. Rough areas, interspersed among the landing areas, were a product of nature—not man—for they were cleared of brush, but were not maintained. It is doubtful such unpatterned integration of fairway and rough would be tolerated on contemporary courses, but recently more target-type golf holes are being built to reduce the impact of golf course maintenance on surrounding environments, particularly in the desert Southwest where the total acreage of maintenance turf is regulated by law.

A middle ground between freeform fairgreens and rigid freeway golf fairways involves contour mowing and contour planting of select grasses (see figure 95). The intent is to design and maintain specific landing areas with adjacent areas of minimally maintained rough. Perhaps, though, a better alternative to the wide expanses of rough bordering each fairway from tee to green would be wide expanses of less highly maintained fairway. These areas would receive less water and fertilizer, and could be mowed less often at the same height of cut than the landing areas.

Traditionally, the form of the fairway was a band of highly maintained turf between 25 to 60 yards wide and usually running from the front of the tee to the back of the green. Lately there has been a trend for fairways to start about 70 to 90 yards in front of the main tee and extend as a free-form ribbon of 30 to 40 yards. Such contour mowing takes out of high maintenance what can amount on the whole golf course to several acres of little-used playing area, while giving the player back a strategic reward for a decently struck shot.

The primary design theme used at Naples National was to provide only three major zones of fairway, scrub sand, or pine straw. Thus only 45 acres is maintained as turfgrass, which is almost one-half of what is permitted in many areas of the desert Southwest, and one-third of that found on a traditional South Florida golf course, but yet almost 100 acres is playable (see figure 96).

Except for uniformity of sprinkler coverage of heads placed down the middle of a fairway, there is no reason for a uniform-width fairway. With contoured fairways, expected landing areas are as generous as the site will permit, extending up to 60 to 80 yards across for less skilled players,

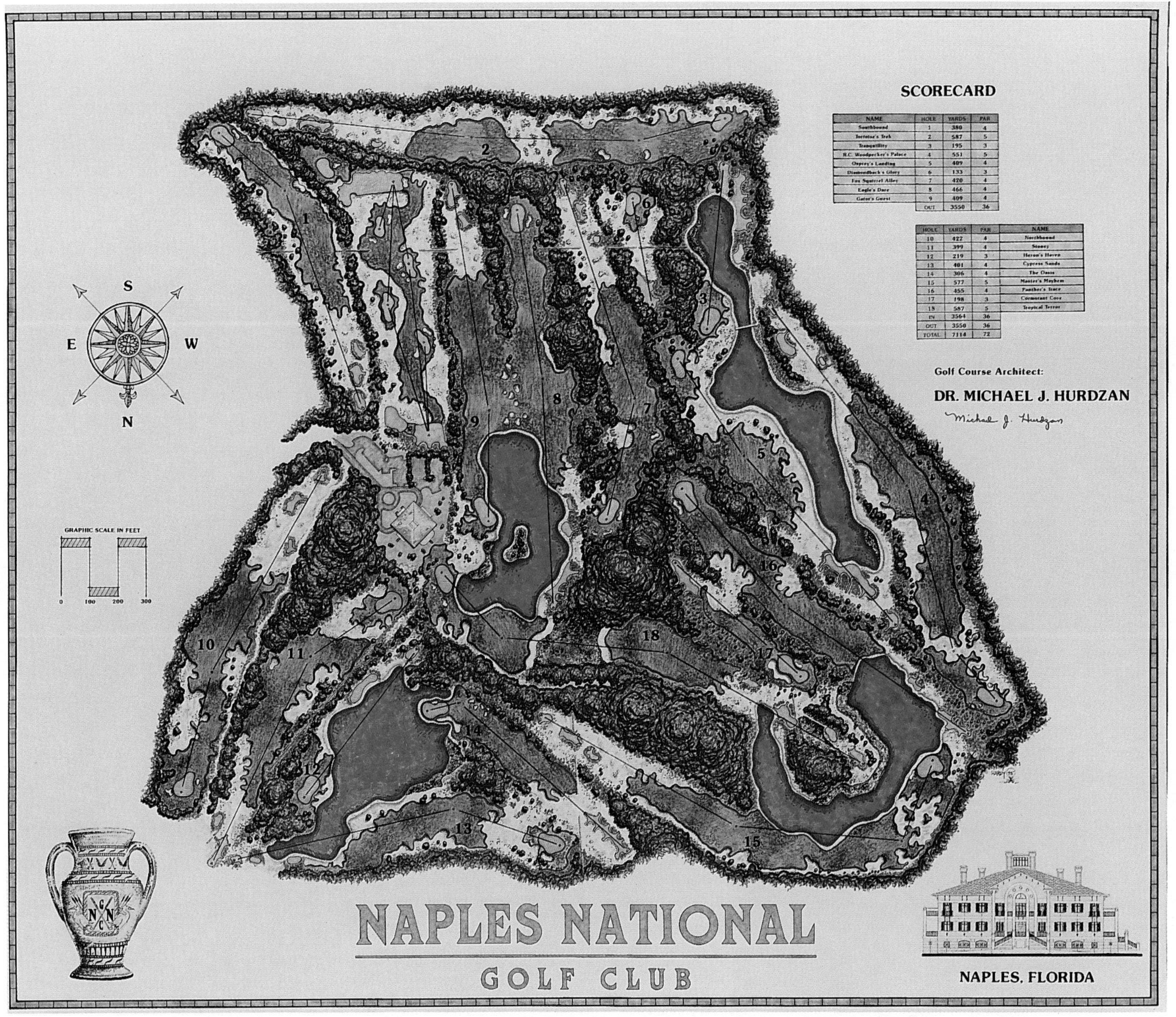

Figure 96. An "as-built" color rendering of Naples National lets your eye compare the relative areas of turf, trees, sand scrub, and pine straw.

Figure 97. The early morning dew on the 10th hole shows how wide most of the fairways are at Cook's Creek.

and down to 30 yards for the best of players (see figure 97). Between expected landing areas the fairway narrows down to 35 or 40 yards wide in slow sweeping mowing patterns. In order to break the monotony of hourglass patterns, contoured fairway lines also accent natural and constructed golf course features, changes in topography, and hazards by sweeping around them in random fashion. By select placement of irrigation heads, watering and fertilizing practices, or the planting of different turf varieties, interesting flowing patterns are developed, much like permanent images of sunlight and shadows cast by puffy clouds on a cool summer day.

6

Individual Golf Holes

An individual golf hole only requires two golf features—a tee and green, and possibly a fairway—to be considered complete. If these elements are properly designed, built, and maintained, nothing more is needed to produce a functional golf hole. However, if the terrain is flat and the surrounding landscape is rather drab, a succession of such holes is boring to play. They may provide good exercise for the body, but they do little to involve or stimulate the mind. Even a flat hole can be given character, interest, and challenge through the addition of that universal spice of golf courses—hazards. The type, manner, and severity of these hazards are dictated by the design philosophy of the architect and his adherence to one of the concepts of penal, heroic, freeway, or strategic golf design (see figure 98).

To discuss the design of an individual golf hole, let's limit the choice of hazards to five mounds and one depression, on a site marked by an out-of-bounds down the left side. Let us examine how each respective philosophy of design would employ these identical hazards. Initially, the accompanying drawings will use symbols to schematically illustrate each hole design from

Figure 98. 18th hole, par 5, St. Albans, Missouri.

only the pro tee position. During the later phase of design development, other features, such as forward tees, greens, bunkers, etc. are added.

Schematic Design Phase

The penal designer would place the depression perpendicularly across the fairway about 200 yards out from the tee (see figure 99), so that any drive that is not well struck would land in the depression and leave a difficult second shot. On such a hole the golfer has to try to carry the depression—for there is no alternative route—or else play short of the depression and face a very long second shot. The penal advocate would also protect the green from imperfect approach shots by placing the mounds all around the front of the green. In such a design the golfer has no choice but to play short of the hazards or to try to play over them and risk their penalty. The average golfer would be humiliated and harassed on every shot. Scratch players might endorse this type of design, for their concept is to test for consistent shot-making and to penalize those who cannot mechanically execute every given shot.

When golf architects realized the fallacy of penal design, they began to modify their placement of hazards to provide relief for the less accomplished golfer. Those who subscribe to heroic principles of design would realize that the longer the approach shot, the more difficult it would be, and that forcing the weaker or unskilled golfer to lay up on his drive made the hole too difficult. The heroic solution would be to place the depression diagonally across the fairway (see again figure 99), so every player could choose as much hazard as he thinks he can carry to a flat landing area. Such a designer might also build something of a dogleg left, so that the farthest point of the hazard was located precisely at the point where the fairway turned. To reward the golfer who carried the greatest amount of the depression, heroic designers might resituate the mounds near the green to provide for an open approach for the most daring tee shot. The other mounds around the green would still serve the same purpose as in penal design—to punish a bad approach. In this manner, we can see that heroic design blunts the harshness of strictly penal hazards, but in making golf more enjoyable and fairer to the less skilled player, it still favors the longest and strongest players.

Freeway golf course designers recognize this inequity, but their solution is to place the hazards to the side of the common line of play in order to penalize the uncontrolled shot-maker and allow the long and straight to reap his fair reward. Although a freeway design is more equitable to all golfers than either the heroic or penal designs, it is also very unimaginative, requires little thought to play, and is not very inspiring of great golf.

The strategic designer takes our sample hole (see again figure 99) and arranges the hazards with the goal of making the hole equitable to all golfers, rewarding the good player, encouraging the poor player, balancing risk with reward, and making each golfer involve his mind as well as his body on each shot. The depression is still used as a heroic-type feature, allowing each golfer to choose how much of the hazard he is capable of carrying with his drive. But the strategic designer values accuracy as well as strength, and uses the mounds in combination with the depression to define various landing areas, with each landing area affording a distinctly different approach shot. The longest carry (symbol B) over the depression is to the smallest landing area between some mounds. It carries the risk of landing in the depression (and facing a hanging lie), or having the player's second shot be blocked by the mounds. The reward is the shortest second shot to the green, with no obstructions to the approach, and approaching the green on its longest axis. Symbol A's drive risks less of the depression but flirts with the out-of-bounds. It is played to the left side of the depression, leaving the only obstruction to the green a mound immediately in front of the golfer. Hit the drive too hard and perhaps the second shot is blocked. The further right that a "safe" drive goes (symbol C or D), the more the next mound affects the resulting approach. Likewise, the axis of the green becomes shorter, thus making the target area smaller. The weakest player can choose to either play left of the depression along a narrow fairway (symbol A), or drive over it to a generous

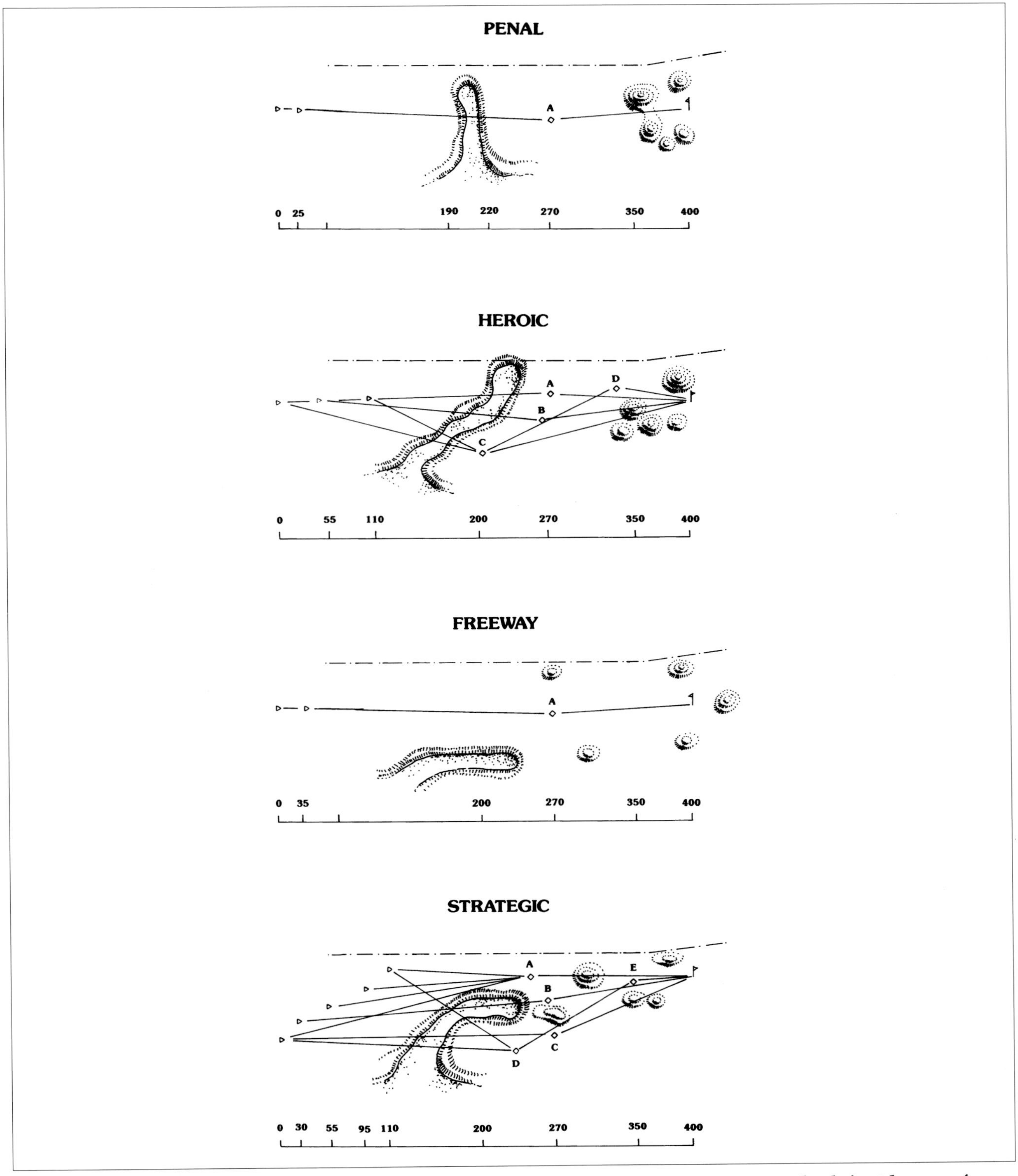

Figure 99. Using the same architectural elements (5 mounds, 1 depression, and a left side out-of-bounds), how advocates of the four major design philosophies would design a 400-yard golf hole.

landing zone (symbol D). The shortest distance across the depression is to the widest landing area, but with no risk of out-of-bounds on the left. However, this short drive leaves the mounds in the direct line to the green for the next shot. This is not really a problem for weaker players, who probably can't reach the green on the second shot anyway. An alternate route (symbol E) for a short second shot, by the way, means that if properly executed it leaves but a short pitch shot to the green.

This strategic hole has all of the same elements of the others, but the placement and manipulation of features, and their extension into the third dimension, creates a golf hole with strategic options. The golfer is given the opportunity to match his skills against the golf course by minimizing his weaknesses and maximizing his strengths. The interesting quality of a strategic design is that the same golfer may choose different routes on various days depending on the weather, his opponent, or his mood. This is why the 14th hole at the Old Course at St. Andrews is so highly regarded.

Design Development Phase

The design process to this point is often called "schematic design," where the basic elements and possible play lines have been established, but no thought has been given to details of each element. The further refinement process is called "design development," which culminates in a master plan that is rich in details influenced by the designer's philosophy about golf and golfers.

Once the framework of a hole is made structurally sound, then it is time to apply, harmonize, and blend the necessary golf course elements, such as tees, fairways, and greens (see figure 100). To begin applying these features, a golf course architect may first try to refine the design to further amplify the strategy of the hole and more precisely balance risk and rewards. He may begin by examining the tee and working his way down the hole to the green. The penal designer wants to maintain the integrity of the cross hazard depression, so he would choose to make the tees small to limit the golfer's option from where to play. If tee space were needed to accommodate large volumes of play, the tee would be made wide instead of long. Forward tees would be grudgingly provided, but they too would be small and located to keep the intimidation factor of the depression for even front tee players. The fairway might have some contour mowing, but it would be kept narrow (30 to 35 yards wide). The green would be small (3,000 to 4,000 square feet), probably round, and tucked up tightly against the mounds, with rough immediately behind the green.

The heroic designer would have opted for a tee that is long and narrow, or perhaps several long and narrow tees, so that the golfer will have more variety in the length of shot to carry the depression. Some days when the tees are back, less of the cross hazard is risked, whereas from front tee positions the golfer can more easily reach the prime landing area. Heroic designers would give a fairly wide (40 to 45 yards) landing area that follows the depression, providing multiple target areas. However, the fairway mowed narrows (30 to 35 yards) as it approaches the green. The green on such a hole would be large (6,000 to 8,000 square feet), free-flowing in shape, and have hole locations designed to favor the heroic tee shot.

Freeway golf holes are characterized as having a square or rectangular tee(s) usually set on the same play line but not providing great flexibility in the total length of the hole. Oftentimes there is less than 20 yards difference between the back and front tee on most holes. The fairway would be cut uniformly about 35 to 40 yards wide, with parallel edges from tee to green. Likewise, rough would border the fairway at a uniform height of cut, or perhaps a 15- to 20-foot strip of low or friendly rough, then the deep rough. Often this linearity is accented with a straight line planting of trees in the rough, or some oval or squarish bunkers all in a row. The green would be round or oval shaped, fairly flat with few or no protected pin positions, but of good size (6,000 square feet).

In our sample hole, the strategic architect realizes that instead of the square tee that yields the needed square footage of tee surface but only permits a minimal front-to-back length flexibil-

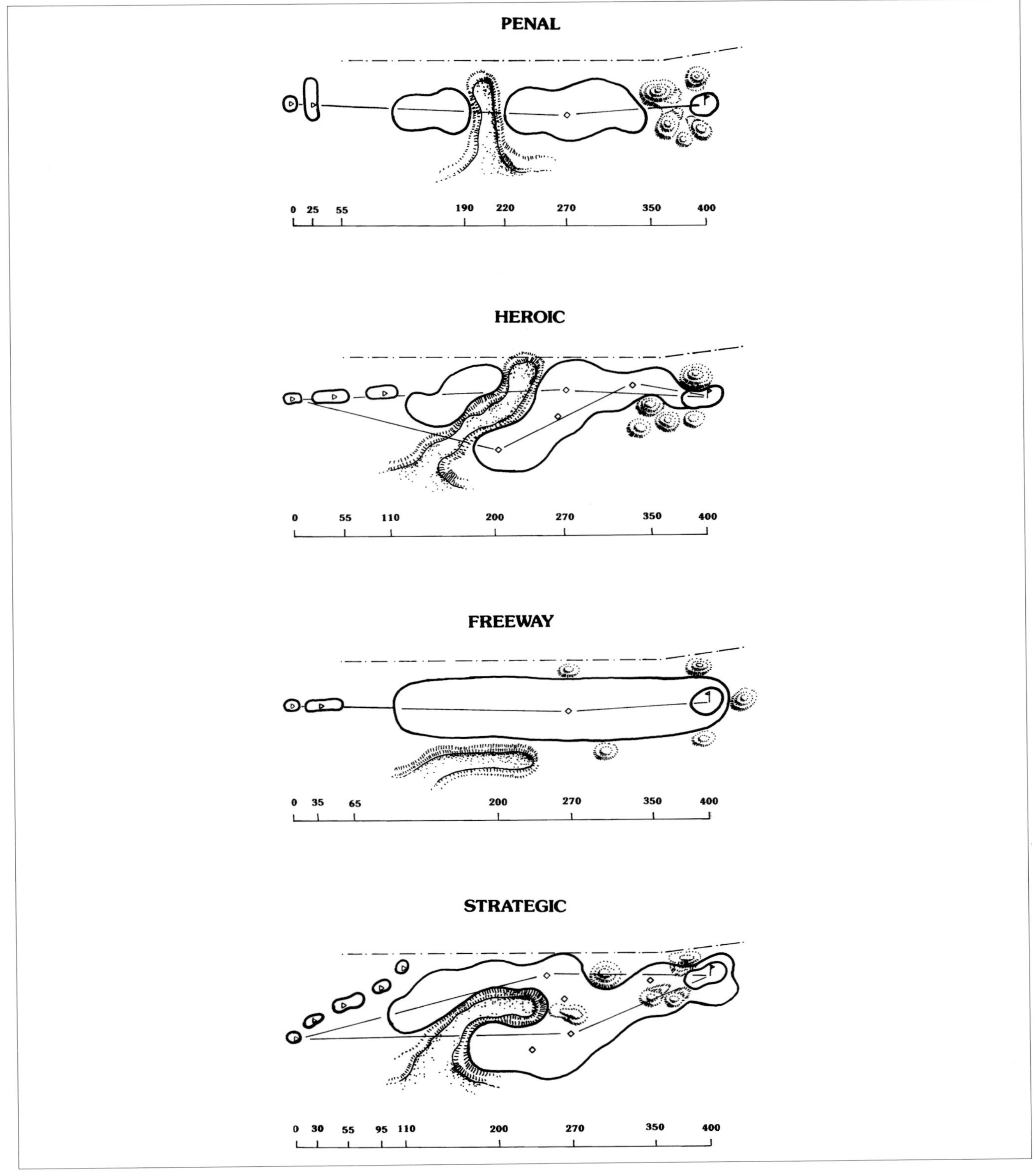

Figure 100. During "design development," each design philosophy advocate would add such details to the hole plan as the sizes and shapes of tees, fairway lines, and green.

ity, he may use a free-form tee that is narrower and longer. In addition, since there will be at least five sets of tee markers, each for players of different abilities, he can adjust the shot value from each tee to fit the ability of the golfer using it. A golf course architect is aware of the relative percentage of golfers who will use each tee, so he will proportion each percentage of the total tee surface to fit the user pattern. The less accomplished player will normally use the front tee, and seeks to avoid the depression down the right side. Placing the front tee as far left as possible allows the weaker golfer to play along a narrow fairway to the left of the depression. Although the out-of-bounds is on their left, these players usually slice the ball, so the out-of-bounds is not as intimidating a hazard as it is for the better player, who tends to hook the ball. He knows that the proper way to avoid a hazard, especially one with the severity of out-of-bounds, is to stand next to it and hit away from it. Therefore, the front tee should be placed as far left as practical and forward far enough so that a 140-yard drive from the middle of the tee reaches the middle of the intended prime impact area. This also permits the less skilled player to slice the ball and have it land in play. In addition, the strategic architect knows that perhaps only 10% of the total rounds played for the year will be off of this tee, and that these golfers do less damage to a tee compared to players of other skill levels. Therefore, this tee can be made small (800 square feet). Since middle tee golfers are the most common and are more accomplished, their tee is largest (3,000 to 4,000 square feet) in size, and located to allow 175 and 210 yards, respectively, from the middle of each of the two tees to the middle of the landing area. These tees are moved more into the center of the site to increase the amount of the depression that must be carried, and to expose these golfers to a greater risk of hitting out-of-bounds. The back tees, used by a small number of very good golfers, can be made small (800 to 1,000 square feet each), adjusted to a middle distance of 240 and 275 yards, respectively, and moved diagonally across the play line to require the longest carry and pose the greatest risk of out-of-bounds. In general, the strategic designer wants to maximize fairway area and minimize rough, so it is not unusual to find strategic fairways two or three times wider (60 to 90 yards) than other design motifs, with almost no rough.

Initiation of Construction Document Phase

At this point the designer's ability to visualize the finished golf hole is brought into play, for now he must assign three-dimensional values to the golf course elements. For our example the designer can make the depression no more than 8 feet deep, and the mounds have fixed heights of 3, 4, 5, 6, and 8 feet, respectively. The arrangement of these elements and their three-dimensional impact must be placed to amplify their philosophy.

The strategic golf course architect will begin to examine the depression and will adjust the severity of this hazard to be in balance with the reward of carrying it (see figure 101). Even though the depression is near the front tee, many front-tee players will dub their drives into it. Therefore, the depression will not be too deep (–2 feet) or steep (5:1 slopes) at this point, and since the slope is enough of a penalty for most players, a portion of the depression may be maintained as fairway. About halfway down the depression, where the middle or back tee players are expected occasionally to mishit their drives, the hazard can be made a little more severe by deepening (–6 feet) and steepening it (3:1 slope), and perhaps by adding an additional hazard of short rough. Near the right end of the depression is the area that is rarely expected to catch the wayward shot of any player. It is at the right end of the depression that the golf course architect would blend the manicured portion of the golf course into the unmaintained or minimally maintained character of the site. Thus the depression serves as both a physical and visual linkage of golf and the natural environment. If surface and subsurface drainage permit, then the depression at this point can be made deeper and steeper than anywhere else, and the area occupied by this end of the depression can be planted in native grasses, wetland plants, or selected scrub or bushes. If drainage does not permit

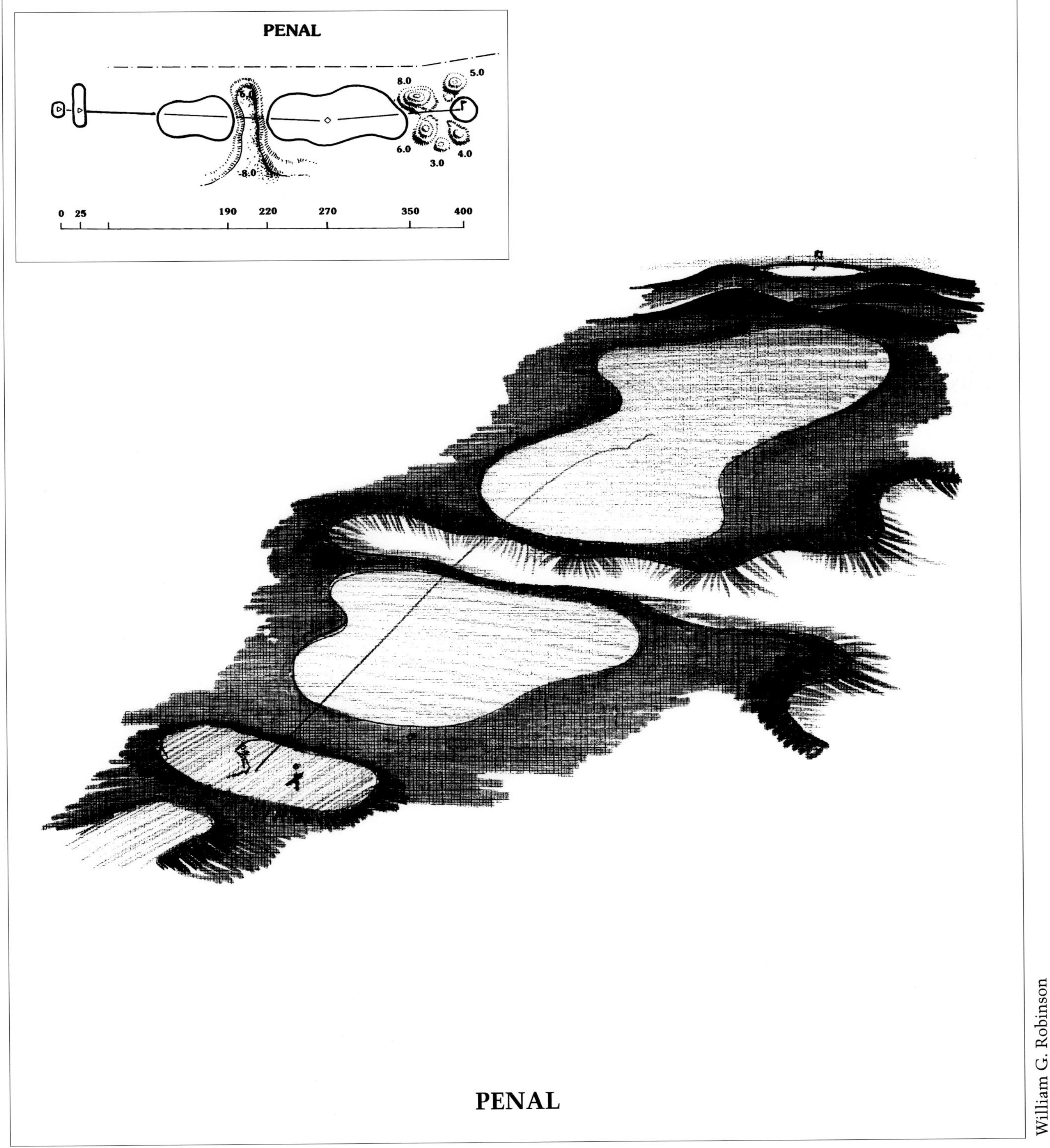

William G. Robinson

Figure 101. To amplify his design intent, the golf course architect must visualize the hole and assign 3-dimensional values to each of the elements. In this case it is a depression of no more than 8 feet in depth, and mounds of 3, 4, 5, 6, and 8 feet in height.

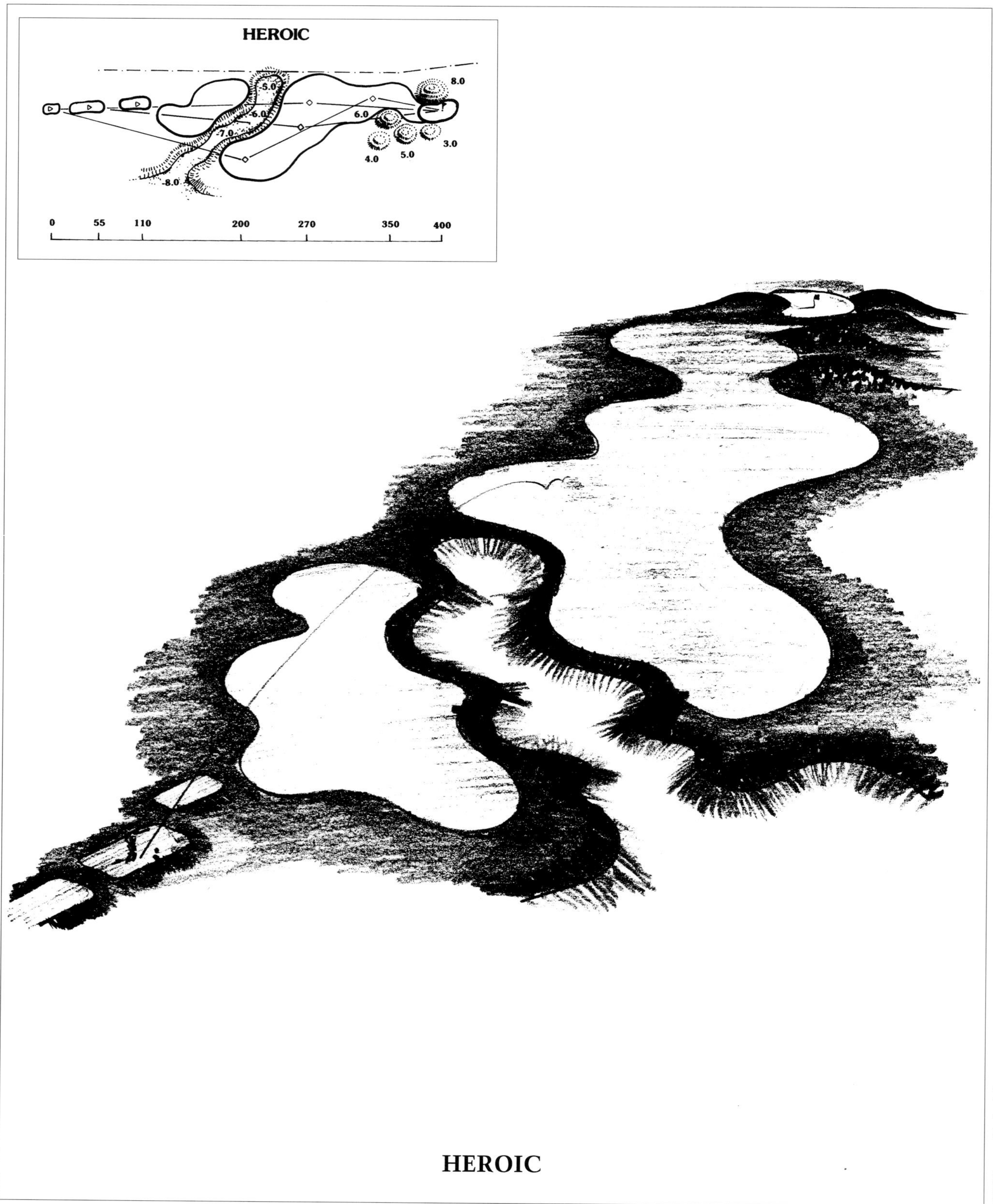

HEROIC

William G. Robinson

FREEWAY

3.0 6.0 8.0 5.0 4.0

-6.0 -4.0 -2.0 -8.0

0 35 200 270 350 400

FREEWAY

William G. Robinson

STRATEGIC

William G. Robinson

making the depression deeper, then it possibly could be made into a water hazard—the most severe of hazards. But whatever decisions are made about the severity of the depression, they are made with the intent to fairly balance risk and reward.

Next the golf course architect would consider the severity of the mounds by analyzing the function of the mound, whom it will affect, and how it will do so. In this example the five mound heights will be 8, 6, 5, 4, and 3 feet, and the side slopes will vary from steep (3:1) to gentle (20:1). Thus each mound can be assigned to a height and outslope that best fits the design intent for that mound. Similarly, the depression can be described with spot elevation such as –4 feet (4 feet deep) with 3:1 (steep) sideslopes.

Penal designers would like to make the depression as steep and deep as drainage considerations would allow. In this example it varies between –6 feet and –8 feet, with 3:1 slopes. Similarly, the mounds clustered in front of the green should be the highest ones, with steep sideslopes, and the lesser mounds as support mounds, but with equally steep faces.

The third dimension of the heroic hole is for a depression of the same proportions as in the penal design, but simply oriented in a diagonal direction across the fairway. The mounds in general would have softer sideslopes (4:1 to 6:1), with the highest mound on the left of the fairway near the green, to frame the hole, and the other four mounds guarding the green on the right. This mound arrangement makes the hole visually attractive and balanced, while setting up a strategy that rewards the bold, long drive.

Freeway design is more concerned about visual balance and symmetry than strategy. So the depression has a uniform gradient upward toward the green, with maintainable sideslope (4:1 to 6:1). The largest mound (8 feet) would probably be placed behind the green as a terminus for the center line or play line of the hole. The other four mounds would be placed and spaced to define or delineate the margins of the fairway and green. The sideslopes of all of these mounds would be rather uniform and would match those of the depression (4:1 to 6:1).

The strategic designer, on the other hand, begins by evaluating the probable play pattern of a golfer using the front tees by mentally playing the golf hole. Assuming the golfer drives the ball properly, he has taken the least risk and therefore should have the least reward, but since he is a weak player his second shot must not be made too difficult. This means that mounds in his landing area must be made gentle enough (4 feet high and 10:1 outslopes) to confound the golf shot without making it impossible to play. Normally, the average golfer in this position will play a fairway wood second shot that will rise quickly with high trajectory and produce little run after the ball lands. This means the mounds near the green must be made very intimidating if such a golfer is to find risk playing over them, so they must be built perhaps 5 and 3 feet high. The purpose of the left side green mound would be to slightly penalize a wayward approach shot, but more importantly to protect it from the out-of-bounds, for if it required an excellent shot to land near it, the shot does not deserve a stiff penalty. That mound needs to be about 6 feet high with long outslopes (20:1) to accomplish its intended purpose, perhaps with some grassy hollows shaped into it. Another alternative for an average player is to hit his second shot between mounds instead of at the green. He is taking almost no risk with this shot and thus deserves very little reward. However, if this "safe" second shot is miscalculated and goes right then he must contend with the greenside mounds. The mound nearest the green can be made as large as desired—in this case 5 feet high with long outslopes of 10:1—and a companion mound can be made 3 feet high with similar slopes. These mounds would then provide definition to the green site, protect pin positions from a safe drive, and cause only slightly imperfect shots to be deflected toward the green. To add visual character to the landscape, these mounds could be planted with accent grasses instead of normal turfgrasses.

Next comes the analysis of the play pattern of the middle tee player, so that we can determine the form of the influencing mounds. For him, the mound in the landing area is pivotal, for the closer he is to it with his drive (but left of it), the easier is his approach to the green. Therefore, such a mound should be made as mentally menacing as possible, for a shot landing near it offers the greatest reward. Thus the golf architect may choose to make the mound high enough to require precision long iron play of anyone behind it, or steep enough to confound the player who drives the ball on its outslope. This mound could be made 4 feet high with at least 5:1 slopes—enough to permit easy maintenance but difficult shot-making. If properly situated, it produces another interesting condition when a player is daring enough to drive the ball directly over it, landing on its downslope. Such a drive would be expected to pick up many extra yards in roll, especially if the back side of the mound is kept dry and hard. However, if the daring drive fails to carry the entire mound and lands instead on the upslope, then he is left with a more difficult second shot, particularly if the upslope is cut as rough or is kept lush by irrigation. Another alternative is to carve a bunker into the front side of the mound, which makes it even more penal as a hazard, though this would be more appropriate on a short hole, whereas on a long hole it would be excessive. The golf course architect might also consider whether a 3-foot-deep depression might not work better. Lastly, the further to the right of the mound the middle tee golfer drives, the more the mounds near the green will require a precise approach shot.

Finally, the golf course architect examines the play pattern of the professional and scratch player in order to arrive at the fairest form for the mounds that confront him. To have the easiest line of approach to the green, the scratch golfer must take the most powerful swing with perhaps the greatest risk, so he should not be strongly penalized by a mound for being only a little off-line with his drive. After all, he not only had the longest carry over the most fearsome part of the depression, but he also had to risk the out-of-bounds. But for the strategy to work, there must be an intermediate intimidation factor of hitting the prime landing zone but being too far left, and hence the menacing influence of the large mound on the left. Therefore, the first left mound should be about 8 feet high, just enough slope (6:1) to fairly penalize a less-than-perfect drive and to reward an expertly played one. The only other mounds that might affect the scratch player are those nearest the green, but their form and function are consistent with the shot value of all caliber of players, so no modifications are necessary.

The last feature that a golf course architect must design is the putting green. Plain geometric figures do not provide much opportunity for protected hole locations. Since such hole positions are, however, a necessary part of strategic design, the golf architect strives to produce small portions of the putting surface that require precision approach play if the ball is to end up near the pin. Two of the most difficult portions of the green to hit in our sample hole are the left rear and right front. The left rear portion is made difficult by the long outslopes or ridgeline of the mound near it. That ridge tends to hide the putting surface and makes distance judgment difficult, so the safe shot is a short shot. The right front is made difficult by the reduced margin of error to stop a ball near this area caused by frontal mounds. It will "kill" an approach that lands on their upslope, while it will also cause a ball that lands on its downslope to run past the intended resting spot. To fairly mitigate the difficulty of this approach, the strategic designer would wrap the fairway around the right side of the green so a bold but too long approach comes to rest on short turf. Donald Ross used this technique often, and these areas became knows as "chipping areas."

Agronomic Influences

In addition, the golf course architect knows that there are many agronomic factors that will also influence the final form of the green. The paramount consideration is surface drainage, which requires not only at least a 75:1 (1.5%) slope but also should be planned in various directions so as not to cause water accumulation in any one spot. Since our hypothetical site is flat, surface drainage requires elevation of the green. With these considerations in mind, the golf course architect begins to mold the circular shape of the green to give competitive hole positions, while at the same time providing for surface drainage. One possible resulting form is a simple three-lobe green that accomplishes all the basic objectives. An added bonus of this shape is that the ridgelines separating the drainage patterns give additional character to the overall putting surface. If, in the opinion of the golf architect, additional protection is needed for the competitive hole positions, then additional or different forms of hazards can be used, with their severity tempered by their function.

Even on a perfectly flat, treeless piece of ground, an interesting and strategic golf hole can be produced using nothing more than a depression and five mounds. No bunkers, water, or trees are needed. No heavy rough stretching from tee to green is necessary. The golf hole is inexpensive to build and maintain.

Construction Influences

But even after the skeleton of a hole has been designed and many of the forms of each feature are decided upon, there are still some practical considerations that must be taken into account. A golf course architect must consider the cost of these features, what construction problems are likely to be encountered, what long-term maintenance problems could arise, and what site limitations might exist. He'll also consider if the construction methods and agronomic solutions are proper for the project, and whether all natural site features have been properly used. Most of the answers to these considerations are products of previous golf course design experience, background, and training.

Construction Cost Estimation

Using our sample hole, an architect would estimate how much it will cost to build it by determining the volume of fill needed to build the five mounds and the green from material excavated from the depression. Such calculations can be readily made via use of cross-sections or a planimeter—a table-top measuring tool by which planners can easily determine surface areas. Then he would measure the area to be occupied by the depression and attempt to balance the size and depth of the depression against the required fill for mounds and the green. If these two figures won't balance out, then he must either borrow fill from another site or haul excess fill away. The actual volume of fill, type of material, and length of haul are all factors that affect cost of earthmoving. Similar calculations and estimations are required for subsurface drainage, irrigation, seedbed preparation, seeding, and green construction.

Since no two sites are alike, every project has a different set of conditions, goals, limits, and problems. For instance, each golf course site has different soil and rock conditions. This means that each site will also have different problems with earthmoving, rock layers, chemical and physical properties of topsoil and subsoil, internal drainage, sand sources, water tables, underground water supplies, and erosion or flood potential. Any or all of these will cause changes in construction costs, construction methods, work schedules, choice of turfgrass cultivars, ideal time of seeding, use and location of water hazards, need for tile drainage, tile drainage backfill, seed rates, fertilizer and lime rates, type of mulch and binder, and post planting care, establishment, and maturation.

All of those items, of course, are a result just of soil and rock conditions, yet each site has many more factors that are just as important and just as variable. An architect cannot ignore specific site conditions and cannot solve them with blanket procedures and specifications. Specifications that are not site-specific can add hundreds of thousands of dollars to the initial construction cost and who knows how much in long-term maintenance. Practical considerations cannot be ignored, and they certainly should not be minimized.

Many times during a review of practical matters, the golf course architect may discover a problem that requires a change in his design, perhaps of just one feature or perhaps of the entire course. The time for such changes is during the planning phase, not during actual construction, when changes are not only more costly and time-consuming but also may not have easy solutions and may substantially diminish the overall design. For all these reasons, practical factors must be considered at the preliminary stages of the design process.

Design Enrichment

Once a golf course architect is satisfied with the skeleton and flesh of his golf course design, he may begin to examine cosmetic enhancement of each hole, or as it is called in architecture, surface enrichment. The purpose of cosmetics is to highlight and accent natural strengths and beauty, visually to obscure weak or offensive features, and to further bond the key elements of the course to the surrounding landscape in order to make them appear more of a single unit. On the golf course, the most commonly used cosmetics are landforms, walls, flowers, flowering plants, bushes, trees, mowing patterns, sand, and natural features of the site, such as rocks, wildlife areas, and established or unique plant communities.

To illustrate this, let's refer to our sample golf hole and sequentially go through the process of applying cosmetics (see figure 102). Since tees are resting spots where golfers may have to wait for short periods of time, it seems logical that tees are where golfers are most likely to recognize and appreciate their functional and cosmetic qualities. Subsequently, the area surrounding the tee can take the form of a resting spot in a garden, with a formal or informal motif depending upon construction budget, maintenance budget, and existing surroundings.

It is always nice to provide shade near tees, and if possible drinkable water and a bench in order to reduce physiological stresses on the golfer. A few shade trees can be planted close enough to each tee to benefit the golfer but far enough away so that shade will not compound normal maintenance. In our example the tees are separated by many yards, so several trees should be planted, at least one or two at each tee. In between the trees it is desirable to plant shrubs, particularly those that flower, bear fruit, or have showy foliage. These shrubs will cast smaller shadows than shade trees, so they can be planted closer to the actual tee surface. Similarly, trees with open or thin foliage that cast light shade—such as locust, palm, or eucalyptus—can be planted closer to tee surfaces. Flowering trees—such as dogwoods, magnolias, or crab apples—can also be nicely integrated into the area around a tee. Tees, especially multilevel tees, are good places to utilize walls of wood timbers or stone to support various levels, particularly where space is limited. Walls also add a different color, texture, and feel to the site. They will most often be the only artificial structure of the golf course, but still be integral to the design. Such walls gain further enrichment by the use of ground covers or flowers at their bases (which are usually unusable and unmaintainable space), growing among the wall members or growing on top and weeping down over it.

In our example, the back tee is elevated 5 feet above grade and is supported by a stacked stone wall. The top of the wall is planted to low-growing creeping junipers that will be allowed to hang over the wall. At the base of the wall and next to the stone steps will be planted ornamental grasses or wildflowers (either annuals or perennials) that are well-adapted to the site and have blossoms most of the season. Immediately to the right and rear of the tee are prime locations for moderate- to tall-growing shrubs that produce flowers, fruit, or attractive foliage or stems. These plants should not be planted so close to the tee or so close together that they impede air drainage across the tee. To provide shade for this back tee, a shade tree well-adapted to the area should be planted.

The middle and front tees can be treated in a similar manner, but since these tees are so much larger, the cost might be prohibitive. Therefore, the middle tee might be elevated 3 feet above grade and the front tee only about a foot above, both with outslopes of 6:1 to give them definition. These tees should also be provided with shade trees and, as an added touch, a fruit tree with edible fruit such as apple, pear, peach, or cherry. Besides trees, these tees might be cosmetically enhanced with an occasional showy shrub, such as laurel, rhododendron, or azalea. Natural fruit bearers, such as raspberry, blueberry, grapes, or wild rose, or small trees such as hawthorn, Japanese maple, or dwarf pine could be used, along with ornamental grasses. These shrubs, bushes, and low-growing trees should provide as much change in color, texture, and growth habit as is practical. Flowers should then be selected and planted to ac-

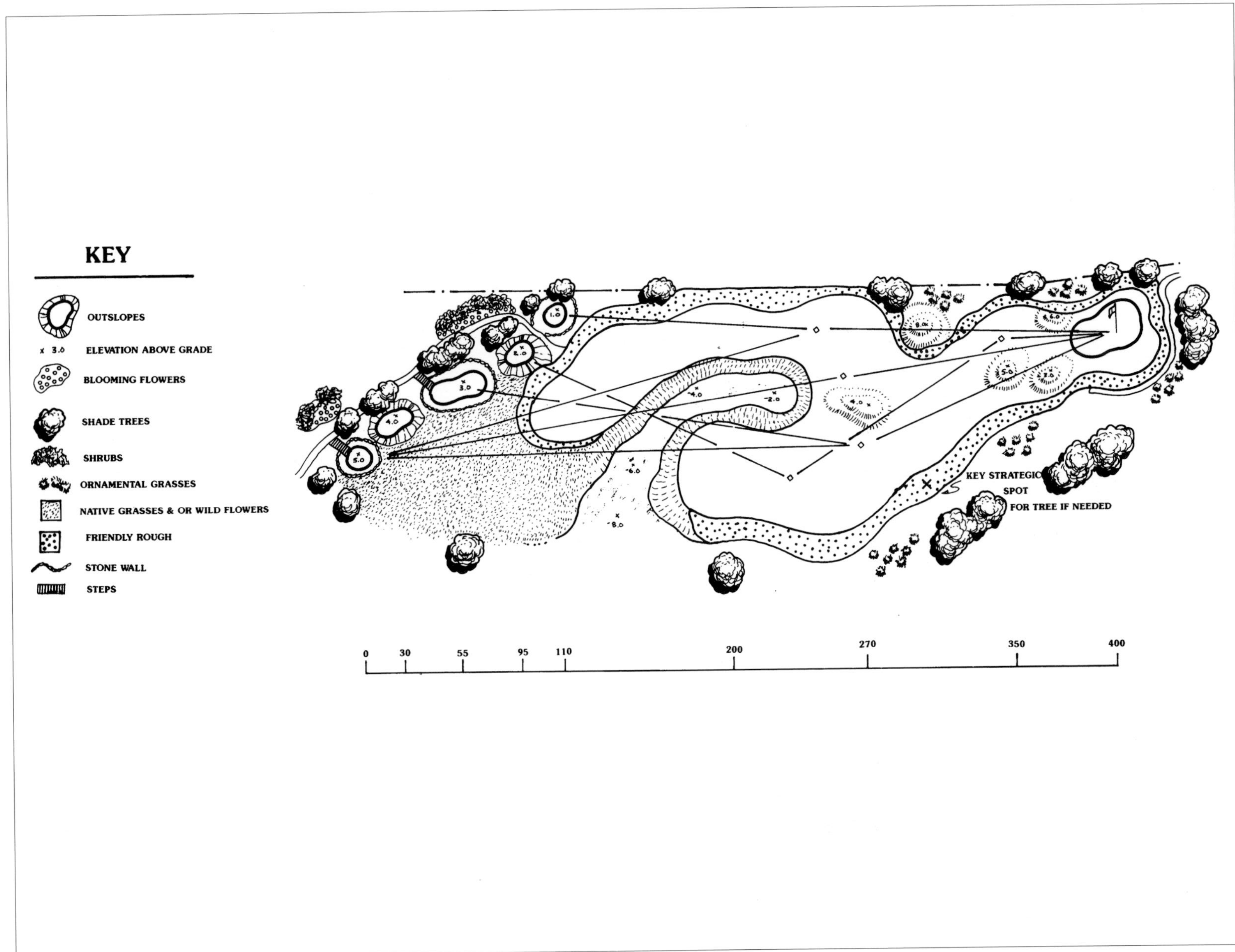

Figure 102. Once the basic hole design is complete, landscaping can be added to create atmosphere and aura, as well as to further amplify the strategy.

cent or define spaces and provide a show of color. In all planted areas, maintenance can be reduced through use of wood chip, bark, leaf, or needle mulches around the plants. The sensitive use of preemergence herbicides will also go a long way toward reducing ongoing maintenance.

Since there are no hard or fast rules about landscaping tees, the possibilities are limited only by imagination and money. Often, after the course is in play, benevolent members will donate money or plants to the golf course, especially if there exists a long-term planting plan. The only rules that must be respected are:

1) don't block traffic patterns or funnel people into narrow spaces unless a path is provided
2) don't plant anything immediately in front of a tee that will grow so high that it would distract golfers or deflect well-hit golf shots
3) select plants compatible with the environmental conditions found around the tee, especially the amount and quality of irrigation water
4) select low-maintenance plants that only need occasional attention, like ornamental grasses, instead of something like rose bushes, which need continual care
5) use as wide a variety of plant materials as possible

A trip or two to a local nursery quickly repays itself in terms of stimulating ideas for plantings.

The area immediately in front of the championship tee and to the side of the middle tee is considered non-golfing ground, for almost no one playing from those tees is likely to hit the ball there. As this area requires little or no maintenance, slow-growing plants native to the area should be planted in it. Wildflower or native grass mixes not only tie the golf course in to the natural landscape but also reduce maintenance. Those who wish to resist such integration of wild plants (which in truth are often nothing more than exotic weeds) should not fear. Such plantings do not increase weed seed production that could contaminate a golf course. Most of these plants do not stand up well under normal golf course maintenance practices. Besides, herbicides are needed regardless, for golf courses are continually bombarded with windborne weed seed that travel prodigious distances.

The area immediately in front of the front tee should be treated as fairway or friendly rough, for it can be expected that some high handicappers will be playing their second shot from this area. The same rough height can be used in the entire depression, or it can be allowed to grow longer at the right or lower end. On the remainder of the hole, rough is used sparingly and only in those areas where that type of hazard is justified. The fairway is made as spacious as possible, particularly in impact areas. The contour mowing pattern of the fairway is in response to the other golf features, changes in elevation, and the design intent of the hole. Wildflowers or native grass mixes are also used to the left of the fairway near the green to reduce maintenance and define the hole.

Very few trees are planted along the fairway or in the rough area, except for some groupings of trees or shrubs planted to mask the straight line of the out-of-bounds markers or fence and define the right limits of the hole. Additionally, accent plantings or evergreens between mounds and the far left side of the green are recommended. Their purpose is threefold: to add definition to the hole; to provide a change in texture, color, and height; and to serve as backdrops to the mounds and the wildflowers. The only other trees are tall majestic ones planted behind the green to aid depth perception and create an attractive backdrop. If, after this was all done, the hole still lacked character, I might consider adding one large tree at one key strategy point (see again figure 102).

White sand is a common material associated with golf courses and is used in bunkers for a variety of reasons, including defining shot values as well as visually enriching the golf course. Good bunkering is an art that few have mastered, but some of the best were MacKenzie, Ross, Tillinghast, Thomas, and one of my favorites, Stanley Thompson. Recently, golf course architects have begun to restudy the work and technique of these legendary designers, and are now much more conscious of the play of light

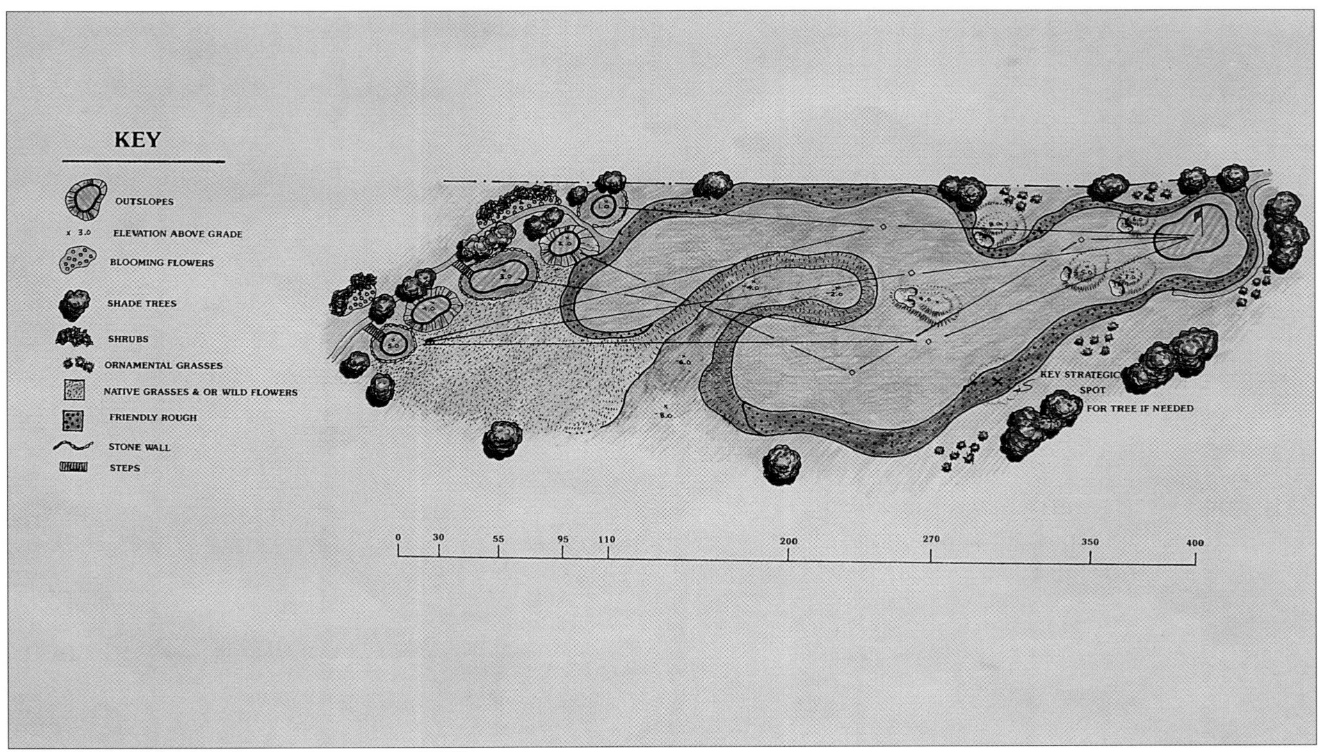

Figure 103. Bunkers can be added to the mounds to increase the shot value of the hole, and hence intensify the strategic intent.

and shadow as well as color and mass in their shaping of the course. There is also a trend away from the bleached white sand that was so popular in the 70s and 80s, and designers are opting for off-white or natural colored sands. This may be an attempt to capture some of the classic look of courses from the 1920s.

If bunkers are added to the sample hole (see figure 103) they should be simple in shape, small in size, and strategic in placement. Since they are light in color, they will read "loudly" on the landscape; or in other words, a little show of sand leaves a strong visual impression on the golfer. Therefore, I would use sand to highlight the main elements of the design, which were the five mounds. Determining the exact size, shape, and shot value of these bunkers would follow the process explained in Chapter 3.

Henebry Photography

7

The Beautiful and the Ugly

"Beauty is in the eye of the beholder," is a familiar cliche whose intent and meaning are clear, but in reality it is an oversimplification of a more complex process. Actually, the statement should read, "Beauty is in the *mind* of the beholder," for recognition of beauty (or ugliness) is not solely a visual experience. Rather, it is a mental experience of interpretation, understanding, and reaction to stimuli. The specific interpretation, understanding, and reaction to any given sensory stimulus are products of both education and instinct. Therefore, if one is to understand what determines beauty and ugliness, one must understand the sensing mechanisms involved, the mental processes, and the emotional and physical responses they evoke. Command of these concepts is important to any artist, designer, or architect who wishes to communicate with others through his art. This includes golf course architects, who can use basic and universal design principles to manipulate the emotional and physical responses of golfers to various planned stimuli, with the goal of enhancing their recreational experience. It may not be too far-fetched to say that both Norman Rockwell and Dr. Alister MacKenzie were masters of their art in communicating values to their audience.

The Visual Process

The starting point for this discussion is with the mechanism of vision. Technically, vision is the absorption of electromagnetic energy of the visible spectrum by the retina of the eye, forming a continuous flow of images of different shapes, colors, and textures, each lasting a fraction of a second, at various depths of field. The brain in turn scans this continuous stream of images and sorts, categorizes, and identifies single images or groups of them. It takes only the faintest image for the brain to go through this rapid process and cause us to believe we saw something as fleeting as a shadowy object on a dark night. In fact, sometimes the less detail that is perceived, the more active the mind becomes, adding information so that the object can be positively identified. This process of recognition, starting with a vague form and adding more detail, is the same procedure used to design or create most things, be it a building, a painting, or a golf course.

Once the visual image is complete and is identified, then the brain may trigger physical or emotional reactions based on experience and on instinctual reactions associated with that image. For example, suppose you are walking through a woods in a very relaxed manner, enjoying the outdoors and appreciating the complexity of nature. Then your eye picks up a vague shape on the ground that is long, narrow, and has moved slightly (see figure 104). Suddenly, a subconscious survival instinct in the brain is alerted and the brain begins to focus the eye on the vague object to add detail to the image. This added detail shows the unknown object is about 3 inches around and 4 feet long, has a checkerboard pattern of earth tone colors, and a texture that appears to be scaly. "A snake," the brain decides. With that visual image identified, the brain instantaneously triggers a physical and emotional response based on your learned experiences and instinctual reactions. If you fear snakes, your reaction will be the classic "fight-or-flight" response. If you've kept a snake as a pet, then you may feel pleased to have another one nearby. If you are a small child who knows nothing about snakes, your reaction might be aroused curiosity and you'll be drawn toward it. If the snake acts in a menacing manner, then your instinctual reaction will be to withdraw from it or defend yourself. This example not only demonstrates the rapid physical and mental process of vision, but also shows that emotional and physical responses to an identified image vary from person to person, culture to culture, and age to age. Therefore, if one wishes to communicate with others using sensory information, he must be able to anticipate what response the information will elicit. These responses are often a product of a particular social culture that assigns general values to various stimuli. But since not all members of a culture may accept its values, a designer must carefully target his message if it is geared to selected individuals or subcultures.

Michael Pogany, Columbus Zoo Original

Figure 104. Visual communication requires both the eye and the mind to sort through what is seen, and to discover what is being looked at. Understanding this process is essential if the golf course architect wishes his work to visually communicate to its users.

Cultural Symbols

Because information is processed by the brain at a very fast rate, common messages are often conveyed by simple symbols, even though their meanings may be very complex. The meanings of these symbols are specific for a given culture or population, so the same symbol may have different meanings to members of distinct human groupings. Depending on the culture, the skull and crossbones symbol may mean poison, or danger, or a motorcycle gang, or pirates. Symbols, then, are shorthand messages to the brain. In general, symbols that evoke instinctive reactions will communicate with great numbers of people with simple messages. That is the goal of logos in advertising (see figure 105). However, as the stimuli become more complex and require greater intellect or experience to understand their meaning, fewer people will get the message. Those who do grasp the more complex meaning will normally experience an equally more complex physical or emotional reaction to it. The best explanation of this concept is found in *The Appreciation of the Arts/Architecture*, by British structural architect Sinclair Gauldie.

Understanding the Visual Message

Reaching this complex level of communication is called "connoisseurship," and is commonly associated with subjects such as wine, music, and art. But it can be experienced with any subject, including golf course architecture. It is assumed that reaching a level of connoisseurship will provide a more intense pleasure, for it involves comparisons between expectations, observations, and experiences. When the meaning of a complex message is correctly read and interpreted, there is likely to be a thrill of discovery and an increased sense of enjoyment or appreciation. The reward for discovering a golf architect's message should be a perceived mastery of the strategy of the golf hole, and should result in feeling that one is capable of achieving a lower score than those who do not understand the message. Sadly, very few golf courses can provide this experience, mainly because most designers have lacked the talent and skill necessary to encode and provide such communication. Sometimes limitations placed on the designer by the site, the budget, or the client preclude such message inscription. But most masterful golf architects have possessed the ability to convey subtle messages in their art, and their works have endured in part because they continually invite rediscovery.

A golf course design is truly sophisticated and complex when one never tires of playing it, when it offers different, achievable challenges and provides opportunities for new discoveries with every round (see figure 106). A golf course can be simply a place to play the game, or it can be a test requiring strategy in both thought and shot-making. The greatest golf courses should not simply be places to play golf shots, but rather places to invent golf shots. The afterglow of experiencing such a course should be a feeling that it didn't demand anything beyond your ability, but it made you think on each shot, and when you did so you were rewarded, and when you didn't you were fairly penalized.

Ideally, a golf course should also offer such sensory diversions that even if one does not play well, one leaves the course feeling mentally and spiritually refreshed. Those are the goals of truly great golf course design: a continuum of challenges, mitigated by a proper balance of risk and rewards, requiring thoughtful shot-making, and presented in such an aesthetic way that the golf course can only be described as beautiful.

Gauldie wrote that fullest enjoyment comes when "one is simultaneously a spectator and a participant." In golf, this occurs when the golf course is not just a setting for human activity but also a site for the adventure of discovery, where sensation follows sensation throughout the round. The best design, says Gauldie, "brings aesthetic incidents together with human activity in a coherent and eloquent way," and the most successful and enduring ones draw their communicative power by stimulating the "emotional associations that are most deeply rooted in the sensory experiences of humanity."

Perhaps this is the reason that the Old Course at St. Andrews has become the point of departure for all golf course design. Its final character and form are products of centuries of thoughtful interpretation by millions of golfers, each of whom has reflected upon the unique interrelationship of nature and golf that constitutes these fabled links. The Old Course is a historical summary of those features and shot values that are indeed the most deeply rooted, emotional associations valued by golfers.

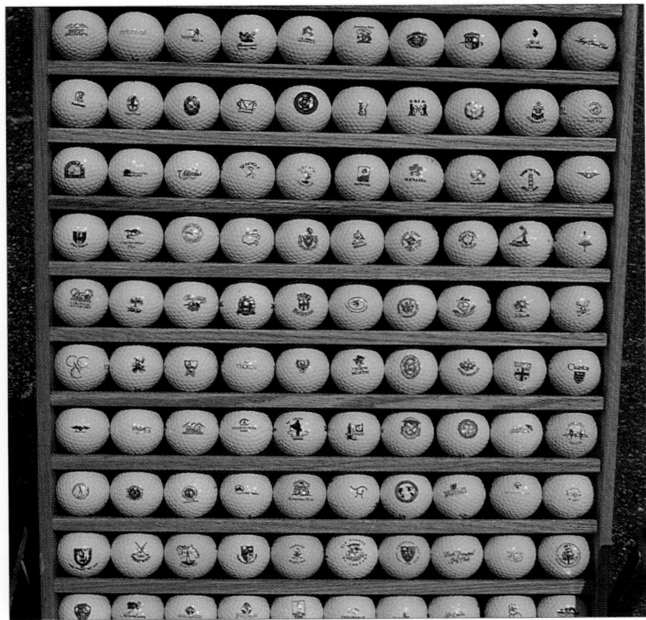

Figure 105. Logos are symbols that abbreviate identification but only carry learned or experienced meanings.

The message presented by any golf hole or golf course is conveyed to the golfer in an architectural language. Such a language is a mixture of common symbols that evoke deeply rooted emotional associations. It also resonates with constantly evolving expressions that are products of the intellectual values of its society. Again, Gauldie states, "every structure is in some degree a historical document, a demonstration of structural technique, a performance test of building materials, a comment on the values of the society that produced it, a reflection of the richness or poverty of its designer's imagination." This is true in golf as well.

For instance, the sand bunker is a very com-

Figure 106. One of the greatest strategic holes in golf is the 359-yard, par 4 5th hole at Royal Dornoch, Scotland. The hole can be attacked from many different angles, but determining which one is best, given the wind, weather, and hole location, requires a great deal of understanding and intelligent play.

mon symbol on a golf course that strikes deeply rooted emotions, but its exact form is linked to the values of the time during which it was built. The earliest bunkers were simply areas within a sandy links devoid of vegetation, with completely irregular form due to the influence of shifting winds, traffic within it, and the strength of plants on its perimeter (see figure 107). As early golf architects strove to build artificial bunkers, they tried to preserve their symbolism but were obligated to give it some form. That form was a product of man rather than nature, an expression of the crude earthmoving equipment of that time, and oval-shaped to mimic the upswept sand face found commonly on linksland (see figure 108). In keeping with the social value of frugality prevailing in the early days of golf design, such bunker forms were the product of the poverty of the designer's construction budget as much as his imagination.

As time went on and inland golf became an acceptable substitute for linksland golf, different structural materials were encountered and social values changed. The form of bunkers became less circular and more flowing. Today, highly individualized—even contrived—forms of bunkers are the accepted norm, and are indeed the collective product of modern construction equipment, improved structural materials, and the societal values that nurture nonconformity and the richness of the designer's imagination (see figure 109). But the success of a particular bunker complex does not derive from the landform itself. Even the most imaginative course designer relies upon the effect of the basic symbol of a bunker eliciting the same emotional associations among

Figure 107. The earliest bunkers were simply sandy wastes, devoid of vegetation.

Figure 108. Early golf courses, built with crude construction equipment, produced rather poor copies of natural linksland bunkers.

Figure 109. Modern artificial bunkers, like these at Westwood Plateau, don't look much like their natural linksland ancestors, but their meaning to golfers hasn't changed.

golfers today that it did hundreds of years ago. How else could one justify putting in pockets of pure white, perfectly raked sand onto a site of red or brown clay, or worse, black peaty soils, and yet expect people to accept it as natural?

Sources of Beauty

Symbols such as tees, greens, and hazards form the basis of our golf course architectural language, but the presentation of these symbols separates the talented designer from the others who have not mastered the language. Masters of the art present them as things of beauty. At the opposite end of the spectrum are those who create features that can genuinely be termed "ugly" (see figure 110). Both invoke intense physical and emotional responses from golfers who play their courses—responses that are obviously poles apart. But the interpretation and appreciation of beauty and ugliness are more complex undertakings than they would first seem, especially when considered in relation to a golf course.

We start with the concept that a golf course symbolizes to the golfer an opportunity to enjoy a recreational experience and to forget his or her immediate worries. So the level of anyone's appreciation of a golf course begins at an instinctive stage of anticipated relaxation. It begins as one approaches the course, by glimpsing a tee or a green, smelling freshly mown turf, or hearing the sounds of golf courses. One can remain at this level of appreciation during the course of an entire round and be fulfilled, but the golf architect seeks to intensify one's enjoyment and satisfaction by sensitive use of the traditional symbols and message of the golf course, all the while presenting them in an aesthetically beautiful way. Many golfers judge the relative worth of a golf course by how well they can remember each hole, so creating mind pictures with whatever means possible has elevated golf architecture to an art form.

Once any golfer reaches the first tee, he or she begins to read the specific architectural language of symbols provided by the golf architect. It may begin as a subconscious awareness of space in the driving area as defined by trees, traps, mounds, lakes, or tall vegetation. From these elements one senses a pattern of risks and rewards and a flow of positive and negative forces offering alternatives of danger and security (see figure 111). Often a visual rhythm of repeated patterns is identified, inviting further inspection. The sensitive golf architect may further define or camouflage his message by the use of color, texture, size, shape, and patterns in the golf course elements. The combination and balance of these characteristics in the design of individual features distinguishes individual golf holes and the entire golf course, and causes the golfer to judge whether the product is beautiful, and therefore memorable, or ugly, and thus unenjoyable.

In his book, Gauldie made the point that the conduct of our personal affairs of life is often a matter of calculating risk against reward. Every day, each of us is exposed to potential risks when riding in a car, crossing a street, earning our income, or eating a meal. But man does not simply react to dangers in the same manner as does an animal. Rather, man foresees latent risks and takes steps to counter them. In golf, this process is played out with every shot (see figure 112).

Figure 110. All of the elements of a beautiful hole are there, but the final work doesn't communicate beauty.

Roots of Ugliness

Our advanced and elaborate thought process will protect us so long as we recognize the initial indicators of any potential risk and act accordingly. Those initial indicators are anything that alerts our security system, and hence are what has been called "the roots of ugliness." Gauldie categorized the elements that alert us to potential risk as "confusing, monstrous, and ungovernable." Confusion is that state of mind which prevents us from clearly identifying a situation. On a golf course it can occur when walking onto a tee and seeing a broad expanse of fairway with no indication of the proper line of play (see figure 113). Such ambiguity causes doubt, insecurity, and irritation about the proper course of action that should be taken. Another example of confusion occurs when an established visual pattern is broken, making us suspect a trick is being played upon us. On a golf course, such a break in rhythm happens when well-defined sand bunkers are clearly presented on hole after hole, only to encounter one with only a small patch of sand visible. We immediately suspect that it must be part of a much larger, but obscured, complex of bunkers. Such a source of confusion may well have led to the edict that no hazard should be hidden.

A second category of ugliness is the "monstrous"—meaning that a form of an element does not conform to an accepted norm, and thus its deviation alerts our security system. A small cat on one's sofa is cute, but a monstrous one the size of a tiger is threatening. In golf, a green that is an acre or more in size is monstrous, as is a sand area or bunker that is 200 yards long (see figure 114). When so far out of scale to its surroundings, such features just naturally cause alarm. Unless there is justification for using such a large scale, the element may well be deemed visually ugly.

Our culture has given us a reference set of expected relative size for objects. Some, such as the size of the noonday sun, have not changed for millions of years. Likewise, some references are specific to each generation, such as the height of buildings in our hometown. Since old references are more deeply rooted, they often

Figure 111. As the golfer steps to the tee at the Pete Dye–designed Austin Country Club, he begins a complex mental process of trying to "read" a flow of positive and negative forces offering alternatives of danger and security.

Rolling Greens Photo

Figure 112. After hitting a good drive on the par 4 8th hole at Glenmaura National, you have about 160 yards to the center of the green. How do you weigh the risks and rewards of this shot, knowing that dark line is the edge of a 30-foot-deep rock quarry? Carefully, obviously.

Figure 113. Walking to a tee and not having a clue on how or where to play the hole illustrates one root of ugliness, which is confusion. One or two of these experiences in a round might be accepted; any more than that will cause the golfer to view his experience with disdain—even on revered linksland.

Figure 114. To many North American golfers, the scale of Irish linksland mounds is considered "monstrous," which demonstrates how values can vary between cultures.

give humans a more secure feeling of what size things should be. Something becomes monstrous when it deviates from its expected size. In golf there is also an accepted norm for minimum expected size of golf features such as landing areas, target areas, and greens. When any of these elements is too small for "fair" shot-making they may arouse a golfer's displeasure, and then these elements may be effectively classed as ugly. In the context of golf design, the golf architect's task is to mitigate normal fears if a feature is utilized that is in a much larger or smaller scale than normally expected. He must think twice about such features, for most people expect symmetry, revere balance, and demand order. However, these principles can be carried to extreme and thus make the golf course seem architectonic instead of a natural appearing landscape.

The final category of ugliness is the "ungovernable"—a state characterized by a lack of control and by the threat of menacing disorder (see figure 115). On the golf course this may take the form of unrestrained plant growth, thick underbrush, or a deeply eroded and crumbling stream bank. The human mind from infancy onward measures and calculates action of external forces in relation to one's own ability to physically control the energy of those forces. Often, judgments of the amount of force needed to dislodge an object are based solely on its appearance, giving rise to the feeling that "I don't think I can move that by myself." Gauldie felt that humans read into an object certain manifestations of kinetic energy which we know cannot exist, but we nonetheless grant this imaginary animation and give it some quality that vaguely corresponds to human control. Examples of this on a golf course are oft-repeated phrases such as "roller coaster greens," "meandering fairways," or "yawning bunkers."

Elements that are confusing, monstrous, or ungovernable threaten our instinctual survival mechanisms and hence constitute the roots of uneasiness and ugliness. But the astute architect realizes the impact of these traits and wisely uses them to achieve a delightful blend of security and fear, which is how a talented golf course designer makes the course "look hard and play easy" (see figure 116).

Chris John

Figure 115. This marshland may seem "ungovernable" and hence "ugly" to some weaker hitters, at the 207- to 146-yard par 3 17th hole at Eagles Landing in Ocean City, Maryland. Others find this to be a beautiful hole.

Levels of Pleasure

If these characteristics of ugliness arouse an unsettling feeling in humans, what then is the basis for pleasure? The lowest level is "survival," that feeling of security achieved when basic human needs are satisfied. The next level is "familiarity," that comfortable feeling of sharing life and memories with family and friends. Above this level is that of "delight," the sensation of a pleasant surprise. The fourth level is "wonder," a prolonged feeling of delight and total contentment, often occurring when one falls in love. The highest level of pleasure is "awe," when delight becomes so intense that it seems mystical and beyond human control. This level of awe is so powerful that it can quickly lead to fear if not properly controlled.

Applying these terms to golf course architecture is easy (see figure 117a & b). We have all seen a "survival" golf course, one only slightly removed from pasture land and simply a place to hit a ball around. It satisfies our basic golfing needs, but nothing more. A "familiar" course is one we played many enjoyable rounds upon, a recognizable golf course without distinguishing features that nonetheless yields pleasant memories. A "delightful" golf course is one that often provides a pleasant surprise. It is on a course of never ending "wonder" that a golfer discovers that by being perceptive and reading the designer's complex message, he can greatly increase his enjoyment, fulfillment, and expectation. Finally, there are the rare "awesome" golf courses, those bordering on the ethereal in nature, where the pleasure is so intensified that it borders on fear.

Not surprisingly, there are very few golf course architects who can achieve this level of awe without creating something that is fearsome

Rolling Greens Photo

Figure 116. "Look hard and play easy" was nicely accomplished at Glenmaura National. The par 5 6th hole from the driving zone illustrates that well.

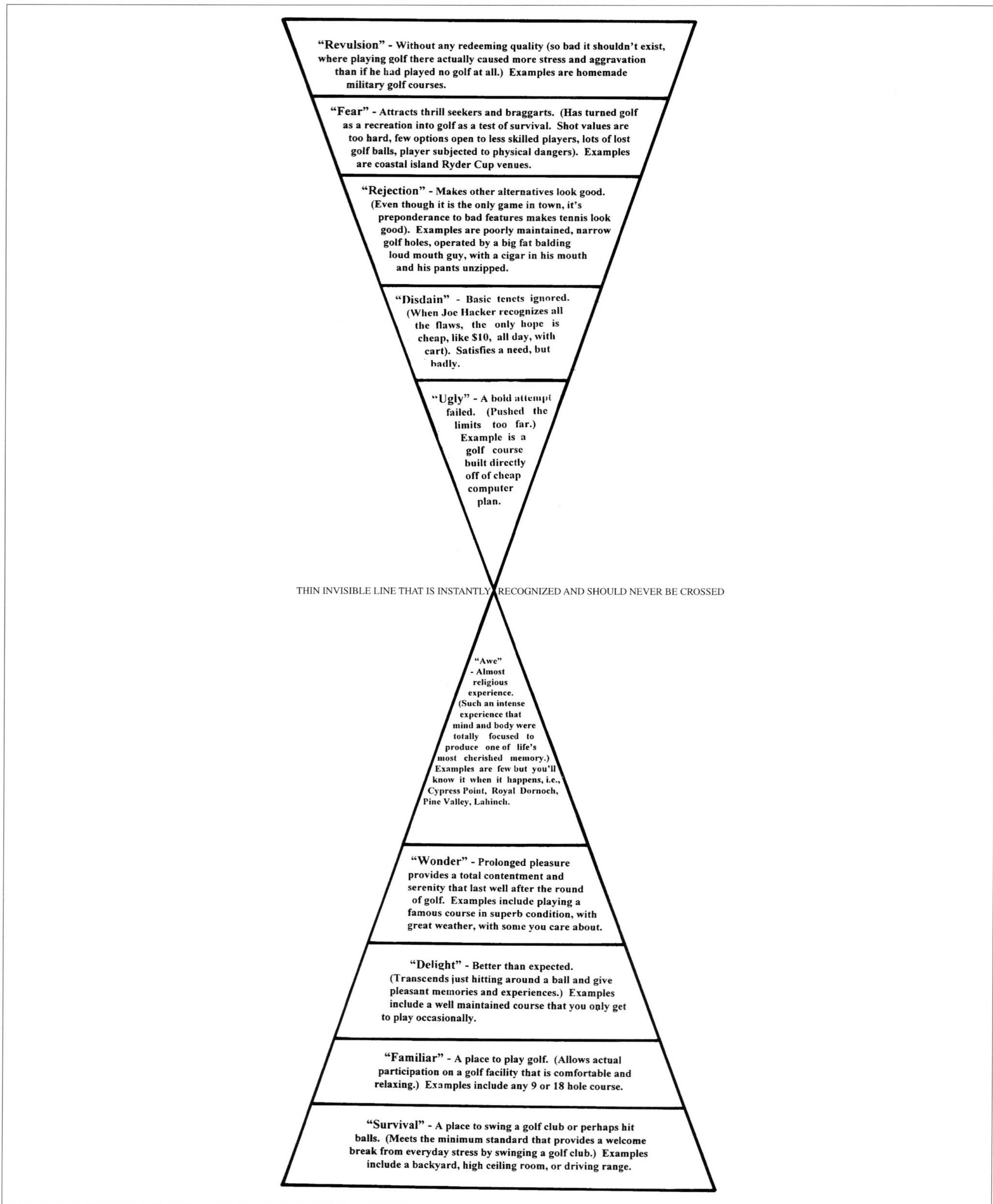
"Revulsion" - Without any redeeming quality (so bad it shouldn't exist, where playing golf there actually caused more stress and aggravation than if he had played no golf at all.) Examples are homemade military golf courses.
"Fear" - Attracts thrill seekers and braggarts. (Has turned golf as a recreation into golf as a test of survival. Shot values are too hard, few options open to less skilled players, lots of lost golf balls, player subjected to physical dangers). Examples are coastal island Ryder Cup venues.
"Rejection" - Makes other alternatives look good. (Even though it is the only game in town, it's preponderance to bad features makes tennis look good). Examples are poorly maintained, narrow golf holes, operated by a big fat balding loud mouth guy, with a cigar in his mouth and his pants unzipped.
"Disdain" - Basic tenets ignored. (When Joe Hacker recognizes all the flaws, the only hope is cheap, like $10, all day, with cart). Satisfies a need, but badly.
"Ugly" - A bold attempt failed. (Pushed the limits too far.) Example is a golf course built directly off of cheap computer plan.
THIN INVISIBLE LINE THAT IS INSTANTLY RECOGNIZED AND SHOULD NEVER BE CROSSED
"Awe" - Almost religious experience. (Such an intense experience that mind and body were totally focused to produce one of life's most cherished memory.) Examples are few but you'll know it when it happens, i.e., Cypress Point, Royal Dornoch, Pine Valley, Lahinch.
"Wonder" - Prolonged pleasure provides a total contentment and serenity that last well after the round of golf. Examples include playing a famous course in superb condition, with great weather, with some you care about.
"Delight" - Better than expected. (Transcends just hitting around a ball and give pleasant memories and experiences.) Examples include a well maintained course that you only get to play occasionally.
"Familiar" - A place to play golf. (Allows actual participation on a golf facility that is comfortable and relaxing.) Examples include any 9 or 18 hole course.
"Survival" - A place to swing a golf club or perhaps hit balls. (Meets the minimum standard that provides a welcome break from everyday stress by swinging a golf club.) Examples include a backyard, high ceiling room, or driving range.

Figure 117a.

and ugly. There are many examples of golf courses where the architect tried to inspire awe but lacked the ability to design those golf holes that fairly tested the mental and physical skills of golfers. These courses are exceedingly difficult, even penal in nature, resorting to gimmickry and bizarre features in efforts to earn a national reputation or notoriety.

Figure 117b. Here, a golf course architect tried to reach "awesome" and ended up with "ugly."

In this author's opinion, there is only one golf course that used a collection of spectacular holes in a powerful setting so sensitively that every human sense is aroused to its fullest, yet the overall feeling is one of awe, not fear. That golf course is Cypress Point, the Monterey Peninsula creation of Dr. Alister MacKenzie. He wisely routed the course to rise slowly to a crescendo of anticipation, climaxing with the infamous ocean holes, numbers 15, 16, and 17, before bringing each golfer comfortably home on the benign 18th (see figure 118). Normally, sustained awe can be emotionally and physically draining, and therefore can only be endured for short stretches. In this regard, Cypress Point offers a one-of-a-kind experience.

If these are the levels of pleasure, what then are the characteristics that produce pleasure? The elemental tools of any architect are form, color, and texture. The skillful blending and embodiment of these elements gives rise to pleasure. Each person has certain learned values and expectations as to what constitutes beauty, just as they do with ugliness.

Reading the Message

For most people it is an intuitive process, like driving down a street and selecting a favorite house after only a fleeting glance. One knows the house is attractive, but if questioned as to the specific features that make it so, one cannot readily respond. Something is attractive or unattractive at a single glance, but the source of this impression is difficult to identify. However, the designer must understand those sources if he is to communicate successfully through his work.

Accordingly, one of the first reactions a person has to an object is consciously or unconsciously to ask, "What is it?" "How close is it?" and "How big is it?" (see figure 119). These also happen to be the most commonly asked questions in a round of golf, for determining distances is essential to good golf. When ready references exist close to target areas (such as a tree next to a green), the task is easier than if only distant landmarks are available to gauge distance to the target.

Those three questions help determine the apparent size or distance because they ask us to establish our own frames of reference from personal experience (see figure 120). Thus, when an

Figure 118. The 16th at Cypress Point is one of the great holes of golf, on a golf course that inspires awe.

object doesn't fit our established reference, we say it is "out of scale." The keen golf architect will often deliberately distort scale to achieve an effect, by locating a bunker or swale well in front of a green to make it appear closer than it really is. To counter such deceptions, touring professionals rely on charts and yardage books for accurate distances. Still, the human mind being what it is, many a pro still falls prey to optical illusions on a well-designed golf course.

The accomplished designer uses a modulation of scale to ward off boredom and to introduce subtle surprises. However, since one of the roots of ugliness is the concept of monstrous, there must be a definite upper limit to this modulation process. An immediate example that comes to mind are those "landing strip" tees that measure 100 yards or more from front to back. Few things are more deflating to a golfer than to hit a poor drive and not have it reach the front of the tee. Great size is impressive, but alone it will not inspire awe for it does not take much imagination simply to make things large on a golf course. In fact, if oversized gimmicks are used too often, the designer will be criticized rather than complimented.

The lower limit of scale modulation on a golf course is always a factor of fairness to the golfer. Landing areas, putting greens, and openings through trees that are too small to allow for a reasonable margin of error will be held in low regard. Small objects are usually thought to be charming rather than inspiring, but by proper positioning, a small object can produce a positive response. A small pot bunker, for instance, if properly placed, can be more menacing, intimidating, challenging, and respected than a huge 150-yard-long bunker (see figure 121).

Geoffrey Cornish

Figure 119. The first time a golfer plays "The Cardinal,"—the 3rd hole at Prestwick, in Scotland—and sees the Cardinal bunker, the questions that enter his or her mind are probably: "What is it?," "How close is it?," and "How big is it?"

Figure 120. Determining "scale" is difficult without frames of reference. A good example is the tee shot on the 7th hole at Royal St. Georges, Sandwich, England.

But scale of individual elements is not the only characteristic of beauty on a golf course. There is also the proportional relationship between elements that influences an observer's impression. Elements of a golf course must relate and be in harmony with one another, for the overall course is most often treated as a single element by an observer. An example is a golf site, made up of bunkers, mounds, collars, putting surface, and perhaps surrounding natural features. There is no set formula or ratio of scale that each of these must be, so its harmonious presentation depends upon the "richness of the designer's imagination." Often this scale is determined by prevailing cultural norms. In the 1960s, putting surfaces of 10,000 square feet were considered fashionable. A quarter of a century later, the accepted size has become almost half that. To ignore the interrelationship of the scale of elements to each other leads to confusion, another root of ugliness. When the proportions of a golf course are correct, they are said to have achieved a facet of visual order. By understanding this principle of design, the skillful golf architect can occasionally use visual disorder to purposely confuse the golfer in an attempt to break his or her concentration.

Figure 121. Although small in size and well out of play, the small sod wall bunker on the par 5 18th hole at EagleSticks in Zanesville, Ohio has become an infamous feature of the course, and has been given the name, "Eye of the Eagle."

Implicit in the concept of visual order is the requirement for balance and symmetry. Organic things that are deformed and thus lack bilateral symmetry alert our internal security systems and are therefore considered ugly or even grotesque. Nearly all biological organisms have an outward appearance of being mirror image halves, and what we find on the right side we expect also to find on the left. The more similar the right and left sides of an organic object appear to be, the more perfect it is considered and the more comfortable is its form to human expectation. However, when an inorganic form is created there is no such strict requirement for equal halves. But there is still the human need for balance between sides to establish visual order. This balance is one of mass, weight, or force, separately or in combination, as mentally calculated by the observer. When a disequilibrium occurs, the observer may become emotionally unsettled and search for stability by resubscribing values to each side or by mentally relocating the fulcrum point. If the designer is trying to communicate stability through his creation, then imbalances are ill-advised. However, if the purpose is deliberately to unsettle the observer, or to portray an inorganic style, then slight asymmetry is an effective tool. By placing balanced bunkers, mounds, or trees on either side of the selected line of play in the common freeway style of design, many golf architects communicate a feeling of security and stability. Their message to golfers is clear: simply hit it between the guideposts and all will be fine. The message is not so clear if one bunker or mound or tree physically or visually dominates an opposite counterpart. The golfer may be confused as to the proper line and the proper way to play the hole. Bunkers in the middle of fairways are more confusing to North American golfers than for European players, who are used to this very old design style. Such visual imbalance causes the golfer to question the circumstances of the situation, make a deliberate decision, and then take what he or she considers to be the best course of action.

Such techniques must be used with caution, for it is a basic human reaction to praise balance and distrust imbalance, especially in visual order. But balance is not just a condition of bilateral symmetry. It can also be a perceived state of stability among apparent mass, weight, and force. The size of a mound or bunker can be balanced by a visual mass of trees or by the visual force of a rapidly flowing stream. There is no common unit of measurement that can be empirically imposed upon each golf course feature to balance it numerically with others around it. Knowing when to balance features and when to create imbalanced ones requires an intuitive sense of correctness and constitutes part of what elevates golf course architecture to an art form (see figure 122). Recognition of this concept has led to a new phrase in golf course architecture vocabulary, called "the look." However, some critics say placing a high priority on the look, such as at the PGA West Stadium Course, ignores playing qualities. The Old Course at St. Andrews, by contrast, has no "look," but lord, does it play well.

Another facet of visual order is visual rhythm. On a golf course, this refers to the pattern of incident and interval set by the horizon line of three-dimensional objects. Vertical rhythm is established by use of a series of peaks and valleys of earthworks or vegetation. Horizontal rhythm, on the other hand, is accomplished through the articulated edges of two-dimensional elements, such as a free-form flowing edge of a sand bunker, a wavy mowing pattern on a fairway, or a gracefully curved water hazard. The more regular the visual rhythm is, the more controlled the element seems and the easier it is to avoid the ungovernable root of ugliness. Visual rhythm can be slow, connoting a stable and near static situation, such as the meandering of a quiet brook, or it can be rapid, portraying the dynamic energy of the tumbling cascades of a mountain stream (see figure 123). When detected by the observer, visual rhythm may either soothe or arouse, both emotionally and physically. If the rhythm is too slow, it may put one's senses to sleep. If the rhythm is too fast or abrupt, the observer may find it hard to relax. The lower limit of visual rhythm is where it is so slow that it becomes boring, and the upper limit is where there is so much tension that it feels unnatural.

The overall topography of a golf course site will often have a distinct rhythm that is so strong that the golf course architect needs only to harmonize the holes with it. But if the site has no distinctive rhythm, it is the golf architect's task to give the site personality through visual movement. The actual undulation of the ground can be enhanced by creation of hills and valleys, or masked by vegetation. Tall trees are often used for the latter because their dominance on the visual scale tends to flatten out the land. Each site is an entity unto itself, with its own characteristic rhythm or lack thereof.

At Naples National the total existing contour interval was about 1 foot—or in other words, dead flat. However, using an average of only three feet of fill on the fairways, but shaping it into a pleasant rhythm of incident and interval, gave the golf course a unique character for a Florida golf course (see figure 124). Some of the best sites have a variety of characteristic rhythms, permitting a golf architect to establish more variety and space in the golf course. A multicharacter site gives the sensitive designer an opportunity to produce a course that transcends the pleasure levels of the familiar and the delightful and approaches the level of wonderment or even awe. I know of no golf course that is a source of wonder or awe that is not on a unique piece of land. Consider, for example, Glenmaura National, or Dornoch, or Pine Valley, or Devil's Paintbrush, or Royal County Down, or my obvious favorite, Cypress Point.

There is a common phrase—"the sweetness of the curve"—that I feel perfectly describes the triumph of visual rhythm. It has been variously used to describe the keel line of an ancient

Figure 122. The par 4 5th hole at Dennis Highlands on Cape Cod illustrates how a balance of light and mass can be artistically present. From the drawing the hole is ugly, although absolutely correct in pure strategic design. Note the use of environmentally intelligent fescue grass, back in the early 1980s.

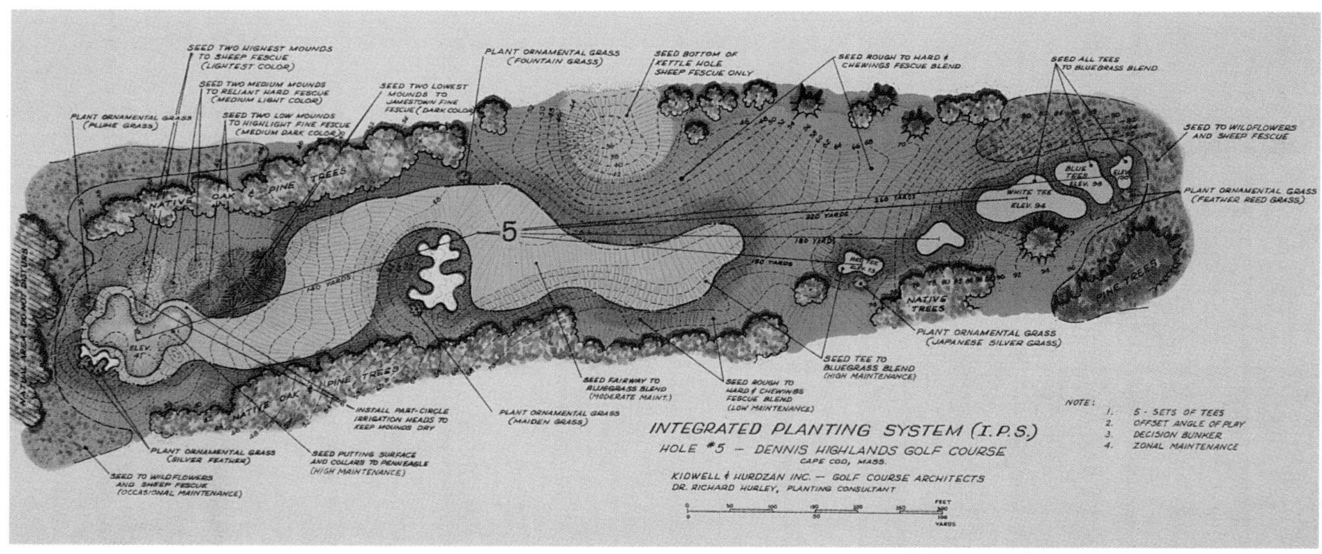

Rolling Greens Photo

Figure 123. The design of the par 3 9th green at Glenmaura National in Moosic, Pennsylvania, was intended to capture the dynamics of the nearby waterfall, and the solid character of the mountainside it sits on.

Viking ship, a path through a formal French garden, and the arch of a classic Roman building. When I've observed such objects, I've found the phrase concisely conveys a feeling of majesty and grace. But since these "sweet" curves aren't related in any way or shape to one another, I've concluded that a certain visual rhythm carries such a sensory connotation of sweetness that it causes all observers to agree that it is near perfection. On a golf course, I've had the same sensation of recognizing this sweetness of the curve. It has occurred when all the appropriate sizes, proportional scale, visual order, and visual rhythm are combined perfectly. When these characteristics are in balance, the course has a beauty and pleasure that inspires awe.

Size, form, and material are commonly associated with great strength, purpose, or importance. We expect that a large suspension cable on a bridge is stronger, and is thus more reassuring, than a thin wire. Likewise, a massive building normally houses an important function, and a big long limousine usually carries an important person. The heavier a material is, the stronger it is supposed to be. A building made of wood does not seem as substantial or important as a building of equal size constructed of thick stone.

Since it is human nature to think of size, form, and material as indicators of something meaningful, designers can use them to convey particular images to the observer. A structural architect who wishes to communicate great purpose may use materials of great weight or strength. If he wishes to communicate openness and lightness, he will use glass or aluminum. It is more difficult to apply this structural concept to golf course architecture, but the same intu-

Figure 124. The Naples National Golf Course site was dead flat (10 inches of contour over 325 acres), but with only an average of 3 feet of fill the land was given a pleasant rhythm of incident and interval. This is the 7th hole, a 410-yard par 4.

itive human value systems are nonetheless at work. At first glance, there might seem to be no set value system for communicating purpose through golf course features, for any golf course feature looks very much like any similar feature on any other course.

A golf course architect can only occasionally express massive forms by manipulating the third dimension on a grand scale. The key is to implement the design without creating something that looks unnatural. This can be done by use of higher-growing plants, or attention-getting colorful or textured surfaces (wood or stone walls), or a grouping of multiple features, each succeeding one at a scale larger than the previous. Since any earthwork or form should appear to be a natural part of the landscape, the golf architect must be cognizant of the steepness of upslopes and outslopes and take care to tie them back into the surrounding contours (see figure 125). The more abrupt this transition from earthwork to earth appears, the more artificial it looks and the more naked is the architect's intent. This unsubtle exposure of intent by the modern architect is usually considered primitive or in poor taste by the golf course connoisseur. (Strangely enough, such abruptness in older golf architecture is revered by connoisseurs because it represents the product of the crude earthmoving equipment of the period, massive expenditure of human and animal energy, and minuscule construction budgets common at that time— see figure 126)

Abrupt or steep slopes are forms requiring costly hand maintenance and should be avoided unless they serve an essential purpose. Even the best modern architecture must occasionally result in some areas that require hand mowing if the golf architect is fully to express his design. For instance, to achieve a particular visual effect of intimidation, a sand bunker face may be made steeper than can be raked with a power rake. Ease of maintenance is compromised for visual impact, and perhaps memorability. Most golf course superintendents clearly understand the designer's intent and seek to preserve it even at a cost of higher maintenance.

Since naturalness of form on the golf course is an expected condition, the golf course architect should try to avoid abruptness of outline. Geometric shapes tend to be too formal and hard-edged for the desired naturalness of the golf course. Rarely does one find in nature perfectly straight lines—or, for that matter, ovals, circles, squares, rectangles, or cubes. If these forms are not found in nature, then why should they be built into golfing ground? Therefore, unless it is the designer's intent to produce a course of architectonic features (which, sad to say, are undoubtedly easier to build and maintain, and have been popular at times), he will avoid expressions of this type. Instead, the designer's goal should

Henebry Photography

Figure 125. Subtle transition from earthwork to earth is shown by the par 4 18th hole at Westwood Plateau in Coquitlam (Vancouver), British Columbia.

Figure 126. By today's standards this earthwork is crude and unimaginative, but since it conveys a historical sense of when earthmoving was done by men or horses it is a natural part of golf.

be more informal, free-form, constantly flowing shapes commonly associated with natural topography. Earthworks should be devoid of straight lines, perfect circles, and formal ovals, and instead should take shapes that are composites of curves without significant abruptness. Perhaps some parts of a golf course lend themselves to simple geometric forms. Tees, which by necessity must be level and raised to provide surface drainage, are normally somewhat geometric. But multilevel, free-form tees are more expressive, memorable, and impressive than simple square, circular, or rectangular ones (see figure 127). If one cannot resist building rigid formal shapes on a golf course, tees seem the logical place to succumb to the temptation.

The use of free-form shapes forces the golfer to read the entire outline of a feature to determine its size and shape. This forces him or her mentally to assess the design. That's one great advantage a golf architect has over a structural architect. It is possible to passively use a building without interacting with it, but it is impossible to use a golf course that way. Anyone using a golf course must sooner or later contend with the architect's intent.

If the golf architect uses very simple forms, the golfer will too quickly recognize the features and will spend very little time assessing architectural intent. Consequently, the more active and articulated a form is, the more time, speculation, and mental energy are demanded of the observer. For example, if a bunker has a rather uniform oval shape, then the eye quickly traces the outline, the brain sorts through its reference file of standard shapes, and quickly identifies it as an oval. Experience has taught us that an oval is almost a circle and thus has just about the same radius on all sides. Once the radius is known, then the extent of the bunker is known.

If the bunker has a free-form shape, when the eye traces the outline the information it provides to the brain does not fit any standard shape, so a bit of confusion ensues. The brain must break the shape down into parts and analyze each part before concluding what shape and size the entire feature is. The more convoluted the form, the more the brain must search and

Figure 127. Tee construction at Naples National became an expression of art by blending together existing trees, coral rock found underneath the site, native plants, and pine straw, with the functional aspect of multiple tees.

identify before reaching a conclusion that will allow the mind and body to react in a secure fashion (see figure 128).

Competing influences of roots of ugliness and sources of pleasure are at work at every level of observation. The designer must be cognizant of this fact in every element he designs. Remembering that visual order is one source of pleasure while the ungovernable is a root of ugliness, it is easy to see why not all free-form shapes are pleasant. If the shape has abrupt sharp edges that break down any rhythm in the visual order, it will appear to be random, ungovernable energy.

On the other hand, if nearly the same shape has the abruptness removed, a flowing visual sensation of rhythm is established and therefore seems more governed and more comfortable.

Two other techniques used to express or reinforce form are the use of complementary shapes and the use of parallel lines. These competing techniques are analogous to singing in unison versus singing in harmony. With harmony, everyone sings the same melody, but does so on complimentary pitches and notes to produce a full sound, such as performed by a barbershop quartet. By contrast, when a song is sung in unison, everyone sings the same note and pitch. The result is the richness and power of a Mormon Tabernacle Choir.

On a golf course, complementary shapes provide the barbershop quartet with fullness and harmony, while parallel lines provide the reinforced power of a choir in unison. These techniques can enhance a landform as well. When designing a green complex, the best integration between forms occurs when there is a harmonious blend of shapes. Bunkers can be visually tied to the articulated edge of the green and given the form through harmonious and integrated composition (see figure 129); or, they can seem detached from the overall complex, with each part remaining a separate entity, complementing nothing.

One use of parallel lines to reinforce form occurs where the fairway, primary rough, and deep rough mowing lines strengthen the outside edge of a fairway bunker. This technique of contour mowing can be a powerful tool of communication to express and reinforce form by presenting features in unison.

Forms communicate well on a golf course be-

Henebry Photography

Figure 128. In the style of Stanley Thompson's bunkering at Banff Springs, British Columbia, the bunkering at the 5th hole at Westwood Plateau, Coquitlam, British Columbia requires inspection by the eye and mind to grasp it.

cause impressions of mass are readily compared visually. Yet the diversity of materials also offers a rich vein of media by which designers can articulate their intent. At first glance it would seem that the golf architect's palette of materials is limited to turf, sand, trees, water, rock, and wood. For the inexperienced designer, that is precisely the case. However, within each of these main groupings are many choices or subcategories of materials. Among available turfs, for instance, are bent grasses, bluegrasses, red fescues, tall fescues, hard fescues, rye grasses, Bermuda grasses, zoysia grasses, and many native grasses. This wide range of turf vegetation offers the golf architect a chance to use materials of various shades of green and brown (see figure 130). Grasses and growth habits can also be altered in ways that complement what structural architects do when utilizing wall coverings, paints, and textures.

Henebry Photography

Figure 129. Integration of form between putting surfaces, bunkers, grassy hollows, and slopes communicates a simple sense of serenity and balance. The 9th green at Westwood Plateau does this well.

To be done skillfully, turfgrass artistry requires a thorough understanding of the life cycle of the plant, its growth requirements, normal habit of growth, and the maintenance procedures associated with it. Here is where the designer depends heavily upon the knowledge and experience of the golf course superintendent. The same is true of trees, which offer a number of choices. The informed designer may choose between open and airy types or dense and foreboding ones, or between short, flowering trees and tall, angular ones.

The choices associated with water and sand are more limited, but exist nonetheless. Water can be made to lie still, move, tumble, spray, or gush. Sand can be white, brown, or yellow, coarse, medium, or fine, or any combination of those characteristics. Each material has its own subtle properties that influence the player and the playability of golf shots (see figure 131).

The incorporation of rock and wood into the golf course dates back perhaps 150 years or more, when timbers were used to shore up bunkers or sand faces on British links courses against wind erosion, and at holes played along and across rock walls, such as North Berwick. Among the most famous of these were the wooden sleeper wall on Cardinal, bunkers at Prestwick, and the stone walls found on various golf courses such as North Berwick, Muirfield, or St. Andrews. Today wood and rocks are considered a natural part of golf course construction, but the choice of materials and how to present them often separate great architecture from poorly done cliches (see figure 132). On contemporary golf courses wood and rock is most commonly seen as walls, supports, and slope stabilizers, and the choice of materials is railroad ties, treated timbers, or utility poles. Rock or stone materials are normally found or quarried on or near the site, so their color, texture, and size are

Doug Ball

Figure 130. By skillful selection of grasses, the golf course architect can make the golf course landscape an interesting and environmentally correct mosaic of greens and browns, such as at Devil's Paintbrush.

Figure 131. Devil's Paintbrush is a blend of colors and textures derived from the various grasses, stone, wood, gravel paths, and natural vegetation.

quite variable. But regardless of the material or use, the more believably functional they seem, the more their use is justified by the golfer, and hence the more they are accepted. The designer who makes randomly and seemingly frivolous use of wood and stone will mostly be seen as lacking creativity.

Recently, flowers and wildflower mixes have been used to add color and variety to golf course landscapes. Such flower patches, especially when meticulously groomed, carry with them a deliberate image of opulence. Likewise, a club with bent grass fairways and white silica bunker sand silently conveys the feeling that the club represents greater wealth and prestige than a club with bluegrass fairways and brown bunker sand. Flower beds don't in any way indicate the shot value or the soundness of a design, but they can attract the kind of regard that often masks weakness in a hole—or perhaps make a good hole or course more memorable. In this way, they are as important as the good icing masking an ordinary cake. One is constantly amazed when visiting a famous club only to find a quite ordinary golf course whose reputation has been based mainly on the aura created by the golf course superintendent's ability to keep bent grass fairways, or meticulous general maintenance, or endless stands of mature trees. If certain materials can cover up a poor design, imagine how much more impressive they can make a great design.

Figure 132. Wood finds a natural place on golf courses both as support walls and steps, especially when the designer wants to communicate heritage, such as at Devil's Paintbrush.

There is an unspoken rule in golf course design that insists, in the interests of fairness, that the same materials must be used throughout a golf course to make it play as consistently as possible. This is not only a false notion but an unrealistic one. If one studies a soil map of any course, one will find great variations in soil types and textures from one end of a course to the other, and even from hole to hole. This quest for consistency throttles the designer's expressiveness. A mixing of turf and sand types adds more variety to the golf course and additional changes in color and texture to the landscape. Further, the game would become even more interesting if golf architects utilized many different plant materials in sensitive ways. Where off-season grasses can persist, they should be used in grass traps or in selected rough areas to guard key landing zones. A northern latitude golfer should be able to experience an occasional shot off of a warm season grass, be it green or dormant (see figure 133). Conversely, a southern player should be allowed occasionally to experience bluegrass or fine fescue grasses to see how they play. Moreover, there is little value in standardizing the sand in all the hazards so that each bunker plays exactly the same, especially when the greatest golf courses demand that golfers invent shots and not just play them. Sand is a hazard, and as such there should be no restriction placed on its consistency. In fact, demanding such consistency limits the range of experiences and risks versus rewards that are the spice of golf.

One final element that contributes to visual order is the force of an object. In structural architecture, force is readily apparent, for there is always the possibility that a building can collapse. But since such a disaster is unlikely to befall a golf course, a sense of force must come from the effect that individual features such as slopes can have on a golf ball. The value of these forces to the golfer is learned from experience and is interpreted by intuition. Although it is possible to calculate, with some sort of vector analysis, the amount of deflection that a given slope will cause in the path of a golf ball, in practical terms it is a matter of individual judgment. We face such judgments of force every time we face a putt. It is called "reading the break." The actual force that we assess is a combination of the linear force of a stroke to a golf ball and the effect of gravity upon it. What is actually being determined when reading the break of a green is the relative direction of the flow of gravitational forces down a slope. On a thoughtfully designed course, such forces must also be considered in combination with other features besides putting surfaces. For small slopes outside the green, the effect of forces is likely to be so small that it will play no part in the overall visual order. However, large slopes most definitely can contribute to the impression of balance or imbalance of mass and weight in the visual order.

Trying to manipulate the apparent flow of forces is very difficult. The golf architect most often only reacts to established force patterns and attempts to mitigate their influence. This is especially true of those features whose effects

Figure 133. Although zoysia grass is best adapted to the transition zone or southern latitudes, it was used on the par 3 13th at Cook's Creek in Circleville, Ohio to cover steep bunker faces and in grass traps.

Henebry Photography

Figure 134. The golf course architect communicates ugliness or beauty to golfers by how he uses scale, composition, materials, and intellectual symbols.

could be considered to be either negative or positive, depending upon how the architect uses them. The best example is perhaps atmospheric conditions, such as prevailing winds or thin air. Long holes into the prevailing breeze emphasize a natural force, while a course of short yardage at high altitude negates another such force.

To summarize, the golf course architect communicates to golfers by stimulation of human senses and invocation of symbols, meanings, and emotions; in precisely the same way, a building architect expresses his art and communicates with his building occupants. A golf course can cause the player to experience fear or pleasure, depending upon how the course is presented. Since golf is a recreation, a preponderance of experiences on a golf course should be pleasant (see figure 134). The level of pleasure that will be experienced is linked directly to the designer's ability to enhance or intensify expectations of pleasure or beauty. The main sources of pleasure are reactions to the scale, order, and rhythm of the apparent balance of mass, weight, and forces of the design. A designer also communicates to golfers by his use of size, form, and materials whose meanings are deeply rooted in human experience, as well as their visual and physical impact on each golfer's game. The ultimate expression of the genius of any golf architect is severely constrained by the site and the available construction budget. An awe-inspiring golf course is indeed rare, for it requires that unique combination of intellect, site qualities, and necessary money in order to approach this ultimate standard of the beautiful in golf course architecture.

8

The Recreational Process of Golf

Although it is easy to wax eloquent about the spiritual and ethereal qualities of golf and golf courses, the golf course architect must understand the recreational process that evokes such passion (see figure 135). That process is not any different than that for any other premeditated human activity, except that golf is the focus. The more thoroughly the designer understands the entire continuum of subexperiences that combine to produce the total experience, the greater is his ability to influence it.

Simply put, the recreation process is a five-part action:

Part 1—Anticipation
Part 2—Travel to the experience
Part 3—The experience
  a. Arrival impression
  b. Preparation
  c. Participation
  d. Cooldown
Part 4—Travel back home
Part 5—Remembrance of the total experience

Anticipation

The first part is when the participant makes a conscious decision to play golf, and for discussion's sake let us say that on Monday a golfer, Macgregor McDuff, decides to play on Saturday (see figure 136). At that moment of decision, Mr. McDuff sets forth a personal set of standards of what he anticipates the experience is going to be. Once these early levels of expectations are established, this is where the total recreational experience begins. Until recreation is complete, McDuff will experience a wide variety of related expectations that will either be met, left unfulfilled, or exceeded. The sum total of all of those substeps will then determine the value of the experience for each individual (see figure 137). The best and most treasured human activity is a continual flow of expectations exceeded.

Going back to our example, the golfing experience actually begins at the moment the decision to play is made. The first step Mr. McDuff might take would be to secure a starting time at his favorite place to play. His expectation level might be a midmorning starting time, at Happy Hollow Golf Club, starting on the front nine, with a foursome of his favorite friends. However, a phone call to Happy Hollow reveals that there is a tournament scheduled for the entire weekend and no starting times are available. This knowledge results in the first unfulfilled level of expectation. However, the magnitude of this disappointment is purely a personal one, depending upon how much weight he places on playing Happy Hollow. Perhaps this is no big deal, for there are lots of other courses as good as Happy Hollow, but to get there will require more arduous and longer travel. On the other hand, this could be such a major disappointment that if McDuff cannot play Happy Hollow, he simply will not play. If the latter is the case, then the total recreational experience will be viewed as one big negative. But for the sake of discussion let's assume that McDuff's attitude is that there is no such thing as a bad golf course, just that some are better than others, and golf with his friends is paramount. So McDuff calls a few alternative places to play but none offer midmorning starting times, only dew-sweeper early hours or sun-lover midafternoon times. Again, another level of initial expectation remains unfulfilled, but at least he has a tee time at Furry Fairways—

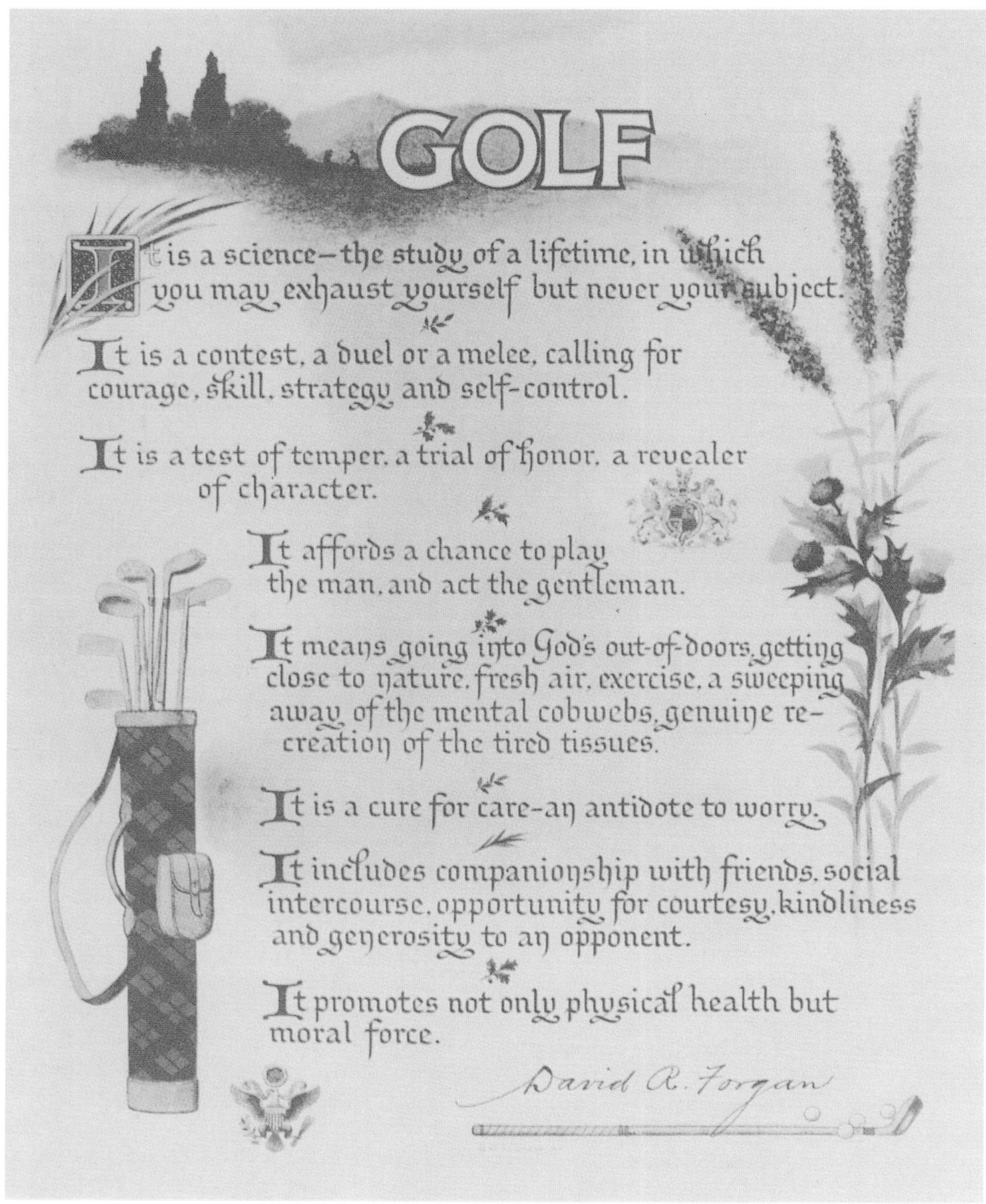

Figure 135. Here is a century-old description of golf that is timeless. This is the true magic of golf. It says nothing about slope ratings, golf carts, celebrity architects, computer-designed clubs, or space age materials for golf balls.

Figure 136. The recreational experience of golf begins the moment the golfer makes a conscious decision to play.

Figure 137. This pre-1920 A.B. Frost print called "Saturday Afternoon" captures the general conditions and formality of golf and golf courses of that period. Despite obvious fashion changes, the same human forces motivate and measure the golfer's experience of today.

but already this golf experience has some negative components.

Next he must call his favorite golfing companions, and his level of expectation is that they will all be available and want to play at the time and place he has secured.

Intuitively one can see that if McDuff's friends couldn't play, or they objected to the golf course or tee time, or if other conflicts arose, it would take a pretty spectacular round of golf to make up for this series of disappointments—and this is still Monday.

But despite a few minor setbacks, the game is set for Saturday and McDuff is well into the anticipation phase. Already McDuff begins to visualize how he will control his swing, master the course, vanquish his competitors, and invest his winnings. He may even go to the driving range a time or two, practice chip shots in the backyard, or tune up his putting stroke on the carpet. With each successive hour or day as it approaches Saturday, his expectation levels rise about what the golf experience will be. As the experience gets closer, fewer routine or mundane thoughts occupy McDuff's mind, and so he is able to more intensely focus and fantasize on golf. Now he is deep into anticipation.

Finally it is Saturday morning and now McDuff's expectations flow at an even faster rate, with more numerous and specific levels of acceptability established, met, dashed, or exceeded. It may begin with a quick look out a west-facing window to visually assess the weather and any impending change like wind and/or storm. This will influence how he dresses and what additional equipment he will take with him to the course. Each decision adds to the total analysis of whether this is going to be a good or bad experience. At last all preparations are complete, and he is ready to leave for the golf course. To this point McDuff alone has controlled the first part of the recreational process called the anticipation phase.

Figure 138. Golf in Japan is experienced with different customs and courtesies that make it memorable, like having two caddies for every golfer. One caddy is in charge of clubs and golf balls, while the other replaces divots, rakes bunkers, holds the flagstick, forecaddies, and helps look for lost balls.

Travel to the Experience

Sociologists tell us that the actual travel to the experience is the second part of the recreational process, and is considered a separate component, because now events are often influenced or controlled by others. For example, one might imagine that McDuff and each of his golfing companions would travel separately to the golf course and rendezvous at an appointed time and place. Alternatively, they might carpool, use public transportation, or hire transportation to and from the golf course. Clearly, driving through crosstown traffic through some tough neighborhoods in a rusted out car is not the equivalent experience of riding comfortably on a train or bus, or, best of all, being picked up in a limo that is suitably equipped with coffee, doughnuts, and the morning paper. So the means of transportation, associated stress, and surroundings are either going to add to or detract from the whole experience.

Of equal or greater importance is the length of travel time to and from the course. It was not uncommon when I played golf in Japan to wake up at 5 a.m., meet my ride at 6 a.m., travel a couple of hours by car, arrive at the course early enough to satisfy the customs and courtesies of Japanese golf, and finally tee off at 10 a.m. (see figure 138). Including a 1 1/2-hour lunch, post-golf bath, and a drink usually resulted in getting back to my hotel at 6 or 7 p.m., for a 12- or 13-hour experience. In the States, I leave my office, stop by my home and pick up my son, and we are on the first tee in less than ten minutes. Two vastly different travel experiences, and each contributing to how I enjoyed my recreative time at golf.

Most market study analysts in the United States define the primary or core market for a potential golf course to be within 20 minutes driving time, a secondary market of being within 45 minutes, and an occasional market requiring greater than a 45-minute drive. However, when golf courses must depend upon customers traveling long distances, or under unpleasant driving conditions, or at some personal risk, the golf course must be exceptional. Such an example is EagleSticks, a public golf course in Zanesville, Ohio, where the *average* golfer must drive two hours or more each way to get there. But the drive is mostly on uncrowded interstates, through rolling Ohio farmland, and at comfortable cruising speeds. Travel to and from EagleSticks has actually become an appreciated adjunct to golf, where people can carpool, share small talk, and decompress from the chaos of daily commitments. (Perhaps the Japanese have the same experiences, except instead of countryside they drive through traffic.) But even though it is a pleasurable experience getting to the golf course, the quality of the golf course must be exceedingly high in order to justify the travel.

So travel to the recreation site can have a profound influence on the value of the recreation, and that is why planners often place lots of emphasis on probable travel routes.

Actual Experience—Arrival Impression

The third step in the recreational process, the actual experience, begins the instant the golf course comes into view; at this point control of the experience shifts from uncontrollable others to the golf course team. That first impression, even though it may be but a fleeting glimpse, will immediately disappoint, fulfill, or exceed very intense levels of expectations within each observer. In 70s jargon, it is a "rush" of sensations that provides such strong impact to the participant that to waste the opportunity to positively influence it is inexcusable. As the ad slogan says, "You get only one chance to make a first impression." Oftentimes that entry experience is confounded by other people or other things, such as zoning, offsite development, owners' demands, or economic or physical limitations. Other times it's simply wasted out of ignorance by the designer. One would ask the reader to pause a moment and recall a pleasant entry experience such as seeing Disneyland or Disney World, arriving at a swank resort or club, or driving into an enchanted golfing mecca like Augusta National. Remember how you felt about that experience, or better yet, the next time you have an exhilarating entry experience, analyze what made it so special.

Sometimes the entry impression is so understated that it too becomes a cherished memory, like arriving at Pine Valley by crossing a railroad track, through an undistinguished chain-link fence gate, up to a charming but old guardhouse, past the maintenance compound, across the 18th fairway, and then up a narrow driveway to an undersized parking lot to a rather homely old two-story house that is the clubhouse of Pine Valley. (God, I remember every inch of the way, for this was **Pine Valley**. Were it any other golf course I probably would have been singularly unimpressed—but this was **PINE VALLEY**.) The entry experiences at Cypress Point and Shinnecock strike one similarly. But rather than use the exception to refute the rule, suffice it to say that as a good designer one should be very sensitive to manipulating the golfer's first view of the facility in the most positive way possible.

Let us be more specific. Care should be taken not to expose golfers to the business side of golf, such as maintenance facilities, dumpsters, or storage areas. Ideally, the first thing that the golfers should see is one of the most exciting holes on the course—a signature par 3 is ideal. This is so important that it should be one of the prime factors considered in deciding among routing plans when many alternatives are possible. This signature hole should occur near the end of the round, so the golfer must patiently wait to satisfy his desire.

If the golf course property is fenced, then "windows" in the fence should be designed so the arriving players get several small views of the course before reaching the entry drive—"teasers," if you will.

The entryway should give a strong sense of arrival, and communicate the specialness of the place (see figure 139b). Waterfalls, flowers, landscaping, gates, columns, guardhouses, etc., are useful tools to enrich the entry. Even a little sign that simply says "welcome" is appropriate and appreciated, and more clever ones are even more so. The entrance drive itself should slow the pace of the traveler and begin that recreative tonic he seeks. If possible it should have a central terminus of the clubhouse with side views of the golf course mixed with the landscape devices used at the entry point. It should be wide and open so even the driver can safely sneak a peek. The best entryway is the one that causes the golfer to experience such a flow of sensations that they are difficult to sort out and become an almost kaleidoscopic blend of natural beauty, devoid of shiny steel, chrome, and paint.

The driveway should lead directly to a building or bag drop, and then turn into a parking area

Figure 139a. "Charming" is the best way to describe the simple clubhouse and pro shop that services one of the world's greatest golf courses.

Figure 139b. Entries should give a strong sense of arrival, for now the actual recreation experience begins.

instead of through the parking lot and then to the building. The parking lot should be paved, or dust-free, and roomy, which can be designed in, since golf courses have predictable and finite capacities. The parking area should be well-drained, well-lighted, and safe. Parking the car should be effortless, so as not to detract from the pleasurable flow of sensations the golfer is experiencing. Naturally, the walk or ride from the parking lot to the pro shop or clubhouse should further complement the euphoric state of mind our patron is feeling by using the same tools of wide walkways, landscape, signage, and golf views. The designer's goal is to exceed expectation—to fill the five senses with pleasant triggers. Sweet-smelling flowers or herbs, sounds of birds or moving water, the soft feel of the path, and distant views of golfers can often be part of the design.

One of the best entry experiences in golf is part of the magic of Devil's Pulpit outside of Toronto. From a great distance the arriving golfer catches glimpses of the green glass and stone clubhouse perched alone atop, but among, some wooded hills (see figure 140a–i). Traveling up Highway 10 is fast enough to go from the city to the course in less than 30 minutes, but slow enough to appreciate the beauty of horse farms, historic farmhouses that dot the land, and ever-rising hills of the unique geologic formation called The Escarpment. Near the property, Highway 10 narrows from four to two lanes as it starts up a long hill, and amid the drab rolling fescue and shrub landscape off to the right, the arriving traveler might catch brief vignettes of golfers and emerald green golf turf.

About halfway up the long grade, a side road exists right where stone pillars and a restored farmhouse/gatehouse mark the front gate and confirm that you have arrived. Once past the subtleties of an elegant but country landscaping treatment, the entrance drive slowly rises and turns to reveal a collage of golden fescue grasses waving in the wind, brilliant green and wide free-form fairways, and an ever-sharpening view of the clubhouse. To the immediate left is the par 3 16th hole (a signature hole) that plays from eight distinct tees across a pond that is edged in huge stones called armor stones. To the right is

Doug Ball

Figure 140a. From a distance the clubhouse at Devil's Pulpit is visible, framed by autumn hills of the escarpment that it sits upon.

the 14th fairway, which fits into a wide valley of fescue-covered hills that with its vertical sod-faced bunkers looks like a hole from Lahinch or Ballybunion. Ahead lies only hills, trees, and the articulated shape of the clubhouse, which stimulates curious observation. It takes a minute or two to reach the bag drop, and many people mistake the golf cart storage area for the pro shop because it is so attractively landscaped.

Once the golf bags have been left in the care of an attendant, you proceed to behind the cart building to a large paved parking area that is below the drive, so you can pretty well see where the open spots are to park before you enter. Almost immediately you are met by a courtesy cart that can carry four or five people,

Doug Ball

Figure 140b. The high-speed travel slows in pace as you first turn onto a gravel side road, then into the club driveway.

Doug Ball

Figure 140c. Once past the formal landscaping of the gate area, the arriving golfer sees a collage of golden fescue grasses and verdant golf course.

Doug Ball

Figure 140d. As the driveway crests, more golf course, cart storage, and distant clubhouse can be seen.

Doug Ball

Figure 140e. A quick look left, about 150 yards past the entrance gate, will reveal the par 3 16th hole.

Doug Ball

Figure 140f. Now moving at 20 mph, the arriving golfer can see the clubhouse more clearly, but his eye is often pulled toward the 14th green and the cart storage area.

Doug Ball

Figure 140g. The bag drop and cart storage building at Devil's Pulpit is often mistaken for the pro shop. Instead, you drive your cart to the top of the hill, where the pro shop is located in the clubhouse.

Doug Ball

Figure 140h. Just before the driveway turns to the bag drop and parking lot, the articulated shape of the clubhouse beckons.

Doug Ball

Figure 140i. On a clear day, the city of Toronto, 35 miles away, is visible and attractive, but it is also the antithesis of the pristine nature of countryside and golf course.

and you will be taken to a golf cart that has your clubs on it. You may choose to hit balls at this time, since the practice area is right by the carts (which is so well-done that many people think it is the golf course, not the range) or you can drive your golf cart up to the clubhouse. No automobile parking is permitted at the clubhouse, only dropoff or pickup stopping. Once at the top of the hill you drive your cart to the pro shop side of the clubhouse, and before you is a huge vista of golf, countryside, and nature that terminates in a view of Toronto 35 miles away. All of this described experience has been by design, with only one thought—exceed expectations. What it lacks in efficiency it makes up for in memorable, pleasurable experiences, no matter how often you visit the club. Before you hit your first drive at Devil's Pulpit you will have many more unexpected pleasures, and then the golf course itself continues that flow for 18 holes.

Preparation

To this point we have only alluded to the human factor in this mix of experiences, for nearly all of these situations have been self-paced. This is not to minimize the importance of human relations in the recreational continuum, but rather to isolate it for greater inspection. Of all the possible inputs, the attitude and demeanor of staff and service people is far and away the most important, for patrons usually come with high expectations of how they expect to be treated. The most innocent human action can destroy a mood or frame of mind. The reason may be that, as products of society, we highly value kind words and appreciative body language more than most other things. Likewise, we abhor bad attitudes, discourteous behavior, and unpleasant gestures from someone who is financially benefitting from us. Again, it is a matter of expectations. We want people to act like they are genuinely pleased we are with them, that they will in fact do whatever they can to help us enjoy the situation more, and that they are there to serve. If something is not right, then immediately every effort is put forth to correct the situation. The Japanese do this very well, as do many other Asian people.

(I recall one visit to Japan being unexpectedly invited to play a very nice course, but I did not have my golf shoes with me. I was perfectly willing to play in my topsiders, but my hosts wouldn't think of such an important guest not being properly equipped. But my shoe size was a 12, and naturally they were not used to having guests with such big feet. They first went through all of the shoes in the golf shop, then the club and shoe storage area, and then through every member's lockers without any shoe larger than a 10. So then they invited me in to have another cup of coffee, and they sent out employees to neighboring clubs to search for a size 12 shoe. The best they could find was an 11, and rather than disappoint them, I stuffed my feet into those shoes. They were so pleased to have found something that worked that I didn't have the heart to reject those shoes, so I wore them despite the pain. I never left my golf shoes at home on successive visits to Japan, and I will never forget to what great extremes some people will go to serve you.)

Even in the Devil's Pulpit arrival sequence detailed earlier, the mood and euphoria of the arrival could have been instantly broken by a surly gate guard, an indifferent or dower bag drop attendant, or a bad attitude courtesy cart driver. But at Devil's Pulpit, or any other business that seeks to exceed expectations, great care is taken to ensure that from the first person you meet to the last that wishes you goodbye, everyone has a warm smile and a pleasant word to say, and is on a mission to make you feel welcome. Great service makes for a great recreational experience.

(I really don't care to remember the number of times that I have gone into a golf shop and had a counter or shop person with a bad attitude ruin my mood for the day. They act as if they are doing me a favor to take my money, I'm using up their personal energy, and I should only expect a minimum amount of concern from them. We have all felt those negative interactions and disliked them intensely, yet they still exist at many places. This is the purview of managers and not designers, but taken together they comprise recreational experiences.)

One certainly doesn't wish to bore the reader with the obvious, but one can still find golf courses with dirty restrooms, poorly maintained golf carts, and litter in plain view of employees. They have bone dry ball washers with missing or dirty drying towels, broken benches, and inoperative water fountains; yet they expect a golfer to pay full price for an inexcusably poor golf course. All of these small things add up to be big things when the final tally is made about whether this was a good or bad recreational experience. Good management would never permit such things to happen.

Participation

The heart of the third part of the recreational experience is the recreation itself, which in this case is a round of golf. The travel phase takes golfers up through leaving their transportation, and it overlaps with their preparation to play, which is the initial part of the experience phase. Once they leave the clubhouse/pro shop and start for the golf course the main part of the recreation begins.

Some years back some researchers were hired to conduct a survey of how golfers felt about the golf course they were about to play and how they felt after they had finished playing. The golfers were polled immediately upon arriving at the golf course and as they were leaving, and the results were surprising.

Arriving golfers confirmed the importance of the entry experience and how it impacted on their levels of expectation. The fact that the pollsters were courteous, attractive college students who sincerely wanted the golfer's opinion probably took a lot of the hostility out of those who would have otherwise gone to the pro shop a little upset or disappointed because of their entry experience. Arriving golfers were initially equally divided on what they expected from the golf course, with some talking about design and others about maintenance. But when asked specific questions about what was most important to them about any golf course, the top answers were usually: 1) condition of greens, 2) condition of tees, 3) condition of bunkers, 4) condition of fairways, 5) condition of roughs, 6) condition of practice facilities, and dead last was 7) design of the course. Departing golfers placed even greater importance on the maintenance of the course, and issues of design always dealt more with what they didn't like as opposed to what they did like. Our survey confirmed that golfers would rather play a well-maintained but poorly designed course, compared to a well-designed but poorly maintained one. The conclusion was that maintenance is more important than design (see figure 141).

One might expect this result, since we have all visited famous golf courses only to find the course design to be completely disappointing, but the maintenance impeccable, which we conclude to be the source of their fame. Few can recognize good design, but everyone can recognize good maintenance. In the ideal world, design should be directed to permit the highest quality maintenance for any given maintenance budget. Although a good bit of lip service is paid to supporting maintenance, too often the concept is ignored to make an architectural statement. Golf courses that are easy to maintain often lack a strong character of features, and do little for a designer's reputation. Working together, the golf course architect and the superintendent must collaborate to find the perfect compromise, which is a balance between being visually dramatic versus being easy to maintain. Too often, maintenance is forgotten during design, unless a golf course superintendent is involved during the early design phases.

Other design considerations besides maintenance can influence whether the expectation levels of the golfer are exceeded. The first is that no golfer likes to lose golf balls, so the fewer he loses the more he enjoys himself. Likewise, golfers like to play from nicely situated or raised tees that offer great vistas of the countryside or the entire hole. Golfers like playing downhill, and they prefer to have their tee shots land in fairways, not roughs. Sand shots should be within their ability, blind hazards are abhorred, and greens should not be too confounding. In other words, golfers like golf courses that look hard and play easy. (One of the compliments I appreciate most is to have someone play one of my better courses, and tell me that they had one of their best rounds of the year there. This tells

Figure 141. Maintenance is more important than design to golfers, as shown by the 5th hole at St. Albans Country Club.

me they loved the place, and that we understand what it takes to thrill golfers.)

Cooldown

Once the round is complete and the golfers are ready to relax, then the central recreational experience of golf is complete, and the afterglow state begins. The golfer's attention and emphasis shift toward facilities designed by the clubhouse architect. The comfort and convenience of a place to have a cold drink and add up the scorecard is considered part of the round of golf (see figure 142). If golfers took showers and stayed for dinner, then this would not be considered part of the golf experience, even in Japan. The round of golf ends with the number crunching on the scorecard and the drinks or light food that follow. Dinner might be considered a subsequent recreational event, and the patron would establish a different set of expectations.

Travel Home

The fourth part of the recreational process is the travel back home after an enjoyable round of golf, and all the issues that golfers must face getting there. An effortless travel experience home does not diminish the central focus, which was golf, and in fact it can even enhance it, but it is beyond the control of the golf course designer. Likewise, if getting home is troublesome, then it can tarnish a round of golf.

Remembrance

The final part of any recreational process is the remembrance of the total experience, with all phases blended together. Remembrance may actually begin while the round of golf is still being played, but total reflection won't begin until after the travel phase is complete. The more average experience is soon forgotten. A

Figure 142. Relaxed clubhouse accommodations allow the golfer to savor his immediate past experience, and start to build his remembrances of it.

fantastic total recreational experience becomes timeless, forever locked in the memory of the participants, and it only gets better with each retelling. Often it establishes new levels of expectation for future recreation.

We in the golf industry are keenly aware that logo items sell best at golf facilities that provide the best total experience. As individual golfers, we buy and display our logo items in hopes that someone will remark about the place, or will start a conversation so we can share our remembrances—particularly if the experience exceeded our expectation.

As designers and managers sensitive to the various phases of the recreational process, it is in our power to positively influence it in order to yield fond memories, triggered by a word, picture, or logo. This is a never-ending quest.

9

THE IDEAL GOLF COURSE ARCHITECT

Thus far, this book has dealt with the theoretical or more ethereal part of the design process, that complex mental activity of producing images of several possible golf course features and selecting the ones that best complement the overall design theme. But conjuring a blend of exciting elements is less than half of the design process. The remaining part, which may be the more important, is the communication of those ideas to the person actually doing the construction. This is the mechanics of design, the construction sequence that is the "nuts and bolts" of actually getting a golf course built.

The basic plan of a golf course is the routing plan, showing the spatial relationship of the elements to each other in a two-dimensional plan view. But to carry out most site modifications, more detailed information is required, usually in the form of drawings and specifications, so that the contractor can understand and construct the exact images that are in the mind's eye of the architect. The more explicit and detailed the information, the better the contractor will understand exactly what is intended.

We've all heard the saying, "A man with an idea, who is unable fully and precisely to communicate the idea, is no better than a man with no idea at all." The key words of this phrase are "fully and precisely communicate." To understand all the various theoretical concepts of golf course design, yet be unable to translate those precepts into physical reality, is of no value except as mental recreation. What separates an amateur golf course designer from a true professional golf architect (see figure 143) is the ability fully and precisely to communicate one's ideas to the people actually doing the work, using terms and symbols that the builder understands so that every aspect of the design intent is realized.

Without clear communications, trial and error result. But trial and error have little place in modern golf course architecture. To build something and then to rebuild it as often as necessary until it looks right and functions properly is wasteful and not indicative of an ideal and competent designer. Given enough time and money, a creditable course can no doubt result from repeated trial and error efforts, but such waste is not necessary if a professional golf course architect is retained.

The skill of a golf architect is measured by his or her ability to mentally formulate interesting, functional, and sensitive design elements and then to communicate the design intentions in the clearest possible manner. The more detailed and precise a golf architect can be, the smaller the chance for misinterpretation of the subtleties of the design, and the greater the opportunity for development of the nuances that often separate masterpieces from ordinary courses. Some designers choose to do minimal drawings but spend maximal time on the site providing construction details, while others choose detailed drawings. But detailed construction documents do not obviate the requirement of the designer to spend time in the field during construction. Ultimately, he is the one to interpret the intent and to develop nuances that support or enhance his ideas. Just as a great piece of music played by skilled musicians requires a conductor, so does a great plan built by a skilled contractor require the tuned eye of the designer to reach truly great results (see figure 144).

Donald Ross (see figure 145) was one of the game's most prolific designers. Yet according to his longtime friend, Richard Tufts, Ross' one great

Figure 143. The American Society of Golf Course Architects represents 80% of North America's most prolific, professional, and dedicated designers. Membership requirements are so rigorous that amateurs need not apply. Founding members are left to right: William P. Bell, Pasadena, CA; Robert White, Myrtle Beach, SC; W.B. Langford, Chicago, IL; Honorary President Donald J. Ross, Pinehurst, NC; President Robert Bruce Harris, Chicago, IL; Vice President Stanley Thompson, Toronto, Canada; William F. Gordon, Doylestown, PA; Secretary-Treasurer Robert Trent Jones, Montclair, NJ; William Diddle, Carmel, IN; and J.B. McGovern, Wynnewood, PA. Three of the original 13 charter members were not able to attend the first Pinehurst meeting: Perry Maxwell, Ardmore, OK; Jack Daray, Chicago, IL; and Robert F. "Red" Lawrence, Boca Raton, FL.

regret was that he didn't do fewer golf courses in his career so that he could have devoted more time to each one. All told, he is credited with having done over 400 golf courses, and this in an era of train travel, when it was no simple matter to spend time visiting and revisiting sites. Thus Ross wasn't able to maximize each site with his personal ideas and interpretations, and had to rely on the judgment of others. The result, not surprisingly, was that not every Donald Ross golf course was his best possible design for its site. But Donald Ross did depend heavily on construction drawings and specifications to produce this prodigious volume of work (see figure 146).

Every design profession must communicate specific ideas that may be unique to the discipline. As a result, a separate set of words or symbols may evolve and become widely adopted to express those discipline-unique concepts. This "jargon" or "standard notation" allows a shorthand method of presenting complex ideas and precise interpretation of their intent to anyone who knows the language. The standard notation in music is the use of a five-line bar upon which are placed notes of varying length and pitch, annotated as necessary. Anyone who can read music will know exactly what the composer has in mind. In golf course architecture, the standard notation of drawings and specifications precisely communicates the designer's intent (see figure 147), particularly using topography lines and spot elevations.

As in music, where there are some successful individuals who are unable to read or write musical notation, there are some successful golf course architects similarly lacking mastery in standard notation of landscaping engineering and agronomics. Ironically, the quality of the end product may be no different, except that in the absence of standard notation the designer or composer must personally attend to every detail of the creation to ensure complete and total implementation of his thoughts. If one does not attend to even the most mundane details, then the final form, because it is subject to interpretation by another person implementing the work, will be a

Figure 144. Great golf courses depend upon a synergy between an inspired designer and a skilled contractor, the way a conductor relates to an orchestra.

Figure 145. Donald Ross, pictured on a 1930 calendar before Pinehurst got grass greens.

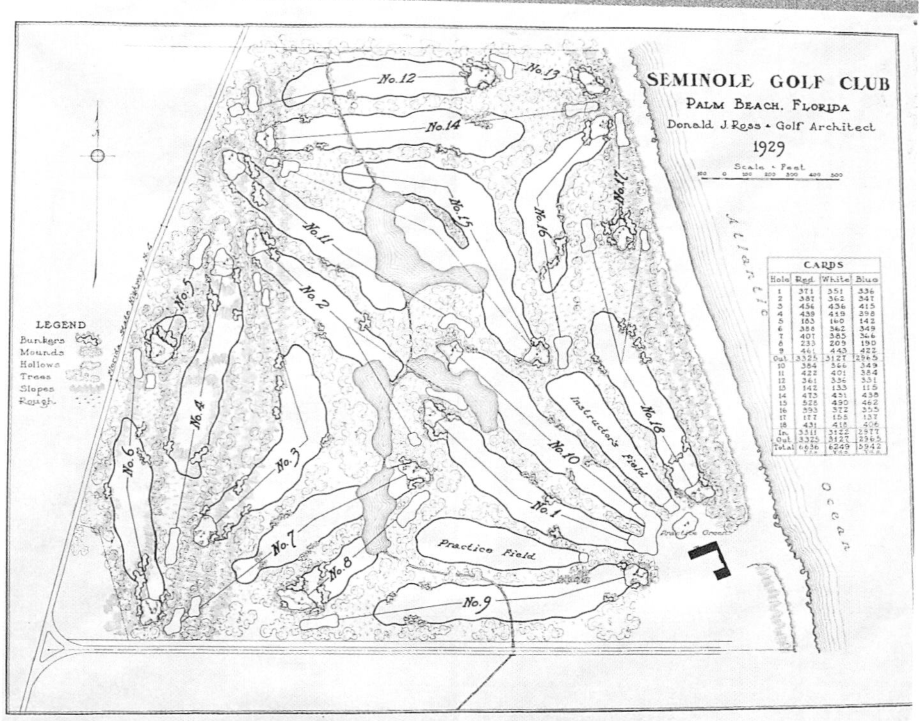

Figure 146. Donald Ross' 1929 plan for Seminole in Palm Beach, Florida was rich in construction details.

reflection of both parties' ideas instead of just the designer's (see figure 148).

This isn't always bad, for there are many instances where a skilled contractor has taken a design and improved upon it. In fact, some designers with notable reputations but questionable skills rely on a particular contractor to make them look good. This explains why some designers insist on using certain contractors, or their own shapers, and also why a particular project of a given designer, built by someone other than his usual contractor, will look different from his other designs. This selective use of contractors may yield good results, but it does not permit competitive bidding between capable contractors to get the best possible price, which is in the client's best interest. It also leads too often to a sameness of design style and a predictability that can stifle originality. Even the most professional golf course architect may prefer one contractor over another, but he or she should be capable of working with any qualified builder to achieve the design goals.

Working with standard notation permits economy in construction, saves time, reduces misunderstandings, and permits the designer to be more productive. One must remember that since all men are mortal and will ultimately pass on, their ideas will die with them unless preserved in pictures and words. That should be an important consideration for a client with a multimillion-dollar project. If a prospective architect does not use formal planning methods and standard notation, what happens to the project if the designer dies?

Alister MacKenzie died just after doing the basic routing plan for the author's home course at Ohio State University (see figure 149). Letters

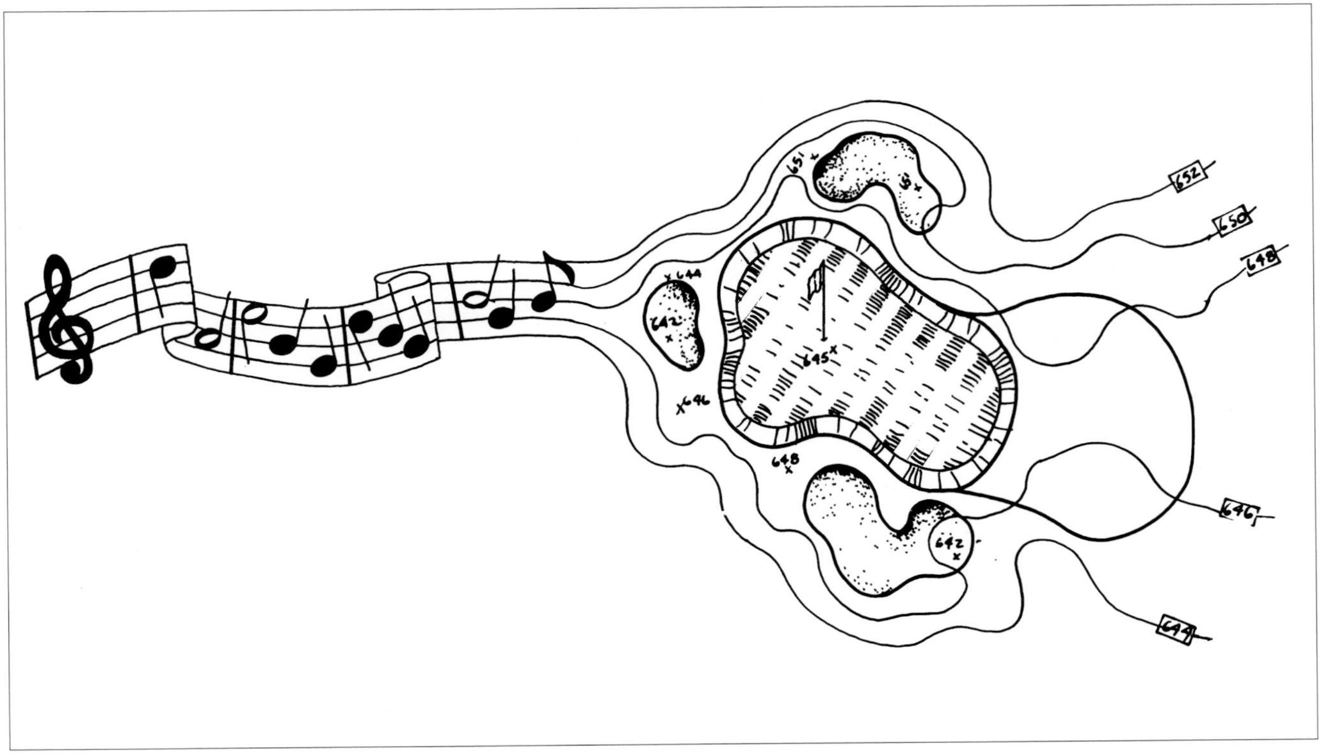

Figure 147. Just as notes of music communicate the composer's intent to the musician, contour lines and elevations convey the design concept to the builder.

Figure 148. My two associates, Dana Fry (in red) as lead designer and Guy Quattrocchi as project coordinator, took my design intent for Devil's Pulpit, Devil's Paintbrush, Ann Briar, and Glenmaura National and added the details necessary to make these projects world class. Thanks, guys.

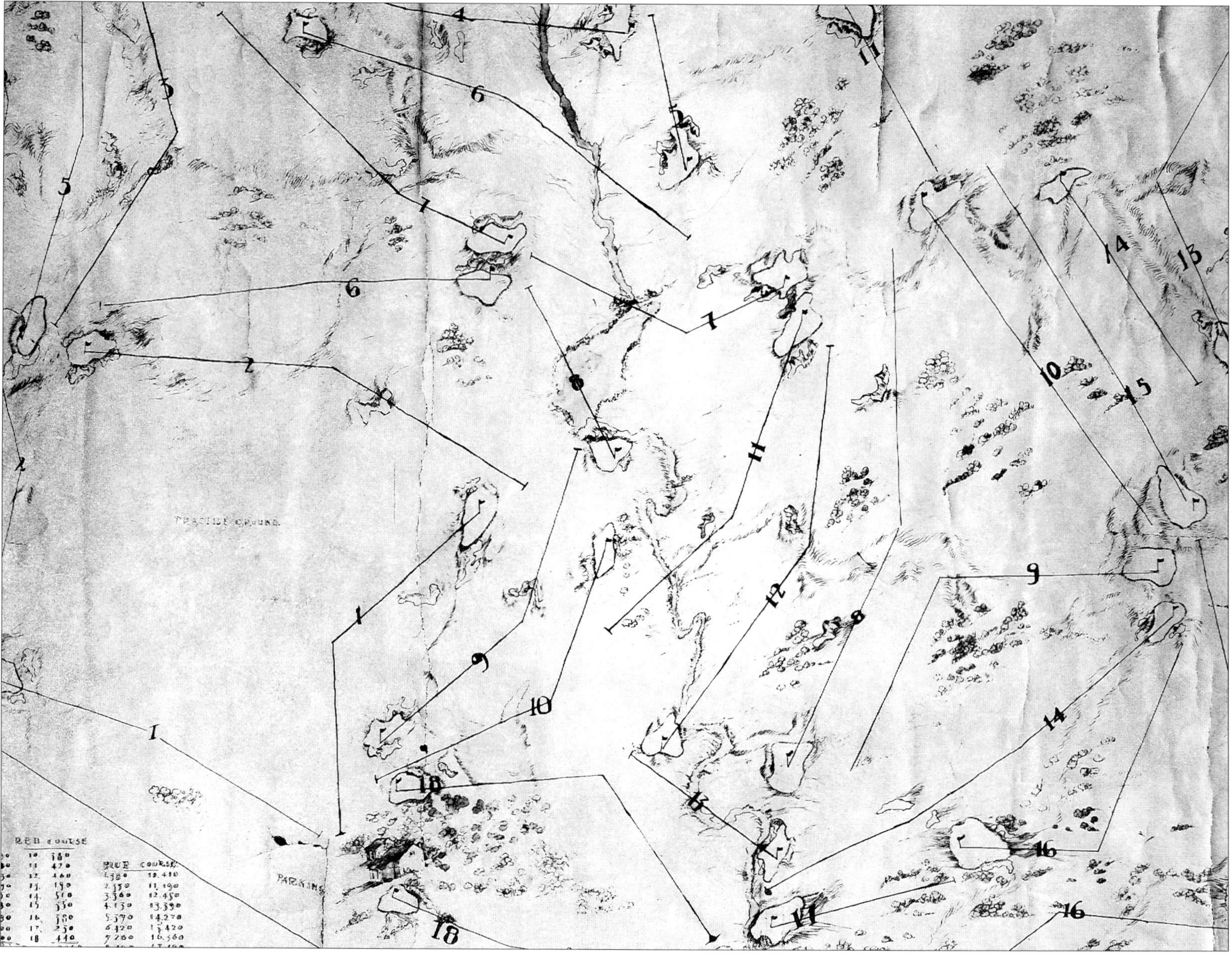

Figure 149. Dr. MacKenzie's initial routing plan for the Ohio State University golf courses.

Figure 150. Since golf courses typically require 150 acres of land, they can have very important influences on the surrounding environment. The better the environmental training and knowledge of the golf course architect, the more positive that impact will be.

to Mrs. MacKenzie, found in the university archives, indicate that after Alister's death, she finished the drawings and sent them to the university. Several people from the university who were completely without golf course construction experience built the golf holes as best they could determine from those plans, with only occasional visits from MacKenzie associate Perry Maxwell. As a great MacKenzie devotee who has studied his creations in detail, I find my beloved home course lacks much of the richness and nuance found at Pasatiempo and Cypress Point, where MacKenzie was available to interpret details.

As modern society becomes more sophisticated in measuring and understanding environmental complexities, the more it seeks to protect those systems through mechanisms of reviews, permits, and monitoring. Normally, design and construction impacts must be assessed, established, and proved before construction permits or approvals are issued. This places a high requirement on producing detailed drawings and documents that facilitate that review procedure. If the golf course designer produces the required drawings instead of an outside consultant who may not understand the nuances of golf course design, the greater the chances are that what is approved will make the best golf facility. The point is that the more skilled the golf course designer is in producing detailed drawings and documents that satisfy environmental concerns, the faster and more complete the submittal will be, without compromising important golf concepts. If by chance the golf course designer is well-schooled and experienced in environmental matters, he or she may be able to improve or support existing ecosystems or develop greater biodiversity on the site that actually enhances the golfing experience (see figure 150).

Accomplishing this technical planning and communication process in the most efficient manner possible requires certain skills and technical information—unless, that is, the designer is willing to handle every bit of construction personally, in which case the genius of personal inspiration will suffice to carry the job through. But even the most inventive mind inchoately gives form to certain technical modes of conveying that genius. If we are to appreciate and analyze what makes that inspiration so distinctive, we would wind up precisely with a body of knowledge and analytical skills that any ideal golf course architect should master. These include:

1. The game of golf
2. The business of golf
3. Golf course maintenance
4. Cartography, or the science of drawing maps
5. Fundamentals of landscape construction
6. Basic agricultural engineering
7. A standard notation of golf course design
8. Construction methods and equipment limitation
9. Soil chemistry, physics, classification, and modification
10. Irrigation and drainage
11. Contract and liability law
12. Ecology and environmental law
13. Horticulture
14. Graphic skills
15. Oral presentation
16. Computer science
17. Ethics and high moral standards

One might think that no one could be knowledgeable and experienced in all of these areas, but most of the master golf course architects have been well-versed in (nearly) all of these fields.

The Game of Golf

First and foremost, an ideal golf architect must know the game of golf and the golf business. He need not be an accomplished player (MacKenzie reportedly had an 18 handicap), but he must understand and empathize with all classes of golfers, from touring pros to rank beginners. One must understand the psyche of golfers in order to design a course that offers each player an individual challenge within their ability and rewards each for successful play. One must also understand how the physical forms of golf features communicate to golfers of varying abilities.

The Business of Golf

An ideal golf architect must also understand the business end of running a golf course so that he can advise on the economic feasibility of a proposed course. He should be able to project revenue, costs, profits, and losses. An ideal golf architect should understand soil classifications, textural limitations, soil physics, soil chemistry, plant growth, and golf course maintenance. Being able to interpret and interrelate such information is important in selecting the most environmentally adaptive turfgrasses for the site, type and performance characteristics of an irrigation system, the amount and type of soil modification required, and internal drainage and water retention potential of the site, among other things. No one can design for efficient long-term maintenance or sustainable environmental protection if he or she is ignorant of its requirements.

Maps, Drawings, and Construction Techniques

The ideal golf architect should be proficient in reading and interpreting aerial photographs, survey maps, and contour maps (see figure 151). He or she should also be able to draw new maps to show proposed modifications. In this area, some background in architecture, engineering, or landscape design is especially helpful. It enables presentation of ideas and concepts in a standard notation and language that can be read and universally interpreted by any capable contractor, engineer, or surveyor. The ideal golf architect should be knowledgeable in engineering in order to review complicated drawings of structures such as water retention basins, dams, waterways, irrigation systems, roads, paths, surface drainage, and subsurface drainage. One should understand the capabilities, limitations, and expense of golf course construction machinery if one is going to minimize costs and build a course without resorting to exotic equipment (see figure 152). After all, even an ideal golf architect is normally working with a strict, or perhaps uncompromisingly low, construction budget and seeks to build more for less. The ideal

Figure 151. The golf course architect must be an expert with maps, for it is a universal language that conveys his ideas anywhere in the world. Here I am, kneeling lower right, in Japan, explaining a plan with very little help from the interpreter, because we all used the universal language of maps.

Figure 152. Chris Haney (in blue)—founder of the Devil's Pulpit Golf Association—and I discuss the design details of the stone wall around the lake he ordered for the 1st hole at the Pulpit.

golf architect should also be schooled in legal matters, for contracts, federal EPA requirements, state laws, and local codes are now part of everyday life in the golf design business. The architect whose work does not uphold such fundamental requirements is likely to have to answer for it later, if not in a court of law, certainly in reputation through the court of public opinion.

Professional Skills

The ideal golf architect also has to be part ecologist and part horticulturist—and why not?, since he or she is often called upon to identify and understand the requirements and growth habits of existing vegetation, evaluate the impact that the golf course will have on the environment, and plan for establishment of a new ecological system involving the golf course, native plants, and small animals.

Within the past few years, and certainly into the foreseeable future, computers have become an essential part of golf course design in order to accurately calculate, amend, or produce information essential for the efficient construction of a golf course. Not only does the ideal golf course architect use computers to assist technically in his craft, but he also recognizes the marketing value to the client of 3-dimensional models, videotapes of holes not yet constructed, and the easy exchange of information with other planning or permitting professionals.

People often ask what is the surest way to become a golf course architect. A good base would be a college degree in civil engineering, a two-year degree in turf science along with two to three seasons of greenkeeping experience, and then employment with a nationally recognized golf course contractor for two to three years. The C.E. degree is essential for handling the ever-restricting permitting process required when building a golf course, and also for learning the standard practice of doing construction document and project administration. The turf background allows the designer to make the golf course maintainable, as well as providing essential knowledge about turf varieties, nutrition, soils testing, greens construction, and environmental impact. Lastly, working for a contractor teaches the proper construction sequence, problems encountered, and how contractors think and work.

Ethics

Finally, the ideal golf course architect should possess impeccable ethical standards and work for only one master—the client (see figure 153). An architect may possess all the ideal skills and knowledge, but if he is dishonest or duplicitous when dealing with the client, the contractor, the golf industry, or the profession, then he is not a true professional, regardless of the quality of the designs he may produce. The golf architect's sole loyalty should be to uphold the finest industry standards in working for his client. The client, after all, has contracted him, and pays for his expertise. The architect, in turn, has the professional obligation to implement the soundest possible design that is consistent with the client's needs and budget. Often the client is a company or group of investors that wants a golf course but has little knowledge of how to properly plan and build one. A golf architect is hired because of a demonstrated ability to understand the client's needs and expectations and to produce a golf course within an allotted budget. Clients must trust an architect's judgment implicitly, for each decision costs thousands or even hundreds of thousands of dollars, and very few mistakes can be tolerated. The golf architect in turn has agreed to provide such services for a fee (which should be his sole source of income from the project). He, therefore, is legally and ethically obliged to protect the best interests of the client when making decisions. This includes notifying the client of any concerns about safety, environmental impact, or legal or ethical practices. A good architect will not work for a bad client.

But even that allegiance has its limits. For instance, a contractor will agree to build a course for a set fee, based upon drawings and documents prepared by the architect—drawings and documents that the contractor trusts are true and accurate. If the plans and specifications are exhaustively detailed and explicit, there is rarely an adversarial relationship between contractor

American Society of Golf Course Architects

The American Society of Golf Course Architects is comprised of leading golf course designers in the United States and Canada. These golf course architects, who are involved in the design of new courses and renovation of older courses, bring years of experience to every project.

Members of the American Society of Golf Course Architects are, by virtue of our knowledge of the game, training, experience, vision and inherent ability, in all ways qualified to design and prepare specifications for a course of functional and aesthetic perfection.

ASGCA members are further qualified to execute and oversee the implementation on the ground of our plans and specifications to create an enjoyable layout that challenges golfers of all abilities and exemplifies the highest standards and traditions of golf. We will counsel in all phases of the work to protect the best interests of our client.

Each member of the American Society of Golf Course Architects is engaged primarily in the practice of golf course architecture, and his/her qualifications have satisfied the ASGCA Board of Governors in all respects.

Figure 153. The American Society of Golf Course Architects' Code of Ethics.

and architect, but rather, some give and take within a context of shared understanding. Such plans provide the normal latitude for the negotiations and compromise that occur, necessarily so, on every golf course project. Adjustments in the field are the rule, not the exception.

Figure 154. A rare photograph of Bill Bell, George Thomas, and Dr. Alister MacKenzie, three men who had a profound and lasting impact on golf course architecture.

Problems arise, however, when the initial plans and subsequent specifications prove faulty. Most disputes between contractors and architects or contractors and clients are caused by insufficient prebidding investigation and planning by the designer. He may have known what he wanted but was not capable of describing it to the contractor; or he simply didn't investigate a matter thoroughly during the planning phase. Sometimes unexpected conditions are encountered, such as an unanticipated rock layer or a wet-weather spring, but in a complete set of plans and specifications there are usually provisions for dealing with such occurrences.

The architect and the contractor should share the common goal of producing the finest work possible within the constraints of the operating budget. The architect should make sure the contractor delivers what is called for and that the client promptly pays all bills and doesn't use withheld payments to exploit the contractor.

A similar relationship should exist between a golf architect and a supplier. The architect must be open-minded about the various products available and specify only those products that are in the best interest of the client. An architect should have no vested interest in any one product, nor should he specify products produced or distributed by companies that offer personal inducements for him to move their goods.

The Architect's Relationship to Golf

Lastly, what should be the relationship of a golf architect to the game of golf? It should be the same as that of any person realizing an income from the game. Anyone making a living in golf, be it as a golf architect, a club professional, a touring pro, a salesman, or anyone else should be committed to making the game of golf grow (see figure 154). We in the golf industry should encourage beginners, strive to keep costs low, and make golf programs accessible to students, senior citizens, the underprivileged, and the handicapped. We should volunteer our time, money, and abilities to introduce non-golfers to the pleasures and benefits of golf. Every person making money from golf should support local and national professional organizations, with membership dues if not time and active participation.

The selection of the golf course architect is perhaps the most significant decision ever made concerning a golf course. Great care should be exercised in selecting an architect. The decision should be based upon the architect's professional abilities, not on his or her golfing accomplishments or playing skills. As the legendary Bobby Jones wrote in his autobiography, *Golf is My Game*, "No man learns to design a golf course simply by playing golf, no matter how well." (see figure 155)

Figure 155. Dr. Alister MacKenzie and his good friend Bobby Jones.

If a golf course developer feels that it is essential to have "a name" to sell the golf course, then he should retain a nationally or regionally recognized golfer for promotional purposes. But he should not be deluded into believing that a touring professional's endorsement or occasional (usually very occasional) appearances can substitute for the time and expertise of a true golf course architect. Golf developers would be wise to follow the "design team" approach that Bobby Jones followed when creating Augusta National. Jones worked with the great architect Alister MacKenzie on the design of Augusta, and he later wrote in his autobiography, "I think MacKenzie and I managed to work as a completely sympathetic team. Of course, there was never any question that he was the architect and I his advisor and consultant."

Part II

Practice

10

The Site Analysis and Feasibility Study

The purpose of a site analysis and feasibility study is to examine all the possible influences on a proposed golf course facility so that an owner can intelligently decide if the project will meet his expectations. Feasibility is like a market study, and is concerned with *pro forma* returns over five or ten years and whether the site itself can reasonably support a viable golf course operation. Normally, such feasibility studies are prepared by a firm or team of consultants who specialize in such economic research. This is usually undertaken in cooperation with a golf course architect, who does the physical site analysis and provides specific information regarding the planning, construction, and maintenance of the potential golf course. The first thing that the golf course consultants must do whenever planning a site feasibility study is to determine the client's needs and purposes. Normally, a client wants ultimately to make a profit from his project, and suspects a golf course can earn money if it serves at least one of three sectors: a stable hometown market; a steady tourist or transient trade; or as an attraction for adjoining home sites or property. Increasingly, golf courses are used by real estate developers to attract clients for the homesites (see figure 156). Indeed, it is rare today to find a client who prefers not to develop property surrounding or even within a golf course site. This is due in part to the fact that with a golf course development project, the enormous cost of a complete golf course (minimum 2.5 million dollars exclusive of land, clubhouse, maintenance

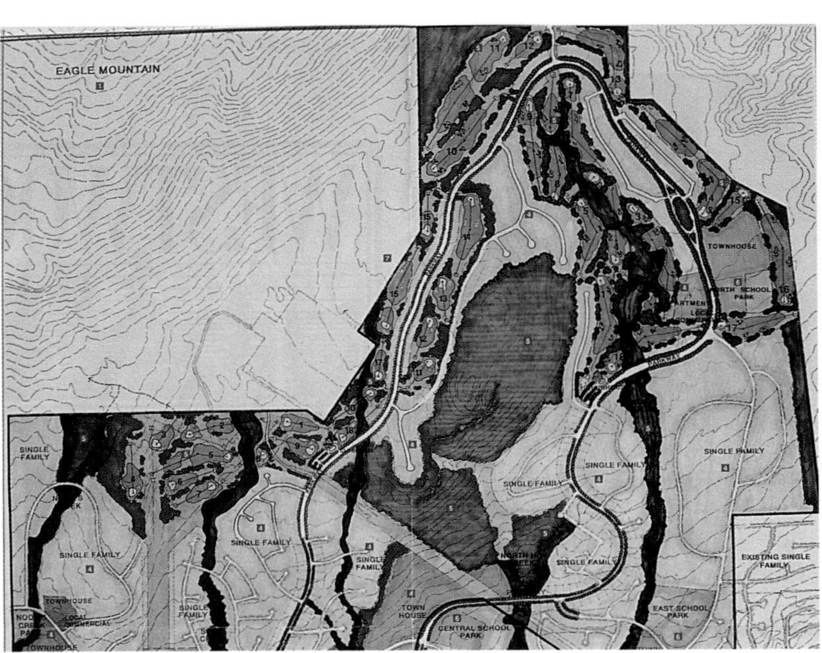

Figure 156. An aerial view of a golf course/housing project.

Figure 157. Clients have many reasons for building golf courses, including enhancing house lots, attracting tourists, making profits, holding professional tournaments, or as fulfillment of a lifelong dream. Each of these is a valid reason, but each requires a different kind of golf course. Client involvement is critical from the earliest stages of planning. Chris Haney (in red) and Scott Abbott wanted a world famous golf course, and they got Devil's Pulpit

building, parking, equipment, etc.) can be spread over a wider income base and need not rely strictly on golf operations to produce a profit.

Other clients view a golf course as a status symbol, and hope to establish prestige by offering a unique golfing experience by keeping membership to a select group or by hosting a big tournament. Still others want a course just to satisfy a lifelong dream (see figure 157). These clients often want to help design the course, or want to utilize a special piece of ground (often one owned by the client's family) or simply to outdo some prominent existing course. This was undoubtedly the motivation of Steve Wynn, Las Vegas casino magnate, who reportedly spent 35 million dollars to build Shadow Creek outside of Las Vegas.

Those are all valid reasons for wanting to build a golf course, but each requires a golf course of somewhat different character. Rarely can a golf course totally satisfy more than one or two of those purposes. Almost all clients want their golf course to be economically self-supporting and not be a long-term financial liability. There are a select few to whom money is no object and who are thus totally unconcerned about financial aspects of the golf course, but few golf architects are ever fortunate enough to work for such a client. For most, a course must be built within a reasonable budget, maintained on a modest budget, and prove attractive enough to accommodate a sufficient number of golfers to be financially self-supporting each year.

Below is a sample balance sheet for a "reasonable," middle-level golf project, showing some ranges of possible costs:

INITIAL COSTS

	Costs	
Item	Low	High
1. Land—175 acres	700,000	3,000,000
2. Golf course proper—modest	2,100,000	7,500,000
3. Clubhouse—basic functional structure	575,000	7,000,000
4. Maintenance building	100,000	600,000
5. Maintenance equipment	300,000	600,000
6. Parking lot, paths, shelters, etc.	125,000	500,000
	$ 3,900,000	$19,200,000

YEARLY OPERATIONAL COST

	Costs	
Item	Low	High
1. Maintenance—golf course	400,000	1,000,000
2. Taxes, insurance, fees	57,500	200,000
3. Clubhouse operations (pro, manager, employees, utilities)	200,000	600,000
	$ 657,500	$1,800,000

YEARLY INCOME

Item	Amount Low	Amount High
1. 40,000 rounds @ $20 to $200 per round user fee	800,000	8,000,000
2. 50 golf carts (net)	75,000	500,000
3. Clubhouse operations (net)	75,000	500,000
	$ 950,000	$9,000,000

ANNUAL BALANCE

Item	Amount Low	Amount High
1. Principal on loan	130,000	3,000,000
2. Interest on loan	162,500	4,200,000
3. Yearly operational costs	657,500	1,800,000
Total annual operating/ debt service costs	950,000	9,000,000
Total annual income	950,000	9,000,000
Yearly net loss/profit	$ 0	$0

This hypothetical balance sheet shows a zero annual balance. The intent is merely to illustrate analysis of the economic feasibility of a project by insertion of applicable figures representative of a particular area. While the dollar value for each item may vary greatly from location to location, as long as each item is assigned a fair market value, a prospective client will have some idea of the soundness of the project. Of course, this is a bare bones balance sheet. There are undoubtedly additional costs and income not listed that may benefit or detract from the project as well.

Note, however, that this initial balance sheet of the low column reflects rather inexpensive land acquisition costs, at a rate which is probably unrealistic for most populated areas. It also assumes a rather low-profile golf course and a clubhouse construction budget to match. In recent years, there have been many projects in the United States that cost far in excess of twenty million dollars for golf course construction alone, with a proportional amount spent on the clubhouse. Some of those projects will never become solvent because they exceed all reasonable income potential.

Reasons for Failure

Nearly all golf course projects that fail do so as a result of underfinancing rather than overspending. It may be annoying for a developer to have to spend extra money at the point where a project is approaching completion, but the sums imposed by such unanticipated expenditures do not compare to the substantial sums invested up front at the outset. Proper planning and financing in advance can therefore mean much more to the success of a project than the most Scrooge-like practices once the capital is secured. That's why an in-depth feasibility study by a skilled golf course consultant is essential to a client. If the total cost and projected income are known in advance, a client can make a reasonable decision and obtain sufficient financing. Of course, it helps if the golf course and building architects live within the set budget, unless unforeseen circumstances dictate otherwise.

Although economic viability is usually the bottom line, the golf course architect must have specific information about the site and the project if he is intelligently to plan the course and prepare a probable construction budget to be part of the feasibility study. All designers assess site parameters, but not all perceive or express it in the identical form. What follows, then, is a model for preparing the golf architect's portion of a site analysis.

Site Analysis

After determining the client's expectations, one should have the client furnish a scaled map showing carefully marked boundary and contour lines, preferably set at one- or two-foot intervals. It is also advisable to have the client provide an up-to-date aerial photograph of the site, enlarged to the same scale as the contour map so the two can be easily matched. Then a site visit is in order (see figure 158). This enables a sound understanding of the relationship between physiographic features, boundary lines, access points, and special assets or problems of the site. After mentally cataloging this information and annotating the map, one can usually start at this point to develop possible routing plans for the

Figure 158. With a contour map in hand, the initial visit to a site is more productive, efficient, and educational.

site, or to identify areas that will need additional study before intelligent routing can be done. If the site is large, with few problems and multiple accesses, then there might be scores of possible routing plans. It is then simply a matter of selecting the ones that maximize the client's main interest—be it housing lots or good golfing features—and that minimize construction and maintenance problems, particularly if the budgets are low. However, if the terrain is harsh or the property oddly shaped, it is entirely possible there might be only one acceptable routing plan, if that. (I have worked a site of nearly 700 acres of West Virginia mountainside and could barely squeeze in a short par 70 course that was affordable to my client.) If money is no object, then some of the worst natural sites can be rearranged to produce some of the most spectacular golf courses possible. One need only consider most of the recent Japanese courses to recognize what can be accomplished on a hundred-million-dollar construction budget (let alone for similar budget lines allocated for purposes of land acquisition, and again for clubhouse facilities).

Soil and Climate

Generating a routing plan is only a small part of the preliminary investigation necessary to produce a site study. The study should also examine the soils found on the grounds (see figure 159). Their textural and chemical properties must be determined, as well as the depth of soil to rock, the type of underlying rock, the depth of soil to groundwater, analysis of each major horizon of the soil profile, and the physical properties of the soils (such as shrink-swell ratios, construction capabilities or limitations, and water retention capacity). Those properties should also be evaluated for their influence on construction and long-term maintenance so that proper soil modification, amendments, and treatments may be identified and their costs estimated.

Unless the golf architect has resided in the locale, he should investigate the climatology of the site for such information as rainfall and snowfall amounts, monthly distribution, normal monthly temperature ranges for the site, dates of the first and last frosts (if any) and the number of days over 90°F. These data, coupled with soil profiles, allow the golf architect to determine the needed capacity and scope of the irrigation system, the best cultivars of turfgrass to specify, the need and possible size of subsurface drainage, the active construction season, the latest planting date and the type of long-term maintenance that must be accommodated.

Figure 159. During the initial site visit it is helpful to dig some test holes, for what looks like productive cornfields on the surface can be a golf course nightmare underneath.

Irrigation Water

Perhaps the most important quality of any golf course site is the availability of water. The issue is not of water as a hazard but water as a sustainer of life. Without irrigation water, no golf course can long exist. In the Midwest, lying between the arid regions of the Southwest and the lush regions found in the Northeast and Northwest, it is generally agreed that fairways need about one inch of water per week to keep turfgrasses healthy. Greens and tees in such locales need about one and a half inches of water per week. Those amounts sound harmless enough, but when one realizes that a typical eighteen-hole course may have fifty acres of fairways and ten acres of tees and greens (including banks and outslopes), the calculations take on a different form:

Calculating Water Requirements for a Midwestern 18-Hole Golf Course

1. Fairways and Near Roughs

50	acres of fairway and rough
× 1	inch of water/week
50	acre-inches/week
× 27,000	gallons/acre-inch
1,350,000	gallons of water/week

2. Greens and Tees (including collars and banks)

10	acres of tees and greens
× 1.5	inches of water/week
15	acre-inches/week
× 27,000	gallons/acre-inch
405,000	gallons of water/week

3. Golf Course

Fairways/Roughs	— 1,350,000 gallons/week
Greens and Tees	— 405,000 gallons/week
Total*	— 1,755,000 gallons/week

*Note: a golf course located in an arid region may require three times this amount of water. (A project I am working on in Scottsdale, Arizona is permitted to use 1,000,000 gallons of water per day for less than 90 acres of turf. Likewise, on an environmental demonstration project just south of Boston, called Widow's Walk Golf Course, I am designing the project to use less than 90,000 gallons of water per day.)

In the Midwest, this means a 300-gallon-per-minute well must be pumped for 97.5 hours per week—the equivalent of four continuous days—to keep up. With such high requirements for water, it is paramount that sources of water supply be thoroughly investigated. This can be done by checking existing well logs or contacting local well drillers to see what water can be obtained from wells (see figure 160). Some communities and regions have water districts that control underground water resources. If the water is to come from a stream, then it must be verified that the stream never dries up, for most often the lowest stream flow occurs at the time of greatest irrigation demand. Also, laws regarding stream flow use must be upheld. A water analysis must also be done to ensure that the water quality is acceptable for long-term turfgrass use.

Figure 160. Local well drillers are an excellent source of information about possible underground water supplies.

Ponds are a poor source of irrigation. Unless they are of great size and depth, rarely does surface runoff into small ponds ever yield sufficient water to sustain a golf course through stressful drought periods. If the water will be purchased from a governmental agency or water district, then a written agreement should be drawn up to guarantee the rate to be charged and continued availability of the water. There are currently several cases where clubs pay in excess of $800,000 per year for water. If nothing else about a potential golf course is investigated, at least attention should be paid to the intended sources of irrigation water. Effluent water has been used on many golf courses, but is not preferred over fresh water. Long-term usage of effluent water has caused problems of soil salinity, heavy metals accumulation, and even diseases that seriously complicate turf maintenance and quality.

Because of the overall importance of water and the normally high cost to buy or pump water, it is vital that information on average rainfall, moisture retention of the native soils, and the cultural needs of potential turfgrasses be cross-correlated with the size and capacity of the pumping plant, the irrigation system, and the watering program. This logical process will permit precise matching of irrigation needs to irrigation capacity so that the system is neither undersized and inadequate nor overengineered and wasteful. Weather stations connected to irrigation controls by computers are gaining popularity because they permit the superintendent to accurately match water application to loss (see figure 161). Additionally, drought-resistant turf varieties and moisture-holding soil amendments are becoming more popular on golf courses.

Existing Vegetation

An inventory of existing vegetation should also be included in the site analysis. Among the crucial areas of interest in this regard are the size, age, health, and species of trees, bushes, ground covers, and grasses (see figure 162). These plants are not only the best indicators of the total integration of climatic and growth factors, but may also influence the design of the course and the cost of construction. For example, in some parts of the country the clearing of woods and disposal of the debris may only cost $1,200 per acre. In other areas, perhaps only miles away, federal Environmental Protection Agency regulations may prohibit burning of refuse. This can force the cost up to $13,000 per acre if the material must be hauled from the site or buried. So the cost of clearing fifty acres can vary from $60,000 to $650,000, depending on the laws applicable to the site. If the construction budget is limited, preservation of woodlands in the overall design becomes a priority. Likewise, an inventory of existing plants may permit a plan for saving certain specimen trees or creating a plant nursery in which young desirable trees may be retained for later root ball transplant. In fact, on the Scottsdale project every significant tree or bush within 50 feet of either side of the golf hole corridor must be identified and mapped.

Figure 161. Weather stations are quickly becoming a necessity for contemporary golf course superintendents, to assist them with irrigation schedules, disease prediction, and long-term record keeping.

Legal Restrictions

Other items often included in a site analysis are descriptions and map locations of available utilities for the golf course, all existing utility easements, any rights of way, and mineral rights agreements. Increasingly, the location and description of any significant archaeological site or formation (see figure 163), or of rare or endangered plant or animal species, or even items of special historical and cultural interest, have become major elements that can affect the prospect of a golf course ever getting built. Those items should thus be noted on the feasibility study. After all, such specimens or artifacts need not be incompatible with the golf course. Many golf holes have been designed around old graveyards, Indian burial mounds, or primitive village sites. Such local touches are not only "politically correct," but they can enhance the overall sensibility of the golf course by establishing its integrity with the natural setting (see figure 164).

Maintenance Cost

Since most clients don't realize the scope or cost of long-term golf course maintenance, it may be useful to include a suggested equipment list with ballpark estimates of costs, a sample maintenance budget, and a projected mainte-

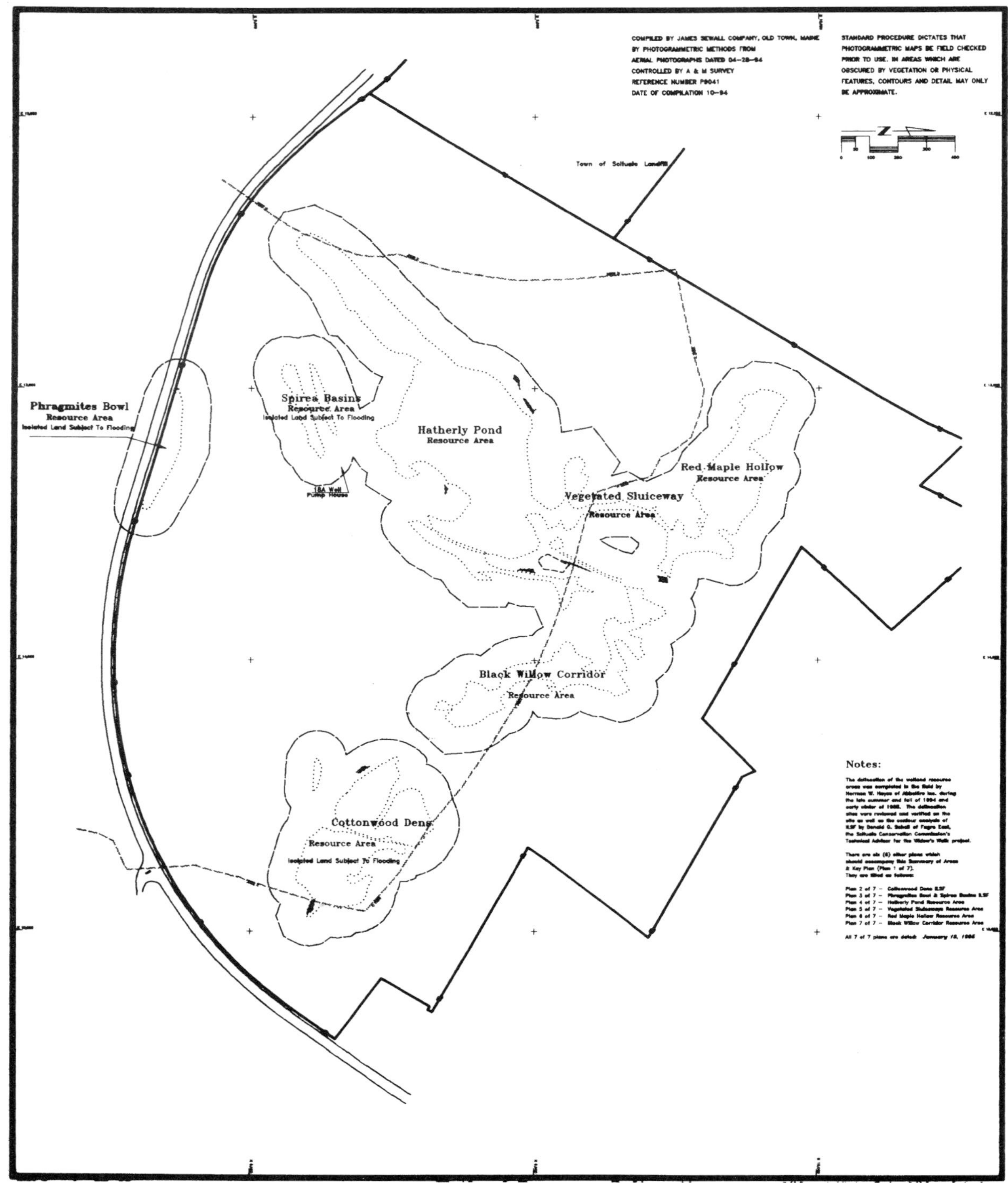

Figure 162. Vegetation and resource mapping of a site are done before any design begins. This map from Widow's Walk Golf Course, a national environmental demonstration project, in Scituate, Massachusetts is a good example of resource mapping.

Figure 163. Ideally, all archaeological work is completed before golf course planning begins, but when possible historical areas are discovered during construction, construction stops.

Figure 164. During a search of historical records for the Devil's Pulpit site it was learned that three young children had died of a mysterious disease and were refused burial in the public cemetery, and were buried on the family farm. The grave site was identified, the 6th hole designed around it, and a permanent marker was installed by the Devil's Pulpit Golf Association.

nance schedule for establishing and maturing the new golf course.

Lastly, if more than one routing plan is possible for a site, then the best two or three may be presented with the designer's comments (pro and con) for each. A possible detailed construction cost estimate for each layout should be presented if there is a noticeable cost difference between them.

Figure 165. All of these studies were done for Widow's Walk in Scituate, Massachusetts, before any detailed designing was complete. The process lasted over a year and cost in excess of $50,000.

Determining Feasibility

Armed with the completed feasibility study, the client should be able to sit down with his attorney, banker, accountant, and engineer and make an intelligent decision about the feasibility of his dream.

It should be clear that preparing a site feasibility study requires a broad range of expertise and a great deal of time. That is why there is an attendant fee of thousands of dollars to cover the costs of such an analysis and study. It may be the most important investment ever made by a potential golf course developer, for it will tell him much about his golf architect, the site, his associates, and himself. It has been this author's experience that only one out of ten projects ever met a client's expectations and was judged to be economically feasible. But in ten out of ten cases, potential clients agreed that the site feasibility study was the best money they'd ever spent. With recent upward spirals in costs of construction, land, and borrowed money, a feasibility study makes very good sense. Nevertheless, potential clients may be reluctant to undertake the investment of several thousand dollars just to find out that their "ideal site" may not be so ideal. If that is the case, then there is only one sure-fire way for them to save a truly substantial sum of money—by forgetting about the project altogether. It takes money to save money. A well-done feasibility study and site assessment is the best place to start (see figure 165).

Clients should be encouraged to select only the general area where they wish to build a golf course, and let the golf course consultant team help select the exact site or parcel of ground. This flexibility allows the developer to save hundreds of thousands of dollars, or perhaps more, by working with a well-adapted site as opposed to one with inherent problems. Rarely does this happen, but when it does the project is usually more financially sound and superior in its final product. (Before I designed Devil's Pulpit, my clients had me rate five possible sites, prioritize them, and then they set out to buy the highest rated site. They did, and the results speak for themselves.)

11

The Design Process

Each golf course site is unique. The lack of topsoil or the existence of shallow, hard rock layers may necessitate importation of soil. Perhaps excessive moisture or shallow groundwater may demand special drainage. Extensive tree clearing or earthmoving may be required. Some sites have unique geologic or environmental features that should be preserved. One site may require a higher construction budget to solve inherent problems than that for another site adjacent to it, yet the former might retain the potential to be a better golf course. An experienced golf architect knows the financial impact such problems present, and he knows that a sensitive routing plan will minimize these problems.

Sensing a Site

The ethereal part of the design process, of "sensing a site" and looking for its subliminal messages, is akin to the statement attributed to the sculptor who said, "In every piece of marble there is a masterpiece; it is only my duty to chip away the excess to free it." Similarly, on most sites there is the potential for a great golf course. The golf architect's duty is to expose and develop it (see figure 166). This same process of sensing a site applies not only to the entire golf course routing, but also to each individual tee, green, bunker, mound, lake, and tree location. This ability to read nature's messages, interpret them, and develop golf features in harmony with

Figure 166. Here I am on my first visit to the site that will become Devil's Paintbrush. Notice the foundations in the background, which are such a sinister part of the 17th hole.

Figure 167. A good contour map and a high hill, like at Widow's Walk in Scituate, Massachusetts, help the golf course architect "internalize" the rhythm and feel of a site.

those messages separates true artists from mediocre designers. However, on some featureless sites architects may compensate for lack of site character by moving huge quantities of fill or by creating artificial features intended to make dramatic statements. Often this works very well, but the designer must be cautious not to make the finished work look too contrived, particularly with repetitive mounding.

As the golf architect initially examines a potential site,he may first sense the rhythm and interval of the topography (see figure 167). This will help him decide possible alignment of major axes, for he knows it is best for holes to flow with the topography whenever possible. The more convoluted the surface of a site is, the more interesting golf features it may provide, but the more time and intellect will be required to internalize its character.

As a golf architect continues to sense or feel a site, he is probably more concerned about problem areas than about the relatively uncomplicated sections of the site (see figure 168). It is very easy to become enamored with the positive features of a site and to become blinded to its problems until they absolutely must be confronted, often well into the construction stage, when they are solvable only at exorbitant cost. More often than not, the client already has some preconceived notions about where certain great holes can be built, with little or no regard for the rest of the site. Architects are all too familiar with the client who shows off the site, and on the designer's first visit proclaims, "You see—there—that will be the signature hole."

Left to their own contrivances, clients might end up with one or two of the most spectacular holes in golf and sixteen others that are practically unplayable. In contrast, a golf architect thinks in terms of sharing certain striking site qualities to produce as many entertaining holes as possible to achieve a sound and balanced golf course. The most gifted architects are able to do what Alister MacKenzie did at Cypress Point. He creatively solved site problems while producing some of the most memorable, challenging, and interesting holes in golf.

Analyzing Drainage Patterns

Having internalized a feel for the ground, the golf architect will then identify major and minor drainage patterns. After all, surface drainage is the single most important surface feature on a golf course. Why, after all, pay to drain the water off with subsurface pipe when much of the surface water can be drained above ground. Without proper surface drainage, a golf course is difficult to maintain. Good design of drainage can lessen the amount of water, fertilizer, pesticides and

Figure 168. As the design team (golf course architect, environmentalist, engineer, golf course superintendent) walks the site, they are looking for problem areas and not the obvious special or natural features.

fossil fuels needed to maintain a golf course. Wet soil conditions encourage weeds to compete with turfgrasses, predispose turfgrasses to more diseases, impair mowing operations, contribute to compaction of soils, and amplify the damage caused by player traffic and (especially) golf carts. If slopes are less than 2%, then surface water will not move across turfgrass. Drainage problems for such flat surfaces must be solved by using subsurface drainage and shaping to get the water to the pipe, but this is expensive, time-consuming, and not totally effective. It is also subject to damage or clogging, and must have an outlet point—a place where subsurface water can be exhausted to atmosphere. At some very flat sites, such as in southern Florida, establishing drainage patterns is both a skill and a science.

At the Naples National site the contour change over 325 acres was about 10 inches, and there was a restricted amount of fill available to create earth forms (see figure 169). That scant amount of fill material was used to raise the center of golf holes into a slowly undulating and believable complex of shapes and slopes, and drain the fairways into the bordering trees, which we were able to preserve as well.

The skilled golf course architect will look for signs of standing water, often indicated by certain kinds of plants or color of soil, for these areas must be avoided or modified. In addition, he will look for evidence of existing surface or subsurface drainage, ground with springs, or wet weather seepage. He will search for rock outcroppings and try to determine the extent and depth of this rock and whether it can be moved without drilling and blasting. After all, ripping out rock with large bulldozers or explosives entails considerably higher removal costs than soil excavation. Rocky areas not only escalate construction costs but also produce shallow-rooted plants, which require more attention in long-term maintenance.

Identifying Environmental Resource Areas

The current environmental situation is that the general public has exaggerated fears of environmental impacts and "environmentalists" have too little information to satisfy those concerns. (Or worse yet, the environmentalists have the documentation but refuse to accept it, because it conflicts with their personal bias.) The result is a rather lengthy and costly permit process during which the golf course developer must prove his innocence instead of environmentalists showing his guilt. Although tomes of recent and mounting research exist that clearly show that a golf course can be safely built and maintained in all but the most fragile environments, this data is often ignored (see figure 170).

Figure 169. Naples National had a relatively small volume of earthmoving, but by concentrating it in the center of the hole, good drainage was gained and trees on the edges were preserved.

Instead, older, unsubstantiated, or unduplicated research using outdated products is often quoted to demonstrate the potential threat of a golf course, which further confuses or upsets an uninformed public. Environmental concerns most often arise because golf courses are highly visible and the public is highly sensitized to environmental degradation. A properly designed, built, and maintained golf course is a far less threat to public health than is the same area occupied by home lawns or gardens, or farmed with conventional techniques. (I strongly support close environmental scrutiny of proposed golf course projects and I endorse asking the tough questions, but when those questions are scientifically answered their responses should not be ignored. End of sermon.)

So as the golf course architect conducts his site assessment he looks for areas that might cause some environmental concern. These are usually certain plant communities, soil types, ground or surface water conditions, evidences of animal activity, or just conditions that depart from the norm (see figure 171). These areas will be annotated on the map or marked for reference, and then the owner is informed of their location. The prudent thing for the owner to do is to hire an expert to study the areas of concern and determine whether they will pose any future problem. If so, then whatever studies are necessary to identify the scope and nature of the problem should be conducted before any design work begins. If the area is to be avoided, then its boundaries should be surveyed and this information made part of the base map. Thus if the area concerned is to be avoided its exact location is known, or if it is to be impinged upon then an amount of impact can be measured (see figure 172). If a site has many such parcels or zones, then the environmental consultant may be asked to prioritize those areas so that emphasis is placed on avoiding the most important ones, and perhaps encroaching on only less important ones.

Soils

The golf architect may check soil profiles at various places on the site by having the client arrange to have a backhoe dig holes 8 to 10 feet deep, or have soil borings made to greater depths, if necessary. By examining these profiles,

Figure 170. Mistakenly, golf courses are sometimes seen as symbols of elitism, cultural dilution, and environmental liabilities. Feelings against golf courses have caused picketing in Hawaii and violence in Mexico.

Figure 171. Even on abandoned sandy quarry sites such as that used for Widow's Walk, establishing natural drainage patterns and depth and fluctuations in groundwater are important. Monitoring wells were installed as part of the site assessment program.

Figure 172. At Widow's Walk, a team of environmentalists reviews the site for its strengths and weaknesses, and assesses how development of the golf course might improve the now badly managed land.

often with the assistance of a soils expert, he will learn about the depth and texture of the topsoil, any hardpan or esoteric soil horizon, the groundwater table, the potential for ponds or lakes, and the internal drainage of the entire profile. This information could influence how he will route the golf course on the site.

Vegetation

During the site inspection process, a golf architect will note the distribution, variety, age, health, and general quality of the vegetation. If he discovers any specimen or outstanding feature, he will note its location precisely on his map so that it may be preserved and incorporated into the golf course. Personal onsite inspections permit a sensitivity that designing from maps and aerial photographs cannot approach. By spending time onsite, an accomplished designer not only maximizes the value of features and can route the course around them, but he can also specify protective devices, such as lightning rods or walls or drainage systems, to ensure the prolonged existence of such features.

Water Courses

If the site is blessed with a bisecting stream or river, a golf architect will determine its high water marks, the swiftness of its current, the cleanliness of its water, and where best to traverse it. If the site has previously supported crops, he may inquire about past farming practices and productivity. He will take samples of the topsoil to be tested for mineral and organic properties and pesticide residues.

Special Features

Lastly, there are many social, civil, and legal features of a site that must be investigated before starting to design a golf course. These include property lines, zoning restrictions, rights-of-way, easements, buried utilities, ancient ways, historical features, common land, and water use rights. These can often strongly influence a design, and need to be identified before the process begins. Like environmental characteristics, each of the "human" factors should be marked on the base maps and aerial photograph (see figure 173).

Establishing Design Goals

But even armed with the knowledge of a site's natural parameters, a golf architect still cannot intelligently begin planning the course. He must first sit down with the client and his planning team, consisting of the golf course architect, engineer, a building architect, land planner, environmental consultant, lawyer, financial advisor, golf course superintendent, and golf advisor. Collectively they determine what goals or objectives the client hopes to realize by building the project, and some generalized priorities and budget limits. After they have a complete base map showing all of the site factors discussed earlier, they determine the probable locations for entry roads, clubhouse, maintenance building, parking lots, home sites, utilities, and any other amenities planned for the property, such as a swimming pool, tennis courts, or hiking trails. Only after having identified these probable locations is he ready to route the golf course.

Schematic Design

The next step is for the golf course architect to go through a process called "schematic design." This is a method of trial and error conceptual planning which allows looking at many alternatives very quickly. Schematic designs are often called stick and ball drawings, because the standard notation is simple, such as a triangle for the backmost tee, a dot for dogleg points, circles for greens, and a straight line between these points to indicate the centerline of play. This method lacks detail and is meant only to show the spatial relationships of the golf course or its skeleton on the property.

The designer begins by identifying each potential clubhouse site and blocking out about 3 to 5 acres of land which would allow for buildings, parking, swimming pool, tennis, etc. Next, the golf course designer tries to locate the golf learning center, which can be anything from a simple warmup range (5 to 8 acres) to a full-service golf

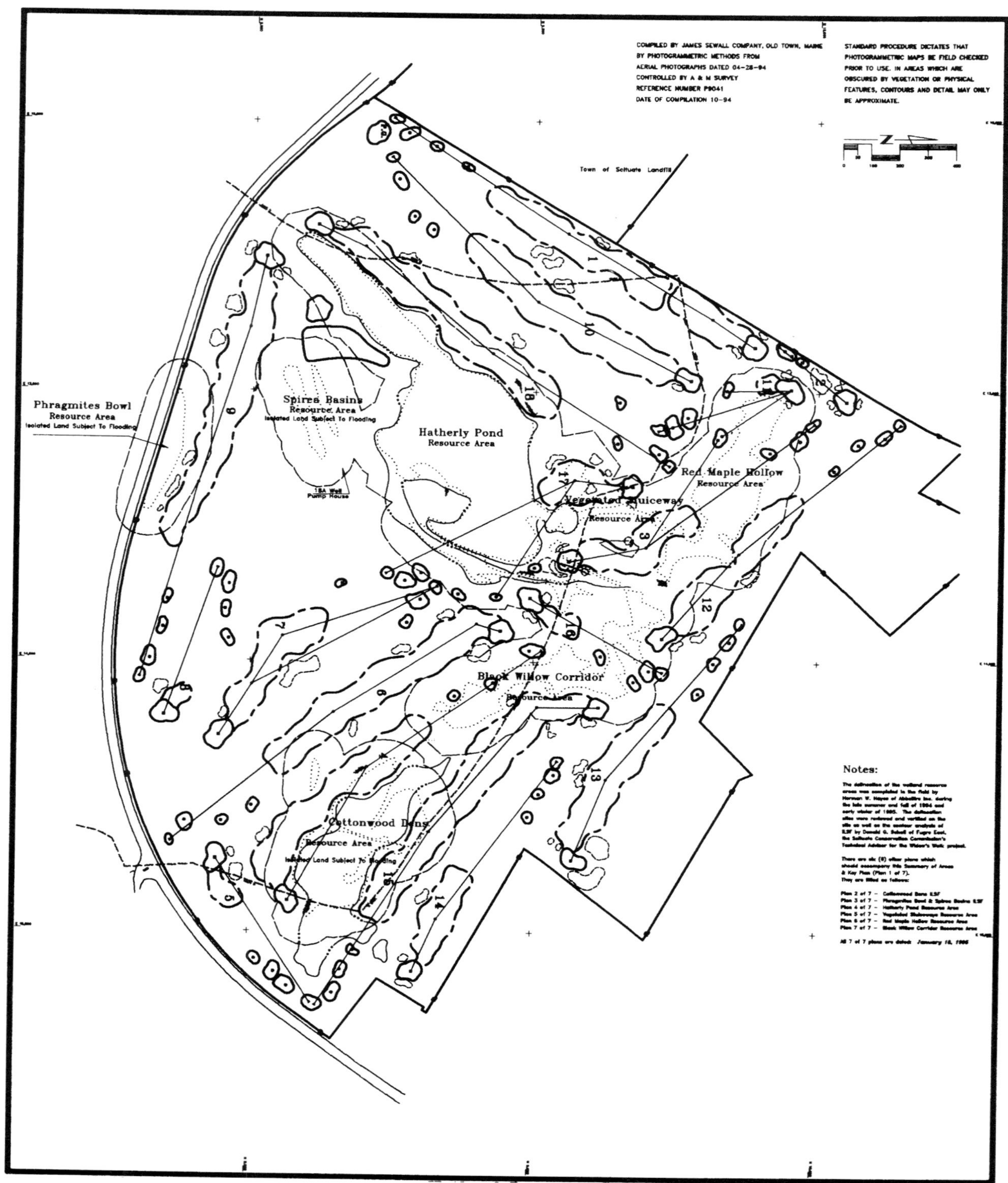

Figure 173. All site factors and resource areas must be transferred to one map and the golf course routed to minimize any impacts on them.

academy that can use up to 50 acres. But whatever the size, the range/academy should ideally be located near the clubhouse, on level or downward sloping ground, and in an area rather devoid of good vegetation. Once these major land gobbling complexes are sited, then the designer turns his attention to fitting in golf holes.

If the course is to be 18 holes, an architect must allow for starting and finishing holes for each nine. These should begin and end in proximity to the clubhouse. He must select those four tee and green positions first, and then make everything else work around them. If the client does not demand or the site does not accommodate returning nines, then he need only plan a first and last hole near the clubhouse.

Rules of Thumb

There are several rules of thumb followed in routing a course. None are sacred, but they do work well when a conventional layout is desired:

1. The starting holes, the first and tenth, should play rather docile to get golfers moving. A rather short par 4 with few hazards on the slice side (for right-handers) and a rather gentle green is ideal. Likewise, so is a medium-long par 5 where players can safely hit second shots without fear of reaching and disturbing golfers on the green. Short par 5's should be avoided.
2. Unless the course is strictly private the first and tenth tees should be positioned near one another so one starter can control play off both tees.
3. If possible, the first par 3 should not occur until the third or fourth hole in order to keep play from bogging down.
4. There should always be adequate safety buffers between adjacent holes.
5. There should not be more than 100 yards of travel between a green and the next tee.
6. Anticipated impact areas should permit a group to view players ahead.
7. A golfer should be able to see the second landing area or the putting surface from the normal approach shot distance on holes that play uphill, so upward grades should be at 4% or softer.
8. Where possible, long uphill climbs should not exceed a 5% slope so that a golfer of average health can walk the course without undue exertion. Also, no uphill slope over 10% should be more than 100 yards, if at all possible.
9. All slopes that are to be maintained by power riding equipment should not exceed 40%.
10. Since a majority of golfers slice the ball, the course should be routed so that few or no out-of-bounds or penal hazards are on the right side of any hole. This means that the course normally flows in a clockwise fashion.
11. A good middle distance for an 18-hole golf course is about 6,300 yards, but the course should be able to stretch to 7,000 yards or more from the pro tees and be as short as 5,000 yards from the front tees. Five sets of tees are preferred, with one set providing a total length of around 5,600 yards and the blue markers giving a course of 6,700 yards or so.
12. Green and tee sites should be appropriately sized to the anticipated wear they will receive and the shot being played to them. They should remain in scale with their surroundings.
13. Harsh hazards should be visible or their locations indicated so that golfers may elect either to risk or avoid them.
14. Great diversity in the length of holes should be provided so that every club in the bag will be tested and monotony avoided.
15. Space should be provided for practice putting greens and, if possible, a practice range with a large tee of one acre or more. Given a choice between a big golf course with a small learning center and a shorter course with a larger learning center, it is best to provide for the large learning center. Not only do good players demand a place to further improve their game, but

learning centers also permit beginners to develop their rudimentary skills.

16. Avoid middle distances of par 3's greater than 200 yards, par 4's less than 300 yards, and par 5's greater than 550 yards.

Noticeably absent from these general rules are the old saws about no holes playing into the setting sun, no parallel holes, or par changing on every hole. While they are valid ideas and are usually desirable, most golf course sites are not large enough to afford all such luxuries. Besides, at least a hundred famous courses violate most of these old standards. Cypress Point, for instance, features consecutive par 5's, consecutive short par 4's, and consecutive par 3's. At the Firestone South Course in Akron, Ohio, fourteen holes run parallel to at least one other hole. Royal Dornoch in Scotland, the golf course laid out by Old Tom Morris—Donald Ross learned his trade—opens with two holes straight into the morning sun, and the closing hole heads due west.

Design Process Example

Once the starting and ending points are determined, the development of a routing plan becomes a series of trial and error in plotting individual tee positions, landing areas, and green sites. At each major play area, a golf architect analyzes its good and bad features and decides what could be done to improve it. The process might best be described as mentally playing the golf course. To help illustrate this process we will use as an example the Ironhorse Golf Course for the City of Leawood, a suburb of Kansas City, Kansas.

The site was part of a private/public agreement where a housing developer gave the city the piece of land for the golf course while he kept the surrounding land for development. This is not an uncommon arrangement, whereby the developer doesn't want to be in the golf business, or he can't finance the golf course, and the city wishes to expand its recreational holding while operating a profit-producing golf course.

The developer naturally took the most buildable land to develop and gave the city a series of hilltops and bottomland of a creek that regularly floods (see figure 174). The site was bisected by a large overhead power line, the creek, a buried oil pipeline, and a storm sewer right-of-way. The creek floodplain had deep soil deposits, while the hilltops were a mixture of thin soils over soft rock, or bare, hard rock deposits. The vegetation varied from poverty grass on the thin soils to isolated pockets of fine old trees.

At Ironhorse the golf course site was further bisected by Mission Road—the main access to the site—which was going to require widening. Since the road was to be rebuilt, a tunnel could then be installed under the road near the creek with only a modest additional cost of about $2,000 per foot. But budgets and topography would only allow for one tunnel. This meant the hole routing had to line up with the only possible tunnel location so it could handle both in and out traffic.

So the challenge was to fit a hole routing that started and ended on top of a 60-foot-high hill, avoided an overhead power line and underground pipeline and sewer, protected Mission Road, required only one tunnel, and had to coexist with an unbridled stream that would regularly flood 3 to 4 feet above its banks. In addition, the course could not be expensive to build despite the steep hills and rocky subsoils, it had to play fun and fast for average golfers, and it had to be worthy of consideration for national recognition. No sweat.

To ensure affordable green fees, the City set reasonable but restricted budgets for total development. With construction funds limited and the site requiring inordinate expenditures for bridges, drainage, rock moving, etc., skillful routing around problem areas was necessary. To exemplify the process, I offer the following internal discourse using maps on accompanying pages, which effectively reproduces my thoughts in the early design phases of Ironhorse in Leawood, Kansas (see figure 175).

Establish Administrative Points

First I must identify a possible clubhouse location that can be serviced with utilities, is easily accessible, provides good views, and allows

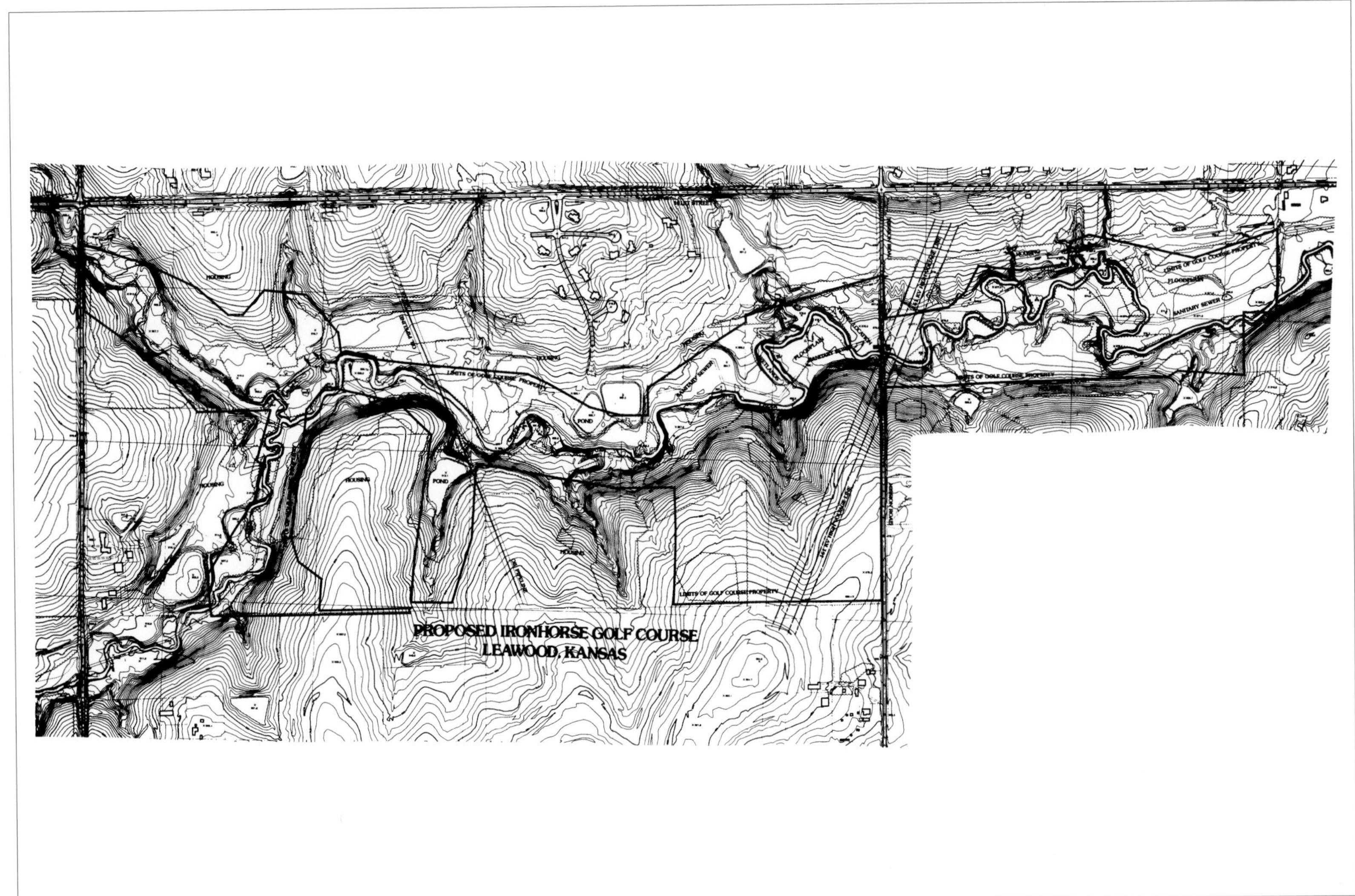

Figure 174. Site map for proposed Ironhorse Golf Course in Leawood, Kansas. Notice that the housing is on the high ground and the golf course must deal with high tension lines, a creek, a floodplain, wetlands, a sanitary sewer, an oil pipeline, Mission Road widening, and installing a golfer's tunnel near the creek.

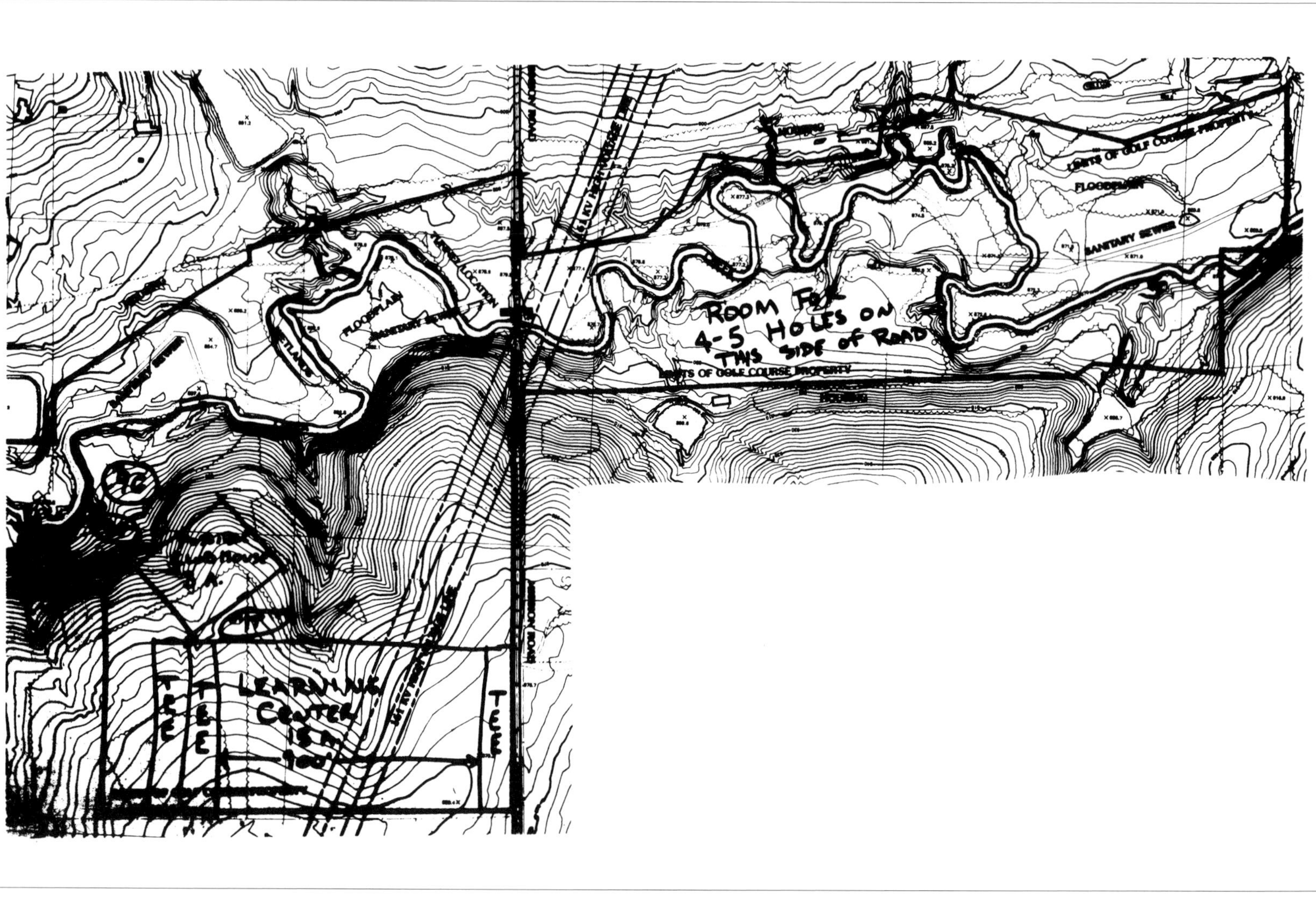

Figure 175. First, I locate a possible clubhouse site, followed by the learning center, since these two features require so much space. Then I locate possible starting (1st & 10th tees) and finishing (9th & 18th greens) points. Lastly, I make a quick determination about how major obstacles (Mission Road) will limit the number of holes that will fit in within a block of ground.

for returning nines. Obviously a central location permits the most variety of routings for the golf course, but at Ironhorse so much of the land is floodplain that my choices are limited to high ground. I study the map and select a hilltop, back about 325 yards from the road, with commanding views of the creek.

"From this possible clubhouse and parking site (for which I have blocked out a 3-acre hilltop), it looks as if the best way to handle the power lines is to put the learning center/driving range under them, so I will reserve 15 acres for it."

(Using my engineer's scale, I now block out an area that measures 1,200 feet by 500 feet that allows for tees at both ends with 45 to 50 stations, and 900 feet from front of tee to front of tee.)

(Having comfortably sited these important and large facilities, I now mentally divide the remaining property into right and left halves for each nine holes. Then I look for starting or finishing points on each half that are within 100 yards of the clubhouse.)

(Using an engineer's scale I quickly calculate that on the other side of Mission Road I could fit no more than five holes, so that means at least four holes have to go on the clubhouse side of Mission. A measurement shows I have easily enough room for three holes but not for four comfortably, unless one or two of those holes could be a space-saving par 3. Still considering only the right half of the site, a map study shows I have at least one decent tee (#1) and green (#9) location near this clubhouse site. The #1 tee was at the top of the hill, and the large fairly flat spot for the #9 green was about halfway up the hill and below the clubhouse site. Perfect and perfect.)

"Assuming these two sites might give me a starting and finishing point, I can now try to fit the first nine holes that work with all the above parameters." (see figure 176)

Fitting in Holes

"This looks like the most extreme back tee position for hole #1, so I'll mark it with a small triangle, and scale out 810 feet to see what the possible landing areas look like for a professional golfer's tee shot."

(Anchored at the tee position at one end, sweeping the scale across the map to form an arc gives me some idea of possible landing areas that include the hilltop straight out toward Mission Road (position "A"), a very narrow and deep valley off to the far left (position "B"), and the hillside in between (position "C")).

"The top of the hill toward Mission ("A") is higher than the tee, so the tee shot might be blind, there are two ugly poles from the power line there, and there is no room for the green unless the hole has a 90° dogleg. So the hilltop landing area stinks."

"The far left ("B") valley, on the other hand, gives a great downhill tee shot, but the landing area is in the creek; the hillside is all rock, so widening it out for a fairway will be expensive; and once I get to the bottom of the hill, where in the world would I go next? I also am infringing a little too much on the possible clubhouse site, so the valley is out, too."

"The only other consideration is the hillside ("C"), which might require some rock blasting to create a landing zone, but it minimizes the ugliness of the power lines, the hole can play slightly downhill, and there is room for a 160-yard second shot with only a slight dogleg to a possible green location (position "D")."

"But to build the hole will require a large pipe across the valley, lots of fill material to cover it and raise the fairway, and I remember from my site assessment that there is lots of rock here. Not the best, but a lot better than the hilltop or valley."

(Next I note the elevations of the tee, landing area, green, and all major high or low spots between these points. These spot elevations tell me if I need to cut away earth, make fills, or just leave things on the existing grade. If I question my sight line from the tee then I will use graph paper to make a cross-section of the hole to help identify more precisely how much earthwork will be required to make the hole function. Similarly, once I have a tentative centerline established, using the scale I make readings either side to determine a rough estimate of cut and fill for the hole, as shown below.)

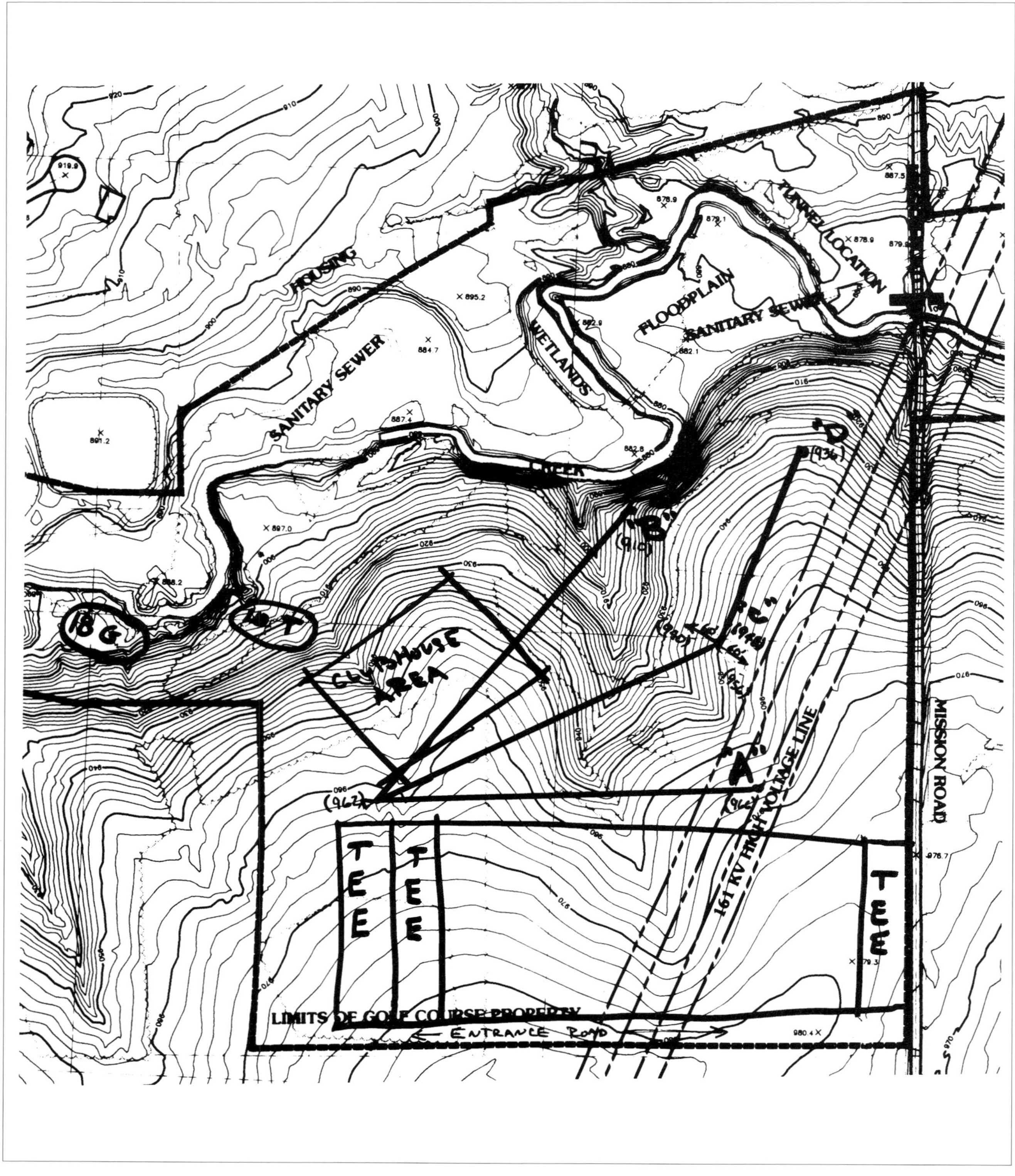

Figure 176. From backmost possible tee location, or pro tee, for 1st hole, various directions for a 810 foot (270-yard) drive are analyzed.

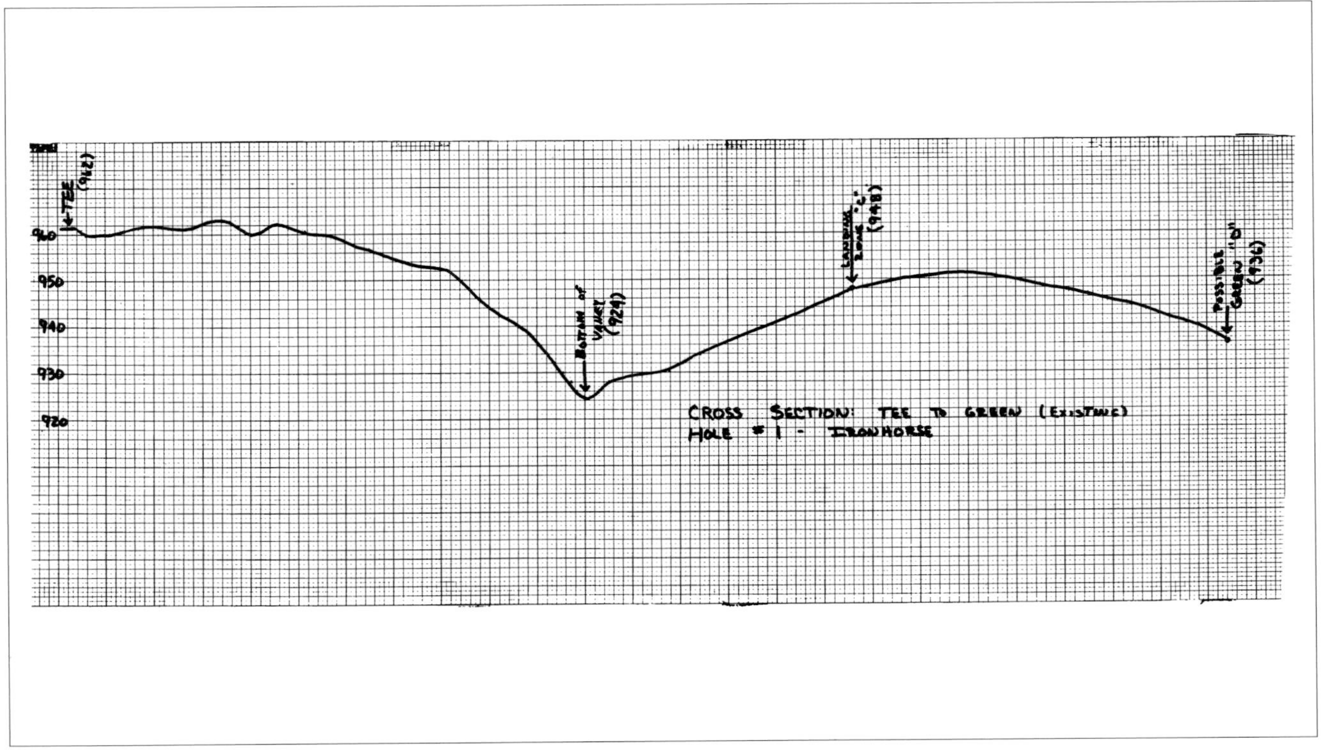

Figure 177. Cross section of topography down the centerline of play (tee to "C" to "D") to help estimate amount of possible earthmoving required.

"Let's see, the existing spot elevations are 962 for the tee, 948 for the landing area, and 936 for the green. Great—the hole is generally playing downhill, but now I must estimate how much I must cut or fill to make it work."

(I graph the centerline with an exaggerated horizontal vector, as shown in figure 177, and I immediately see that the valley in front of the tee must be filled, the hillside landing area must be leveled out, and the ridge between the landing area and green must be cut.)

"So I know I will cut and fill on this hole, but how much, and will the amount of cut balance the fill requirement?"

I have simplified the above thought process, for it is probably as boring for the reader to follow as it is intuitive for me to do. Mastering the art of routing golf holes only requires the ability to read and visualize topography, an analytical and creative mind, and lots and lots of practice. The basic skills to sensitively route a course can be taught, as can the basics of playing a musical instrument, but to reach the status of virtuoso requires a great measure of hard work and a touch of divine blessing. Some golf course architects go through an entire career without truly showing the genius in routing that could distinguish them and their courses. Massive earthwork and artistic shaping can somewhat mask an indifferent routing, while a superior routing—such as at Pine Valley, Dornoch, or Cypress Point—works naturally.

Earthmoving

"I want the fairway landing area to be at least 40 yards wide and I want to save the trees on the left side of the fairway, so I don't want to disturb their roots with cut or fill. So I measure over 20 yards from the centerline to find the left fairway edge and I note the elevation at that point, which is 940. Then I measure over 20 yards to the right fairway edge and find an elevation of 956, so now I know there is 16 feet of right-to-left fall across the fairway and I only want 4 feet of pitch, or approximately 3%. So if I leave the left edge at natural grade 940, the center of the fairway must become 942, and the right edge will be 944. The existing elevation of the center of the fairway is 948 and I want 942, so a 6-foot cut is required at the center point and a 12-foot cut at the right fairway edge."

For rough calculations I say the *average* cut to get the fairway is going to be 6 feet deep over an area of 200 feet wide by 200 feet long. The total cut volume is then calculated as:

$$\frac{200\text{ ft} \times 200\text{ ft} \times 6\text{ ft}}{27\text{ cu. ft./cu. yd.}} = \frac{240{,}000}{27} = 8{,}888.9\text{ cu. yd.}$$

or 9,000 cu. yd. for rough estimating purposes

Using the graph paper, I see that to fill in the valley in front of the tee will require a 10-foot average fill, which I calculate to be 3,000 cubic yards (80 feet wide × 100 feet long × 10 feet deep ÷ 27 = 2,962 or 3,000 cubic yards.)

"So I generated 9,000 yards of cut in the landing area and used 3,000 of it in the valley, so I still have 6,000 cubic yards of material to use up. Perhaps I can raise the back tees and use 3,000 yards and lose the rest on the driving range tee near by. I will leave the final decision on what to do with this excess fill for a later stage of refining the work called design development."

(Now I know the center of the fairway must be at 942 to save left-side trees, so I plot this on my graph paper and now determine what this does to the green site, which is at an elevation of 936. The green is blocked out by a ridge, which peaks at elevation 952 about 40 yards in front of my dogleg point. By drawing a line on my graph from landing zone elevation 942 to green elevation 936, I see that I must make a 10-foot cut in the fairway to see the green. By quick calculations, this means about an additional 15,000 cubic yards of fill material, too, for a total cut of 24,000 cubic yards.)

"This is a lot of excess fill, so perhaps I can lessen the cut and use some fill by raising the green elevation a few feet—besides, I remember some hard rock surfaces showing up about the 940 to 942 elevation, and this will help avoid it." (I verify the rock by looking at my field notes.)

"Okay, let's raise the green by 3 feet to elevation 939 and see what this does (see figure 178)." I regraph the new elevation and "eureka, it works." (Not only do I reduce the ridge cut to 10,000 cubic yards, but I also might be able to use about 4,000 cubic yards of excess fill in the green complex, since the green site is falling away from me, or is on a reverse pitch.)

"So far I know that with a little adjustment to the clubhouse area, hole #1 as I have sited it will generate about 19,000 cubic yards of cut to build. I can only use about 10,000 cubic yards in raising the tee, filling the valley, and building the green, leaving about 9,000 yards to haul away to the range. I might hit rock in the landing zone or ridge cut that will require blasting, and I must install a 24-inch or 36-inch pipe in the valley to handle upslope runoff, but the damn hole will work, so now let's find hole #2."

Fitting the Second Hole

"Let's see. Between the first hole and the creek I have left a small portion of hilltop, and then it falls steeply into the creek (see figure 179). Better stay off that steep hillside at all costs to avoid wiping out all the trees growing there, messing with the rock poking out everywhere and the steep slope that terminates into the creek. But I do have enough room for a skinny tee if I play back toward the clubhouse, and it looks like the landform over there will accept a landing zone."

(Again I select and mark the extreme back tee position, anchor one end of the scale there, and sweep an arc to determine the possible landing zones across the steep valley and up onto the hilltop.)

"This line of play works fine and there is sufficient room for tees on this side of the valley, but if I leave the clubhouse where I initially

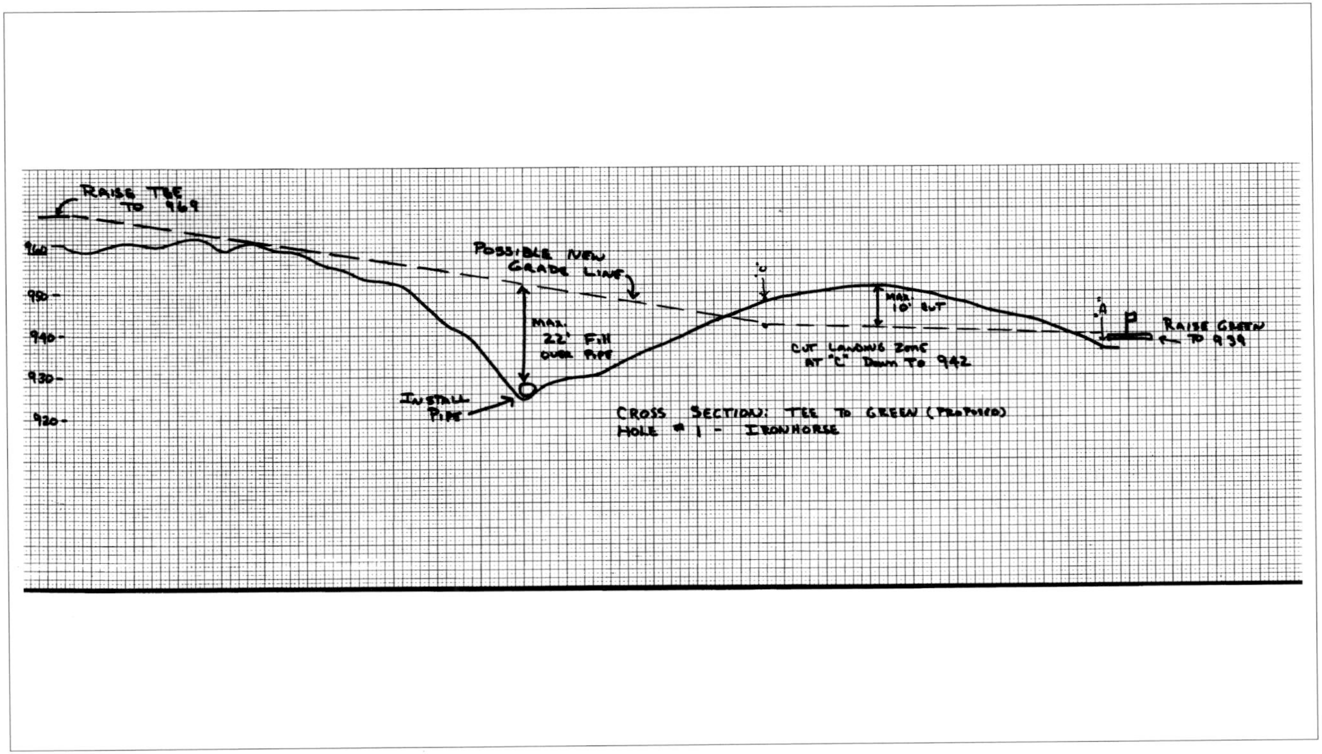

Figure 178. Possible gradelines for 1st hole are determined by cross-sectioning grade adjustments.

spotted it, drives will land in the clubhouse patio (map symbol "A"). Since this violates one of my safety guidelines, should I move the clubhouse—or make the second hole a par 3? I don't like par 3's until at least the third hole unless there are some strong reasons to violate that guideline."

(I know this could be a good clubhouse location and the range and the first hole work well, so being open-minded I continue to sweep the scale, noting distances to possible par 3 green locations.)

"Here is one at 240 yards at the top of the hill right in front of the clubhouse (map symbol "B"). A par 3 might look great from there and would avoid the hard rock layers that I know exist on that hillside. But the front tees must be built on this side of the valley so the shortest distance this par 3 would play is 170 yards, but it would be uphill and may be blind. This would be an unplayable hole for weaker hitters. So the green at the top of the hill idea is a last resort. A very last resort."

"How about this little flat place about one-third of the way down the hill? Back tee distance is 200 yards (map symbol "C") and the front tee shot is only 110 yards across the valley to a green at about the same elevation. That works. Now let's check grades."

(On par 3's I usually don't graph the centerline, but rather just note the tee and green elevations and visually inspect what the contours are doing in between.)

"For Ironhorse #2, the tees are at elevation 924 at the back and 928 at the front, with the green at 933. Oh heck, it's still an uphill par 3, with the front tee higher than the back. But it does fit the space if not the topography, so let's do some grade manipulation to see if it works."

(First I will use some of the excess dirt from

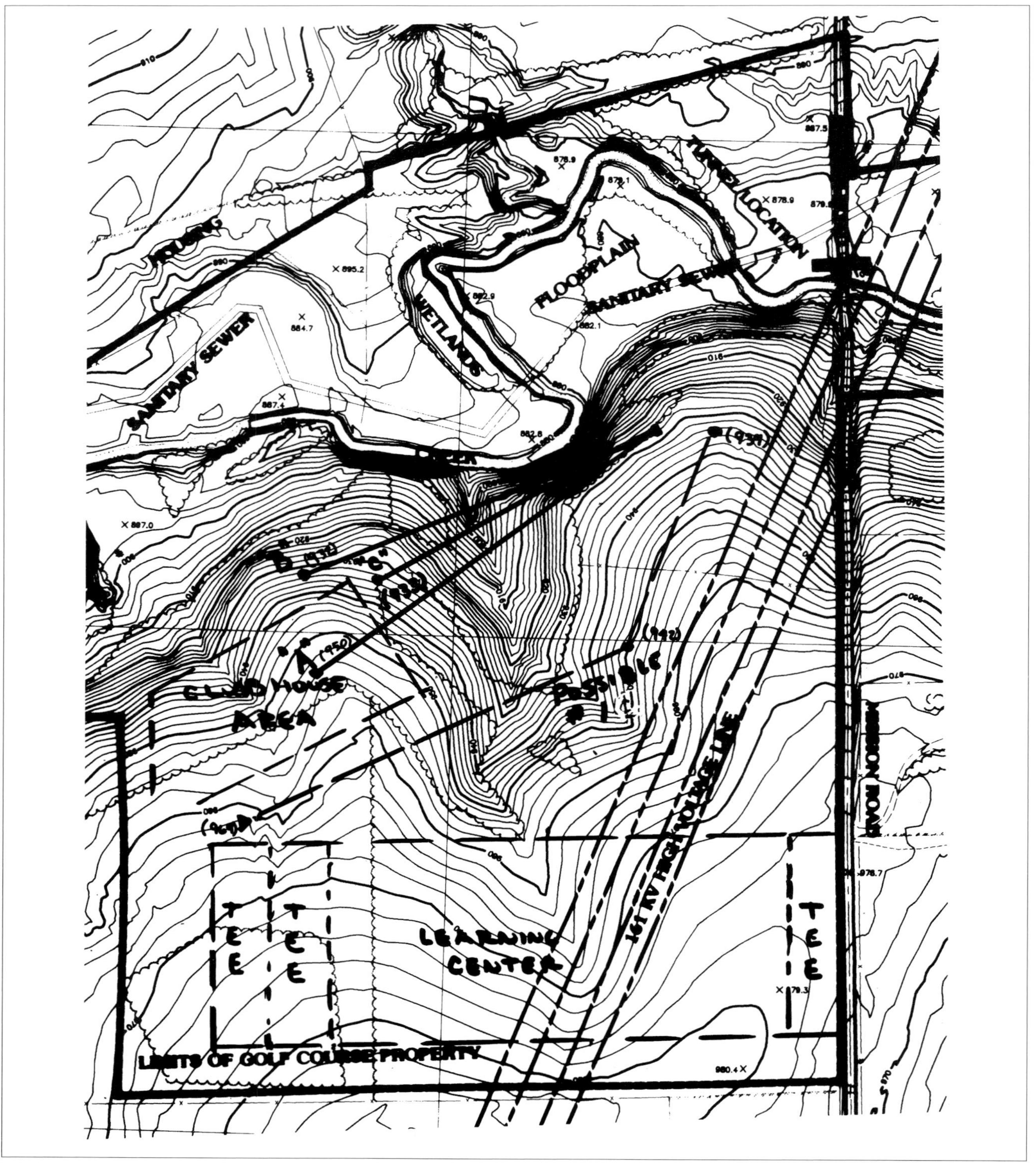

Figure 179. The same trial and error process, or war gaming, is done to find a possible location for the 2nd hole at Ironhorse Golf Course in Leawood, Kansas.

#1 to raise the back tee about 4 or 5 feet to 928 or 929. Then I can cut in the front tees to get line-of-sight from the back tee over the front tee, which is now also 928. I will try to drop it to 924, even though I know the hard rock layer starts at 927 or so. This may require drilling and blasting, but I will worry about that later.)

"The tees work, but the green must be cut into the hill at least 6 or 8 feet to elevation 926 or 928. Seems I wrote in my field notes—and I was right—that the hard rock layer starts at 927 or 928, so again I am faced with rock blasting to achieve the proper elevations. Not only don't I have enough budget to do much blasting, but this is only the second hole. However, the hole fits the space, it saves trees, the rock faces will look nice—so let's move on to see where the third hole will fit."

Fitting the Other Seven Holes

Fortunately, the third hole fit perfectly into the land available by placing the tee on the hill beside #2 green, driving across the creek in the valley to a wide landing area, and then across the creek again to the green (see figure 180). It was a downhill hole, except that the green has to be raised to stay above the flood elevation of 885. But best of all, this hole lined up perfectly with the tunnel location to get to the hole on the other side of Mission Road.

At this point I have located three golf holes on the ground and I have used only symbols for the tee(s), land area, and green. At each symbol I write the elevation at that point and sometimes the elevation I want the finished feature to be, if it is important. I continue this process until I locate all 18 holes using only this stick-and-ball format. But as skeletal as it is, it permits me and the other planning team members to evaluate one possible way to use the ground. I normally try several schematic designs out of each clubhouse site, using a thin tracing paper material so I can overlay one upon another for comparison to analyze the strength and weakness of each plan. As you can see by the Ironhorse maps I was able to get hole numbers 4 through 8 on the isolated piece of ground, line up with the tunnel again, and get hole #9 back up to the green location I initially selected at the beginning of this exercise. Sometimes routing plans can be done in hours; other times it takes days of trial and error map work—measuring, graphing, calculating, and trying every option.

If housing is to be part of the plan, then I draw in boundary lines I think I will need to safely construct the golf hole(s) to form a golf corridor.

Reviewing Schematic Design

Then I present my schematic designs to the other team members, along with my logic that resulted in each particular routing. At this point others on the team critique the plan based upon their area of expertise, and we agree to discard the seemingly nonfunctional ones and refine the best ones. Those schematic designs that seem to make sense then go to the other planners, who try to work in their designs along the golf hole corridors. We meet often, visit the site, and further evaluate which plans work or need to be modified, until it is generally agreed to limit our options to one or two "best" possibilities.

Design Development

Once the routing works, then it is refined during a process called "design development," where more detail is added to the golf course skeleton. At this stage the golf course architect begins to evaluate locations, sizes and shapes of additional tees, fairways, green complexes, bunkers, hazards, and water features.

The goal of design development is to reach a "master plan" of the project that has addressed every possibility and detail of the plan, short of working drawings. So now I start to add the muscle, sinew, and tissue to the golf course skeleton by using standard symbols for golf course features. It is during this phase when the golf course is actually designed, for it involves thinking about such issues as golf strategy, drainage, earthmoving, maintenance, integrating environmental resources, allowing for integrated pest management, and visual and sensory impacts. The most important of those design issues is reasonable safety for golfers, maintenance personnel, and adjacent land users. After that,

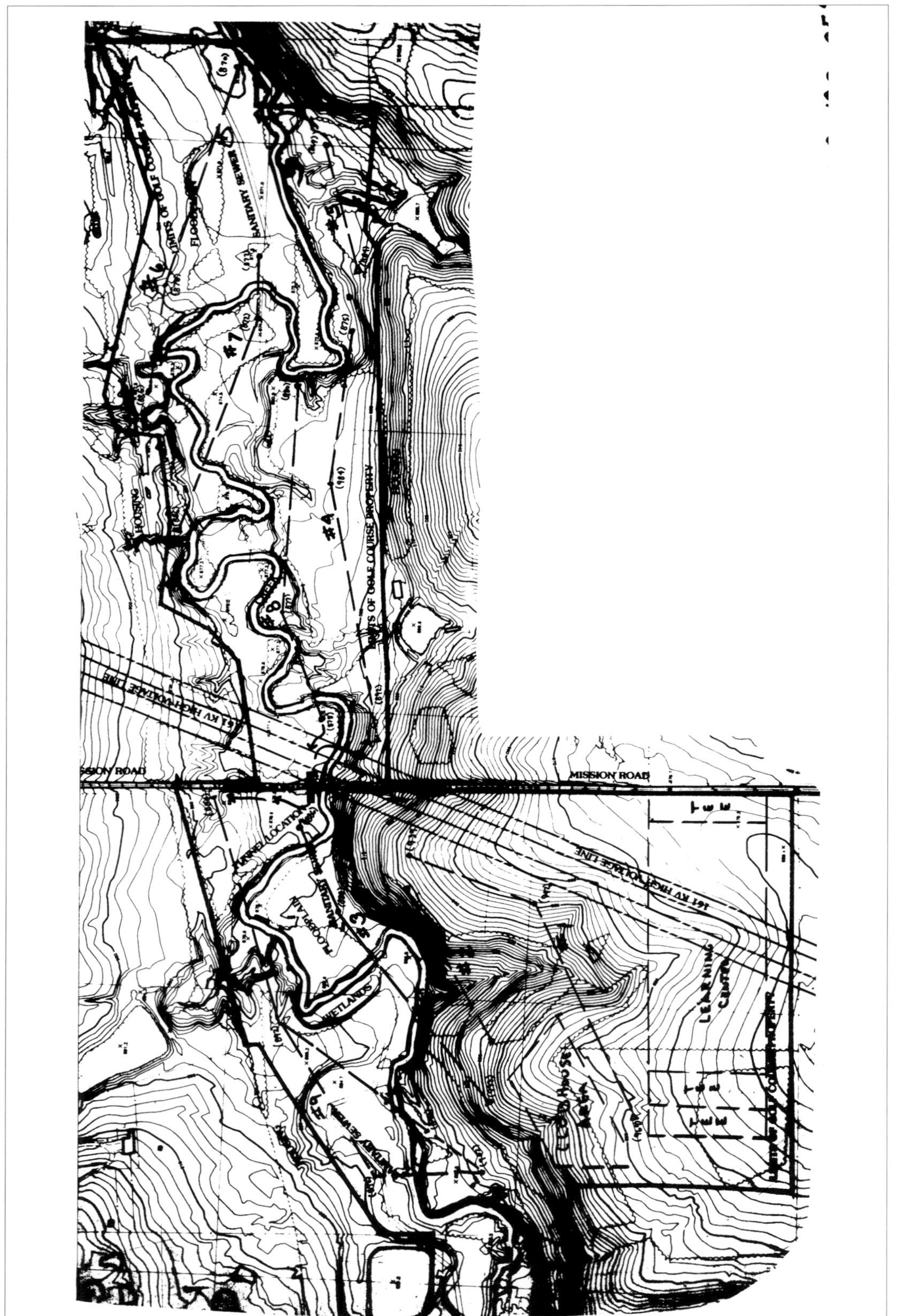

Figure 180. Schematic design of the first nine holes at Ironhorse Golf Course. Triangles represent location of pro tees, dots symbolize landing points or greens, and elevations are given for each key location.

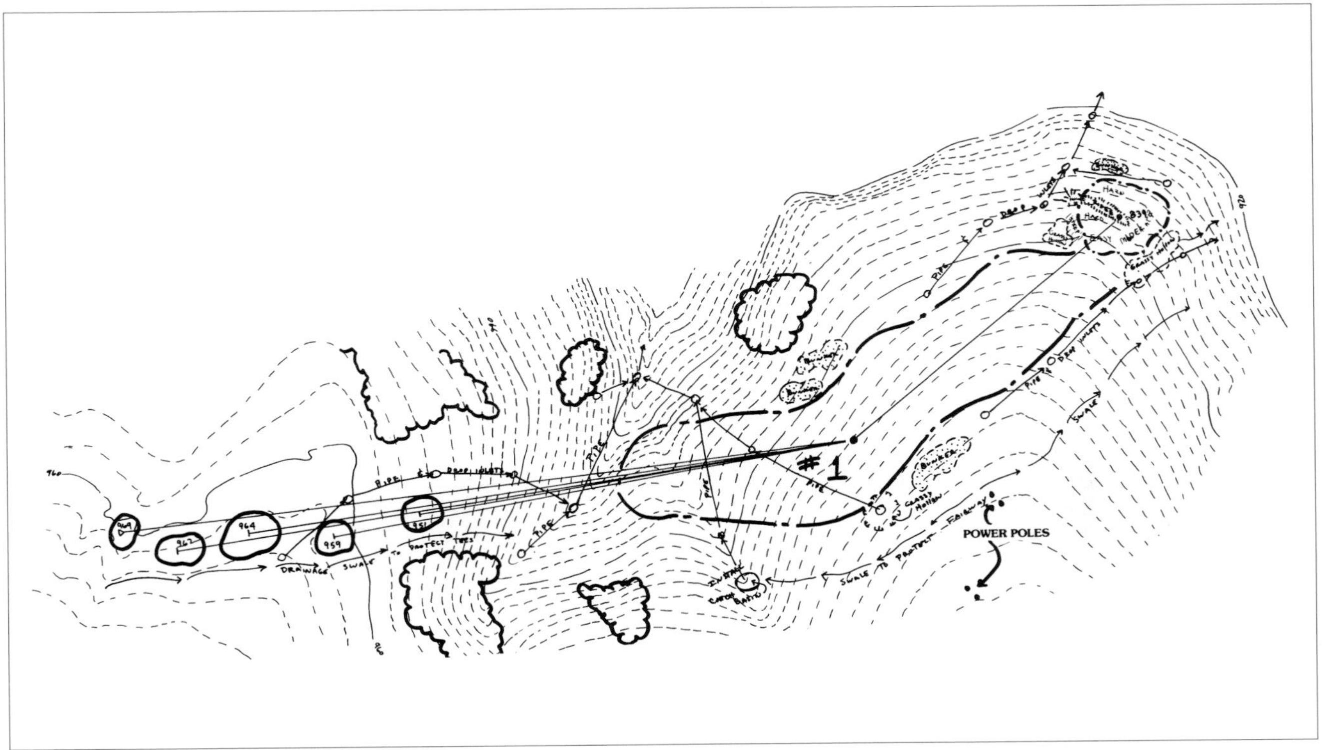

Figure 181. During design development, the golf course architect not only places and sizes the golf features correctly, he also considers drainage and strategy.

drainage shapes the golf hole by dictating flow patterns, earthmoving, and shaping of drainage basins or containments. Once the golf hole is physically correct for drainage then the strategy issues determine hazard placement and together allow a further refinement of earthmoving.

Planning Drainage

My drainage thought process for the first hole at Ironhorse might read as follows.

"First, I see that the tees are at or above grade, so surface water drains away from them (see figure 181). But I do need to intercept the surface water off of the hillside in front and to the right side of the tee."

(Checking my field notes, I verify that the valley in front of the tee had an erosion that was 4 feet deep and showed evidence of extensive turbulence.)

"Well, we'll put a corrugated metal pipe under this fairway to handle this water, and the erosion must be filled. But I wonder about how large of a pipe we must install?"

(Going back to my contour map, I outline the watershed into the valley. Then, using a planimeter I determine the watershed area to be 100 acres. Using standard formulas, I compute the size of the needed pipe, based on watershed size, slope, vegetation cover, and a 50-year rainfall maximum.)

"Okay, I'll need a 36-inch corrugated metal pipe through this valley, starting at just behind the tee and terminating 700 feet away on the left side of the fairway. I'll also specify a flared end section at the head of the pipe, a concrete headwall, and a rip-rapped plunge pool at the bottom end. To handle this water, plus what will enter the valley from side hills, I should plan a grass waterway from the terminus of the pipe to the little creek way down the valley toward the second hole. Good—that should handle the stormwater and make this hole very playable for all golfers."

"Above the fairway cut I also need a drainage swale to stop water from running down onto the fairway, but I don't want golfers to see it so I'll put it 8 feet above the playing surface and hide it with earth shaping. I'll also stop water from crossing the fairway by cutting in a series of grassy hollows along the bottom of the cut, then tile drain them across the fairway."

"The green is raised above grade except on the right side where I expect water to drain toward the green. I'll catch it in grassy hollows and drain them with pipes. This means the putting surface will be about 30 feet away from the right slope of the hill cut, and the shape of the hill lends itself best to a long thin green that runs diagonally to the play line."

Selecting the Green Site

(Using my scale, I make a few measurements to get a rough idea of the site. Since I want a putting surface of about 6,000 square feet, I look for an area that is about 100 feet long by 60 feet wide. At this point I'll either use an easily erasable pencil line or an overlay paper to sketch some possible putting surface shapes. By trial and error and past experience, I choose what I believe is the best shape and sketch it onto the map.)

"Since this hole is short and I have some slope to work with, I think I'd like to split the green with a 2-foot-high ridgeline that comes out of a mound on the left side and tails away to nothing in the middle of the green. That's the easiest part of the green to hit from the right side of the fairway. But in order to reward the skillful player who plays boldly to this left rear pin position, and to defend against indifferent shot-making, I'll leave this left front mound with a steep front slope. Shots played short will land on the sharp slope, which I'll leave as a grassy hazard. Behind the ridgeline on the left rear of the putting surface I'll build a sand bunker to challenge the overly aggressive player. But this was a pretty good shot that ended up in the bunker so I'll make the bunker shallow and as flat as possible to make recovery easy. This bunker will also give this green a strong visual backdrop. The easiest shot to the green is from the right side. So I think I'll defend the right side of the fairway with a sand bunker that starts out about 230 yards from the middle of the tee and flows out into the fairway, making the landing area at 260 yards (300 yards from the pro tee) only 30 yards wide. The light color and intimidation factor of this bunker will draw the golfer's eye down to the ground and away from the power poles, and it will help visually turn the hole. The left side of the fairway is protected by the trees I left, but to visually balance the hole I need to add some accent right at the corner of the dogleg, so say hello to a second bunker. Both should show nicely from the tee."

"Let's see, for everyday play, 80% of the green is open to receive shots from anywhere on the fairway. But during competitions, when the pin is on the left rear, the best drive is close to the right fairway bunker in order to have the best angle to the green. The less bold can play safely to any part of the green, but they'll have a more difficult putt up across the ridgeline. This hole should look nice and play quickly. Oh well, let's move on to the next hole."

All of that mental calculation, graphing, plotting, and evaluation served simply to map out one hole. The same process is applied to each individual shot for each hole for the entire routing plan. By using this method, a skilled golf architect can make intelligent decisions concerning safety, construction problems, probable construction costs, playability, and the character of each hole and of the entire golf course. As he designs he'll have to make trade-offs, compromises, and sacrifices to try to plan a golf course that is enjoyable to play, easy to maintain, and in harmony with natural contours and environmental resources—and that can be built within an allowable budget.

Field Checking

After a golf architect has developed what he believes is an acceptable routing plan, he will then go to the site and field check his routing plans to make sure they work as well on the ground as he imagined them in his mind and on paper. He may centerline all of the holes, or he may simply select key points and locate them in the field. It is not uncommon for the golf course site to be obscured by heavy vegetation, high water, or crops, or to be inhabited with some not-so-friendly wildlife, like poisonous snakes, wild dogs, or pesky insects. In such situations he does the best he can until he feels confident that his plan will work.

The Master Plan

Finally, the master plan of the golf course that evolves should be sensitive to all the parameters that were set out initially as the owner's goals and objectives (see figure 182). But even this master plan is just the start of many more modifications to the routing that will take place to respond to concerns of environmentalists, permit agencies, zoning and legal restrictions, other development, etc. The Willowbend project on Cape Cod required 29 major master plan presentations until it was approved for construction by all the permit agencies. I estimate that the developer had a total investment in legal, engineering, architectural, and environmental professional services of nearly 2 million dollars.

Construction Document Phase

Once the master plan, sometimes called the feature plan, represents the golf course that he wants built, then the golf architect must produce construction documents (usually drawings and specifications) that communicate the details of the design to the contractor (see figure 183). This involves taking the conceptual plan and turning it into a "hard line" drawing that uses contour lines, spot elevations, and other symbols common to the profession. A complete set of detailed construction documents may require 400 to 500 man-hours if drawn manually, or one-quarter of that if a computer is used. As previously discussed, some designers prefer to do very specific drawings with less construction observation, while others prefer the reverse. I firmly believe in both, doing detailed documents for bidding and then providing intense personal attention to details and nuances in the field to get the best features possible. But whichever process is opted for, this is the next logical step. Often during the construction document phase the design will change because problems not previously discovered will arise whose only solution is a departure from the master plan. Situations which most commonly dictate such alterations are the requirement to balance cut and fill volumes in a given area, rock layers, blind areas, newly discovered features which must be protected, or changes in property lines. This phase of the work will be discussed in later chapters.

As an architect methodically develops his routing plan, he measures and estimates the volume of each phase of work (see figure 184). The major items may be clearing, earthmoving, large size drainage, tile drainage, soil amendments, areas to be seeded or sprigged, and irrigation. By estimating some rough totals for these quantities, he can apply realistic unit prices to them and prepare a probable construction cost. This cost is not firm, nor is it a bid. It is simply a ballpark estimate of the construction cost at that point in time. It is only after the detailed working drawings and specifications are finished and exact volumes measured that close approximations of anticipated bids will be possible. Even then, it's the bidding climate at the time of the bid opening that really counts. If there are few bidders, many other projects to bid on, or rapidly escalating costs for labor and material, then bids for a project could be significantly higher than if none of those conditions existed.

Most golfers never consider the design process of a golf course. They're aware of the finished product, but know nothing of the process used to create that product. To understand and appreciate the process will increase one's enjoyment or connoisseurship of a golf course (see figures 185a–n).

As a personal example, I recall the first time I played the 130-yard 15th hole at Spyglass Hill (see figure 186), just after it had opened. This beautiful Robert Trent Jones–designed par 3 plays from an elevated tee across a small pond to a wide shallow green. Because of the natural-looking amphitheater setting, the hole would have been fine without the pond. But with it the hole was all the more memorable. My curiosity

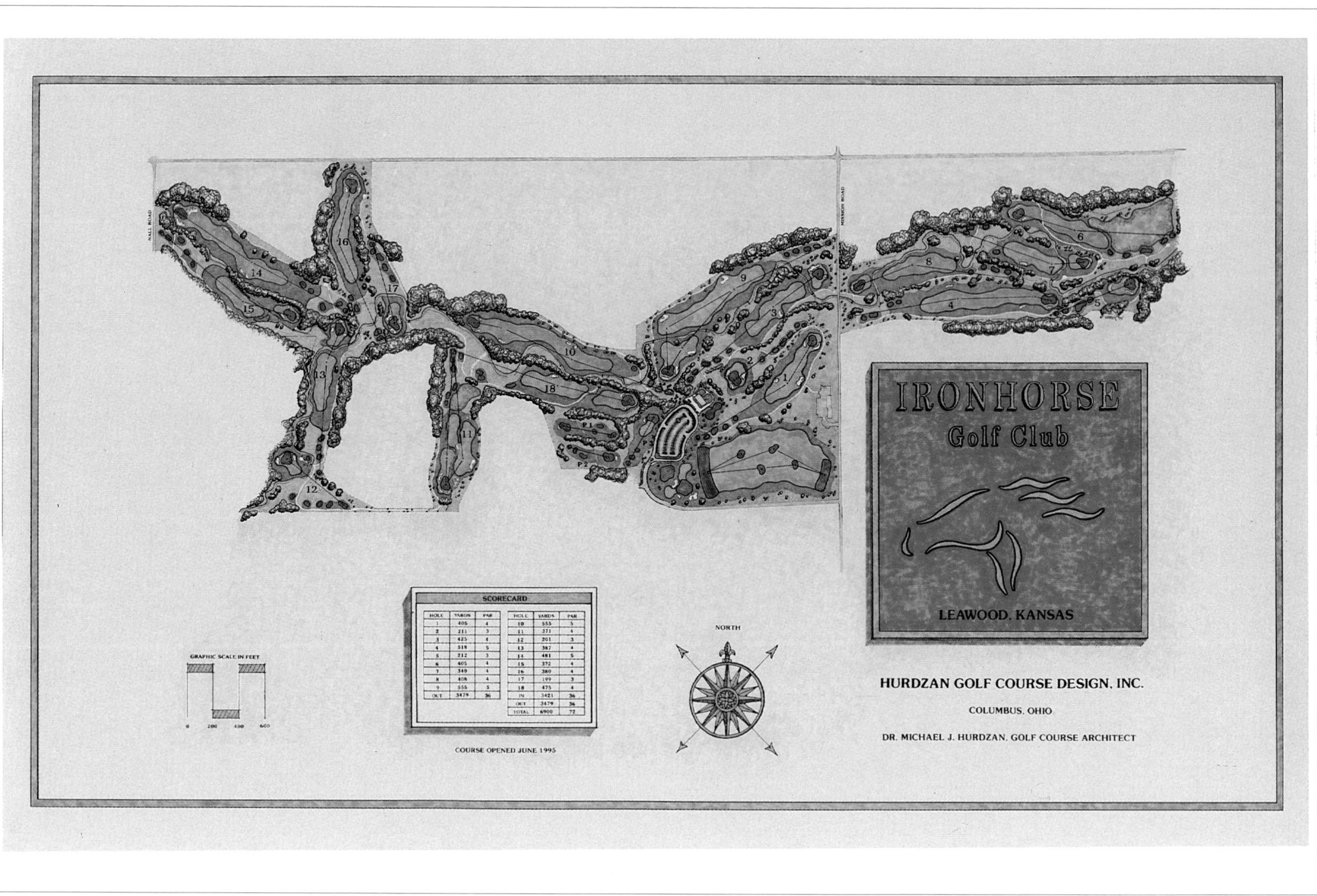

HOLE	YARDS	PAR	HOLE	YARDS	PAR
1	405	4	10	555	5
2	211	3	11	371	4
3	425	4	12	201	3
4	518	5	13	387	4
5	212	3	14	481	5
6	405	4	15	372	4
7	340	4	16	380	4
8	408	4	17	199	3
9	555	5	18	475	4
OUT	3479	36	IN	3421	36
			OUT	3479	36
			TOTAL	6900	72

Figure 182. After the schematic or skeletal routing plan is approved, then the design development phase begins, where the designer adds tees, greens, fairways, bunkers, and hazards to develop his strategy. This leads to the master plan shown here. Notice that the learning center consists of a practice range, a short game center, and three practice holes (P-1 to P-3).

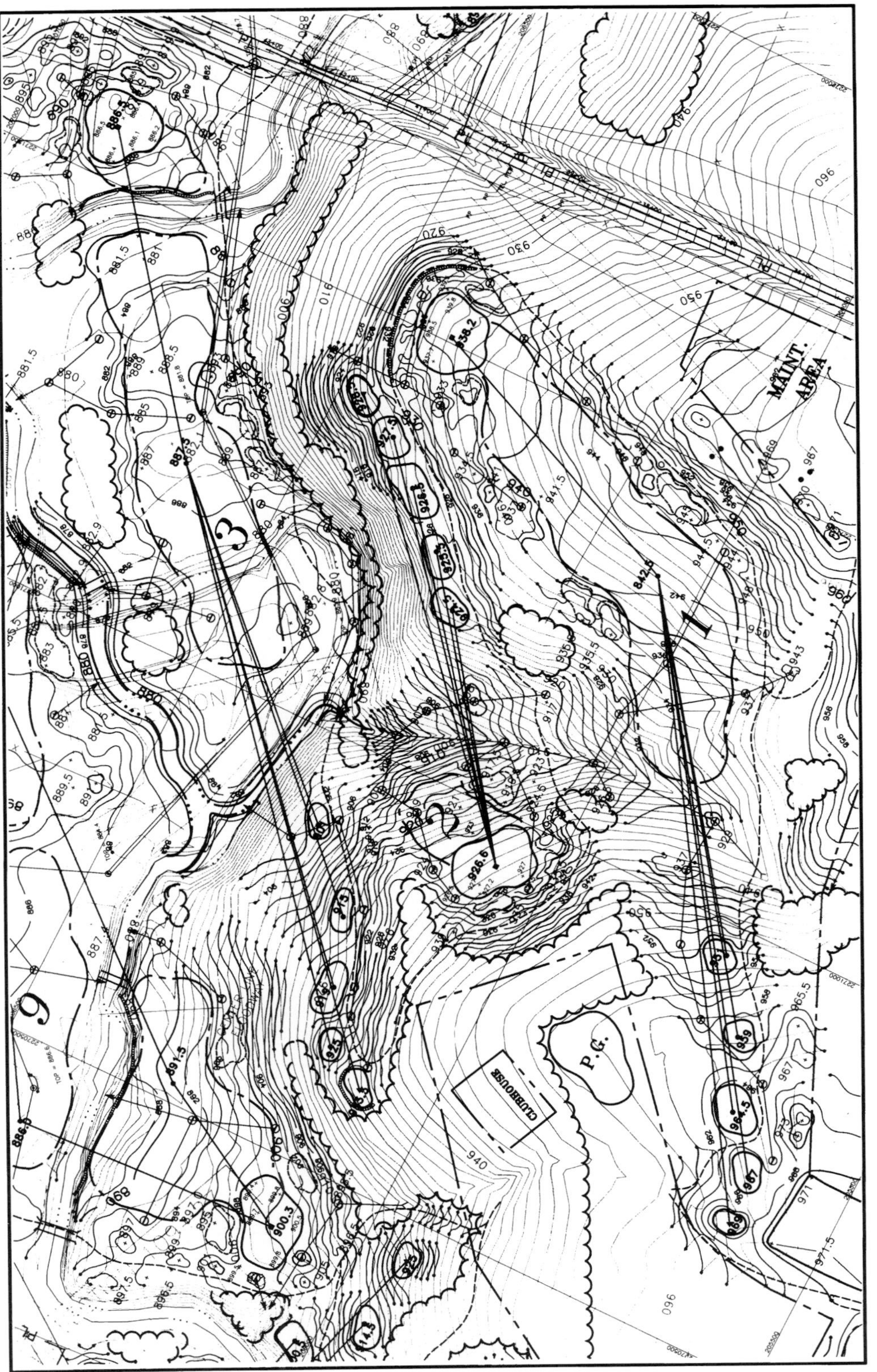

Figure 183. Detailed or working drawing for the 1st, 2nd, and 3rd holes at Ironhorse in Leawood, Kansas. From a drawing of all 18 holes, qualified contractors can bid and build the golf course with the greatest economy of time, energy, and money.

QUANTITY ESTIMATE

PROJECT NAME - CITY OF LEAWOOD, KANSAS

ITEM & DESCRIPTION		GOLF COURSE QUANTITY	PRACTICE RANGE QUANTITY	PRAC.HOLES SHORT GAME CENTER QUANTITY	TOTAL GOLF FACILITY QUANTITY
1 MOBILIZATION	ls	1			1
2 EROSION CONTROL					
A. Silt Fence	lf	20,000	500	1,000	21,500
3 CLEARING & THINNING					
A. Total Clear	ac	44	1	5	50
B. Selective Thin	ac	22	1	2	25
4 TOPSOIL STRIP & RELAY	cy	99,000	9,000	5,000	113,000
5 EARTHMOVING	cy	228,000	18,000	13,000	259,000
6 DRAINAGE					
A. Major (> 12")	lf	5,175			5,175
B. Minor (8, 10, 12")	lf	16,570	1,405	1,430	19,405
C. Field Lines (6")	lf	12,035	602	1,203	13,840
D. Exit Lines (4")	lf	11,580		900	12,480
E. Large Catch Basins	ea	210	9	15	234
F. Small Catch Basins	ea	173	3	10	186
G. Headwalls	ea	18	1		19
7 GREENS CONSTRUCTION	sf	108,754	3,000	44,820	161,574
8 TEE CONSTRUCTION	sf	125,436	67,500	17,003	209,939
9 SHAPING	hr	2,430	150	340	2,920
10 BUNKERS:					
A. Edge & Place	sf	71,252		14,216	85,468
B. Purchase	tn	2,001		399	2,400
11 IRRIGATION HEADS	hd	665	46	48	759
12 PUMP STATION	ls	1			1
13 PLANTING PREPARATION	ac	122.7	11.0	6.0	139.8
14 SEEDING:					
A. Greens	sf	108,754	8,000	44,820	161,574
B. Tees	sf	125,436	67,500	17,003	209,939
C. Fairways - Zoysia	ac	27.9			27.9
D. Fairways - Blue/Rye	ac		1.8	1.8	3.6
E. Prim Rough	ac	16.9	7.3	2.0	26.3
F. Sec Rough	ac	63.4	1.7	1.7	66.8
15 SODDING	sy	44,255	1,156	4,425	49,836
16 MULCH	ac	85.6	10.8	5.1	101.5
17 GERMINATION	ls	1			1
18 WALLS					
A. Stone Stream Bank	lf	1,000			1,000
B. Stone Retaining	lf	600		220	820
19 CART PATHS					
A. Base - 8′ wide	lf	29,430	1,244	500	31,174
B. Extra - 2′	lf				
C. Curb	lf	9,000	150	100	9,250
20 BRIDGES					
A. Cart - Long Span	ea	12			12
B. Cart - Short Span	ea	4			4
C. Foot Bridge	ea	12			12
D. Culvert Crossing	ea	3	1	2	6
E. Road Underpass	ea	1			1
E. Street Crossing	ea	1		1	2
21 CONTINGENCY					
A. Earthwork	cy	20,000			20,000

Figure 184a. A volume estimate of each phase of work allows the architect to prepare a probable construction bid.

LEAWOOD, KANSAS
PAY APPLICATION NO. 1 11-11-93

LANDSCAPES UNLIMITED

ITEM NO.	CATEGORY	UNITS	CONTRACT QUANITY	UNIT PRICE	UNIT TOTALS	QTY. COMP. TO DATE	AMOUNT COMP. TO DATE	MATERIALS STORED TO DATE	TOTAL COMP. & STORED TO DATE	% COMP
1.00	- MOBLIZATION	LS	1.00	$60,000.00	$60,000.00	1.00	$60,000.00		$60,000.00	100.00%
2.00	- EROSION CONTROL									
	A. SILT FENCE	LF	10750.00	$2.50	$26,875.00	2129.00	$5,322.50		$5,322.50	19.80%
3.00	- CLEARING/THINNING									
	A. TOTAL CLEAR	AC	50.00	$1,600.00	$80,000.00	17.33	$27,728.00		$27,728.00	34.66%
	B. SELECT THIN	AC	25.00	$1,300.00	$32,500.00	0.00	$0.00		$0.00	0.00%
	C. WASTE REMOVAL-TIRES	LS	1.00	$2,000.00	$2,000.00	1.00	$2,000.00		$2,000.00	100.00%
	D. WASTE REMOVAL-TRASH	LS	1.00	$2,000.00	$2,000.00	0.00	$0.00		$0.00	0.00%
4.00	- TOPSOIL STRIPPING/SPREADING	CY	100000.00	$1.60	$160,000.00	22519.74	$36,031.58		$36,031.58	22.52%
5.00	- EARTHMOVING	CY	243000.00	$1.50	$364,500.00	86191.46	$129,287.19		$129,287.19	35.47%
6.00	- DRAINAGE									
	A. MAJOR									
	15" ADS	LF	1,850.00	$10.00	$18,500.00	0.00	$0.00	$969.00	$969.00	5.24%
	18" ADS	LF	1,080.00	$12.00	$12,960.00	0.00	$0.00	$998.00	$998.00	7.70%
	24" ADS	LF	1,100.00	$17.00	$18,700.00	0.00	$0.00		$0.00	0.00%
	30" ADS	LF	800.00	$24.50	$19,600.00	0.00	$0.00		$0.00	0.00%
	36" ADS	LF	400.00	$31.84	$12,735.00	0.00	$0.00		$0.00	0.00%
	B. MINOR (8" TO 12")	LF	18940.00	$6.50	$123,110.00	0.00	$0.00	$8,233.00	$8,233.00	6.69%
	C. FIELD (6")	LF	13840.00	$4.00	$55,360.00	0.00	$0.00	$3,096.00	$3,096.00	5.59%
	D. EXIT (4")	LF	12480.00	$3.00	$37,440.00	0.00	$0.00	$1,600.00	$1,600.00	4.27%
	E. 9X9 C.B.	EA	234.00	$80.00	$18,720.00	0.00	$0.00		$0.00	0.00%
	F. 12X12 C.B>	EA	186.00	$200.00	$37,200.00	0.00	$0.00		$0.00	0.00%
	G. HEADWALLS	EA	19.00	$300.00	$5,700.00	0.00	$0.00		$0.00	0.00%
7.00	- GREEN CONST	SF	161575.00	$1.20	$193,520.00	0.00	$0.00		$0.00	0.00%
8.00	- TEE CONST	SF	209939.00	$0.13	$26,460.00	27623.56	$3,481.58		$3,481.58	13.16%
9.00	- SHAPING(MIN)	HR	2910.00	$103.09	$300,000.00	318.58	$32,842.11		$32,842.11	10.95%
10.00	- BUNKERS:									
	A. EDGING & CONTOURING	SF	85468.00	$0.35	$29,913.00	0.00	$0.00		$0.00	0.00%
11.00	- IRRIGATION DIST. HEADS	HD	759.00	$657.24	$498,843.00	0.00	$0.00	$109,242.78	$109,242.78	21.90%
12.00	- PUMP STATION	LS	1.00	$82,000.00	$82,000.00	0.00	$0.00		$0.00	0.00%
13.00	- PLANTING PREPARATION	AC	139.00	$700.00	$97,300.00	0.00	$0.00		$0.00	0.00%
14.00	- SEEDING									
	A. GREENS	SF	161574.00	$0.14	$22,036.00	0.00	$0.00		$0.00	0.00%
	B. TEES	SF	209939.00	$0.13	$28,190.00	0.00	$0.00		$0.00	0.00%
	C. FAIRWAYS	AC	3.60	$1,347.22	$4,850.00	0.00	$0.00		$0.00	0.00%
	D. PRIM ROUGH	AC	26.30	$637.26	$16,760.00	0.00	$0.00		$0.00	0.00%
	E. SEC ROUGH	AC	66.80	$809.43	$54,070.00	0.00	$0.00		$0.00	0.00%
15.00	- SODDING									
	A. ZOYSIA	AC	24.90	$12,453.82	$310,100.00	0.00	$0.00	$25,000.00	$25,000.00	8.06%
	B. BLUEGRASS	SY	49836.00	$1.53	$76,471.00	0.00	$0.00		$0.00	0.00%
16.00	- MULCH	AC	50.00	$350.00	$17,500.00	0.00	$0.00		$0.00	0.00%
17.00	- STONE WORK									
	A. STEAM BANK	LF	1000.00	$40.00	$40,000.00	0.00	$0.00		$0.00	0.00%
	B. POND ROCK EDGING	LF	1000.00	$17.00	$17,000.00	0.00	$0.00		$0.00	0.00%
	C. RETAINING WALLS	LF	820.00	$60.00	$49,200.00	0.00	$0.00		$0.00	0.00%
18.00	- CART PATHS									
	A. 8' WIDE CONCRETE	LF	31174.00	$10.59	$329,979.00	0.00	$0.00		$0.00	0.00%
19.00	- DELETE SHORT GAME CENTER	LS	1.00	(36,000.00)	($36,000.00)	6.55%	($2,357.84)		($2,357.84)	6.55%
20.00	- DELETE PRACTICE HOLES	LS	1.00	(48,000.00)	($48,000.00)	6.55%	($3,143.79)		($3,143.79)	6.55%
					CONTRACT TOTALS $3,198,092.00		$291,191.33	$149,138.78	$440,330.11	13.77%

ORIGINAL CONTRACT AMOUNT	$3,198,092.00
CHANGE ORDERS	$0.00
REVISED CONTRACT AMOUNT	$3,198,092.00
TOTAL DUE CONTRACTOR	$440,330.11
LESS 10% RETAINAGE	$44,033.01
LESS PREVIOUS APPLICATIONS	$172,066.49
TOTAL DUE THIS APPLICATION	$224,230.61

PHILIP S. GIBBS, P.E.
LEAWOOD GOLF COURSE PROJECT MANAGER
CONTINENTAL CONSULTING ENGINEERS, INC.

Figure 184b. A detailed cost estimate showing a quantity for each phase of the work, a unit price, and a total. This estimate is not only good for forecasting money flow, but also ensuring that the scope of work matches the construction budget.

Figure 185a. Installing pipe in swale between tees and driving zone of the 1st hole at Ironhorse.

Figure 185b. Looking from the fairway back toward the tees at the first hole at Ironhorse. Note rocky fill going into the valley.

Figure 185c. Earthmoving on the 1st hole at Ironhorse to deck in fairway, build up tee and green pad, and fill valley in front of the tees.

Figure 185d. Drainage installed on the 1st fairway at Ironhorse, looking back toward the tee.

Figure 185e. Retopsoiling fairway after earthmoving and drainage completed. Looking back toward the tee.

Figure 185f. Topsoil being replaced in front of the 1st green at Ironhorse.

Figure 185g. Finalizing drainage patterns and subgrades on the 1st green at Ironhorse.

Figure 185h. First hole at Ironhorse after all grading, shaping, and topsoiling are complete. Now begins the work of seed bed cleaning and preparation.

Figure 185i. First fairway at Ironhorse being sodded with zoysia sod. Note watering of freshly laid sod.

Figure 185j. First fairway at Ironhorse completely sodded. Areas to be seeded are being prepared. Note drainage tile left high until after grow-in.

Figure185k. All areas of the 1st hole at Ironhorse are planted either by sod or seed.

Mike Klemme

Figure 185l. Golf hole is complete and ready to open.

Figure 185m. Completed 2nd hole at Ironhorse. Note rock ledge at front tee.

Figure 185n. Completed 3rd hole at Ironhorse.

Figure 186. The par 3 12th hole at Spyglass Hill, with a natural-looking pond that can't be natural because of grades around it.

Figure 187. This pond was cleverly "floated" above a piped drainage swale, or it would not have otherwise been possible to build. The art is in hiding the art.

was piqued by the contours on either side of the pond and the great watershed above it, with no apparent provision for handling floodwaters. Upon close inspection I found that Mr. Jones had respected all of these influences by building the pond on top of a pipe large enough to handle floodwaters (see figure 187). The pond was completely detached from the landscape, yet was thoroughly natural in its appearance and function. I was impressed by the genius of the course architect for having so skillfully hidden the mechanics of the design process. The adage, "the essence of art is in hiding the art," applied perfectly. A less skillful designer might have built the pond in front of the green, but would have drained the watershed to it. Without the buried pipe, the pond would have been silted in or washed away by the heavy rains. I don't recall what I made on the hole, but I will always remember the thrill of understanding that tiny bit of the design process engaged by such a master of golf course design.

12

Use of Computers

The application of computer power has touched and changed nearly every industry, including golf and golf course design. Yet the computer is still in its infancy. Therefore, it is logical to assume that even this chapter on the frontiers and thresholds of computers in course architecture may be viewed in a few years as a charming period piece.

Early Computer Applications

Computers first invaded the golf course architecture profession in the mid-1970s with word processing. This assisted in written correspondence and specification editing and reediting, and also in accounting and spreadsheet applications. By 1980, a few software packages written for earthwork and mining calculations were being applied to golf course planning, and they proved helpful in doing cut and fill calculations.

Irrigation designers really led the movement of computer applications into golf course planning and construction, because there was sufficient demand and application to warrant developing specific software packages for irrigation design (see figure 188). The computer could quickly and accurately compute pipe sizes, allowing for friction loss, elevation changes, and water demands. In addition, computers became the newest way to control complex irrigation systems once they were installed, so golf course superintendents quickly became computer literate. Not only was irrigation design more thoroughly engineered by the computer than in the past, but also the operation of the sprinklers themselves, which results in savings in water, greater pump efficiency, and more optimal water distribution. Even today the greatest sophistication in computer applications to golf courses is with irrigation.

Since golf course design was still a cottage industry, most firms tried to find software that could run on the personal computers they were using for word processing. Only a large engineer-

Figure 188. Larry Rodgers pioneered the use of computers for irrigation design.

ing or architectural firm could afford the mainframe computers. Even when powerful computer networks were available to golf course designers, almost none of us were computer literate enough to use them. So we relied on designing the golf course as previously described, using the trial and error method of overlay paper, cross-sectioning, and intuition built on experience.

Until about 1987 or 1988, designs still had to be visualized in our minds, set down on paper in the form of contour lines, and verified by graphing techniques. Once we had generated a grading plan, we simply took it to a computer technician, who converted it into the appropriate computer language and gave us the cut and fill results we wanted—or perhaps a computer-drafted plan of our hand-drawn plan. This computer application was much faster and more accurate than manually computing cuts and fills using a planimeter, but this was all much more a function of checking a design as opposed to doing it on a computer. We were not yet designing directly into and with the computer.

Why not? First, there were only about 200 to 300 real golf course architects in the world at that time, so the demand for a specific software package was too small for a programmer to worry about. Of this small number, probably only about 10%—that is, only 20 to 30 design shops—saw a need for computer design techniques. Most of these fellows were either intimidated by computers or unable to justify major expenditures for mainframes. The result was that only a few adventurous (and young) designers kept trying to use word processing type computers—with ill-adapted civil engineering or mining software and with limited time to experiment because of the great demand (in the heady days of the late 1980s golf boom) for their conventional-style designs. But as the scope of golf course construction projects rose in terms of earthwork volumes, engineering complications, and environmental constraints, the search to use computer technology design began anew. The American Society of Golf Course Architects started making computer applications in design work a regular part of its professional development seminars in 1986. By 1990, computer applications in golf course design were regular professional development seminar topics at the annual ASGCA meetings.

Although interest in computer-aided golf course design was rising, existing programs designed for landscape architects, site engineers, and buildings architects that could run on low-cost, medium-power machines were inadequate when it came to golf courses. First, you couldn't design in the computer; you could only digitize in a design for calculations after it had been done on paper (see figure 189). Next, available programs couldn't handle large complex sites with correspondingly vast numbers of data points.

Figure 189. Digitizing in schematic design or design development drawings is still the norm, but once the data are in, subsequent refinements can be done right on the screen.

Nor could the computers. The closest design activity to golf courses was found to be civil engineering packages utilized for highway planning. But even these were not well-suited because a roadway is usually relatively flat, narrow, with uniform slope, and is not meant to be very aesthetic. And who would want a golf course that looked like a highway?—aside from those who subscribe to the freeway design philosophy of the 1950s and 1960s.

Early Golf Course Applications

A major contributor to computer applications in golf course design came from golf course renovation and a smart guy by the name of Ed Connor. Ed had worked as a golf course builder for years, and had seen the application of a surveying tool called a Theodolite, which was coupled to a small data collection "computer" (see figure 190). Ed could survey an existing or perhaps historic green, like the 7th at Pebble Beach, lock all of the data points into a small 64K microprocessor, go back to the office and couple the microprocessor to a desktop computer, and produce 3-D images of the green on the screen (see figure 191). Then the green could either be redesigned or modified, this information inputted to the computer, and in turn downloaded to the field microprocessor, and resurveyed and grade staked for construction (see figure 192a & b). Using Ed's methods and equipment, now old greens with poor rootzone materials could be rebuilt and every wrinkle in the original green restored (see figure 193a & b). Even golf course architects could see the value of this, so Ed got many of us to recognize that sooner or later, we were going to have to enter the computer age—all but Pete Dye, of course.

About this time, I had working for me three bright men of completely different backgrounds and experience: namely, a skilled landscape/golf course architect with a strong computer background; a civil engineer who used to design highways and was learning golf course architecture; and a draftsman who had the ability to absorb very complex situations and then manipulate elements within that situation to a achieve a desired end product. In addition, I had a contractual need that could only be solved by computers: a 36-hole golf course complex in the mountains of Japan that ended up requiring 8,000,000 cubic meters of earthmoving. This synergism of three gifted minds and a fabulous opportunity produced a quest to truly apply computer technology to course design.

When we started, we, too, tried to apply ill-adapted software packages on low-power machines to our golf course project, but our collective experience told us it wouldn't work. We spent months listening to salesmen and watching meaningless demonstrations, but whenever we said, "Here, use our Japan project for the demonstration," it never worked. We resigned ourselves to the belief that low-power, less-expensive systems wouldn't suffice.

The solution came to us as it often does in business—by chance. One of our designers happened to meet a computer salesman on a plane who said that his company was instrumental in designing space capsules for NASA. After hearing about our needs, he said he could do what we wanted. But the only way to see a demonstration was to buy time from Ohio State University's mainframe, just down the road from our office. Yet this meant we couldn't afford the product. But at least we knew something was out there that worked.

All of our clients and subcontractors knew what we were looking for, and one day we were introduced to a small Colorado company called HASP Engineering, which our mapping firm thought would satisfy our demands. After a couple of demonstrations and a three-day visit with their programmers, we too believed it would satisfy our demands, and would cost only about $100,000 stripped down, or twice that much with extras. After months of bargaining, discussing, arguing, and consideration, we struck a deal and bought the computer. A couple of years later we purchased CADMAP (now owned by Zeiss, Inc.), for its ease of editing and its lack of point limitations. CADMAP also bridged the gap with its translators, so that we could more easily communicate with other software.

With this system we could design in the computer. It could accept the vast quantity of data points, it could do perspective views, make vi-

Figure 190a & b. Ed Connor with his Theodolite surveying in an existing green; this one happens to be the 7th at Pebble Beach.

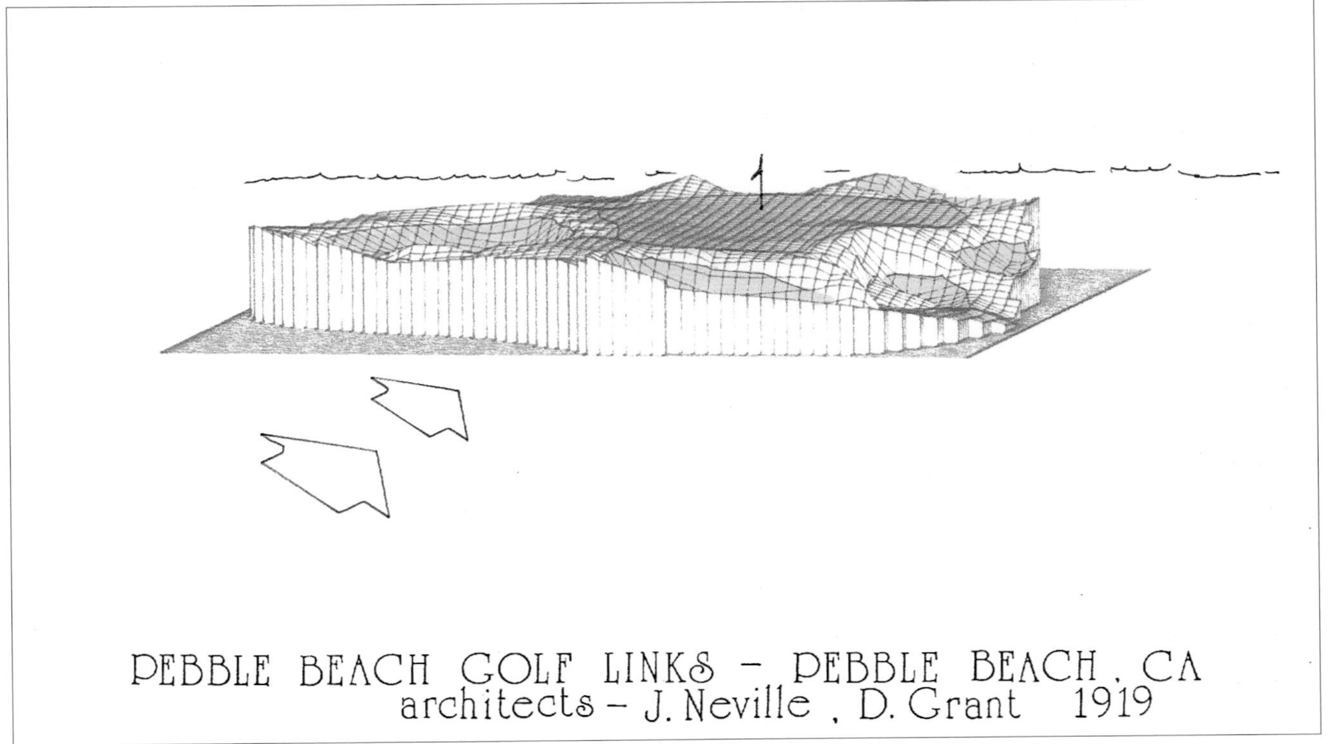

Figure 191. The 3-D computer image of the 7th green at Pebble Beach as reproduced by Ed Connor's equipment.

sual models, and identify areas blind to an observer, and it was fast and flexible. But it was cumbersome to use. While most software packages advertise that they are easy to use, the ease comes at the expense of data manipulation. In other words, more power of the computer is used to make it "user friendly," and thus less power is left for actual applications. We decided to go with a more complex system that would do more things. This meant extensive and expensive training for operators and reduced initial production, but with a long-range goal of greater data point flexibility. Bill Kerman, who started life as a civil engineer, and Scott Kinslow, our draftsperson and now computer guru, were chosen to receive the schooling, with the rest of us learning from them. But this technology is changing so quickly that only Scott has been able to keep current, and hence that is his main responsibility within the firm. In fact, I sincerely believe that a golf course architect can never stay current, and he must always rely on a Scott, who is dedicated to nothing but handling computer applications.

Computer Application Example

To demonstrate how this system might be used to design in the computer, I will lead you through a thought process similar to the traditional one described in the last chapter, but this time using a computer.

First, the topography of the site must be digitized, either directly by the cartographer from the stereoscopic flight photos, or from an existing manually drawn map. For illustration I will use my project called "Westwood Plateau," located in Vancouver, British Columbia, Canada

Figure 192a. Ed Connor finishing the 7th green at Pebble Beach.

Figure 192b. The box blade that Ed Connor is using with his finish tractor is operated by a "laser" rotating beacon that allows him to carry perfect grade. This system is best adapted to tees or greens with very little or no pitch.

Figure 193. A finished 7th green at Pebble Beach that is indistinguishable from the original, except for bunker changes made by Jack Nicklaus.

(see figure 194). The site is on about 1,700 acres of mountain foothills and plateau which rise and fall some 700 feet on about 3:1 slopes. Since the base map was developed in Canada for our client, the Wesbild Company, it made the most sense simply to digitize the maps they furnished instead of trying to go back to the source of the maps and develop them from the original flight photos. To digitize this site took about 250,000 data points and approximately four to five days (see figure 195). Then the map had to be thinned to reduce the extraneous data points and smooth out any lines that were a little too jagged. By doing this we reduced the computation load for the computer and left more power and points for the design process. This thinning process happens almost instantaneously. However, due to the data point limitations of the software, the data needed to be separated into a few file levels.

Figure 194. An aerial view of the Westwood Plateau site before planning and construction began.

For previous preliminary studies, I had drawn the golf course concepts using traditional methods of thin sheet overlays because it was easier given the nature of the project, the need to interface drawings with other professional firms associated with the project both in Canada and the United States, the requirement for metric measurements, and our inexperience with the new system. Once we had a reasonably accepted routing concept, it was time to develop a meaningful and accurate grading plan.

The computer does not obviate the need for the experience and intuition of the designer, but rather permits him to make the same choices faster. I found that my thought processes are still the same whether using the traditional method or the computer.

From preliminary studies with other members of the professional team, we established the general location of the clubhouse site, main entrance road, areas we couldn't use, and special site features that had to be preserved. So I generally knew the location of the starting and finishing holes, but no specifics as to elevations, play lines, hazards, internal contouring, etc. So I began as I had before when using traditional methods.

We place the existing topography map on the monitoring screen and confine our view to about 20 acres (4 hectares) or so around the clubhouse site at an approximate scale of 1:2,000 (see figure 196). Since the map is configured in meters, I will design in the metric system and convert later. So I'm looking at a 19-inch high-resolution color monitor which affords a rather small view with lines cramped close together. Shortly afterward, as it turned out, we bought a 45-inch big-screen TV to work on so we could see more of the map at a small scale, but this did not work because the image was too fuzzy. Perhaps as large-screen, direct-projection, high-density TVs are more fully developed, we will try the experiment again, since a monitor larger than 19 inches really is needed. But for now I am looking

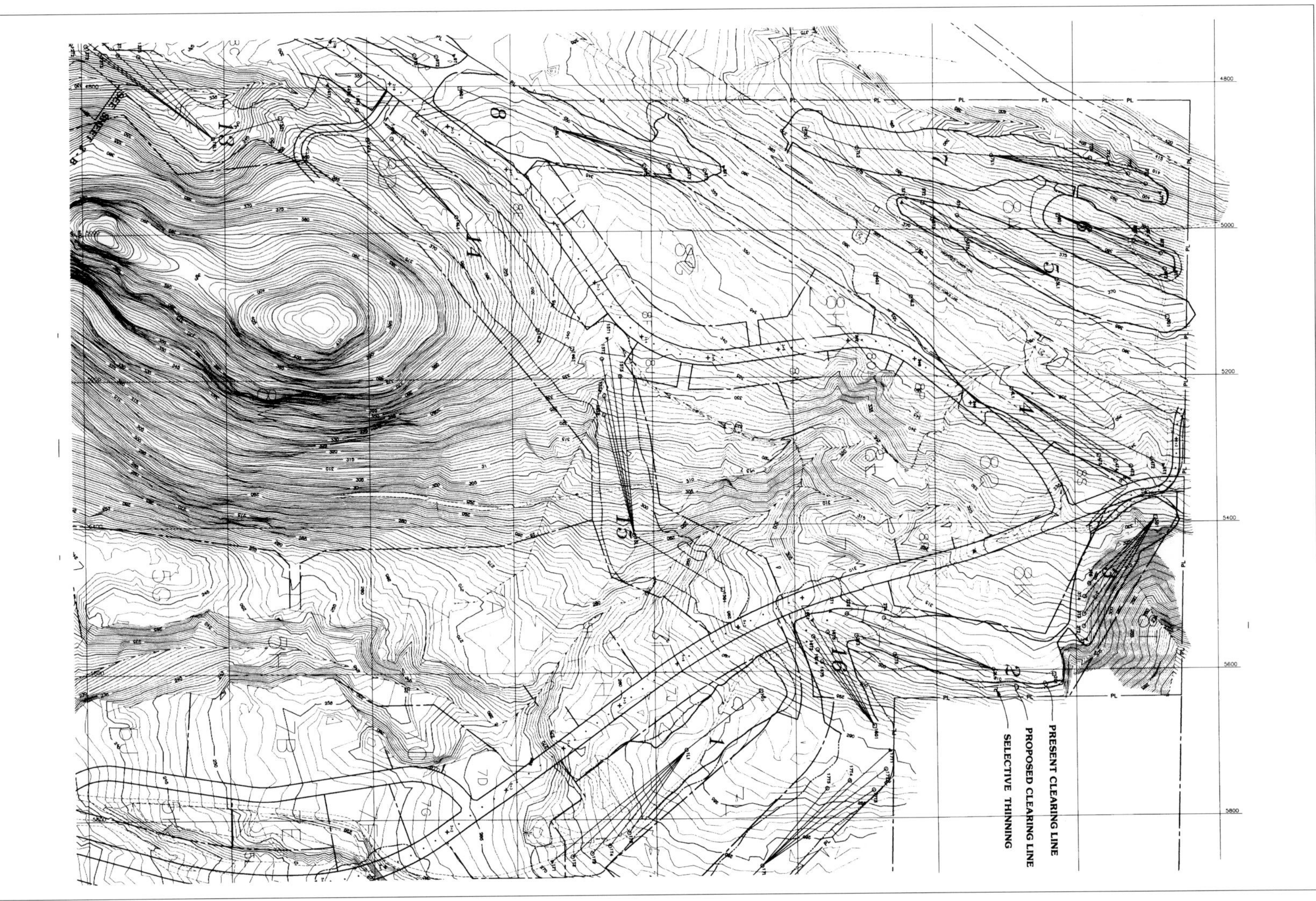

Figure 195. A topographical map of Westwood Plateau in Coquitlam, British Columbia that shows the enormous amount of data that may be required for inputting.

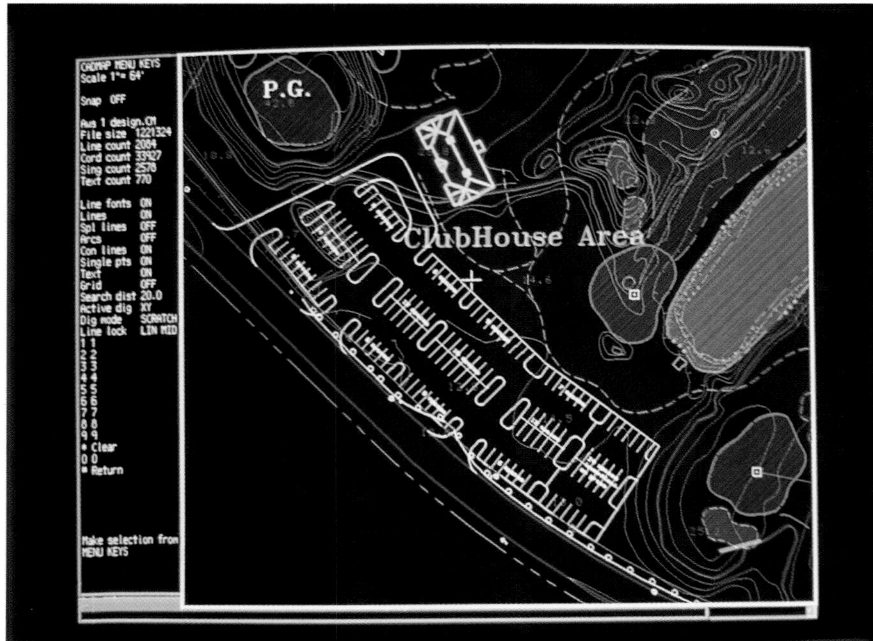

Figure 196. A computer screen showing clubhouse location and possible site use.

at a the 19-inch screen with 10-meter index contours in purple and 2-meter intermediate contours in red, and I'll use yellow lines for designing (see figure 197). I find a ridge that looks like a good starting point so I move the "mouse" or cursor control until a small white arrow on the screen indicates precisely the point I have selected for the backmost or pro tee. I touch the "mouse" and lock down one data point for the back tee, and from it start to draw out a line segment which follows the white arrow on the screen.

Schematic Design with Computer

Then from studying the maps during preliminary designs, and having physically examined the site on three occasions, I have an intuitive notion that this hole might play across and up a westward slope. This seems like a reasonable place to start, and if I cut the fairway into the slope I'll have the topographic features of hills on both sides define and contain the fairway (along with some 100-foot-high hemlock trees as well.)

So I next move the mouse on the mouse pad until the arrow on screen has moved to a possible landing zone some 250 meters out from the back tee location. I know the distance from the tee data point to the landing zone data point because the computer is measuring the length of the line segment as it follows the white arrow. This distance is displayed for me in a small text window next to my graphics. At 250 meters, I touch the mouse button to punch another data point at the landing zone and leave a line segment between the tee and landing zone points which represent a "line of play." Then I look for a good green site for this hole so I can punch in another data point and line segment to complete the hole and play line (see figure 198).

(But there are several possible green sites—at the base of a 10-meter-high ridge, at the top of the ridge, or halfway up it.) I choose the bottom option for the first attempt and then I will adjust to the upper green sites if needed. I again use the mouse to snap down a line segment from the landing area to the green, and ask the computer to tell me the length of each line segment and hole.

(I can now see more of this topography map and I spot a fairly flat ridgeline. Using the white cursor arrow, I stretch a line segment and see that the distance from the landing point to the possible green site is about 120 meters—a bit short for my liking, but still workable. With some good bunkering it could be made exciting.)

Now I am almost off the map that I have displayed on the monitor, so I must rewindow the screen to move the topography map to a more central view.

Figure 197. On a paper map the convention is to either use lighter or dashed lines for existing topography, and solid or heavy lines for proposed. In the computer you can use colors and then assign a line weight for distinction between the two before printing; or you can print in colors, but this reproduces poorly.

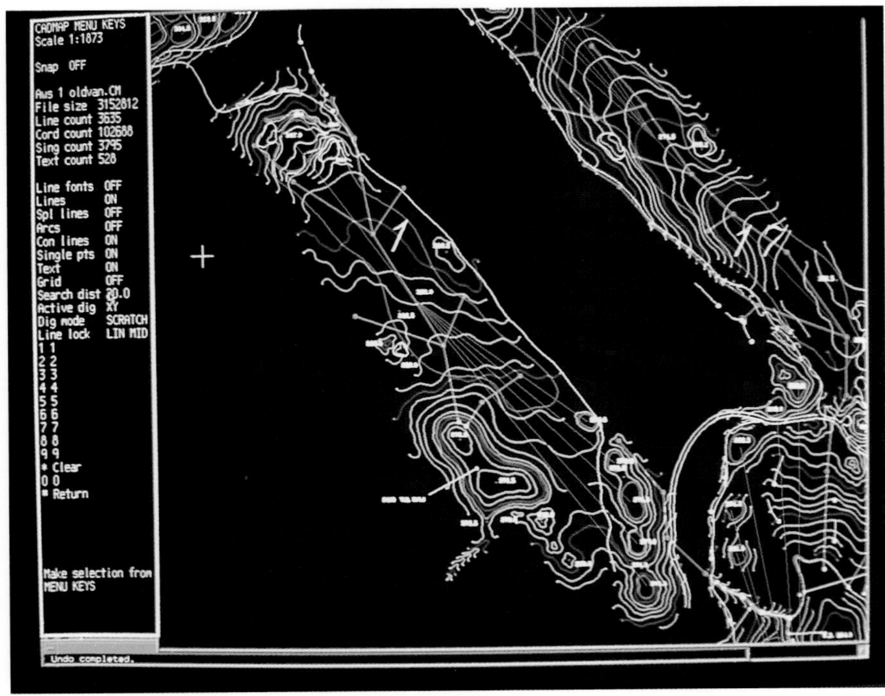

Figure 198. The line of play for the possible 1st hole at Westwood Plateau is locked down in the computer. Like using a swale, you can quickly evaluate landing zones or green position to get the desired length of hole.

Figure 199. Schematic design of a golf course on a computer screen, showing only the skeletal play lines for each hole.

I continue this process until I have laid out all of the holes and had them defined by data points for the backmost or pro tee, with a line of play segment to a data point for the landing zone, and another line and point for the green (see figure 199). None of these "holes" has any elevations attached to them, nor possible contour changes, because I am only interested in seeing how golf holes fit the site. Naturally, I am aware of the elevations and grading that might be required, for the holes must fit the land as much as possible, but at this point I assume that I will not be limited by budget or construction technique in making cuts and fills as necessary.

Assigning Elevations and Grades

Finally, I have a routing plan that works, in that it provides a great combination of holes and shot values. Now I must see if my beautiful creation will be raped by the reality of golf course construction. To determine this, I identify spot elevations for each teeing area, landing zone, dogleg point, and green (see figure 200). This is done by simply moving the "mouse" to an appropriate point on the routing plan displayed on the screen and typing in or registering an elevation. Initial selection of these elevations is by intuition and experience, as well as by the guidelines set out by my client. In this particular case, Wesbild instructed me what the Vancouver golfer has come to expect:

1. Total contour changes from tee to green should not rise more than 10 meters.
2. The rise from the previous green to the next tee should not be greater than 10 meters.
3. Tees are placed close to previous greens when possible.
4. Fairways must be 50 meters wide in the landing zone, flanked by at least 10 meters of rough on each side.
5. Greens will be fairly large (minimum of 6,000 square feet) and of bent grass.
6. Hazards should be visible to all golfers.
7. Golfers do not necessarily have to return to the clubhouse after finishing the front nine.

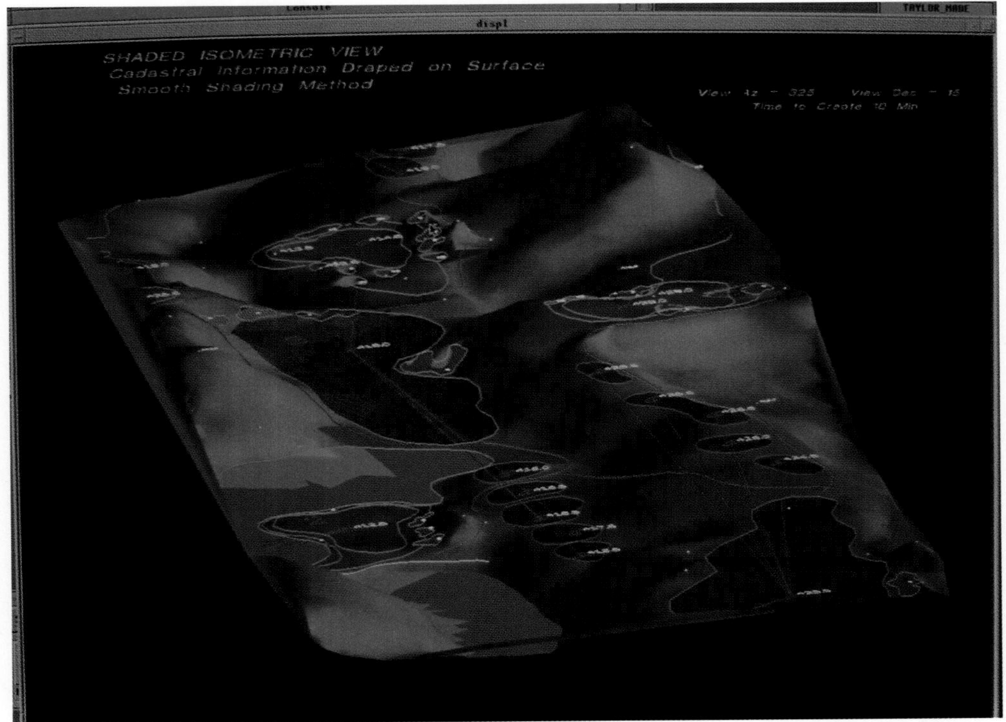

Figure 200. Once the routing works spatially on the site, elevations can be assigned to each key point following the design criteria specified by the client, and shown in 3-D.

8. Golf cart usage is highly probable for most golfers.
9. Bunkers should not be deep, and should be easy to play out of.
10. Views of mountains are required, but views of surrounding development should be avoided.
11. Remember always that most golfers are not very good players.

Given these requirements, I had to "grade out" the site and attempt not to violate any of these guidelines, yet produce a golf course that would be world famous and capable of hosting an international championship. Without the computer this goal could not have been accomplished on paper, leaving the only alternative to do a rudimentary grading plan and just keep moving dirt until the golf course was done. Unfortunately, some new courses there look exactly as if they had been done in such a haphazard manner. I saw one course where earthmoving volume was initially estimated too low to properly build the course, and the budget was not flexible enough to do the earthmoving correctly. This resulted in exaggerated high walls and steep perimeter embankments, too-narrow fairways, and too-short hole length. The golf course was forced onto the land, and it sorely showed.

Previewing the Design

The way in which the computer can reduce if not eliminate this problem is by permitting the designer to preview or test his design decisions before putting them on paper, or on earth. The process amounts to war gaming, where various combinations of solutions can be altered quickly and cheaply to determine the best course of action.

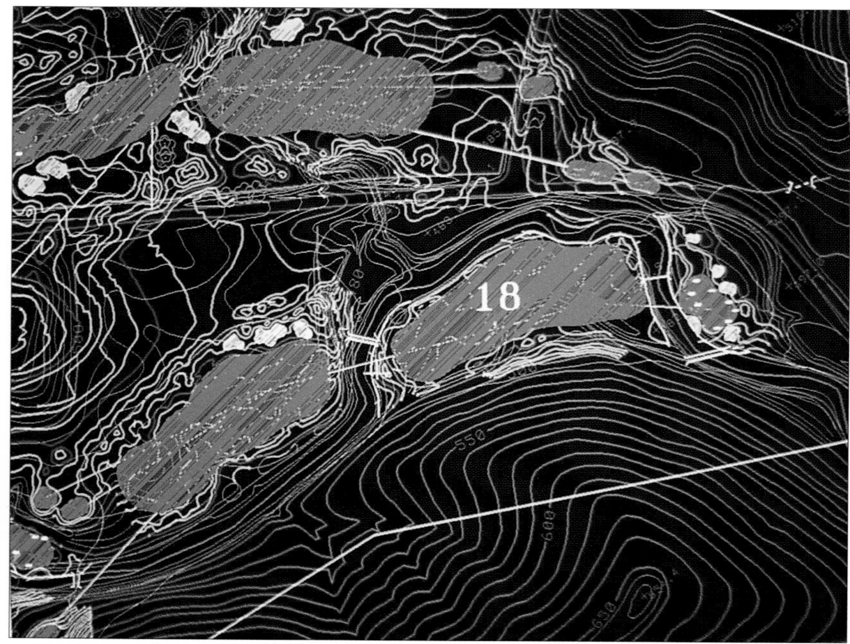

Figure 201. The computer software has been written to identify the desired elevation of a location (tees, green, dogleg point, etc.) and have the computer grade it back into existing contours. For instance, the computer can be instructed to take a dogleg point, lower it 2 meters, level the fairway for 25 meters on either side of that point, and tie into existing topography on a 4:1 slope.

Once the centerline of each hole is established and an elevation assigned to each of these points, rough cuts and fills can be made right on the computer screen by measuring 25 meters from each side of the fairway center point (yielding a 50-meter-wide fairway), assigning another elevation to the fairway edge, and then letting the computer draw in slopes of 3:1 or 4:1 or whatever is desired. Once the computer completes this procedure (in a matter of seconds), we can analyze slopes for their impact on the surrounding land (see figure 201). Next the computer can produce a three-dimensional model of these proposed contours at any observer position we choose. Usually we begin at the back tee at eye level of 5 feet above proposed grade, then work out toward the landing zone(s) and in toward the green. At each observation the computer can be commanded to draw a map delineating all areas visible to the observer, and those areas that would be blind (see figure 202). Armed with that information, we can adjust our elevations upward or downward in a few seconds and evaluate the impact this has on the hole. Similarly, with a small degree of manipulation by a computer operator, grades can be adjusted and pretested to appraise their impact upon the proposed total grading.

As this process continues I turn to my "super-symbols" file, which contains a mix of tees and greens of many sizes and shapes (see figure 203). These three-dimensional "super-symbols" are tied to a control point. I can rotate this "super-symbol" green along any axis and alter its size to fit the area. The same goes for my "super-symbol" tees. Once these symbols are placed down on the screen, their contents (lines, points, symbols) become components of the design.

Checking Earthwork Volumes

We should check our earthwork volumes before we commit ourselves to further design (see figure 204). We can enter a highway design program that allows us to make many templates to attach to our greens and tees. These fairway templates will create a "mock version" fairway for proposed grading. The templates from tees and greens will create proposed grading coordinates. We can specify with all templates to return to grade at a 5:1 slope (or any slope), and if this does not happen within 10 to 12 meters (or any assigned distance), then continue at 3:1 slope (or any desired slope). We will use templates at this stage because they are easy to at-

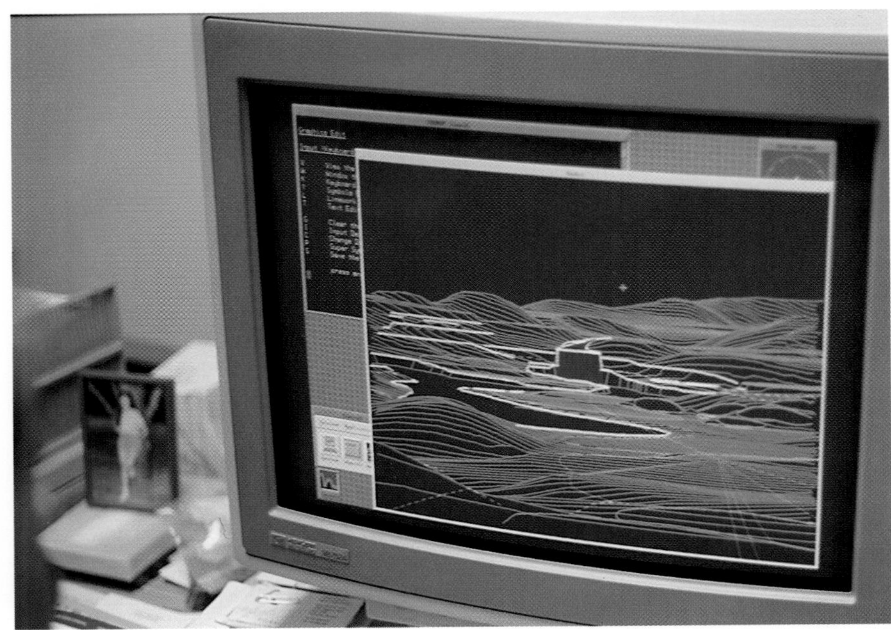

Figure 202. Blind spots in steep ground can be easily checked for by the computer in minutes. This might require hours or days to do with graph paper cross section.

tach to our intended line of play. They give slopes and distances without requiring that we spend much time creating numerous data points.

Now we'll ask the computer to create a three-dimensional model from our preliminary design (see figure 205). We can view this isometric model from any direction or elevation, or even stand at any point and create a perspective view. We will ask the computer to compare the existing topography model with our new proposed model. It will create an "inner-surface" model of the positive and negative voids between the two models. These positive and negative voids are in direct relation to cuts and fills, which we can ask the computer to determine for us. When the volumes are printed, usually only 45 seconds or so later, we can further modify our proposed design to reach a closer balance. We can instantly increase the depth of lakes and raise or lower tees, greens, or entire fairways to accomplish our earthwork balance.

Having arrived at an acceptable design that is, indeed, in earthwork balance, we will ask the computer to "contour" the model, replete with desired contour intervals. This will remove the templates and create a contour map of the *proposed* topography.

Now we can analyze this new map and move on to the next step, furthering the design by modifying the shapes of tees and greens (see figure 206). For this we need to put in two-dimensional lines to define our fairways and bunkers. We can also modify our newly created contours and give them a rolling character, and at the same time create drainage swales and mounds and ridges for the safety of players as well as for future development. We also add numerous spot elevations to define tops and bottoms of our hills and depressions. These allow us to build in extra definition.

Plotting Options

Before we do any plotting, some cleanup will be necessary. We need to separate any proposed grading from existing topography. We should also separate any design elements (greens, tees, fairways, bunkers, lines of play) for a design development file. With these combinations we can plot or print the following at any scale (see figure 207):

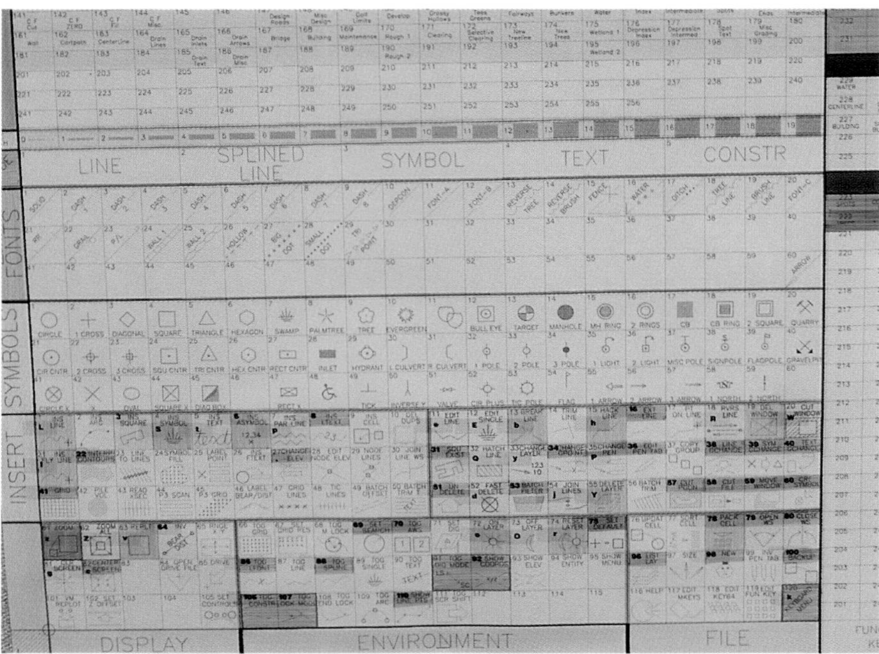

Figure 203. In the figure below, Scott Kinslow selects from the super symbol menu. Super symbols are shorthand ways to have the computer preliminarily size and grade key golf course features like tees and greens.

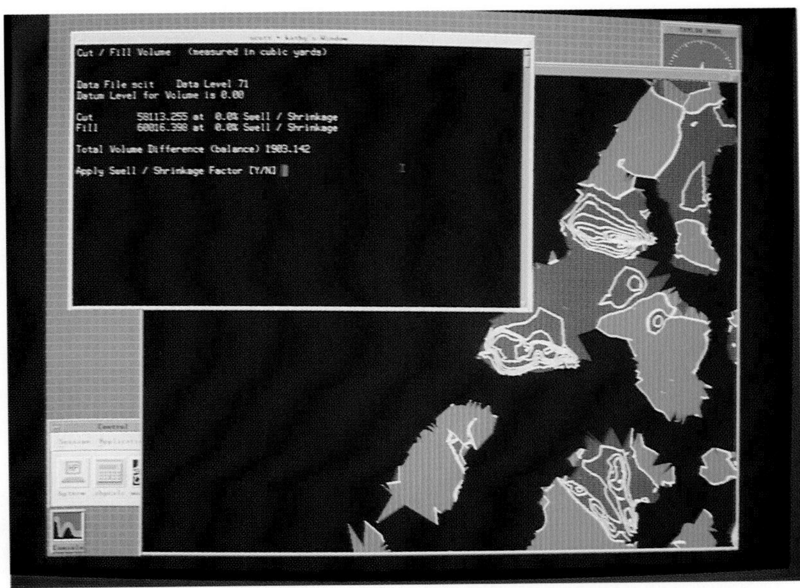

Figure 204. Earthwork calculation can be done quickly, so the golf course architect can completely balance the cut and fill on a site for the working drawings that follow.

Figure 205. Three dimensional perspective drawings can be done on the computer screen and then printed or transferred to videotape for later viewing. If a client wants, for a reasonable additional cost, a "fly-through" of the golf course on videotape is possible, even before construction begins.

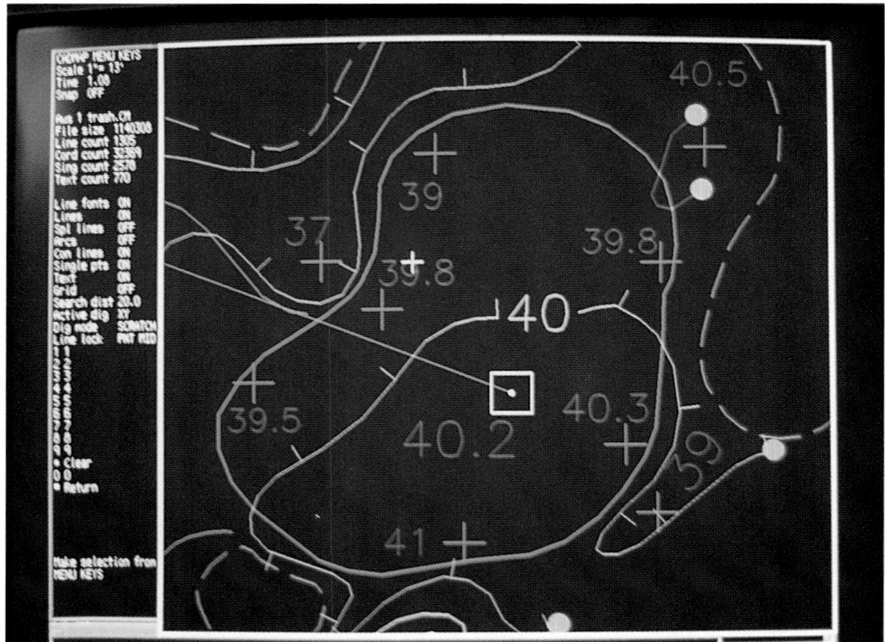

Figure 206. Individual golf features—such as tees, greens, lakes, etc.—can be designed or modified on computer.

Figure 207. An electrostatic plotter, producing working drawings in one-hundredth the time of hand drawing.

1. Original topography map
2. Proposed grading
3. Design development
4. Cut and fill contour map showing depth of cut or depth of fill
5. Three-dimensional isometric views at any distance range
6. Perspective views to any direction from any height
7. Grading analysis—computer-generated analysis of visibility (differs from visuals of perspective and isometric views)
8. Plan and profile cross sections and place on gridded sheets

As indicated at the outset of this chapter, advances in computer-aided design are likely to be rapid. What, then, can golf course architects expect from new technologies and applications that are likely to find their way into the office? Consider the following:

1. The spread of hardware and software is increasing nearly two times every six months to one year.
2. File size limitations are expanding, soon to disappear entirely for higher-speed machines.
3. Software packages are becoming more "user friendly."
4. Peripheral costs are coming down, e.g., large-format color plotters are now affordable for medium- to small-sized design shops.
5. Multitasking allows users to do many tasks simultaneously, such as plotting, copying to or from tape drives, printing fields, orienting the digitizer, working within files, and modeling of files—all at once.
6. Solids modeling: turning wire frame files into solid models, fully colored, with movable light sources for shading, freeze-frame walk-through (for slower machines), real time fly-by (for faster machines), ray tracing, sectioning/capping, radiosity, and contour mapping.
7. Complete output of graphics to videotape.

With future golf courses likely to be planned for land that is not well-suited for the purpose, site constraints will increase. Certainly, the accumulation of regulatory controls over environmental, hydrological, and engineering parameters means ever greater demands upon golf course architects. In all of this computers provide an indispensable technical aid. They will never replace the architect's imagination and dedication. But they can make them more effective.

Ultimate Use of Computers

The first step in the ultimate use of computers in golf course design has just been taken by a large computer design software company that has introduced 3-D viewing of golf course designs. This company has taken my design for several holes and manipulated the data so that an observer wearing battery-powered 3-D glasses can virtually walk down or fly over each hole. The effect was almost as entertaining as that experienced at amusement parks like Disney World with Captain EO. Not only will such 3-D viewing assist the designer in previewing his plan, but it will also help the developer market the project. Further, potential lot or home buyers can view the "golf course" from their lot, or patio, or second story window, before the construction even begins.

In the near future I expect to see the time when I will put on a glove and goggles connected to a computer, and on the screen I will shape and mold the earth into the 3-D shapes I want to see on the golf course, and then have the computer generate maps of my vision. This will almost be like photographing a dream, but technologically it is just around the corner.

13

ECONOMICS OF COURSE CONSTRUCTION

Let us assume that after some deliberation on the feasibility study and site assessment procedures described in Chapter 9, a client decides that a golf course project is still in his best interest. The next step is to secure adequate financing. This financing should include funds for land purchase (if necessary), golf course construction, clubhouse construction, maintenance building construction, maintenance equipment, parking lots, roads, paths, bridges, shelters, an initial maintenance and operational budget, special amenities such as swimming pools or tennis courts, and finally a contingency fund of perhaps ten percent to cover emergencies and unforeseen expenses (see figure 208). All of these are major items that will require an expenditure of funds before any revenue will be realized from the project, unless, of course, house lot sales are to be factored in. Therefore, financial planning should be given consideration for each of these items, for nothing shocks a client more than the discovery that he needs to spend an additional $500,000-plus for maintenance equipment and initial "grow-in" just about the time the course is to be planted. Knowing all of his possible expenses allows the client to plan his finances properly.

The methods of financing are as individual as the projects themselves, but most are variations of either ready cash, conventional loan, partnership, stock sales, or secured loans. There are

Figure 208. A complete golf course development package must include funds for land, golf course, clubhouse, maintenance facilities and equipment, roads and paths, other amenities, and funds to operate them as well.

additional methods available to government agencies—mainly bond sales, leaseback arrangements, joint public-private venture bonding, or a surcharge added to green fees on existing courses. Despite the climate of municipal budget scrutiny, and a general reluctance of taxpayers to foot the bill for public amenities (regardless of its utility or profitability), there is some room for publicly sponsored (if privately cofunded) arrangements that will supplement conventional means of either private equity or speculative investment.

A significant share of the front-end money for a golf course project can go for the purchase of land. There are several options that can reduce this expense. One method is to use less land by building a more compact golf course. This doesn't mean lessening the safety buffers between holes, for those should never be sacrificed. But it does mean building a regulation course as efficiently as possible. With a properly shaped site—one of gently rolling topography with no odd corners or protrusions or unusable areas—it may be possible to build an 18-hole, par-70 course on as little as 120 acres. But that is a rare site indeed.

Or one could build a shorter golf course. Reduced length should not be a stigma, and in fact is scoffed at only by long hitters who rely upon their length to gain advantage over their opponents. Reducing the length of a course doesn't lessen the challenge of the game. Shorter golf courses are equally challenging if their design requires skillful shot-making. More often than not, the course records on venues placing a greater premium on accuracy are higher than the course records of their longer brethren. Shot-making, by definition, is a skill, whereas length can be readily overcome through sheer strength. While golf equipment is making longer courses play shorter, it has no effect whatsoever on making players more inventive shot-makers.

By popular definition, a full-sized course requires a par of at least 70. A course with a par below 70 to as low as a par of 55 is commonly known as an executive course, on the idea that a busy business executive could play a quick 18 on it in a couple of hours or less (see figure 209). The distinct advantage of such a course is that a par 62 executive course, with four par 4's and five par 3's on each nine, can be built on all of 70 acres. I designed such a course for the Hamilton County, Ohio Park District, called Meadow Links, which is one of the most heavily played courses of their seven total. Moreover, well-designed executive courses may produce the greatest income for money invested, and may be a client's only realistic option for entering the golf business.

The only physical difference between an executive golf course and a full-sized course is the length of fairways. Tees, greens, sand traps, water hazards, and mounds are identical in size, shape, and appearance on both courses. In fact, I've had clients walk an executive course for several holes before they realized it wasn't a full-sized layout. Since an executive course seldom has par 5's and usually has fewer par 4's than par 3's, it requires less land, less maintenance, and can be fit onto an oddly shaped or problem-plagued site. A well-planned par 62 course can even require the accomplished golfer to use every club in the bag, and may demand more finesse shots than required on a longer course (see figure 210).

Not only does the executive course appeal to a greater market of golfers, but it is also faster and less expensive to play. The real advantage of an executive course is that it is less expensive to build and maintain, as demonstrated by this sample balance sheet, which can be compared with budgets for a full-size course shown in Chapter 9:

EXECUTIVE COURSE BALANCE SHEET

Initial Cost

Item	Costs: Low	Costs: High
1. Land—70 acres @ $4,000/acre	280,000	1,000,000
2. Golf course construction	1,000,000	3,000,000
3. Clubhouse—small but efficient	210,000	600,000
4. Maintenance building	50,000	175,000
5. Maintenance equipment	100,000	250,000
6. Parking lot, paths, shelters, etc.	50,000	100,000
Total initial cost	$ 1,690,000	$5,125,000

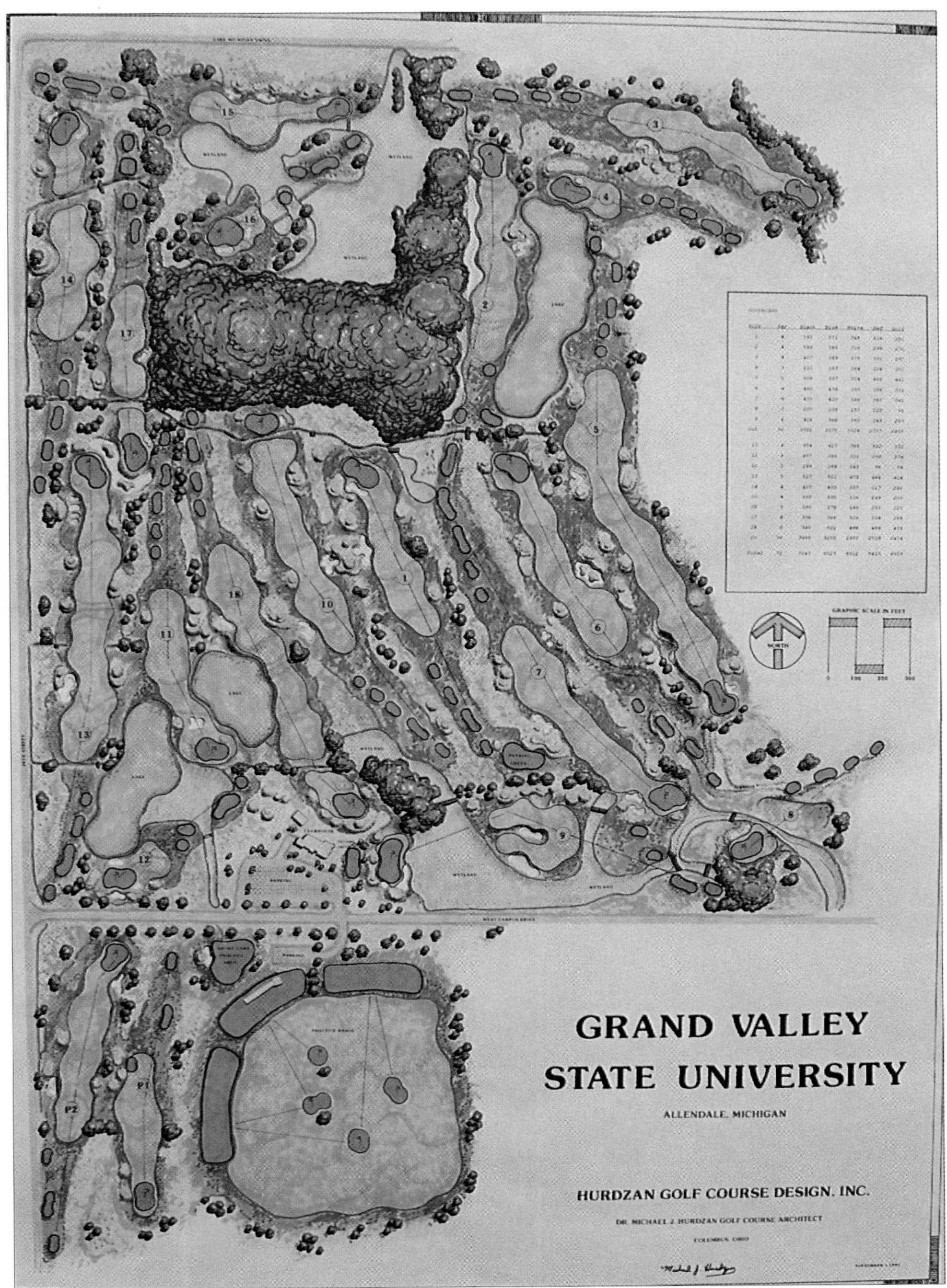

Figure 209. Grand Valley State University placed a great deal of emphasis not only on a fine 18-hole golf course, but also the best in learning facilities. Non-golfers can have a pleasant entry level experience into golf by learning swing fundamentals on the practice tees, the short game on specially designed target greens, and by using the practice holes. This is ideal for a university environment, and it produces excellent income.

Figure 210. Shorter golf courses or forward sets of tees are essential to maintaining interest and producing the golfers of tomorrow.

Yearly Operational Cost

	Costs	
Item	Low	High
1. Maintenance	200,000	500,000
2. Taxes, insurance, fees	30,000	100,000
3. Clubhouse operations	70,000	550,000
Total operational costs	$ 300,000	$1,150,000

Yearly Income

	Amount	
Item	Low	High
1. 40,000 green fees	400,000	1,600,000
2. golf carts (net)	65,000	100,000
3. Clubhouse operations	60,000	200,000
Total income	$ 525,000	$1,900,000

Balance Sheet

	Amount	
Item	Low	High
Principal (20-year loan)	195,140	597,192
Interest (20-year loan, 10% interest)	26,760	80,808
Yearly operational costs	300,000	1,150,000
Total yearly costs	521,900	1,828,000
Total yearly income	525,000	1,900,000
Yearly net profit	$ 3,100	$72,000

At modest green fees per round, this low-cost executive course shows a modest profit. Granted, it isn't a spectacular one, but it generates a surplus nonetheless. Many clients would prefer a small steady profit year in and year out from an executive course than the higher startup costs of a full-sized layout or an upscale executive. An executive course makes great sense in a housing development since 80% of home buyers are non-golfers and couldn't care less about par of the course they live on.

Another successful method of reducing initial cost is by using some creativity in securing and selecting the land. At one club where I am a member, the organizing committee searched until they found a site that had two qualities: excellent natural features and land that could be leased for 99 years (see figure 211). By leasing the land at slightly higher than what farmers paid in rent for cropland ($60 per acre per year), the club committee eliminated a huge front-end cost. Since we obtained construction money by stock sales, and thus didn't need to use the land as collateral for a loan, it didn't matter if the land was leased. The owner who leased it was satisfied, for he not only had a guaranteed income, but

Figure 211. Hickory Hills Golf Club in Grove City, Ohio was built on leased farmland that kept initial development cost very low, without which the club might not have been built.

Figure 212a. Cook's Creek was built on floodplain land that produced an additional 70 acres of wetlands for wildlife habitat, besides adding beauty to the golf course.

Figure 212b & c. The learning center tee complex at Westwood Plateau, which used power line rights-of-way that would have otherwise been unusable.

also saw the rest of his land triple in value. In future years, it's possible that the club may have the money to buy the land outright. I have had several projects in the past few years where land is given free to a golf course developer.

A related method of land procurement for projects intended to be open to public play is to approach a government agency with an offer to build a course in exchange for a long-term lease. This system usually involves a city or county leasing its land at a nominal cost for 20 to 30 years, with a provision that upon expiration of the lease term, the golf course and all its amenities will become its property. If the site is good and near a large population center, this can be a very profitable arrangement for both parties.

Still other methods include use of low-value land such as floodplains, garbage dumps, airport flight paths, or power company rights-of-way (see figure 212a & b). Successful courses have been built on each of these.

Minor savings in the construction costs of a golf course can be realized by specifying certain methods or products, but such decisions should be made only by the golf architect. Used maintenance equipment can halve startup costs, but selections should be made by the golf superintendent.

Perhaps the most effective method of reducing the high initial cost of a golf course is to hire a golf course architect who is capable of properly assessing the site in early phases, and then preparing detailed plans and specifications that permit competitive bidding by golf course contractors. The more detailed the drawings and specifications, the less guesswork the contractor must engage in, and the lower the bid for the job will be.

14

Plans, Specifications, and Bidding

After funds are secured, the next phase of golf course development is preparation of detailed plans and specifications (see figure 213). These plans and specs, together with legal information and documents, comprise the construction documents (CDs). A complete set of CDs should leave nothing to chance, for all items should be either clearly defined or provisions should be made for dealing with them.

The purpose of working drawings is to define the exact quality and quantity of the proposed construction, to provide protection to both the owner and the contractor by defining the rights, responsibilities, and obligations of each party, and to serve as a basis of decision in any arbitration. It is not uncommon for an 18-hole golf course to require more than 60 pages of drawings and perhaps 100 pages of printed information to cover all items adequately. It may take the golf architect two months or more to prepare working drawings, so preparation costs are substantial. But these are essential to a successful project, since they are the primary means of communicating design intent to the contractor in the field.

Once the golf architect has written approval to prepare the working drawings, he begins by refining the routing plan. After reaffirming the client's expectations and the site data, he then again verifies the routing plan by visiting the site. He checks not only the continuity of the course but also every single tee, green, bunker, and mound location in order to design golf features that are sensitive to each particular site. After a thorough site evaluation, the golf architect will make his final adjustments to the routing plan. This will become the base map from which all other plans are drawn. The scale of this base map should be no smaller than 1″=200′ and can be as large as 1″=50′. (For metric maps we commonly use 1:2000, 1:1000, and 1:500 scale maps.) Most designers prefer to work at 1″=100′ in order to show sufficient detail without the hassle of huge sheets of paper. From this scale it is easy to reduce maps photographically or in the computer to sheets of a 1″=200′ scale that are more manageable for field work, or to enlarge them to do detailed drawings for tees, greens, and other features as required.

Base Sheets

There is a series of maps within the base map sheets. The first sheet may be a location map or a staking plan which fixes the exact location of golf features on the site (see figure 214). This can be done by gridding the entire site and working off the grid, but this may be costly if surveyors are used. Another method is to select a known permanent point (such as a corner of a structure or a cement post) and then extend an azimuth and distance from the reference point to the golf feature. This method is less expensive but is a little less accurate and can be time-consuming, especially if the golf course site is heavily vegetated or widely dispersed. I expect we will soon use coordinates and vectors off satellites as in global positioning systems (GPS) used in aircraft, instead of magnetic, grid, or polar coordinates—perhaps by the year 2000.

The most commonly used method is to indicate on the base sheet all existing reference marks (such as fence rows, large trees, trails and streams) that can be seen and located from the aerial photograph. This method is fast in the field, does not compound initial error, and is accurate enough for most golf course projects to confirm surveyed points.

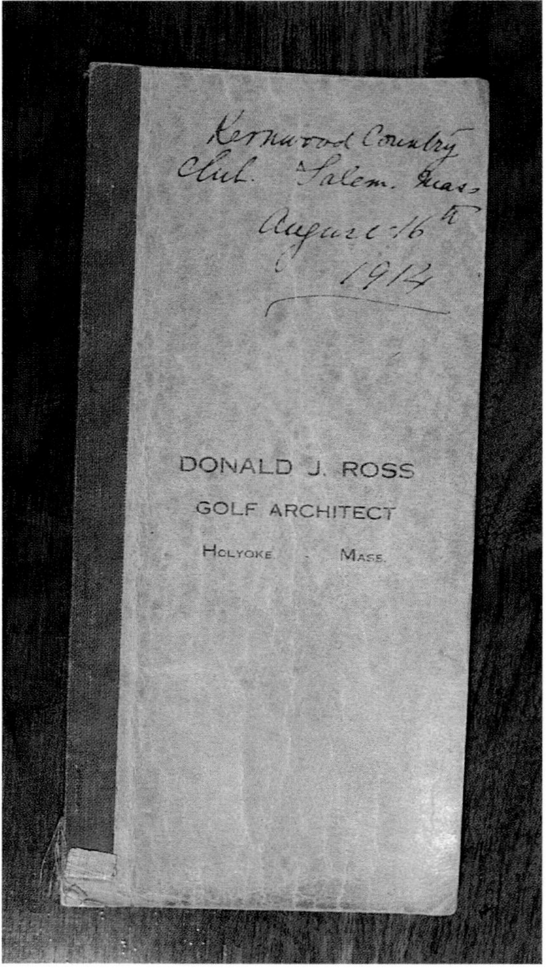

Figure 213. As early as 1914, Donald Ross was doing plan books which consisted of a small-scale drawing of the golf hole with his handwritten notes on how he wanted each feature built.

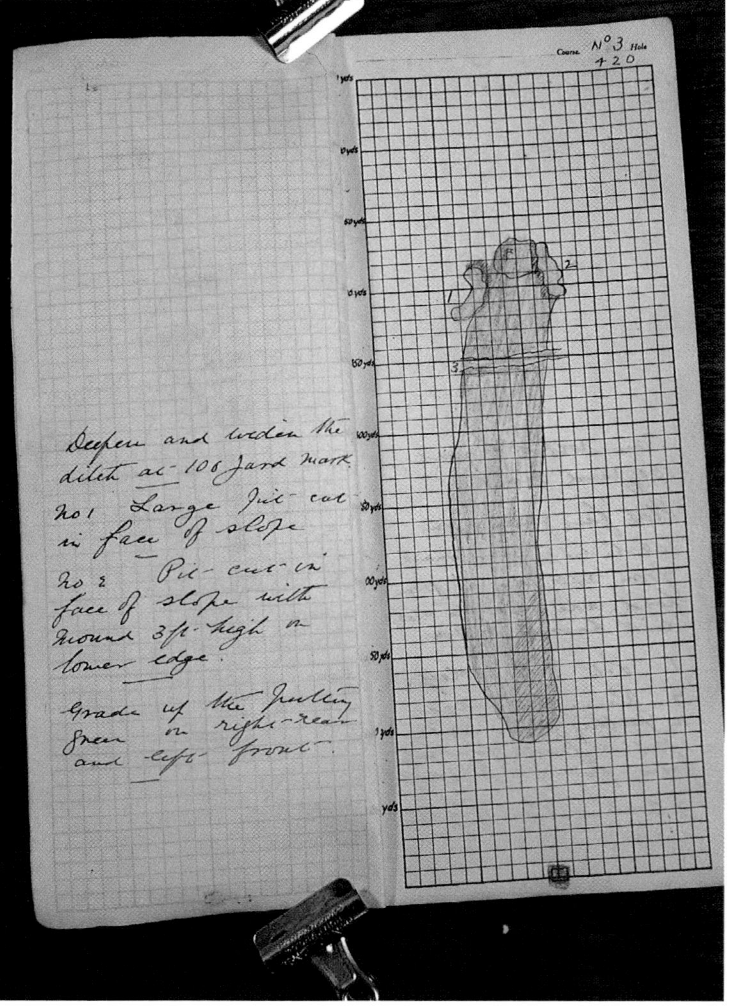

Figure 214. Feature plan for Ironhorse showing final routing and general size and location of greens, tees, fairways, hazards and site characterizations.

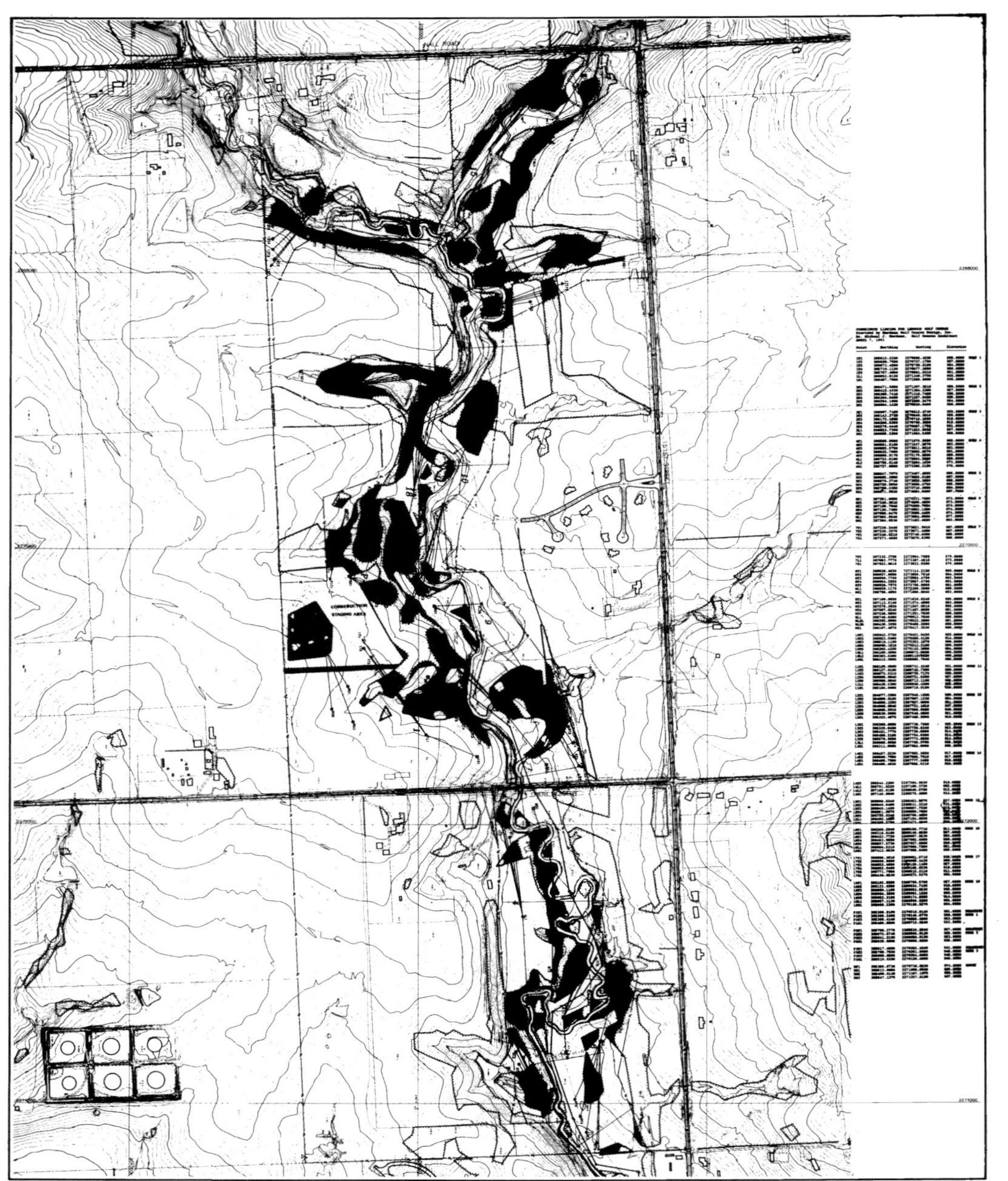

Figure 215. One critical base map is the "staking plan," for it should permit an accurate locating of all major features of the golf hole. This one is using the universal grid system of northings and eastings, and also delineates areas to be cleared.

Figure 216. Perhaps the most important and most used base map plan is the grading and drainage plan. It controls an enormous expenditure in men, equipment, and materials, so it should be extremely accurate and reliable.

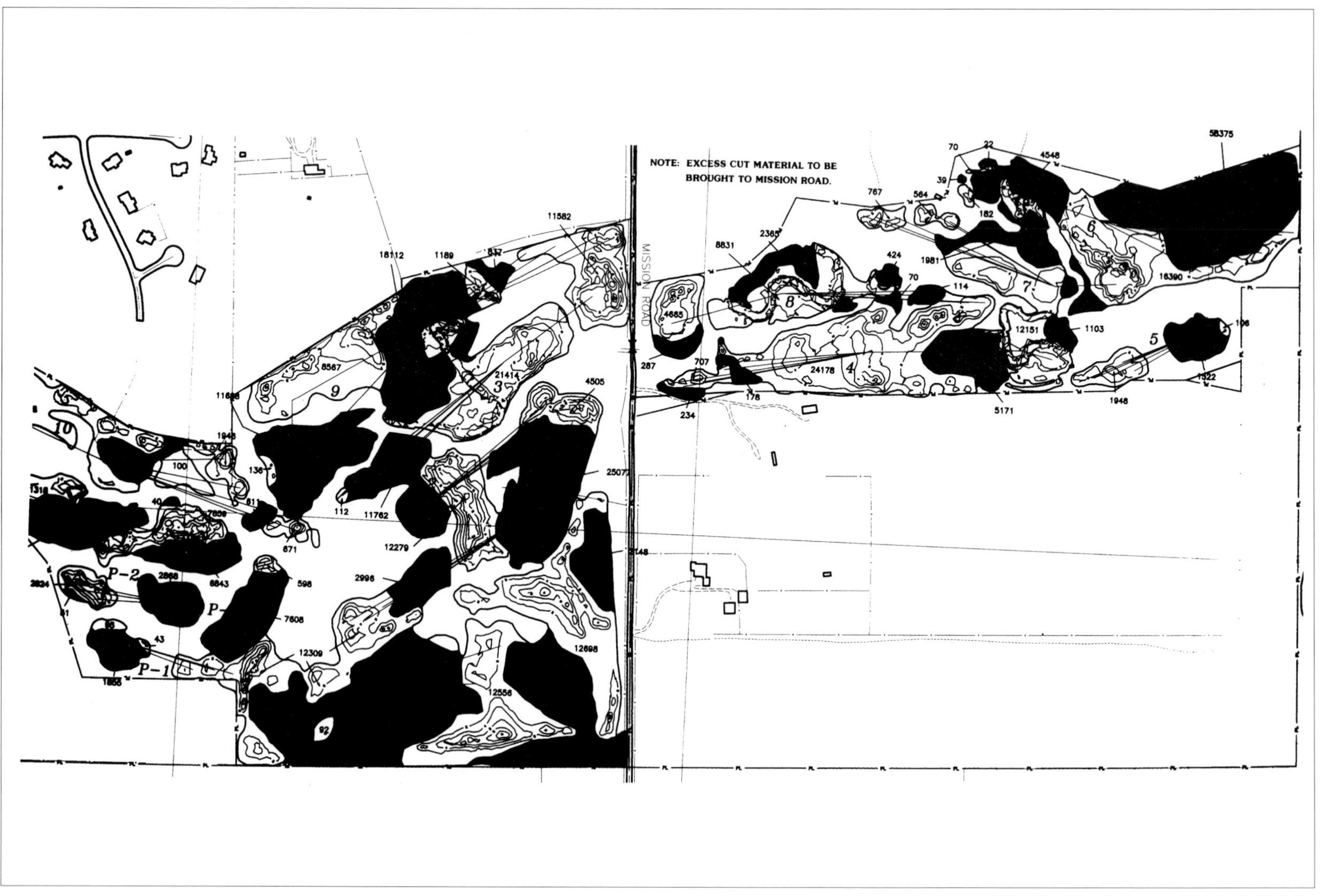

Figure 217. A bulk earthmoving plan is generated by the computer and shows areas of cut or fill and the quantities of earthmoving involved.

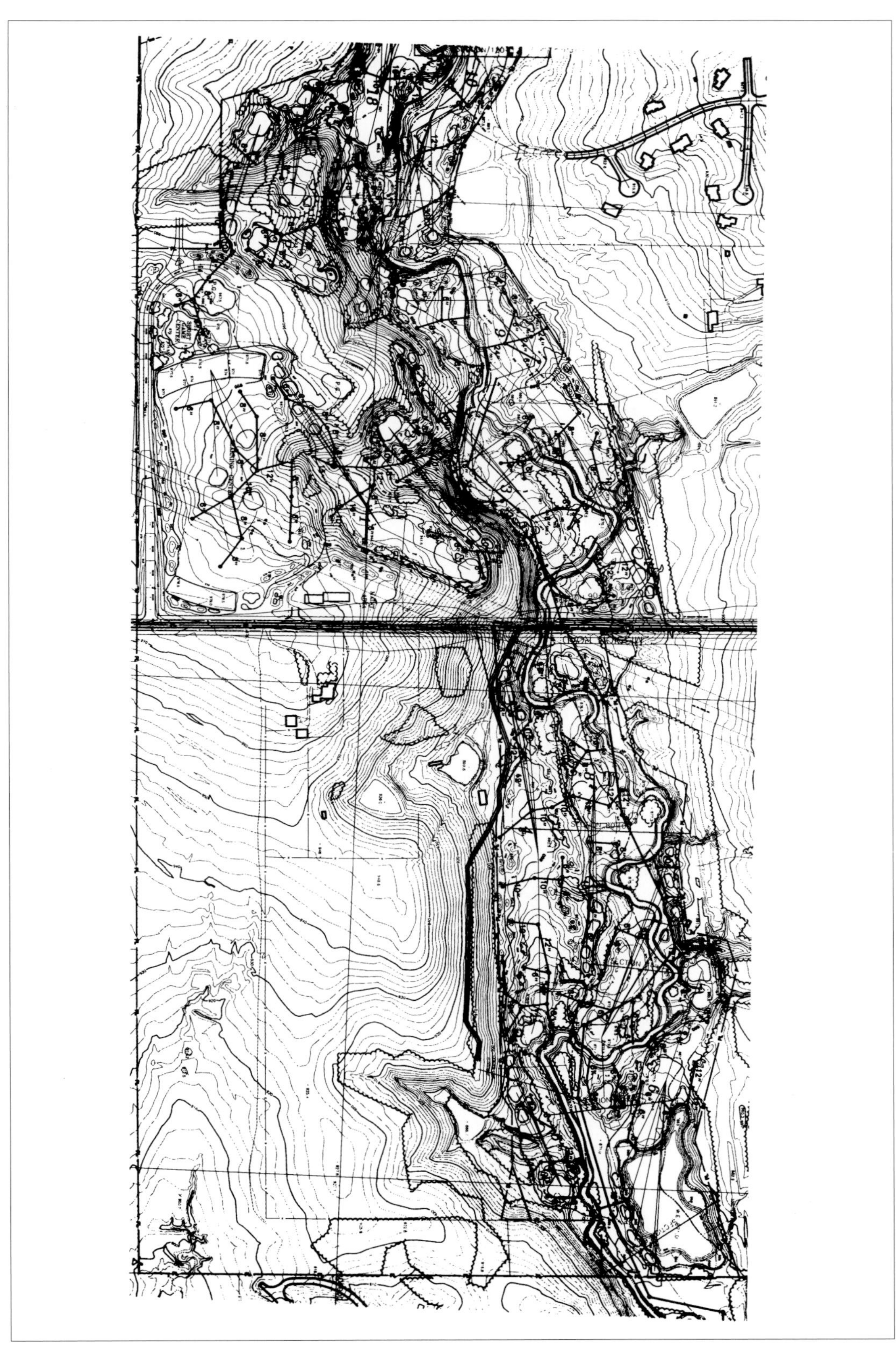

Figure 218. The major subsurface drainage system is shown on a composite grading plan. It gives both locations and sizes of pipes required.

Figure 219. The irrigation plan locates and assigns a controller number to each sprinkler head, along with pipe sizes, controller and valve location and pertinent site characterizations.

Figure 220. Grassing plans show the general scheme for planting various grasses on and around the course.

A second base sheet will show anticipated clearing, thinning, grubbing, and disposal operations so the contractor can estimate the work (see figure 215). It is helpful to show burial or burning sites so that the contractor can figure the volume of the work as well as the distance he must move the debris. The specifications spell out what is to be done, but also indicate how trees or facilities damaged in the clearing process are to be treated or repaired.

The next base sheet may be the overall grading plan, clearly distinguishing existing contours from the proposed contours (see figure 216). Many architects, including me, feel excavations shown at a scale of 1″=200′ or 1″=100′ are not sufficiently descriptive, so we will also show excavations at a scale of 1″=50′ or even 1″=20′. Similar scale choices are also used for the next base sheet, which shows subsurface drainage systems. The more explicitly such work is shown, the less overestimation a contractor will do, and hence the lower and more accurate his bid will be. If, for instance, all subsurface drainage pipe, catch basins, head walls, and end sections are accurately described and specified, it obviates the need for an experienced contractor to add a contingency factor for unforeseen problems. It also instills confidence in the contractor that the architect is thoroughly competent and, thus, less likely to make capricious field changes. After all, confidence in the architect also helps keep construction bids reasonable.

Among the many items that a golf architect will indicate on the base sheets are lime and fertilizer rates (see figure 217), planting, mulching (see figure 218), irrigation (see figure 219), tree locations (see figure 220), suggested bridge and roadway locations, maintenance or nursery areas, fencing, water lines, utilities, shelters, drinking fountains, traffic circulation, wildlife areas, borrow sites, and any other pertinent information for the entire golf course.

Detailed Drawings

Besides the base sheets, most golf architects make detailed drawings of individual holes showing tees, greens, and hazards on a scale of 1"=50' or less. (For other features such as ponds or drainageways, it is best to use the largest possible scale in order to keep the feature on one page while showing maximum detail.) Greens are usually drawn at a scale of 1"=20', with 1-foot or even 6-inch contours. Such drawings were previously discussed in Chapter 4.

Although there are many methods to depict the designer's intended size, shape, and slope of a green or bunkers, the most universally accepted method is continuous contour lines. This method uses conventional notation by showing the existing contour line in halftone or dashed lines and the proposed contours as bold, continuous lines that tie back into the appropriate existing contour. Having the proposed contours blend back into the existing lines tells the contractor the extent or limits of the grade change. Using the contour line method, a designer can show mounds and depressions, surface drainage patterns, undulations, and slopes, all in a very precise and defined manner.

But such descriptive drawings do not exclude the need for the designer to guide or define the precise shaping he wants in the field. The best designs are products of a fertile mind and a talented shaper. From detailed drawings, however, the contractor can accurately calculate the amount of cut or fill needed to build each feature and, knowing the limits of the work, he can safely make his lowest possible bid. Although panoramic sketches showing an oblique view of a proposed green look impressive, they aren't very descriptive to a contractor, who may overestimate the work to be sure he doesn't lose money. Such overestimation can run into thousands upon thousands of dollars.

Base map drawings (1″=200′ or 1″=100′) visually show the following site or construction data:

1) Staking plan or location map
2) Clearing, thinning, grubbing, and disposal plan
3) Grading plan
4) Subsurface drainage plan
5) Liming and fertilization plan

6) Planting and mulching plan
7) Irrigation plan
8) Tree planting program
9) Suggested roadway and bridge locations
10) Maintenance or nursery locations
11) Fencing or property lines
12) Existing utilities and planned utilities
13) Shelters and drinking fountain locations
14) Traffic and circulation flow (if necessary)
15) Natural, wildlife, or historic areas
16) Borrow or storage sites
17) Any other information pertinent to the project

Note: Not every project needs all of these base sheets, but most projects do need the majority of them.

Detailed drawings are usually done at scales of 1"=50', 1"=25', 1"=20', or 1"=10', and are used to show construction details of:

1) 18 individual greens plus practice green
2) All individual tees plus practice tee
3) All sand traps and mound complexes
4) Pump station, electrical circuits, wet wells, etc.
5) Construction details of bridges or shelter houses
6) Dams, waterways, revetments, etc.
7) Drop inlets, overflows, headwalls, or end sections
8) Typical interior tee or green construction
9) Typical irrigation information
10) Any other pertinent detail that will further define the quantity and/or quality of the proposed construction.

Not all golf course architects prepare such elaborate plans. They might instead use other methods for providing the contractor with the proposed quantity and quality of the work. However, it is my belief that such methods may be subject to errors that cannot be easily checked, and hence there is no basis for arbitration if a problem arises. In many instances bonding companies will not bond work that is not explicitly detailed and supported by detailed specifications; nor will lending institutions fund them.

Specifications

Detailed specifications are a written expression of the quality and quantity of the work, and provide all contractual, procedural, and legal aspects of the project. Thus, the specifications need not be redundant to the drawings, but should be consistent with them and should serve to amplify or clarify operations or procedures related to the work.

Usually written specifications deal with three main topics. The first involves instructions to the bidder and includes general conditions. It establishes the overall formality of the work and the relationship between the client and the contractor by covering such topics as:

1) Definition of terms
2) Basis of contracts
3) Proposals, bonds, and bonding procedure
4) Standards and substitutions
5) Damages for delays and extensions of time
6) Changes from the original plans and addenda
7) Owner's right to do work and terminate contract
8) Materials, employees, and guarantees
9) Documents required prior to signing contract:
   a) insurance and workers' compensation certificates
   b) division of contract or unit price schedule
   c) bonding companies
   d) financial, insurance, and legal foundations
   e) state registration to do work
   f) corporate power of attorney
10) Progress schedule and lists of materials and subcontractors
11) Basis of payment (retainage, partial and final payments, etc.)
12) Contractor's rights and responsibilities
13) Insurance coverages and responsibilities
14) Use of premises, visitation of the site, and consultation with engineers
15) Taxes, equal employment statements, and wage scales

16) As-built drawings, shop drawings, and material samples

For either party to begin work without some understanding of these topics is to court financial disaster or the possibility of an adversarial confrontation.

The second main topic of written specifications is the detailed specifications of the work. This portion describes or affixes the manner, extent, quality, quantity, schedule, and contingencies of the actual work. In establishing standards for the overall workmanship and quality of the final product, this portion of the specification is what begins to separate the highly competent golf course architect from the hopeful Walter Mitty designer. Now the architect must demonstrate his knowledge of turfgrasses and of currently accepted practices and technologies for their maintenance. The experienced golf course contractor reads these specs not only to guide him in bidding and doing the work, but also to ascertain the relative competence of the architect. Without such knowledge, the contractor would not be aware of possible extra charges he could make, or inadvertently incur, after the work has begun. The contractor must also identify any potential loopholes by which the contract could be legally manipulated, even if in violation of the spirit or intentions of the specifications.

Loopholes can sometimes be as subtle as whether the seed is to be tested on a 1-gram sample or on a 25-gram sample, or whether the seed is to be tested before shipping or after delivery. I know of one example where weak testing procedures were adhered to. Although the seed bore the proper certification tags, it contained enough *Poa annua* seed to contaminate all the newly seeded greens. To rid the greens of the weed, it cost tens of thousands of dollars and two years of vigilant work by the golf course superintendent. It's no exaggeration to say that I have read specifications so poorly written that the client could have saved one million dollars simply by having had the specifications rewritten by a competent golf architect.

Using the example of topsoil, let me show how a seemingly self-evident parameter must be fully and carefully specified. Because most sites have a limited supply of topsoil, and because topsoil is so important to the future health and management of the grasses to be planted on the course, it must be treated as a precious and expensive resource. If from his site inventory and soil profile inspection a golf architect determines that topsoil will be in short supply, he will write specifications to protect it. He may begin by defining topsoil as "the plow layer" only, or "down so many inches," or as "all soils above a certain zone," or a "profile layer." Others define topsoil in regard to its textural classification based on percentage of sand, silt, clay, and organic matter content.

Whatever method is used to define the topsoil layer, once it is identified the contractor will be instructed to remove all surface growing vegetative matter and debris before stripping the layer. Then all topsoil in all areas of grade change greater than a certain number of inches will be stripped to a specified depth. The location of topsoil stockpiles may be further specified for areas beyond the immediate zone of excavation and that possess good air and water drainage, are easily accessible to normal earthmoving equipment, and are free from contaminating sources of runoff. There may be a specification that requires the addition of a soil amendment to the stockpile, or that weed control be practiced or periodic mowing take place. The topsoil section of the specifications may indicate the manner, locations, and depth that the topsoil will be replaced. Those specifications may describe how to treat it with soil amendments and may even require fine grading of the subgrade before the topsoil is placed back. The specs will also indicate how the topsoil will be amended, packed, and graded once it is repositioned. Such detail on a topic as seemingly simple as topsoil may seem excessive. But loss of topsoil through erosion, burial, or mishandling causes many problems for a golf course superintendent long after the golf architect and contractor have left the site. The more the surface of a site is changed or molded with construction equipment, the more attention must be paid to topsoil.

The final topic of written specifications is the bidding and contract documents. These too are a product of evolutionary forces seeking to make

Figure 221. A prebid site inspection is made by the designer and contractors, so they know exactly what they are bidding on.

contractual obligations safe and equitable to all parties. This section usually includes:

1) Notice to bidders
2) Statement of bidder's qualifications
3) Time of completion
4) Form of proposal
5) Form of bonds
6) Substitution sheet
7) Bid schedule or bid sheet
8) Form of contract

In addition, some clients require a state registration form, a federal equal opportunity statement, a statement of net worth, and the corporate power of attorney for officers. Since all of these forms have significant legal implications, it is wise for both parties to have an attorney review the documents.

Bidding the Work

Once the working drawings have been completed by the golf architect and have been reviewed and approved by the client and his advisors, the next step is to put the work out for bid. This is done by publishing a notice to bidders in a newspaper or periodical and by contacting golf course contractors in the region. The contractor will then contact the client to purchase or make a deposit on a set of plans and written specifications. The client should keep a detailed list of names, addresses, and telephone numbers of anyone getting a set of plans so that they can be contacted if any changes or addenda are necessary.

Contractors should be given about four weeks to prepare their bid, during which time the golf architect will conduct a prebidding site inspection (see figure 221). In this walkaround, the golf architect tours the entire golf course routing plan with any interested bidders, identifying the work to be done and answering specific questions. A walkaround is usually scheduled at least one week and preferably two weeks before the bid opening.

The bid opening is usually scheduled for a specific day, at a given hour. With public bids, all bidders are invited to hear the sealed bids read aloud; on private projects, bid openings can be conducted in private. During this bid opening it is up to the client to decide if he will read aloud the golf architect's estimated cost for the project. Having the architect prepare an estimate in the same manner as the bidders permits the client to evaluate what is the lowest and best bid. If a bid is ridiculously low, the client may counsel the bidder and allow him to retract his bid if he wishes, without penalty. To accept a bid that would break a contractor is not only inhumane but is injurious to the industry.

Another approach is to solicit proposals rather than bids. A bidding process implies that the lowest qualified bidder should be given first consideration for the contract. But if proposals are sought then no such implication exists and the client is free to bargain with bidders as best suits his interest. Bidding does not provide this freedom.

Normally, a bid bond accompanies each tendered bid. This bond or certified check is usually at least 10% of the contractor's bid. This proposal bond is the contractor's commitment to honor his bid. If he is the low bidder and then refuses to sign the contract, or is in some other manner negligent, the client is entitled to keep the bond or check without obligation to the bidder. Bids remain valid for a period stated in the invitation to bidders. The usual period is 30 days, after which all bids and bonds are considered nonbinding. Assuming that the client selects a bid, he will next contact the successful bidder and instruct him to prepare all the necessary insurance forms, work permits or licenses, an actual contract and, most importantly, a division of contract. Unless the project was bid on a unit price basis with no lump sum items, a division of contract becomes the contractor's basis to request payment for work completed.

Division of Contract

A hypothetical division of contract looks like this:

Division of Contract

Item	Labor	Material	Total
1. mobilization, bond insurance	$ 8,000	$ 12,000	$ 20,000
2. clearing, thinning, grubbing, disposal	$ 50,000	$ 17,800	$ 67,800
3. earthmoving and grading	$500,000	$121,016	$ 621,016
4. drainage:			
corrugated metal pipe	$110,200	$116,300	$ 226,500
polyethylene tile	$ 75,650	$ 76,750	$ 152,400
5. amended soils for:			
greens			
mason sand	$ 6,500	$ 58,000	$ 64,500
peat	$ 2,500	$ 24,000	$ 26,500
mixing, hauling, compacting	$ 11,000	$ 8,000	$ 19,000
6. irrigation	$200,000	$276,000	$ 476,000
7. pump station or wells	$ 26,000	$ 46,500	$ 72,500
8. seedbed preparation (lime & fertilizer)	$103,200	$112,800	$ 216,000
9. planting, mulching	$ 41,000	$ 46,000	$ 87,000
10. establishment of turf	$ 45,000	$ 25,000	$ 70,000
11. sand traps	$ 14,150	$ 24,200	$ 38,350
12. bridges & cart path	$ 64,000	$228,000	$292,000
13. shelter & drinking fountains	$ 15,200	$ 13,900	$ 29,100
Totals	$1,272,400	$1,206,266	$2,478,666
Total Contract Price			$2,478,666

This division of contract becomes part of the contract and will determine the amount of payment due the contractor for work completed or materials delivered to the site. For instance, the total cost for clearing is $67,800. When the clearing is certified by the architect to be 50% completed, then the contractor is entitled to 50% percent payment, or $33,900. The division of contract indicates that the bridge materials will cost $28,000. When these materials are delivered to the site and are properly stored, protected, and insured, the contractor is entitled to payment for them.

Method of Payment

This method of payment, establishing the contractor's payment based on work completed, protects the client. Since the contractor is only paid for work that is certified by the golf architect, there is incentive to finish the project. In addition, the client usually retains a small percentage (5%) of the due payment as a further guarantee that the work will be properly done. This amount is stated clearly in the general conditions of the specifications and is commonly 5% of the total contract price. The usual mechanism is to retain 10% of the first half of the contract. This money is held until the golf architect issues a statement of final acceptance, meaning the entire project is completed to his satisfaction. If the work is not done to his satisfaction, the architect notifies the contractor in writing and gives him a short but reasonable time, normally two to ten days, to correct any deficiencies. If the contractor doesn't do so, the retained money can be used to hire another contractor to make the corrections.

Besides the retaining mechanism, proper execution of the work can be assured by requiring the contractor to secure a performance bond and a maintenance bond. The performance bond is issued by a surety or bonding company for an amount equal to the total contract price. The bond states that if for any reason, other than acts of God, the contractor defaults on his work, the bonding company shall be responsible to finish the work as specified, at no greater cost to the client. Although the intent is to ensure that the work will be properly done at the contracted price, it is my opinion that such bonds are worthless; the bonding company will try to find every way possible to avoid payment. After all, if a contractor only paid the bond company 1% of his bid for the bond, why would the bonding company step in to pay 5% to 10% of the project's cost to complete it? In short, they won't. Contractors advise me to require a bid bond to verify a contractor's financial stability to do the work, but skip the performance bond (unless required by the lender) and just do good project management.

Construction Calendar

The best mechanism to protect the client is to have the contractor prepare a construction calendar or timetable to make sure all milestones are identified (see figure 222). Probable monthly expenditures for each phase of the work can be placed on the calendar so the client can adjust his cash flow to meet the payment schedule for the work completed. Then, at each request for payment this calendar should be reviewed to see if the project is on schedule, and if not, what the contractor will do to get it back on track

A maintenance bond goes into effect after final acceptance of the project, and is usually in force for one year. This bond guarantees the labor and material that went into the job, so that if errors in workmanship are discovered or materials fail, the bonding company will pay for their correction. This bond is worthwhile.

These methods are common to most building trades, but may be modified as situations dictate. Some golf course projects started with nothing more than a sketch on the back of a napkin or envelope, and the finished product was acceptable. But a client is always taking a risk with such informality. Occasionally, even today, the most professional golf architect may not have the time to prepare a complete set of plans and specifications if favorable planting dates are to be met, so he may elect to work from base sheets and simple shop drawings. But unless the contractor is working on a time-and-material basis, it is the contractor who is taking the chance that the architect's estimates aren't accurate. The client is also taking a risk, for he probably doesn't have the security of performance and maintenance bonds, and has no way of knowing if he is receiving the quantity and quality of work he expects.

Because golf course development is so costly, its most important phase is detailed planning. Only under mitigating circumstances should golf course construction be pursued without such planning, and even then only under the personal direction of someone skilled in golf course architecture.

Schedule of Construction and Monthly Draws for Vail Valley Golf Club

WORK ITEM	1993 SEPT.	OCT.	NOV.	DEC.	1994 JAN.	FEB.	MAR.	APR.	MAY	JUNE	JULY	AUG.	SEPT.	OCT.	NOV
Mobilization / Survey / Staking	125000														
Clearing / Grubbing / Thinning	38250	76500	57375			76500	57375								
Erosion Control	30000	2000	2000	1000	1000	2000	2000	2000	2000	2000	2000	1000	1000		
Topsoil Stripping		40000	30000			40000	30625								
Earthmoving		261750	261750			349000	349000	349000	174500						
Shaping		25000	37500			50000	50000	50000	50000	50000	39500				
Drainage		48000	72000			96000	96000	96000	96000	69005					
Walls / Bridges							96000	96000	91000						
Topsoil Replacement								48000	48000	44625					
Greens Construction								63000	63000	63000	31500				
Tee Construction								30000	30000	15000					
Irrigation / Pump Station									333800	333800	333800				
Cart Paths									160000	130950					
Planting Preparation									30000	40000	40000	14000			
Seed / Sod / Mulch / Germination										132000	176000	171970			
Bunkers Construction								24000	48000	48000	39099				
Landscaping											60000	60000	60000		
Retainage and Contingency *															49657
Billable	193250	453250	460625	1000	1000	613500	681000	758000	1126300	928380	719899	245970	60000	– 0 –	– 0 –
Less Retainage	19325	45325	46062	100	100	61350	68180	75800	1466	– 0 –	– 0 –	– 0 –	– 0 –	– 0 –	– 0 –
To Pay Contractor	173925	407925	414563	900	900	552150	612900	682200	1126300	928380	719899	245970	60000	– 0 –	– 0 –
Cumulative		581850	996413	997313	998213	1550363	2163263	2845463	3970297	4898677	5618576	5864546	5924546		642112

* 50 % of work complete by early May and no retainage withheld after that date.

Figure 222. A proposed construction calendar and possible amount of contractor's request for payment.

15

Aspects of the Construction Sequence

When the contractor is selected and the contract finally signed, there remains one last item of protocol before actual construction begins. It is the preconstruction meeting, conducted at the site and attended by the golf architect, the contractor, the subcontractors, the client, representatives of any utility with existing or planned installations, and other engineers or architects involved with the project. The purpose of a preconstruction meeting is to formalize cooperation among all people involved with the site or the proposed project. This face-to-face meeting establishes the lines of responsibility and personal points of contact for all parties involved. There is an exchange of specific information about construction sequences, exact locations, time schedules, necessary coordination, and any site data that have changed or are expected to change since the plans were drawn. This coordination process must begin before construction, for once the golf course contractor begins work, it is often at a six-days-per-week, 14-hours-per-day pace that requires instant answers to unforeseen situations, with no time for meetings. To facilitate communications, a roster of everyone involved is made with names, addresses, work and home phones, and areas of responsibility.

Preconstruction Considerations

The information exchanged at a preconstruction meeting is specific to any given project, and hence so variable that there are few common guidelines. Some usual points of discussion include where the golf contractor will set up the field office, toilets and employee areas, the equipment and fuel storage areas, material storage and security systems, and entrance roads, gates, locks, and parking areas. Schedules and deadlines have to be established, such as: the last date to have power to the pump site; the last date any utilities crossing the course must be completed; the earliest date to have phone and power installed at the field office; the starting dates for subcontractors; dates when invoices will be submitted (and probable lapses of time until payment); and the probable starting dates of ancillary construction projects, including roads, sewers, and clubhouse.

Construction Sequence

The construction sequence is also broken down by operation and location. Where and when will clearing operations start? When does subsurface drainage installation begin? How will the successive phases of clubhouse and road construction coordinate with final shaping of golf course features? For instance, it hardly pays to have completed a particularly sensitive area of the golf course only to find that the bulldozers waiting to clear the clubhouse parking lot have to trample across the green site.

To the uninitiated, it may appear that golf course construction is a melee of men and equipment with little coordination or control (see figure 223). However, the trained eye will detect a carefully orchestrated and rigidly enforced sequence of operations that is never violated by experienced professional golf course builders.

Staking

The first step is staking the course, physically locating the center of each element of the golf course and any property lines not previously marked, and then designating them with a stake or flag (see figure 224). Most of the time, the

Figure 223. To the uninitiated, golf course construction may seem unstructured, but it is actually a highly organized effort. This is especially true on a project like Westwood Plateau.

Figure 224. Key golf course points are surveyed in and marked with a pole and flagging for future reference. Other stakes are added to mark installed or constructed features. This is the Citadel, under construction in San Angelo, Texas.

client pays a surveyor to do the centerline staking of each hole because he is usually the person most familiar with the maps and site. However, the contractor may be required to do the center staking and the golf course architect only verifies it. The most common method is to place one stake at the back of the pro tee, another at the center of the landing zone(s) or dogleg(s), and one in the center of the green.

Clearing and Grubbing

The second operation is clearing and grubbing (see figure 225). This entails removing trees, brush, vegetation, and debris to expose the topsoil for earthmoving and seedbed preparation. Each contractor has his own method of clearing and grubbing. Whatever the method, the result must be the same. The desired result is complete removal of all trees, brush, saplings, roots, stumps, vines, rubbish, structures, and debris from all fairway lines or areas of grade change. This is commonly done first either by cutting down and salvaging usable timber and removing stumps with a large hydraulic backhoe, or using a bulldozer with a clearing blade to push out the biggest material, followed by a bulldozer with a root rake, and finished with a tractor-pulled rake or a large root disc (see figure 226).

Figure 225. After staking, the limits for clearing and thinning are tied out in the field, usually by the golf course designer. At first the hole is cleared narrow, and then edges are adjusted for the second clearing.

Clearing usually involves cutting 100-foot-wide swaths down the centerline of the hole, then allowing the golf course architect to view it and then adjust the second cut width to save or highlight trees or vegetation along the edge of the golf hole. The removed material is pushed into burning piles or pits, hauled away, buried in preselected, non-play areas or shoved up into large piles for wildlife habitats in out-of-view locations. During the clearing and grubbing operation, every effort is made to save the topsoil, for it is frequently the most precious resource on a project. Also, efforts should be made to dispose of debris, for if debris is buried haphazardly it may interfere with earthmoving operations, complicate tile drainage or irrigation installation, impede seedbed preparation, and complicate long-term maintenance.

Selective Thinning

Once the total clearing operation is completed, the contractor begins the selective thinning process in areas adjacent to playing areas. The purpose here is to preserve some vegetation, yet permit long-term, efficient turf maintenance (see figure 227). From the standpoint of golf, the idea is also to provide a chance for the errant shot-maker to find his ball and continue his game. In selective thinning in the Midwest, we usually designate that the contractor remove trees of less than a 4-inch caliper at the base (unless those are the only trees present) and any trees closer than 22 feet apart. Remaining trees should have limbs lower than 8 feet removed,

Figure 226. A root rake on the front of a big bulldozer cleans out roots, small stumps, large rocks, and other details.

Figure 227. Selective thinning of wooded areas to remain permits grassing it and maintaining it so golfers can find errant shots, and light and air can flow freely across the golf course.

and cut or injured surfaces treated with a wound compound within 24 hours. These sort of specifications allow larger trees to remain far enough apart so that tractor-pulled equipment can be used to maintain the area. By removing low branches, the area is easy to walk and play golf through. Such thinning not only encourages turfgrass growth in what will be lightly shaded spots, but also more vigorous growth of the remaining trees.

Figure 228. Bill Kerman, one of my chief designers, is setting out the work limits for clearing and selective thinning. There is no substitute for the golf course architect personally selecting these limits.

The golf architect should personally mark—or verify the marking of—all clearing and selective thinning limits (see figure 228). In delicate situations, he should mark every tree that is to be removed or preserved. This sort of personal attention to detail often determines whether the golf course is average or spectacular. By virtue of its size, production, and formulation process, an aerial photograph is insensitive to the vegetation it portrays. Although an aerial photo may clearly show the location and limits of vegetation, it does not identify age, health, species, or conformation. And no matter how meticulous the early stages of routing and planning that follow, no one can fully determine clearing and thinning plans from an office. Slogging through the mud may be indispensable to finding all of the unique properties that characterize a site, including its specimen trees, or simply those worth saving.

I recall one particular hole that my mentor Jack Kidwell rearranged to save a unique low-growing cluster of sassafras trees. Those trees were masked by the thick brush both on the aerial photograph and on the ground, but they caught Jack's eye as he was marking the clearing lines. He redesigned that hole and several others near it to save and highlight those interesting trees. Because of that attention to detail, the golf course has been enhanced, especially in the autumn when their foliage adds an aura to the hole that no architect can build in; he can only bring it out. Had the trees been removed as planned, no one would have been the wiser. But thanks to sensitivity and experience, a pleasant hole was made memorable.

Major Drainage

After the clearing, thinning, and disposal are completed, the contractor can begin installing a major network of large-sized subsurface drainage (see figure 229). These are usually poly plastic, metal, or cement pipes of sizes ranging from 8 inches up to 8 feet in diameter. The size of the pipe is determined by the area it must serve, and its location depends on how it relates to the golf holes. Thought and care must be given to the location of subsurface drains, for where the water enters and leaves the pipe there will usually be an area of water turbulence. First, it must be determined where the end points of the pipe lie

Figure 229. Major subsurface drainage pipes go in immediately after clearing and selective thinning, because all other minor systems must connect to them.

and the amount of fall that will occur between these points. Using a transit or level, elevations are determined for the exact bottom of the pipe, called the invert elevations (see figure 230). By knowing how deep the pipe bed is to be, the contractor knows how wide his construction area will be and how far back he must strip the topsoil. After the topsoil is stripped and stored, the pipe bed is prepared by digging or filling until the bottom of the pipe bed is smooth and has a uniform pitch. Then the pipe is laid on the bed and stabilized while clean fill or sand is placed around its haunches. After the connections are reexamined, the pipe is carefully buried to ensure that large rocks or chunks of dirt in the covering fill don't dislodge or disturb the pipe. The fill may be replaced in 10- to 12-inch layers and compacted or allowed naturally to water settle. Once the fill is up to design subgrade and is harmonious with adjacent slopes, the topsoil is replaced as specified. Finally, at the ends of the pipe, the contractor will install end sections, headwalls, revetments, rip-rap, or plunge pools as required.

Earthmoving

After the major subsurface drainage is installed, the golf contractor turns his attention to earthmoving. The contractor first strips and stores any topsoil—for it is one of the most valuable natural resources on the site—to ensure healthy turfgrass on the finished golf course (see figure 231). He then establishes field controls to guide the operation. From working drawings he determines the site and extent of cuts or fills. Then by using grade stakes (wooden stakes on which existing or proposed simple elevations are marked), he lays out the work. For cut-and-fill operations, only a few grade stakes may be needed, but for something more complicated, such as a green and sand trap complex, as many as fifty to sixty grade stakes may be necessary. These stakes should be maintained until all the earthmoving is completed and the finished feature is ready for topsoil.

There are various degrees of refinement associated with earthmoving operations. The crudest is where the fill or dirt is simply dumped in piles as shown on the grading plan and only slightly graded out; this is called "rough subgrade." When the fill has been worked and graded to conform to the required grades and is ready for topsoil, it is called "design subgrade." When the topsoil is placed down but has not been worked, then "rough finish grade" has been reached. After working and grading the topsoil to a smooth and harmonious grade in conformity with planned evaluations, the site is in "design finish grade."

The equipment used for earthmoving operations depends on the scope of the operation, the distance the earth must be moved, and the conditions of the site. The most common instruments are bulldozers, earthmovers (also called

Figure 230. To ensure drainage systems work as required, a transit or level is used to establish the invert elevations (or bottom of the flow line) of the drainage lines. The rock at Westwood Plateau made this particularly difficult.

Figure 231. Topsoil is stripped from all sites that will require any earthmoving or extensive shaping.

scrapers), pans, backhoes, trackhoes, power shovels, trucks, dredges, and pumps. Since each of these has advantages, disadvantages, and limitations, each will be considered separately.

The average person most quickly associates the bulldozer with earthmoving operations, perhaps because bulldozers are so ubiquitous (see figure 232). But, in fact, a bulldozer is better suited to grading than earthmoving. Except for short distances of no more than 100 yards, a bulldozer is quite inefficient in moving large quantities of earth. The amount of actual material that stays on the blade and is moved by a dozer is quite small for the time and power expended. But a bulldozer is useful in tight working spaces, on steep slopes, or on moderately soft ground. But generally most contractors treat bulldozers as machines better suited for grading, pushing, or ripping hard surfaces.

If large quantities of fill must be moved within a site over distances ranging from 100 to 500 yards, the most efficient tool is an earthmover or pan. A pan is either pulled by a dozer or tractor or has a self-contained power source of one large engine for two-wheel drive, or two engines (one front and one back) for four-wheel drive. The most common types used for golf course construction are the rubber-tired two- or four-wheel-drive types. The pan is efficient because it can usually load itself, carry large volumes, and is fast in transporting fill. Its primary disadvantage is that it is very heavy, and thus requires firm dry working conditions so that it doesn't slip, spin or get mired down. The pan is not very maneuverable and must be given adequate room between grade stakes and for turns.

There are two distinct methods of pan loading. One is a slicing action, performed by a bottom blade of the hauling compartment, much like a cheese slicer (see figure 233). This method is fast and especially efficient in loose, friable material. Pusher assistance may be needed, however, in more plastic materials such as moist clay that tend to resist breaking. In those situations, the cutting action of the bottom blade of the pan acts as a great plane, cutting thin slices of earth, which curl much like wood chips from a wood plane. As these huge curls are loaded in the pan, they collapse upon one another and form pockets or voids. If, after this material is dumped it is not sufficiently worked by dozers to remove the voids, they will collapse at a later time. I recall once being summoned to a course where in the spring of one year a golfer had sunk up to his waist while putting. As I suspected, the course had been built years earlier with a slicer-type pan and care hadn't been taken to remove the voids from the fill material.

Figure 232. Bulldozers are good earthmovers only for short distances (100 yards or less) and for poor material like mud, rock, and rocky soils.

The other kind of pan is the self-loading or elevator pan (see figure 234). This piece of equipment has a conveyor belt with beater bars mounted immediately in front of the slicer blade.

Figure 233. One type of pan or earthmover is a slicer type, which usually requires a pusher bulldozer, but it is well-suited to wet conditions or hard or rocky soil situations.

Figure 234. Earthmovers can be self loading—that is, they don't require a pusher bulldozer—and are best adapted to dry, clean soil conditions.

As the fill leaves the blade, it is met by the beater bars, which break it up into small clods to prevent large voids. Material moved by a self-loading pan is easier to grade after being dumped, will settle at a more uniform rate, and is best suited to stripping and replacing topsoil. Also, the choice for golf course work in plastic soils is the self-loading pan. Incidentally, all pans serve not only to move fill, but also to compact it as they run over it to dump their loads. Such compaction is usually sufficient, and additional compaction by machines is only required in special situations or under foundations or roadways.

Another method, called top-loading, moves earth by power shovels or loaders and dump trucks or pans (see figure 235). This method is the most efficient and economical at distances greater than 500 yards. Trucks have the advantage of fast transport speeds, they can place the earth in small working areas and, because they are not as heavy as pans, they can work in softer conditions (see figure 236). But since trucks are loaded by a shovel or loader, there's always a chance that small voids may form between the piles. Another disadvantage with trucks is the high concentration of manpower involved, which can compound the chance of a costly mistake or a slowdown in construction. Also, the small loads most trucks carry necessitate many trips, so good haul roads must be maintained.

A last method of earthmoving is by dredge or sand pump. Such equipment is used where a high water table prevents earthmoving by more conventional means, in coastal areas, swamps, or where planned lagoons or waterways are to be built. The cost of moving earth in this fashion is not high, but it is slow and the fill can only be pumped a limited distance from its source.

No matter what the method of earthmoving, the purpose is to alter the existing grade to conform to the golf architect's plan. The initial stage of such design work is called rough grading. It entails working the land to within 2 to 3 feet of finished grade and bringing the bulk fill material in place and at the approved design subgrade.

Shaping

The next step, before replacement of the topsoil, is to bring to life the features that will characterize each hole. This is what is called "feature shaping"—the real artwork of course design (see figure 237). Here, the surface features are brought to within six inches of final grade.

Figure 235. A dozer pushes wet, sloppy soils to a backhoe, which in turn toploads it into a pan. Since this dirt is handled three times, the cost is much higher.

Figure 236. Some trucks are designed and built to handle tough hauling jobs within a site. These have to be toploaded, but they are best suited for hauling rock.

Figure 237. The real "art" in golf course construction is called "shaping," where bulk fill is given personality and character. Lots of people can run bulldozers, but very few are shapers.

Figure 238. Great shapers can take a flat field and make it look like the 14th hole at Cook's Creek in Circleville, Ohio.

Shaping has become a more important part of golf course construction as a result of the recent importance placed upon achieving "the look" associated with such contemporary projects as PGA West, Cook's Creek, and Devil's Pulpit (see figure 238). The bulldozer operator with imagination and exceptional hand-eye coordination to mold dirt into features associated with these golf courses is no longer a dirt mover, but is considered an artist and can earn two to three times more salary than can an ordinary dozer operator. Many golf course architects jealously keep a stable of shapers who are their exclusive employees and work only on their projects. Oftentimes, a shaping budget for a golf course project will be higher than either the earthmoving itself or the golf course architect's fee. It is not unusual for a shaping budget to allow for 3,000 hours or more of bulldozer time, which is the equivalent of five shapers working for four straight days on *each* hole. In fact, some golf course contractors are often selected not for their artistry, but rather for the artistry of their shaping crew.

There are many reasons for this emphasis on shaping in modern golf course architecture (see figure 239). One reason is the photogenic qualities of golf holes—often at the expense of playability—in order to get publicity in golf magazines. (One architect has earned quite a bit of notice for a couple of golf course designs that can only be understood from a helicopter view. Otherwise, from the ground, it is difficult to tell if a bunker is shaped like a fish, or whether a hole is an earth sculpture of a mermaid.) Another reason for extensive shaping is to build visual interest in a golf hole through the contrasting qualities of sunlight and shadows (see figure 240). This is the origin of the term "shadow

Studio A Advertising

Figure 239. Some golf holes fit the land so well that no earthmoving is required, only shaping. As an example, consider the 14th (playing out of the opening in the trees on the right) and the 15th (par 5, uphill) at Blackthorn in South Bend, Indiana.

Figure 240. Shadows emphasize shaping lines and make bunkers seem deeper than they really are, like at the 15th green at Naples National.

Figure 241. Wood walls have been part of golf courses for about 150 years. Here is an example from Westward Ho! in North Devon, England.

bunker"—a feature designed as much, if not more, for its contrasting visual qualities and for its vertical relief as for its strategic position in the scheme of shot values.

The increased emphasis on shapers seems to have paralleled the emergence of celebrity designers who usually lack professional skills to formulate and present design concepts in a conventional manner, and who, therefore, must rely on skilled shapers to make them look good. In essence, the shaper is the real designer, but is willing to let the celebrity take the credit. Yet golf course architects use many different shapers, because this permits them the freedom to do less detailed plans and simply rely on the shaper to build in the detail or nuances in the field. But the golf course architect can pay a price for this in terms of quality and consistency. As alluded to earlier, it is not uncommon to find that one golf course by a certain golf course architect is masterful and another by the same architect is miserable, depending upon who the shapers were. An architect is only as good as his ability to communicate his design intent to the shapers.

Shaping is also an integral part of drainage. As previously discussed, at least 2% pitch (3% on warm-season grass) is required to allow water to surface drain across turfgrass. Additionally, one should never allow water in active play areas to drain more than 150 feet before it enters a tile or is out of play. If (like the author) one prefers fairways to be as wide as possible, one should try to avoid drains in fairways, and shaping must be done to skillfully direct the water and hide catch basins or drop inlets.

Walls and Bridges

Stone and wood walls have been part of golf course architecture for about 150 years (see figure 241). Oftentimes they are used only to add color or texture to the golf course, but are most appreciated as an integral part of the course when they also seem functional, and/or very old. At Devil's Paintbrush, the walls are over 100 years old, while the walls at Naples National are new, but in both cases the walls add an unmistakable charm (see figure 242a & b). At Westwood Plateau and Glenmaura, the boulder walls are purely functional in that they stabilize banks and slopes that would otherwise collapse (see figure 243). Construction of these walls sometimes requires a good bit of engineering and special construction techniques or equipment. A civil engineer should be consulted on the bigger walls, and an experienced contractor should be used to build them.

Figure 242a. Most of the stone walls at Devil's Paintbrush were built by pioneer farmers, and are a significant part of the hazards on the course.

Figure 242b. At first, the stone walls at Naples National were planned to be purely aesthetic, but they are actually functional in that they saved precious fill material and trees by building vertical walls on tees. They also make the golf course seem older or more mature.

Figure 243. Westwood Plateau walls are purely functional, extensive, and necessary because of the mountainous terrain.

16

Tee, Green, and Bunker Construction

Tees are not as simple to construct as they seem, but by using some proven methods, good results are likely (see figure 244). First, the topsoil should be stripped from the area and any unstable subsoil or foundation material removed. Then, using the plans, the contractor sets his grade stakes to show the base or bottom of the outslope of the proposed tee. If the tee is to be raised above grade, earthmovers deliver the fill to the tee site. A small bulldozer then shapes it to the grade stakes in shallow (6-inch) lifts, compacting each lift as it goes down. Once the tee is at a state of design subgrade, the golf architect inspects the tee, makes whatever alterations are necessary, and approves it for topsoiling or the addition of sand or other soil amendments (see figure 245). After topsoiling is done, the golf architect inspects the design finish grade so that any subtle changes can be made before installing irrigation.

Unless a tee is constructed like a green, using green mix and underdrainage, tees cannot be perfectly level, for drainage must be provided for. The golf course architect usually specifies the di-

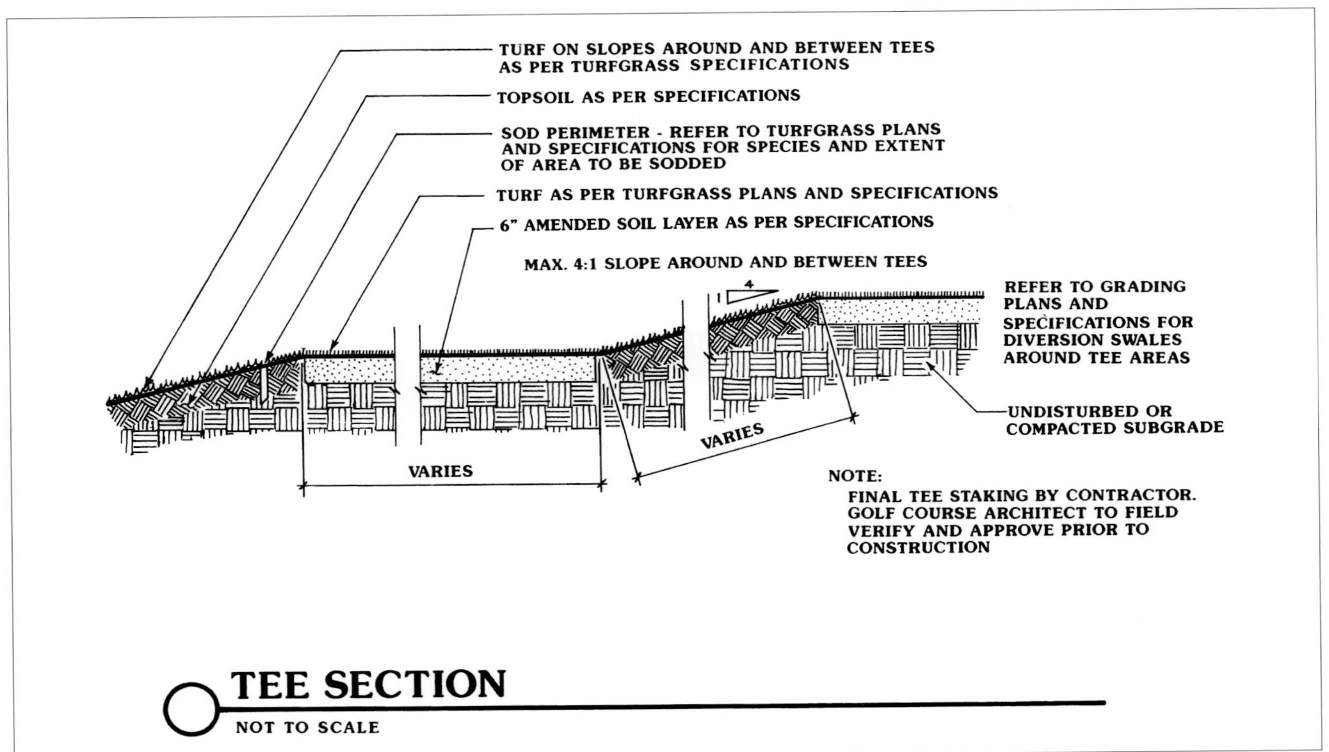

Figure 244. Typical construction detail for tee construction.

Figure 245. The topsoil or amended rootzone mix is spread on the 6th tee at St. Albans Country Club. Grade stakes are removed and the planting bed is prepared.

rection (back to front, left to right, etc.) and slope (1%) of the tee's surface drainage, and the contractor must use a surveying instrument to ensure that tee surfaces will indeed drain. Before irrigation, the tee should have all the appearance of a finished tee except for fine grading and planting. Requiring the tee to be in this state of completion eliminates the possibility of damaging the irrigation heads, control wires, or tubes during finish grading, and ensures a uniform topsoil or amended soil layer over the tee surface to permit uniform turfgrass growth and management.

Greens

The building of greens, while done in a fashion similar to tees, is a great deal more complicated. First, the contractor strips the topsoil or sod from the green site and sets his grade stakes (see figure 246). The stakes should be placed 20 to 30 feet apart to give plenty of working room for the earthmovers, yet close enough to identify the shape of the green. It is best to establish the perimeter of the green with a grade stake placed at every change in direction or elevation as shown on the plan (see figure 247). Each grade stake is marked with the proposed elevation at that point. If conditions permit, grade stakes for bunkers or mounds can be set at the same time and in the same manner, or the contractor/ shaper roughs in the bunker and makes the necessary adjustments after the golf architect inspects it. Even for a person experienced in reading working drawings, it may take several hours or more to grade-stake one green and its surrounding features.

Once the stakes are in place, the earthmovers begin bringing in or cutting away fill to build up the green (see figure 248). A dozer then grades the earth to conform to the grade stakes, compacting the fill to about 90% of full compaction as they go (see figure 249). This process continues until the green is at design subgrade. For greens built to existing grade or built below existing grade, the construction machine of choice depends on working room, scope of work, and material, but is usually done with a large bulldozer. Once the desired basic gradients are achieved, the distinctive aspect of greens construction have to be confronted.

At the point of rough grading, the golf architect reviews the work and makes whatever necessary changes are needed. Then the contractor will install the tile drainage as shown on the plan or as laid out in the field by the course architect (see figure 250). After the tile drainage is approved, the contractor places the topsoil around the outside perimeters of the putting surface and around the sand line of the sand traps (see figure 251). This operation is called "ringing." When ringing is finished, the inside of the

Figure 246. Contractor strips sod and topsoil from green site. Topsoil is saved for later reuse; sod is disposed of. This is the 2nd green at Hillcrest Country Club in Batesville, Indiana.

Figure 247. Existing irrigation is removed and grade stakes set.

Figure 248. Excess fill is cut away from the old 2nd green at Hillcrest Country Club. This stage is called "rough" subgrade.

Figure 249. A small bulldozer works the green site soil to shape it to the architect's plan (2nd green at Hillcrest C.C.)

Figure 250. After the architect approves the design subgrade of the green, tile is installed. At Westwood Plateau several greens were tiled using flat tile laid directly on the design subgrade. This eliminated expensive trenching in the very rocky soil.

Figure 251. At Westwood Plateau, conventional trenching and gravel backfilled methods of tile installation were also used. After tile trenches were cut, topsoiling or "ringing" of the outside of the green began.

Figure 252. The greens at Westwood Plateau are California method, so pure sand is dumped at the edge of the green and pushed over the tile. Notice the tile was flat, and all of the grade stakes used to control depth of sand.

green and sand trap look rather like empty pie shells waiting for the filling.

It is amazing to realize that many of the country's finest classical golf courses built before 1960 had greens comprised of the available local soil. Most greens today, by contrast, are built of a high percentage of sand, often blended with a laboratory-determined percentage of organic matter, with no soil whatsoever.

Green Construction Methods

There are many methods of green construction that produce acceptable results, but two of the most popular are the USGA Method and the California Method.

If the California Method is chosen, then after the tile lines are in, pure laboratory-tested and specially selected sand is placed directly over the tile without any layers (see figure 252). The top few inches of the sand is amended before seeding with supplemental fertilizers or organic materials like seaweed extract. The USGA Method uses a 4-inch base layer of small gravel, overlain with 2 to 4 inches of coarse sand, and capped with 12 inches of laboratory-tested and carefully selected sand blended with a small amount of organic matter. The USGA Method functions by "perching" the water table within each layer to conserve water in the rootzone (see figure 253a & b). The California Method, on the other hand, seeks rapid drainage by having no layers and using pure sand. There are strong proponents of each method, and there is no research that definitively concludes that one method is superior to the other. If the golf course designer wants to conserve rootzone moisture he chooses the

---

For additional information on green construction I recommend the following sources of information:

1) *The Evolution of the Modern Green*, by Dr. Michael J. Hurdzan, available from ASGCA, 221 North LaSalle, Chicago, Illinois 60601 - price $5.00.

2) *USGA Method of Green Construction*, by USGA staff, USGA Golf House, P.O. Box 708, Far Hills, NJ, 07931 (908) 234–2300.

3) *The High Sand Putting Green*, Publications, Division of Agriculture and Natural Resources, University of California, 6701 San Pablo Avenue, Oakland, California, 94608-1239, or (415) 642-2431 (publication #21448).

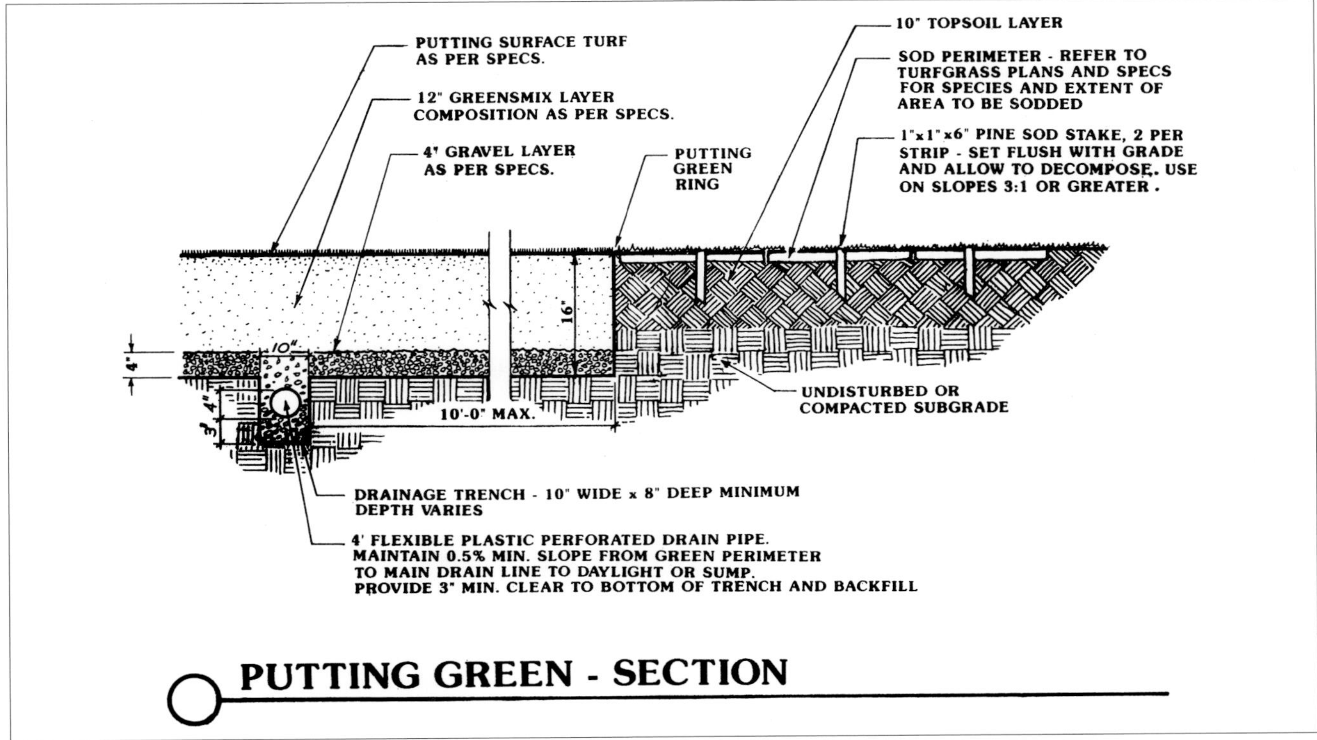

Figure 253a. USGA-recommended method of green construction showing elimination of optional intermediate sand layer.

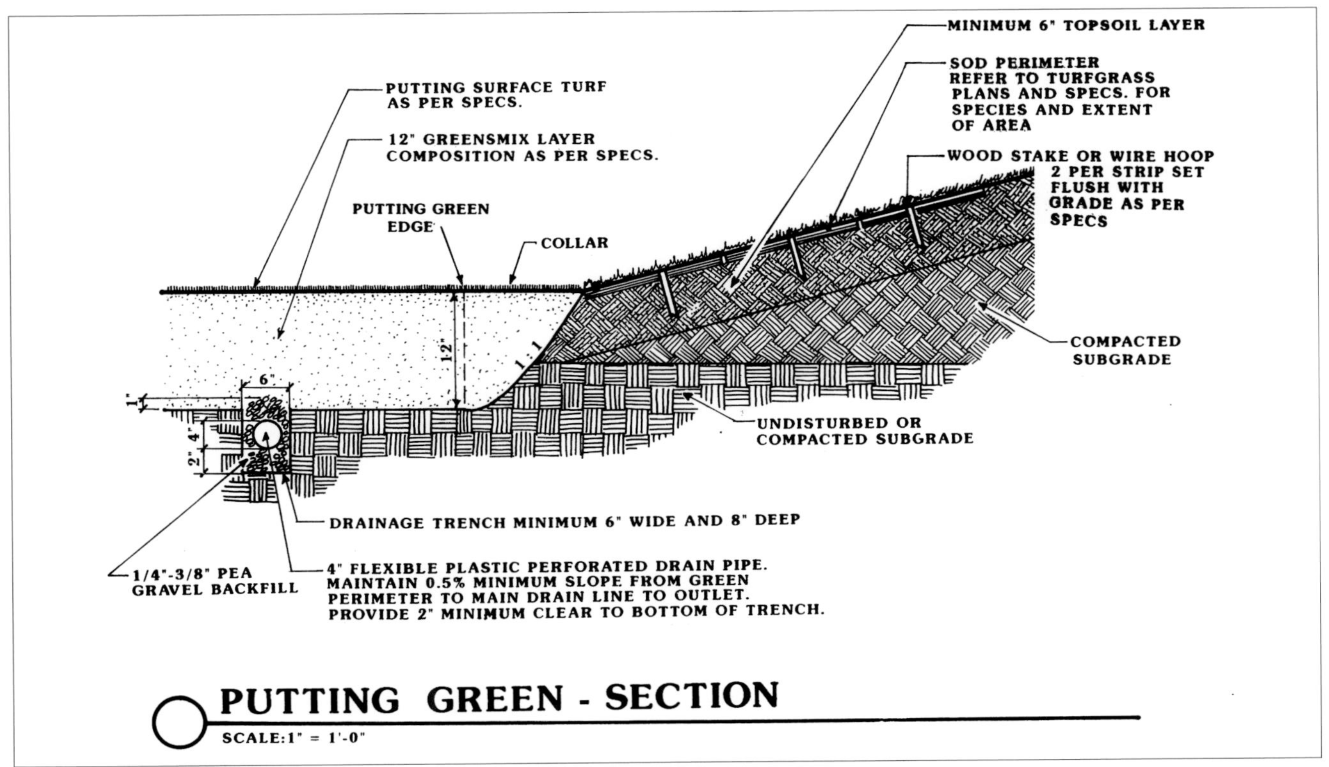

Figure 253b. California method of green construction.

USGA Method, but for rapid drainage he may choose the California Method. Recently I have experimented with a simplified version of the California Method in an area that gets 120 inches of rain per year, and it has worked very well (see figure 254)

If the green is to be constructed using the USGA method the 4-inch blanket of stone is installed over the tile line. Then inside this pie shell of a green and over the gravel may be placed an optional 2-inch to 4-inch layer of coarse sand (see figure 255), and then the sand–organic matter mix, most often called "amended soils." Around the perimeter of the green it is advisable to install a liner that will keep water from being pulled from the amended soil by surrounding native soil, which leads to a dry or droughty ring at the edge of the green (see figure 256). This amended soil mix can be blended together in a central mixing area and hauled out to each green (see figure 257), or the constituents can be brought to each green site and be mixed onsite (see figure 258). Offsite mixing is preferred for the best quality control.

Architect's Approval

But even before ringing, the design subgrade must be approved by the architect, who applies several criteria (see figure 259). The primary consideration is whether the contours of the design subgrade—but without amended soils in place—have the exact configuration as the contours of the proposed finish grade. The design subgrade should be as smooth and compacted and of such a configuration as the contours of proposed finish grade, but without amended soils in place. The design subgrade should look like the finished green, but at a lower elevation. The reason for this is a principle of soil and water physics, which says that the amount of water retained by a soil profile against gravity is inversely proportional to the depth of that profile.

This means that the deeper a soil layer is, the more water will be removed from the top of that layer by gravitational forces, and the shallower the profile, the wetter the top surface will be. So the practical implication of this is that if the contours of the subgrade do not exactly match what the finished contours will be, the amended soils that cover the subgrade will be of different thicknesses, and hence will have a different moisture content at their surface after gravitational water is removed. If the amended soil layer varies in thickness, the water content of small areas of surface will also vary, and will require individual attention. The green will be dry in some areas and spongy in others. When such a situation exists, the golf course superintendent is faced with the dilemma of either: 1) overwatering the turf growing on shallow profiles while properly watering the turf on deeper soils; or 2) hand watering individual spots on the green. For these reasons, a golf architect may be particular about conditions of the design subgrade.

Another criterion the golf architect applies to the design subgrade is its firmness, or compaction. If it is too soft to bear construction equipment or if it appears that it could settle into a distorted surface, the architect will instruct the contractor to compact the subgrade more completely or allow natural settling processes to occur before submitting it for approval prior to ringing. Similarly, if the surface is too rough or has chunks of fill or rock on it, it will not be approved until it is smoothed. If vegetation has started to grow on the subgrade, it must either be removed or killed so that it doesn't contaminate the amended soils with weed seeds or hamper the ringing and grading operation. Finally, the golf architect will check all measurements, elevations, and slopes of the green to ensure they conform to the plans. If all criteria are met, the design subgrade will be approved.

Tile Drainage

Some contractors prefer to ring the green before installing the tile drainage in the green (see figure 260). Others may install the tile first so that the soil from the tile trenches won't contaminate the topsoil ring. But whichever sequence is chosen, the end result must be the same. The tile must be installed and gravel backfilled to the design subgrade surface, all spoil from the tile trenches must be removed, and clean topsoil must be installed around the green. There is no

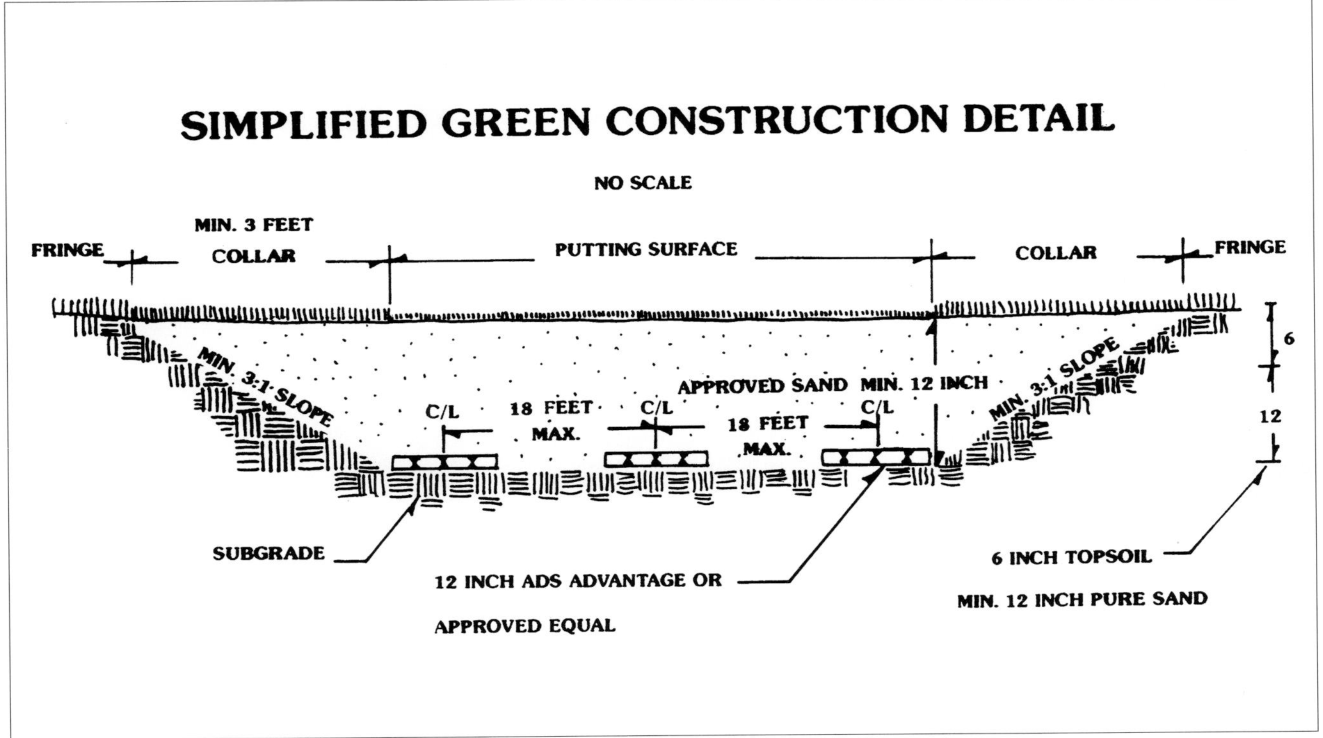

SIMPLIFIED GREEN CONSTRUCTION

Greens are to be constructed in the following manner:

1. Shape subgrade to design subgrade allowing edges of green core to slope back at a 3:1 ratio from designated putting surface, to permit a transition of sand with surrounding topsoil for growing of a collar.
2. Once the interior part of the green putting surface core is compacted and smoothed, and approved by the golf course consultant or his designated representative, the contractor shall flat-tile drainage directly on the floor of the core. This operation will eliminate the trenching and gravel backfilling of all tile. The flat tile shall be 12″ wooden stake or wire staple designed for that purpose.
3. The outflow from the green core shall be 4″ N-12 ADS tile as specified and shown. Outflow tile shall terminate to atmosphere with a 10′ long section of PVC or metal pipe that is fitted with an animal guard device.
4. After the tile is installed and approved by the golf course consultant or his designated representative, the contractor shall install a minimum of 12″ layer of unamended and approved sand inside the collar and green core, that matches and flows uniformly over the design.

Figure 254. A simplified version of the California method using flat tile and no trenching. Rely on laboratory test results before using this experimental method.

Figure 255. A coarse sand layer is spread over a gravel blanket, as per USGA recommendations.

Figure 256. The coarse sand layer and plastic liner are in place, ready to receive amended soils, in accordance with USGA recommendations.

Figure 257. An offsite blending together of sand and organic matter to form an "amended soil." This is a highly controlled operation which is periodically checked (every 1,000 tons on the average) by a quality control laboratory to ensure that the proper blend is achieved. A front end loader adds sand and organic matter to the blend, then loads trucks that have amended soil to go to the green site.

Figure 258. Onsite mixing involves spreading sand uniformly over design subgrade, applying an even layer of organic matter, and thoroughly and repeatedly mixing until homogenous. Offsite mixing is much more accurate.

Figure 259. Before "ringing" the green, the golf course architect will usually approve the work up to this stage, applying several quality control criteria. This is the last chance to identify and correct weaknesses in the foundation of the green.

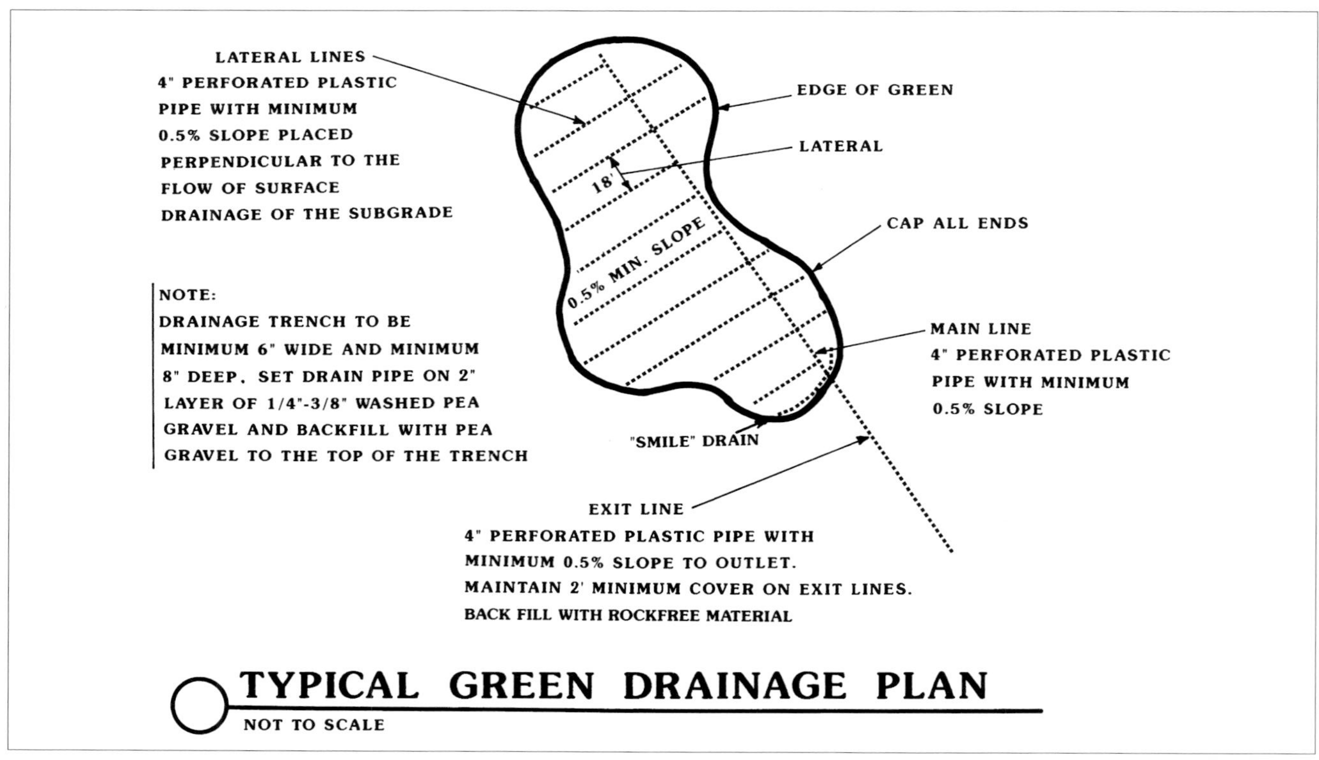

Figure 260. Green drainage detail, using a grid system of layout which the author prefers.

easy way to install tile. It requires additional handwork after the trenching operation. Removal of the excess soil produced from the trenching operation can be accomplished by raking the soil back away from the trench and using a small loader to place it into trucks, conveying it directly from the trencher onto a truck, or by bulldozing it off the green, taking care to run the machine between the trenches and not across them. The bottom of the trench is then filled with a few inches of pea gravel or drainage stone (1/4 to 3/8 inch size), smoothed out, and then meticulously checked for elevations to ensure that the fall of the tile bed measures at least 0.5%. The tile is placed on the tile bed and secured while gravel is shoveled around its haunches to stabilize it. The trench is then filled with the gravel, mounding it up a couple of inches higher than the subgrade surface to reduce the probability of silt being deposited over the tile line by rain, wind, or other construction operations (see figure 261).

Irrigation

Following tile installation comes installation of irrigation, because many of these lines intersect and the trencher would surely cut irrigation pipe that had been previously installed. Because it is easier, cheaper, and faster to repair a cut drain tile than a cut irrigation pipe, the contractor would rather risk cutting a tile line. Various schemes have been tried to preserve tile lines while installing irrigation, such as putting the tile deeper at possible crossing points or installing markers, but neither works without reducing the capacity of the tile. Dips in the tile to avoid irrigation pipe become sediment traps, and markers hamper the settling process (see figure 262).

The exact location of irrigation heads on a green or tee is usually determined and marked on large-scale detail drawings, but it is best to select their precise locations in the field after the feature has been built. Since the size of the sprinkler head is determined by the size of the area to be watered and the rate at which water will infiltrate into the soils in that area, those two factors ultimately determine the spacing between the heads. This distance can vary from 45 to 90 feet, with the most common spacing about 60 feet apart. Knowing the spacing between heads and having the green already built, it is a matter of using a tape measure to plot the locations on the green or tee, and then doing the "as-built" plan of the installation. Lately architects and contractors have been employing irrigation designers to do this layout work, especially in areas where moisture control is critical.

Since the front approach to a green is so important, it is best to begin by locating two heads 60 feet apart, perpendicular to the line of play and far enough forward on the green so that when the green sprinkler patterns are interlocked with the fairway sprinkler patterns the water from the fairway heads just touch the front of the putting surface (see figure 263). This is necessary because fairways require a different amount of water at fewer frequent intervals than do greens. Separation of the influence of fairway irrigation at the front edge of the green permits the golf superintendent to program and control the greens watering as discriminately as possible.

Once the first two heads are located, the rest of the greens irrigation heads are placed in relation to them at the appropriate spacing. Other factors that influence sprinkler head locations are prevailing wind direction, slopes, surface drainage patterns, and proximity of other sprinkler heads. Of course, the overall irrigation design is influenced by the course budget. It is now becoming commonplace to add another set of heads to water only the greens banks, and/or small lawn-type sprinklers are installed on every mound or high spot, and as many as ten additional heads are spaced around each green. Such baroque installations may be economical, but only if conditions are such that the mounds and high spots would otherwise require daily hand watering.

Once the sprinkler head locations are selected, the contractor trenches for the pipe installation around the outside perimeter of the green, never through or across the green. In addition to the sprinkler heads and pipe, he installs the sprinkler control system (hand valves, electric or hydraulic valves, wire or tubing), and finally at least one quick-coupler valve to allow

Figure 261. Gravel should be about an inch above the sides of the trench to protect against silt closing over the tile line.

Figure 262. Irrigation should follow tile installation, or be coordinated with it, so that trenching does not cut the irrigation system or block drainage tile.

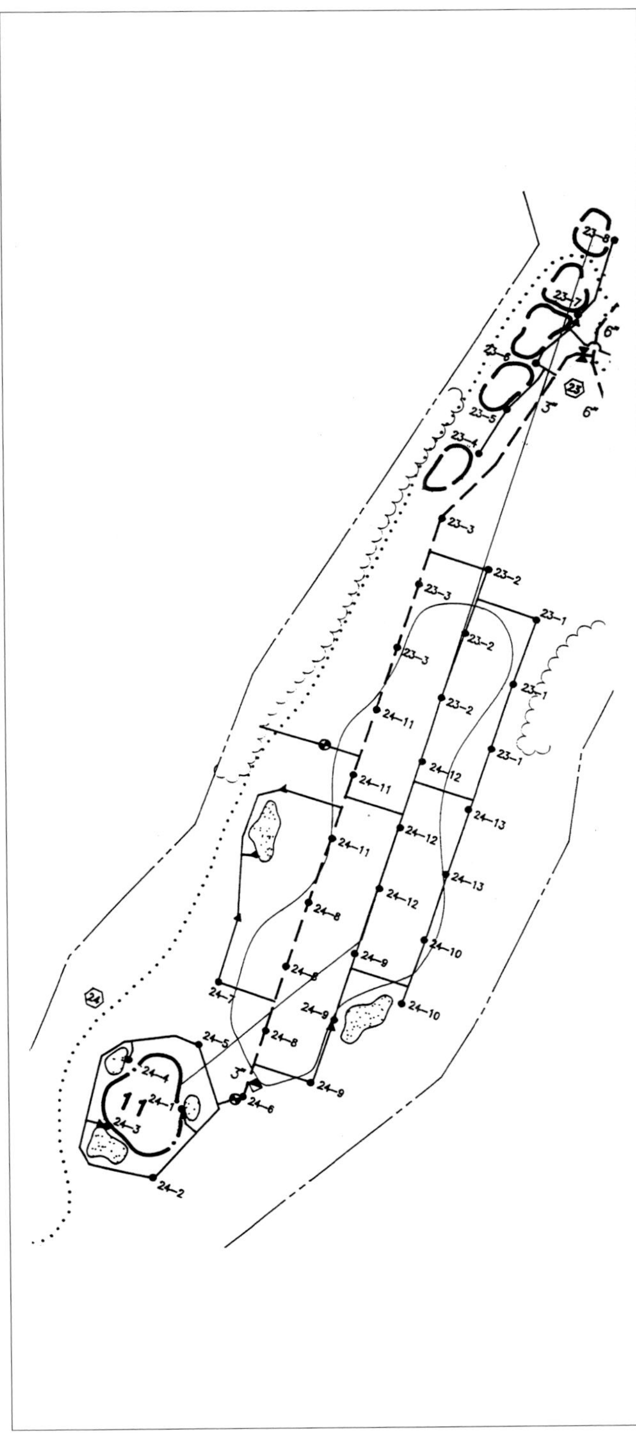

Figure 263. A typical irrigation plan for the 11th hole at Ironhorse in Leawood, Kansas. Although this plan is complete, it must be field adjusted to allow for the subtleties that develop during shaping.

use of a hose for hand watering when necessary. If the system is in a region where freezing temperatures can cause breaks in the pipe, he may install drain valves in low areas or he will grade the pipe bed so that it drains to one location that can easily be purged of water in late autumn. In areas such as the Colorado Plains that experience little or no snow cover, but temperatures low enough to make the turf go dormant, a winter irrigation system is installed below the frost line, 4 to 6 feet deeper than summer irrigation. This winter system is necessary to periodically water the dormant turf to keep it from freeze drying in the winter winds and being permanently lost. Some other courses cover their greens with engineering cloth in the winter for the same reasons.

As in any pipe or tile installation, the contractor will ensure that the pipe bed is smooth, without humps or holes, and will recheck the pipe connections before covering them. He then stabilizes the pipe while backfilling, and backfills in a manner that doesn't damage the installed equipment. Since these lines must be fully settled before planting, the contractor may compact the backfill by wheel rolling, use of a tamper, or flood settling. Lastly, since the spoil from the trenching operation has probably contaminated the topsoil with fill material or rock, the irrigation contractor is responsible for removing any foreign matter and reestablishing the topsoil layer. After this is done he will adjust the height of the sprinkler heads to 3 to 4 inches above the proposed finish grade and mark them so others can avoid damaging them during planting and grow-in. After the turf is matured the heads will be lowered to match the finish grade.

Some contractors like to bed the sprinkler head and swing-joint in sand so that it quickly drains excess water that may slowly leak from the nozzles (see figure 264). This sand backfill also allows for easier adjustment of the heads to grade. Usually the ring of the green becomes so distorted during the tile and irrigation installation that it must all be regraded to reestablish design finish grade. Only after the golf architect is satisfied with the workmanship of the tile and irrigation installation, the regrading of the out-

Toro Company

Figure 264. A properly installed swing joint that is bedded in sand is easier to adjust and handles excess water around the sprinkler head.

Figure 265. Blending surroundings into the green is slow, hard work, but is important to produce an artistic green complex like the 13th green at Westwood Plateau.

side of the green to design finish grade, and the inside of the green to design subgrade will he permit the contractor to install the amended soils (see figure 265).

Amended Soils

First the green's interior is grade-staked to control the depth of the amended soils (and gravel if it is USGA construction). Then the amended soils (and perhaps gravel) are hauled to the green and dumped just inside the edge of the green or between the tile lines. This material will then be graded to conform to the grade stakes. Usually, a small bulldozer is used for this operation. Once the amended soil is in place and conforms to the grade stakes, the stakes are pulled out and the entire putting surface is packed and smoothed with a small tractor and grading attachment or a power sand trap rake. The contractor must blend the amended soil portion of the green to harmonize with the topsoil ring without contaminating the amended soils. This requires a great deal of experience and a great deal of time. The ability to tie these surfaces together into one flowing contour is a skill that separates true construction artists from dirt movers. The personal attention and pride of workmanship of the man applying the final grade establishes the character of each feature of a golf course. For this reason, it can be expected that the golf architect will critically examine each contour, mound, and swale, and will be particular about approving them for seedbed preparation.

Many of the same construction principles and methods used for greens are also used for tees, especially if the client wants them dead level, with no surface drainage. Sand traps, too, are built using similar techniques as those for greens, except that the pie shell of a bunker is filled with sand. The design subgrade of its interior must be as clean, smooth, and compact as that of a green. Likewise, the tile installation is exactly the same for both, and the same standard of workmanship is applied.

17

Irrigation

At least two months prior to the expected planting date, the contractor should begin installation of the irrigation system and pumping plant. Before any irrigation equipment can be installed, all other work preceding it in the construction sequence must be completed at least to the state of design rough grade. That means that all planned clearing, grubbing, disposal, earthmoving, tile drainage, retopsoiling, and initial grading are completed to within a few inches of design finish grade.

Laying Out the Work

With that work completed, the contractor feels reasonably sure that subsequent operations of seedbed preparation will not damage the fragile irrigation equipment that he is about to install. From the beginning of the project, after all, the contractor had to anticipate the direction he wanted the irrigation installation to follow and he had to plan and schedule all of his other work accordingly. There is no set pattern that irrigation installation must follow, but in all cases the contractor realizes his greatest efficiency and quality of workmanship if he does not skip around between work areas, but instead follows a continuous path of irrigation installation from a logical starting point. Most contractors choose to start either at the pump station and radiate outward or at the furthest element and work back toward the pump station. Frequently it may be necessary to use a combination of the two, but in all instances he tries to minimize the number of places where he must stop and restart the installation process. All things being equal, both the golf architect and the contractor would prefer first to install the pumping plant and then work outward. Having the pumping plant installed and in operation early in the construction schedule permits the contractor to use it to test his lines, controllers, and thrust blocks, or to flood settle his trenches.

Selecting the Pump Station

The pumping station (see figure 266) is the heart of any irrigation system and is one area where it is simply foolish to cut corners. This is particularly true on newly planted golf courses, where young shallow-rooted plants require frequent light waterings of perhaps 8 to 10 times per day.

Until a few years ago a pump station was a collage of pumps, motor, valves, pipe, and controls that were delivered to the site as single pieces and assembled by the contractor. This method was plagued by mismatched pieces, incorrect sizes, inexperienced workmen, and imprecise plans for assembly and operation. More headaches, indigestion, and arguments have been generated by a single pump station assembly than by the rest of a golf course project combined.

For these reasons most experienced golf architects, contractors, and superintendents now recommend a package pump station (see figure 267). This is a complete pumping system that has been factory assembled, matched, tested, and balanced to achieve its design efficiency. It is then delivered to the site as a skid-mounted package that is set on the specified pump pad and simply wired up. Most package pump station companies send one of their field engineers to the site to fine tune the system, so the net result is a reliably coordinated pump station, most often for less cost than a do-it-yourself model. Some exceptional irrigation contractors can put

Figure 266. The heart of the irrigation system is the pumping plant.

Figure 267. A package pumping plant, even as large as this one, can be delivered to a job site preassembled in 2-sections.

together a pumping station as reliable, sophisticated, and smooth in operation as a package system, but they are rare.

Not all pumping requirements can be solved simply by installing a package station. There are many different approaches to pumping plant design, depending on the source of water and site conditions, but no matter the source or site condition, the ultimate goal is always the same. The pump must provide a sufficient volume of water to permit irrigation of an entire course over a given period of time at a minimum of working pressure to the base of every sprinkler head, no matter its proximity or elevation. Determining the needed volume and pressure is a complex process based on the daily requirements of the grass plant during drought periods, the area to be irrigated, the soil texture and climate of the site, the slope and topographic extremes of the site, the power source to be used, the time to complete one total golf course watering, and the money available. Since each of these factors varies at each golf course site, the advice of an experienced irrigation consultant should be sought to determine the exact pressure and volume needed.

Sources of Water

Most sources of water can be grouped into three general categories:

1) Subsurface water—wells, springs, natural underground reservoirs
2) Surface water—ponds, streams, or lakes
3) Processed water—city water, sewage effluent, desalinized, or the like

Each source can be used independently, but is often used in combination, depending on the yield of the supply. For example, if we need a volume of 1,000 gallons per minute (gpm) at a pressure of 120 pounds per square inch (psi), we could satisfy this requirement from subsurface sources by developing one well that can withstand a sustained pumping of 1,000 gpm or two wells at 500 gpm or four wells each at 250 gpm, or some other combination. If water comes directly from the well to the irrigation system, then the well pump must be sized so that it not only lifts the needed volume, but also pushes it at the given pressure. However, if it is found that only 250-gpm wells are possible to develop, then it may be more expedient to develop two wells at 250 gpm pumping directly into a holding pond where another pump station of 1,000 gpm can be used to charge the irrigation system. This is commonly done because few places produce high-yield wells. Also, if effluent or purchased water is used it often comes at a slower rate than needed for irrigation and so it is stored up over a longer period of time. By pumping the two 250-gpm wells for twice the running time of the 1,000-gpm relay station, the pond stays full over most of the 24-hour period. Since the wells are being pumped into a holding pond, there is no need to size the pump and motor to the 120 psi level, but rather only to atmospheric pressure (15 or 20 psi), so smaller motors and pumps will suffice. (There is a trend to use lower-pressure (60 to 80 psi) pumps and sprinklers, for they can conserve electric power, stress the piping system less, and deliver larger droplets of water. However, smaller heads must be used, which increases initial cost.)

Surface water sources and processed water sources can generally be handled by one of the wide variety of package stations available to boost pressure and volume. Or the packing station can be custom-fitted to accommodate a particular site limitation by the pump suppliers.

Installing the Pump Station

Once the contractor has decided on the configuration of his irrigation installation, the source of water, and whether to use a package pump station, the golf architect marks the exact location of the pumping plant and the contractor installs a wet well (see figure 268). A wet well is a pipe or box within which the pumps will pick up the water. It is supplied by water from whatever source by an inlet pipe. After backfilling and settling the fill around the pipe and wet well, he pours a cement pad around the wet well (see figure 269). This pad will support the package pump station and serves as the floor of the pumphouse. The pad should be nearly level, but it should drain slightly toward the wet well. In

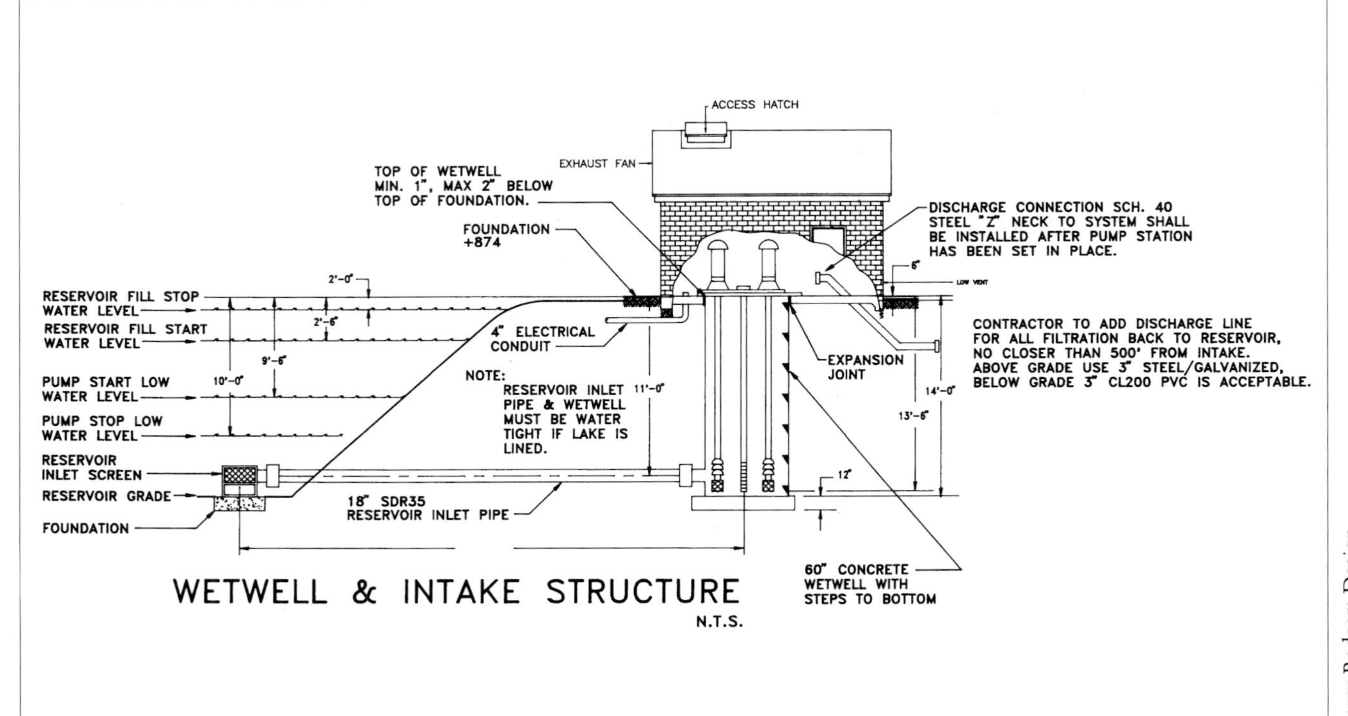

Larry Rodgers Design

Figure 268. Typical detail for wetwell and intake structure.

most instances, the owner is responsible for supplying the electrical service to the pump station site, including the lines, meters, transformers, and main disconnection. All the golf course contractor must do is pick up the electrical power, bring it on to the pad, and wire up the package pump station once it is delivered. As soon as water is available to the pumps, the plant can be turned on and tested. It is good practice to enclose the pump station within at least a high fence, if not an actual pumphouse, to reduce vandalism and to protect people or animals from the high-voltage electricity and the powerful equipment.

Once the pump station is complete, the contractor must route his lines away from the raised pump station and get it into the irrigation pipe for burial in the ground. The pipe that starts the irrigation system should be of a heavy metal until it reaches a place where slow curves of pipe are planned. The metal pipe can then be connected to plastic irrigation pipe. Sometimes this is only a few feet away from the pump pad; other times the metal pipe may run several hundred feet before it is connected to the plastic pipe. After the transition has been made to plastic pipe, the contractor adheres to the irrigation plan for the planned pipe location and size. Since an irrigation plan is drawn to a small scale and is usually not sensitive to conditions, there may be many instances where deviations from the plan are permitted. Such deviations should be approved by the golf architect or irrigation consultant before being attempted, and they must be carefully and faithfully noted by the contractor on a "drawing of record"—the permanent scale drawing of the irrigation installation that is given to the owner upon final acceptance of the job. This drawing of record aids all future golf superintendents, who use it to locate and define

Figure 269. The wetwell and inlet pipe for a pump station can be a big construction job unto itself.

the size of irrigation lines. A similar drawing of record, by the way, should be made for tile installations.

Adjusting Head Locations

The proper laying out of the irrigation system requires that a contractor work from greens back toward tees. Frequently there occurs a compromise between desired sprinkler overlap and actual spacing of heads. It is far better that such compromises are made near a tee, which receives less golfing activity and has more compatible water requirements than do greens. Once the irrigation system is staked out, the architect may wish to inspect the location of the marking stakes and make whatever subtle adjustments he may feel are necessary. Laying out satellite controller locations is done in the same manner.

Locating sprinkler heads may at first seem to be rather routine and require little judgment, but actually the converse is true, especially on the best golf course sites. Such sites are characterized by undulating terrain and changing wind patterns, have holes framed by trees or other vegetation, and usually have many different conditions of soils and microclimates. Since the purpose of the irrigation system is to sustain plant life in the most efficient manner, the best location, size, and type of each sprinkler head must take all of these factors into account. For instance, if it is expected that a hillside will shed water more quickly than the soil will absorb it, then the proper sprinkler head should be of a lower volume and located higher up on the hill than a sprinkler located on a more gentle slope with more porous soils. Similarly, south-facing slopes need more water than ones facing north, and trees are stronger competitors for water than grass plants. These factors should be considered in selecting and locating sprinkler heads.

Areas subjected to winds are especially difficult when selecting the locations of sprinkler heads (see figure 270). Although it is commonly known that winds have a drying effect on grass and thus demand supplemental watering, few people other than superintendents are aware of the devastating effect wind has upon a water stream once it leaves a sprinkler head. Winds not much stronger than those that rustle tree branches can literally atomize a stream of water into a mist. To combat this situation, one can locate sprinklers upwind of prevailing winds, use a lower-pressure water stream or lower-angle sprinkler heads and smaller and more closely spaced sprinklers, or provide quick-coupler valves for supplemental watering. The location and size of each sprinkler head must be given careful thought.

Although sprinkler heads are located by measuring from the green back toward the tee, this does not mean that the irrigation must be installed in the same direction. Once the location of heads is fixed, it does not matter in which direction one proceeds as long as sufficient control

Figure 270. Areas of strong or sustained winds must use extra care in the design, placement, installation, and operation of the system to avoid needless water loss.

wires and tubes are laid with the pipe to service all the planned heads. Generally the materials used in golf course irrigation are polyvinylchloride (PVC) pipe, polyethylene pipe (poly), galvanized or black steel pipe, or asbestos cement pipe (AC). Although popular in the 1950s and 1960s, asbestos cement pipe and steel pipe are not used much because they are difficult to work with and expensive, but occasionally their use is required by law in certain areas. Poly pipe is flexible, safe for potable water, and inexpensive, but in large sizes it does not have the life expectancy or reliability of other materials.

PVC Pipe

The material most widely used is PVC pipe, because it is strong, light, inexpensive, reliable, and easy to work with. There are two categories of PVC pipe, defined by the method of connection. Solvent-weld PVC pipe is joined together by first applying a primer or cleaner to the inside of the connecting fitting of one pipe and to the plain end of the other pipe. Then, a light coating of solvent-weld cement is applied to both the fitting and the plain end. The plain end is then quickly inserted into the fitting, given a quarter of a turn and allowed to dry undisturbed for three hours. The cement actually softens the fitting and the pipe and allows them to bond together as if welded. Hence its name: solvent-weld pipe. If properly done the joint will never separate, so solvent-weld pipe is most applicable in areas where pressure surges or uneven pressures are expected, such as around tees and greens, dead ends or tight turns in the system, or in loose soil conditions. The disadvantages of solvent-weld pipe, however, are its long drying period (which is often ignored by its installer) and the chance of an improper weld or a permanent softening of the pipe caused by too little or too much cement.

The other type of PVC pipe is the bell and spigot type. This type is joined together by seating a rubber "O" ring in a bell-shaped portion of one pipe and then slipping a spigot portion of an adjacent pipe into it. Once water pressure is applied, the rubber ring expands and secures the joint. Without even pressure on the ring, the pipe is free to slip, so this type of PVC pipe is best suited to long straight runs or slow curves. At locations of fittings, pipe size changes, and directional changes, the bell and spigot pipe is subject to separation. To reduce its tendency to separate, the contractor must install thrust blocks—small volumes of concrete poured around the pipe or fitting in those areas that are most subject to movement and subsequent separation. This is especially true in loose or unconsolidated soils that are themselves subject to movement. Because of the inherent characteristics of these pipes, the golf architect may specify both types of pipes on a project: the bell and spigot for long straight runs such as on fairways, and solvent-weld for all other applications (see figure 271).

Figure 271. Large PVC "O" ring main line, with a saddle clamp connection to a solvent-weld lateral, at a major isolation valve that has been thrust-blocked with concrete. Notice the sleeve under the cart roadway to protect the pipe, and supply and control wires on each side of the main line.

Swing Joints

Sprinkler heads do not directly fasten to the pipe. Instead they are joined by swing-joints, a system of fittings and nipples that permits the raising and lowering of the sprinkler head without raising or lowering the pipe. A sprinkler head must be able to move up and down in order to be properly set at grade once the turf is established and the soil settles. A swing-joint also affords some protection for a sprinkler head that might get hit or snagged by a piece of maintenance equipment, or at least it will usually absorb a blow without breaking the underlying pipe.

In the 1980s, the most common swing-joint was made of galvanized steel fittings and nipples. Today, the choice is swing-joints made totally of very thick PVC components and preassembled at the factory. All threaded unions utilize a Teflon® tape to improve the seal between the components and to reduce the necessity to screw down the PVC fittings much. Unlike metal pipe, PVC fittings will fatigue and stretch if tightened down too tightly. Whatever the material or method, a contractor should install a swing-joint under each sprinkler head.

Another element of an irrigation system is the quick-coupler valve. Usually one quick-coupler valve is installed at each green, and others are spotted throughout the golf course wherever it is anticipated that infrequent watering may occur.

The irrigation contractor will also install isolation valves used to turn off water in one section of the golf course to make repairs or additions while other sections can continue to have water. Sometimes he must install drain valves to purge low spots in the water system during prolonged freezing spells. In instances of extreme topographical changes, the contractor may install pressure reduction valves on the irrigation lines to counter added line pressure caused by gravity.

Control Systems

If the sprinkler heads are activated automatically by electric or hydraulic controllers, or by radio remote signals, then the contractor must be concerned about the hundreds of wires or tubes that must be carefully inventoried so that each is correctly connected to its assigned station on the controller. At each controller, he must also install suitable lightning protection using copper rods and wires. To install miles of control tubes or wire is not unusual. This makes recently refined radio controllers practical in some instances.

After the irrigation system is completely installed, the golf course architect will normally demand both a 24-hour pressure test and a cycle test. In a 24-hour pressure test, the irrigation pump is turned on and all lines are charged to 120 psi. When that pressure is reached, the pump is turned off. After 24 hours the pressure on the lines is measured again. If the irrigation system is tight, then the pressure should not have fallen over that period. If the pressure did drop more than a couple of pounds, it is a clear indication of a leak in the system. Leaks are located by walking each line until an abnormal wet spot is found. After all leaks are repaired, the 24-hour pressure test is repeated. When the system finally passes this rigid test, the contractor then operates each sprinkler head from its proper controller or valve. If the system is malfunctioning, the causes must be located and repaired.

Such testing may seem overly demanding for a new and complex installation, but the irrigation system is the key to rapidly establishing a newly planted area, and thus it must be reliable. If a break occurs, it usually results in a sloppy wet area that is difficult to rework once the repair is made and can cause erosion that can disrupt acres of newly planted areas. For these reasons it is not uncommon for the golf architect to prohibit any planting in an area until the irrigation system has been proven sound and operative.

All modern, fully automatic irrigation systems are also connected to a personal computer of 1 megabyte RAM or larger. Mainframe and PC manufacturers are developing new computer technologies in a very competitive environment, so frequent updates or revisions of software are made. The computer usually acts through a satellite controller which may itself be a smaller, simpler computer or a mechanical-electrical device that activates and deactivates the valves controlling a sprinkler or group of sprinklers. Using a computer permits course superintendents to exercise tight control of the irrigation cycle, which normally results in applying exactly the right amount of water in the right spot, and thus saving water, keeping the pumping plant running at its most efficient peak, which saves power and reduces manpower to water the golf course.

Water-Saving Devices

Two other devices common to a modern irrigation system are soil moisture sensors and weather stations. Such stations feed information to the central computer, which on the basis of this data can adjust the irrigation cycle based upon plant requirements and daily water loss. These devices taken together are not gadgets but are essential tools for water conservation.

Another means of water and power conservation is a concept of irrigation design that used a sprinkler head that operates at about one-half of the pressure and volume of a conventional system. This low-volume, low-pressure design uses many small heads in place of one larger head. With some refinement this concept may become the standard of the future, especially because environmental constraints now mean that golf courses of the future will have to do with less water than in the recent past. If, indeed, municipalities impose sharp limits on the water available to golf courses, the design and efficiency of golf course irrigation will become all the more important to the game. Clearly, the use of recycled or effluent water is in the future.

18

Seedbed Preparation and Planting

As the construction of the physical features of a golf course near completion, the contractor must turn his attention to the laborious task of seedbed preparation.

Methods of Planting

Whether the area is to be sprigged, sodded, or seeded, the soil preparation is the same. The process actually begins when the contractor first clears and grubs the site and strips the topsoil. The first concern is unwanted vegetation. Chunks of old turf or weeds interfere with proper grading of the seedbed, prevent seedlings or sprigs from growing properly by blocking light and water, and often reestablish themselves in competition with the desired turfgrasses. The contractor removes unwanted vegetation by stripping it, spraying it with an herbicide, or plowing it under. For large areas, plowing the weeds under a few months before planting is the preferred method. It not only recycles the vegetation into a decaying fertilizer, but also permits easy incorporation of soil amendments and expedites the final grading operations. Even fairway and rough areas altered by earthmoving may be plowed to loosen the soil. Usually some weeds will rejuvenate even after a thorough plowing, so the plowed area should be retilled as often as once a week to mechanically control the weeds (see figure 272).

Figure 272. Areas to be planted are first plowed, disced, rock picked, and then tractor raked and smoothed.

Soil Preparation

Once the soil is loosened and relatively free of live vegetation and large rocks, the contractor applies corrective applications of fertilizer, lime, and other soil amendments as determined from soil tests and prescribed by the specifications (see figure 273). Normally the contractor will use large farm equipment for bulk-spreading materials intended to adjust the pH and major soil nutrients over the seedbed. These materials will then be lightly worked into the soil. Sometimes

Figure 273. Soil amendments have been spread on the 1st hole at Cook's Creek, ready to be lightly tilled into the top 2 to 3 inches of the soil.

if large quantities of corrective materials are needed, the operation must be repeated two or three times.

Final Grading

After the required amount of amendments have been incorporated, the seedbed undergoes a final grading. Each contractor has his own personal method of final grading, but the goal is to break up large clods of dirt, remove rocks larger than 2 inches, roots, stems, and other debris, and fill in the low spots while topping the high ones. Perhaps the most common approach is to disc the soil thoroughly, followed by rock raking with a rock remover and then a tractor-pulled landscape rake to windrow the debris, finishing with a hydraulically controlled land leveler, box scraper, or finishing rake. The disc breaks up the clods, chops any existing vegetation, and floats up any rocks. The landscape rake combs the soil for rocks and debris and places them into windrows to be picked up with a pan or front-end loader. The land leveler, which works on the same principle as a road grader, grades the seedbed to near perfection on flat sites, while floating grading tools are preferred on undulating sites. On certain features—such as tees, greens, sand traps, and mounds—this large equipment may destroy or distort shape and height, so small equipment or hand labor must be used (see figure 274). It is not uncommon for contractors to use hand labor to spread the soil amendments, work them in, pick up rocks and debris, and rake out the green and tee surfaces and banks. Although this is expensive, it normally produces the highest quality.

Architect's Approval

After the seedbed has been prepared and the contractor believes it is ready to be planted, the golf architect inspects the work, for it must meet his approval before planting. The golf architect may ask to see another performance test of the irrigation system by running through a complete program and observing every head. This is done because once the golf course is planted, it must immediately and continually be watered until the turf is mature (see figure 275).

Figure 274. Hand labor is used to work around sprinkler heads and bunkers on hole #1, at Cook's Creek.

Figure 275. The irrigation has been tested and cycled to ensure smooth operation, the trim areas around bunkers have been sodded, and the drainage basin has been protected with straw bales and erosion control nets. The area is ready to be seeded.

Not only does an irrigation leak or problem jeopardize the life of the young plants, but irrigation repairs can disrupt the seedbed extensively. The golf architect might therefore delay planting until he feels the irrigation system is able to sustain newly planted areas.

Another criterion the golf architect will apply when evaluating the seedbed is how firm or fluffy it is. If the top surface is too compacted to permit young plants to establish deep and dispersed root structures, then the seedbed requires more cultivation. On the other hand, if the seedbed is not stable or is muddy it could rut badly during planting. It may not be approved until it reaches a more moderate moisture level. Likewise, if the soil is too dry and powdery so that proper finish grades are not possible, then planting will not be approved until a more favorable soil moisture is realized.

The architect may check for adequate topsoil over zones that are expected to receive lots of golf activity. He will look for proper incorporation of soil amendments, acceptable removal of debris, the absence of large rocks and roots, and a soil structure of small soil particles. For some soils it can reasonably be expected that no stones over 1/2 inch in diameter should remain in the seedbed, while other sites and soils can only be cleaned down to the 2-inch-size stone remaining. The architect may spot check elevation readings to establish proper surface drainage, and he will look for areas that may develop into wet spots or puddles. No matter how carefully the contractor prepares the seedbed and the golf architect or his representative inspects it, there are always problem areas that must be corrected after planting but before the course opens.

Preplant Amendments

When the seedbed is finally approved, the contractor starts the planting operation. First comes a preplanting application of a complete fertilizer at normal maintenance rates. The most commonly used fertilizer has at least one-third of its nitrogen source in a slow-release form to provide some long-term availability and to ensure that the development of the young plants will not be retarded by low nutrition. This preplanting fertilizer may be worked lightly into the soil, but that's not entirely necessary, for the planting operation itself will mix some of it in.

Planting Sequence

Normally, first to be planted are greens, including the putting surface, the collars, and outslopes to a point just beyond the reach of the greens sprinklers (see figure 276). Planting greens this far out allows each green to be watered immediately without causing muddy conditions in areas not yet planted. Greens are normally planted using hand labor because most machines are too large and heavy and can cause distortion of the finished grade. In addition, the working area may be limited and the changes in direction and elevation may be too sharp for normal planting equipment.

After the seed, sprigs, or sod is applied, it is good practice to roll the planted area with a light roller to ensure proper contact with the soil (see figure 277). Then the planted area should be mulched to reduce evaporation losses, minimize erosion, and lower soil temperatures during the day and conserve soil heat at night (see figure 278). Mulch also clearly marks the areas that are planted and encourages people to treat them tenderly.

Concurrent with the planting of greens will be the planting of tees, bunker edges and outslopes, catch basins, pond and ditch banks, and all other areas that need special attention. Where these areas are large enough, power planting equipment is used; hand labor is used only supplementarily. Often these areas are sodded, which reduces the probability of erosion during establishment.

Next comes planting of fairways, followed lastly by the roughs. This sequence permits rather free access for men and machinery to move about without crossing newly planted areas. If paved cart paths are in place, they prove very useful in servicing new turf areas without damaging them. The roughs become the corridors to service the planting and mulching of other places, for roughs can be regraded and planted and mulched in a retrograde fashion

Figure 276. Green and tee complexes are completed first, and then work begins down the fairway and finally out to the rough.

Figure 277. Planting can be done by seeding as shown here, by sprigging, by sodding, or by a combination of methods. Seeding with a Brillon-type seeder is preferred because it gives the best soil-seed contact, which is critical for best germination.

Figure 278. All seeded areas, including greens, can benefit from mulch, be it straw, wood or paper fiber, or a synthetic plastic coating. This straw operation shows use of an asphalt binder or tacking agent to resist displacement by wind or water.

Figure 279. Early germination and growth on hole #1, at Cook's Creek.

much like a painter paints his way out of a room.

Immediately after the planting and mulching, the irrigation system is put to full use. The aim is to never allow the top surface of a newly planted area to dry out. Sprigs and sod are living tissue that must be watered to survive. Seed must be kept wet if it is to germinate quickly (see figure 279). It is not uncommon for an automatic control system for the irrigation to be programmed to cycle sprinklers on greens as often as ten to fifteen times per day for twenty minutes per cycle during hot, dry periods. During this watering phase, motor vehicles should be used on the course only when absolutely necessary. Unthinking workmen and curious observers can easily destroy a newly planted area by compacting wet soils, making tire ruts, or getting vehicles mired in soft wet soils.

At this point the golf course looks complete except for having no turfgrass covering it except sodded area. In fact 95% of the work is complete. But until the planted area grows to a point of being able to resist erosive rains and drying winds, everything done so far could be lost in one major weather event. To say that this is the most critical phase of golf course construction is a gross understatement. The next 6 to 8 weeks after planting are in the hands of God, being feebly assisted by the efforts of the "grow-in" superintendent. Making a 3-foot putt to win the Open is less stressful than growing in a golf course.

From this point forward in the golf course construction sequence, the burden of producing a good golf course shifts from the golf course architect and contractor to the golf course superintendent.

19

Turfgrass Establishment and Maturation

Of all the operations that go into building a golf course, none is more important than establishment and maturation of a fine turfgrass sward (see figure 280). No matter how creative, imaginative, or challenging the golf course features may be, if they are not covered with a strong, healthy mantle of fine grasses they will not be appreciated by average golfers, to whom maintenance is more important than design. So establishing and maturing a good stand of turfgrass is a prime concern of the golf architect and contractor, but usually is the responsibility of the golf course superintendent or a "grow-in specialist."

Figure 280. Once the golf hole is planted and mulched, like the 8th hole at Glenmaura National, the job of establishment and maturation begins, which is usually under the control of a golf course superintendent.

Stages of Establishment

The task is not a simple one, for it requires an understanding of the various physical and physiological stages of turfgrass growth and development. To best understand this in the simplest terms possible, consider that a grass plant goes through three main stages of development, much as a human does. These three stages are: "infancy," when the plant needs constant attention to survive; "juvenility," when the plant looks like an adult but is still physiologically immature; and "adulthood," when the plant is able to sustain itself and vegetatively propagate new plants. The total time from infancy to adulthood for a grass plant is about 10 to 12 weeks.

A plant is an infant from the time germination begins or the sprig takes root until it is able fully to support, nourish, and maintain growth itself using its root system and metabolic mechanisms of photosynthesis, respiration, and other energy-dependent processes. This period usually lasts for about four weeks after germination or planting. The juvenile state lasts as long as the plant continues to grow as a single-stem plant trying permanently to establish itself. It is not physiologically developed enough to be able to spread out vegetatively by means of either belowground rhizomes, aboveground stolons, or new stems. If the juvenile plant is subjected to stress or injury, it may die completely, for once a single stem of a juvenile plant is killed, the whole plant will not survive. An adult plant is able to spread, and thus can recuperate from conditions that would kill single-stemmed plants. Sprigs, sod, or stolons are adult plants, but can often be badly shocked by the planting operation. They act as infants for only a short time, then quickly start toward adulthood, effectively skipping the juvenile phase. Only when the plant reaches adulthood is it suitable to stand the rigors and stresses of an actively used golf course. Grass plants on a golf course must be able to spread and regenerate in order to recover from divots, ball pits, spike marks, pedestrian traffic, and golf cart damage, as well as from diseases, insects, and maintenance machinery damage. Therefore turfgrass plants must have a minimum of 10 weeks of ideal growing conditions before golf should begin.

Since most golf contractors are not turfgrass experts, it falls to the competent and experienced golf course superintendent to guide the maintenance program properly during the phases of germination, establishment, and maturation. Even if the owner had the foresight to employ a qualified course superintendent, he *sometimes* must be guided by the golf architect unless he has grown in a new course before. The requirements of early growth are so distinct as to pose problems for which few are prepared.

Erosion Threat

Until the turf is firmly established, erosion from one severe storm can easily cause hundreds of thousands of dollars worth of damage (see figure 281). Sometimes specifications make the contractor responsible for all damage until the turf reaches adulthood, although "seed or sprigs in the ground" contracts are more common.

Factors Affecting Germination

Four main factors control the rate of seed germination and plant growth: proper soil moisture, balanced nutrition, adequate light, and favorable temperatures. In reality the contractor can directly control the first two, but the superintendent can only indirectly influence the latter two. His acumen in properly manipulating all four factors to the greatest extent possible will determine his success in maximizing seed germination and plant growth.

To further complicate the task, he must recognize that as a plant grows older its needs change, so he must continually adjust his establishment program. To understand the establishment process, consider the chronology of plant growth and related cultural needs.

Figure 281. Water erosion is the greatest threat to establishment and grow-in, for one brief rainstorm can do thousands of dollars of damage to each tee, green, or bunker.

Temperature

We begin with seed germination, since in most parts of the country that is the most common method of planting. (Since regions rely totally on sprigging or sodding warm-season grasses, suitable reference will be made when applicable.) Germination is initiated by the embryo and endosperm of the seed imbibing water under suitable temperatures. These soil temperatures vary for different plants, but for turfgrasses it is generally accepted that 70 to 75°F soil temperatures are optimal, with the range extending from 45 to 90°F. Under optimal temperature conditions, it is common for properly moistened bent grass and ryegrass seed to germinate in five to seven days, fine fescues in 8 to 10 days, and bluegrasses in 12 to 14 days. Under cooler soil conditions the rate is progressively slower. When soil temperatures go under the 45°F mark, no germination will take place.

Since the contractor has no means to warm 150 acres of golf course, he can only indirectly influence temperature regimes by adjusting his planting date. In the Midwest the ideal planting time is from August 15th to September 15th, and in any case no earlier than August 1st nor later than October 1st. Before August 1st there is a much higher frequency of convective thunderstorms that produce the rampant erosive forces, and after October 1st the soil temperature will usually start a rapid decline. These dates are considered optimal. Some people have been successful with July and November seedings, although more often than not they experience tragic failures. Knowing this, an intelligent contractor won't gamble on the weather and will plan the entire golf course construction sequence to meet an ideal seeding period. In southern areas, where sprigging is the common method of planting, sprigging begins about mid-May and is ideally completed by mid-July to afford optimal temperature to establish and knit together the sprigs.

If a fall seeding date is missed, it is not advisable to try a spring seeding. Most experienced golf architects will not permit spring seeding without written permission from the owner that acknowledges the potential poor results of such seedings, and that absolves the contractor of the resulting quality of the turf stand. Instead, most will insist that the contractor practice suitable weed control of the seedbed over the summer and begin seedbed preparation early enough to take advantage of ideal fall seeding periods. The reason for a strong prejudice against spring seeding is that most soils contain countless numbers of viable weed seeds which germinate and rapidly produce plants at temperatures too cool for desirable turfgrasses. The net result is that 50% or more of seeded areas become populated with weeds that cannot be chemically controlled without injury to the young turf seedlings. These weeds grow at a more rapid rate than the seedlings and can shade them out. Weeds also tend to grow in clumps, distorting the finished surface of a seedbed. Even if weeds are not a problem and only turfgrass seedlings grow, there is still a high probability of seedling mortality caused by high temperature stress of summer, diseases, insects, and the fact that seedlings are unlikely to produce tillers, and thus have little or no recuperative ability. Young plants are not usually deep-rooted enough nor close enough together to resist erosive forces of summer rains. Thus, spring seeding is a costly gamble with a low percentage of success.

The contractor should plan all his work in order to meet a seeding date that has optimal soil temperatures. The optimal planting dates for warm-season turfgrasses are in the early summer. Since warm-season grasses compete well against summer weeds, especially in high temperatures, it is desirable to have all sprigging done between June 1st and July 15th. These planting dates allow spring weeds to germinate and be controlled properly before sprigging. Since sprigs are mature plants, they quickly establish and begin to spread vegetatively if they are kept continually moist and well-fertilized for the first four weeks. In addition, chemical weed control of sprigged areas is possible only a few weeks after sprigging.

Light

Another environmental factor that a grow-in specialist can only indirectly influence is ade-

Figure 282a. Properly mulched area that appears to be without germination until the straw is lightly parted.

quate light. One strategy is to adjust the planting date to benefit from long days and high sun angles. But such conditions can produce extremely high soil temperatures that can injure seedlings and cause rapid surface evaporation of soil moisture. To reduce the severity of these conditions, yet realize the advantages of adequate light, an experienced golf architect specifies a suitable mulch for all seeded areas. The best mulches are wheat or oat straw, or wood fiber materials bound with an asphalt or synthetic binder.

Mulch is applied through a mulching machine that separates and shreds the straw or wood fiber and mixes it with a spray of asphalt or synthetic binder. The binder gives structure to the mulch covering by binding the mulch with the soil. Another method is to blow the mulch on without any binder and then use a specialized tool that looks like a disc but actually crimps the mulch into the soil without cutting it into small pieces. This makes it resistant to displacement by wind, rain, and traffic. Any residual seed left in wheat or oat straw that may germinate will help establish the cover crop over the winter and will die from the winter temperatures or during subsequent mowing of the turf. The contractor applies mulch at a rate of about a ton and a half per acre with up to 90 gallons of binder per acre, or crimps it with a straw crimper to reduce the deleterious effects of the sun while gaining the advantage of high light and warm temperature. A properly applied mulch should produce a shade equivalent to 50% screen. In other words, when one looks down at the mulched area he should see an equal proportion of soil surface and mulch (see figure 282a & b).

The mulch on all areas except greens is never removed, but rather is left to rot away. On greens, however, about half the mulch is removed when the seedlings are about 2 to 3 inches long. To remove the mulch, a leaf rake is used to lift lightly and roll the mulch layer away from the young seedlings (see figure 283). Great patience is needed to avoid pulling up shallow-rooted seedlings in the process. The remaining half of the mulch will continue to protect the young plants and will in time either decay or be picked up by mowers.

In some areas it has become popular to seed the golf course with a hydroseeder, using mulches compatible to this machine. Most often these machines leave deep tire marks, the materials often separate within the spray rig, and poor germination results because of poor soil-to-seed contact. A hydroseeder is best left to the purpose for which it was designed—to seed steep highway banks inaccessible by normal equipment—and use of a hydroseeder is the exception, not the rule.

Figure 282b. Pulling away the straw reveals lots of germination.

Figure 283. My mentor—and one of the finest golf course architects to contribute to the game—Jack Kidwell, shows how to lightly remove straw from a green with a leaf rake.

Moisture

Up to this point the contractor has indirectly aided establishment by adjusting the planting date and properly mulching seeded areas. He can exercise more influence over turfgrass establishment by assuming direct control of soil moisture and applying proper nutrition. During the seed or sprig bed preparation, he will have applied soil amendments needed to adjust the soil pH, supplied any missing nutrients, and assured a suitable organic matter content to permit early, healthy plant growth. Immediately following planting and mulching, the irrigation system is used to moisten the seed or sprig bed. Never permit the bed to dry out until the young plants have enough root system to withstand occasional arid conditions. The better the contact between soil and seed or sprig, the better the transfer of water to seed or sprig and the less fluctuation there will be in their water content.

Even after the seed germinates and sends the first shoots upward and the first fragile roots downward, the seedlings will be sustained mostly by the stored food of the endosperm for two to three weeks (see figure 284). After this food storage is depleted, the plant must be of sufficient size and vigor to carry on nutrient uptake and photosynthesis or it will perish. But water is not stored in a seed, so it must be continually available to the seedling through its small, shallow root system. Soils dry at different rates under different environmental conditions, so watering programs must be adjusted to particular soils contexts, never allowing the soil surface to dry during the first three to four weeks after planting.

Frequent and light applications of water to seed beds are the direct opposite of the infrequent but heavy waterings given to established swards (see figure 285). The pattern holds in the case of nutrition: young plants are given several light feedings of quick-release nutrients, whereas established turf is allowed the normally infrequent but heavy applications of long-lasting fertilizers.

Nutrition

It is common for the fertilizer used on high-sand-base greens to be mainly a fine particle uniform-release nitrogen applied in frequent light applications. Chief among the preferred fertilizers are those balanced with equal amounts of nitrogen, potassium, and phosphorus in a 1-1-1 ratio, applied for 8 to 10 weeks (see figure 286).

Figure 284. Young seedlings, growing vigorously through the mulch, start to produce substantial carbohydrates 2 to 3 weeks after germination.

Figure 285. The early watering program for establishment should be light and frequent, so as to never let the soil surface dry out.

Figure 286. Fertilization should be frequent and light to keep the young turf actively growing.

In some locations environmental concerns may require adjusting this rate downward or using only organic-source fertilizers at higher rates. Considerable water will be passing through the sand profile of such greens, leaching away the nutrients at a faster rate than that once turf is established. Microbes in the organic matter of the soil amendments, organic fertilizers, and mulch compete with the plants for the nitrogen. Mulches commonly have a carbon-nitrogen ratio of 70 or 80 to 1 and must be reduced to about 10 to 1 before they no longer compete actively with the turf. As time goes on and less water is applied to the seedbed, the turfgrass root system becomes more extensive and the microbes are more balanced. The fertilizer application can then be altered toward practices more commonly associated with mature turfgrasses, and almost no leaching of fertilizers takes place. Long-term EPA studies on several Cape Cod golf courses have proven that properly managed golf courses actually protect water supplies, not pollute them.

On tees, banks, fairways, and rough, followup nutrition is in the form of a second large application of a complete-analysis fertilizer, usually four to six weeks after germination. This can be applied even on frozen ground not subject to runoff if necessary. Winter fertilization of young turf is not wasted. Even though top growth may have subsided, root growth may continue for weeks and start up in the spring weeks earlier than top growth. On steep ground, winter fertilization is not recommended unless at least 1/2 inch to 3/4 inch of young turf is established to check potential runoff.

Micronutrients

In addition to proper major nutrients, special attention should be given to micronutrients, or trace elements. Shortages of the micronutrients severe enough to seriously impair proper plant growth and development can commonly occur during establishment, particularly on high-sand-base greens (see figure 287). Since the function of micronutrients is to assist in the metabolism of major nutrients, deficiencies are difficult to recognize and identify. The absence of micronutrients can produce disastrous results. Trial applications of likely elements can be made to small areas, and if dramatic improvement in the vigor of turf is observed, then the element in question should be applied to all similar areas of slow

Figure 287. The hardest part of a fertility program to balance on a grow-in is the micronutrients. Here only epsom salts (magnesium sulfate) was applied to the turf to get a dramatic green-up in only 3 days. Magnesium is the center of the chlorophyll molecule, and calcium-to-magnesium ratios need to be 20:1 or lower, with the ideal being 7:1.

growth. Trace elements most likely to be deficient are magnesium, iron, sulfur, manganese, zinc, and copper. Soil tests may prove helpful, but the testing lab should be clearly instructed that tests for micronutrients are required and the results needed quickly.

Biostimulants

In recent years a whole class of plant growth enhancers called "biostimulants" has become widely accepted in the turf industry, especially on sandy soils or rootzones. This class of naturally derived products includes cytokinins, humates, vitamins, and beneficial soil organisms. Although their mode of action is not completely understood, practical experience has shown slow and subtle positive effects, such as increased disease resistance, healthier roots, and more active top growth during or after stressful climatic periods. I personally endorse these products, particularly those derived from seaweed materials.

Mowing

Under normal conditions, newly planted areas should be mowed when the majority of the plants are 2 inches or longer and the soil firm enough to support a small, light mower. Putting greens should first be mowed at 1 inch and slowly lowered to 1/2 inch until turf is tightly knit. In the snowbelt area, the greens should winter between 1/2 and 3/4 inch in height. Bermuda grass greens should be mowed no lower than 3/8 inch until fully established. It has been found best to roll greens lightly before mowing them to remove any surface distortions caused by settling, foot traffic, or animals. Care should then be taken to walk flat-footed on the soft surface to eliminate foot or heel prints. Likewise, power equipment should be operated slowly, making as few turns as possible, ensuring that the turns are slow and gently sweeping. Once the putting turf is well-established (6 to 8 weeks of active growth), the cutting height can be slowly lowered to the final playing condition. On areas other than greens, the turf should be maintained during establishment at about twice the height it will be mowed when mature, but in any case not greater than 2 1/2 inches for any area. The frequency of mowing depends on the growth rate, but once per week is the minimum.

Pesticides

The use of chemicals, such as herbicides, fungicides, and insecticides, is usually not required on young turf and should be avoided when possible. Young plants have a lower resistance to phytotoxic effects of some chemicals and may be seriously injured by pesticides. As the plants mature they respond with more tolerance, so that by the time they are ten or eleven weeks old they can usually be treated with normal precautions. Some grass weeds, such as crabgrass, foxtail, or sedge, can become extremely vexatious in greens during the early stages of turf growth. The best control method is to spot-treat each single weed with a suitable chemical or to cut it out with a weeding tool. After seedlings are well-established, the use of preemergence grass weed preventer or other barrier product is permissible.

Tillering

Most turfgrasses are selected for their normal growth habit of spreading by means of either aboveground stems, called stolons, or belowground stems, called rhizomes. These stolons and rhizomes are collectively called "tillers" and are a means of spreading out to cover the soil surface, repair wounds or divots, and produce a closely knit turf. Very few desirable turfgrasses simply grow in clumps. However, tillering is a physiological function triggered by certain internal mechanisms after the plant has reached a requisite stage of development. In cool-season turfgrasses, it has been found that tillering is strongly initiated by repeated mowing and subjection to cold temperatures (see figure 288).

Before winter or cold dormancy, most seedlings are growing as single individual plants with little evidence of tillering. However, in the following spring, these seedlings, if mowed a couple of times before the prior winter, will initiate tillering.

Once tillering occurs, the maintenance proce-

Figure 288. Mowing programs should allow the plant to grow as high as practical, for the longest time possible, to build carbohydrate reserves and develop root mass. As opening approaches, slowly lower mowing heights, but don't be misled into thinking that close mowing forces vegetative spreading.

dures change from establishment of young plants to maturation of juvenile plants into adults. Maturation is that phase of postplanting care concerned with growing and grooming of adult plants to a condition associated with golf course standards. During maturation the same categories of maintenance procedures are practiced, but their objectives and principles are slightly different. The watering program is shifted more toward single daily watering of longer duration, except for special areas that need some continued supplemental water. The nutrition program is dominated by slower-release fertilizers applied at monthly or bimonthly intervals. Comprehensive soil tests should be made of all greens, tees, and fairways, with the application rates for fertilizers to be determined by these tests.

Continued monitoring and evaluation of micronutrients should be observed for the first few years of growth. The mowing frequency is increased to at least five times per week for greens at 1/4 to 3/16 inch in height. Teeing surfaces and greens collars should be mowed three times per week, and all other areas are mowed twice weekly, with the cutting height slowly lowered each week. The use of preventive pesticides is on an "as needed" basis, with weed control measures the same as for routine golf course maintenance. Spot-seeding, hand watering and some sodding may be necessary to improve some slowly maturing areas. The ability of putting green turf to withstand wear is dependent upon an underlying layer or cushion of 1/4 to 3/8 inch of thatch or mat. Topdressing causes destruction of the mat and thus should be avoided until at least a 3/8-inch mat is present. The topdressing can occur as necessary to maintain the mat layer within the appropriate range. In this way the maturation process slowly evolves into routine maintenance procedures. Too much topdressing is the biggest factor in delaying the maturation of golf greens.

Other Tasks

During the maturation process it is expected that construction deficiencies will be found and corrected. Such things as clogged or broken tiles, irrigation leaks, settled trenches or holes, and the development of wet-weather springs are commonly discovered. Once the edges of the bunkers have a good sod cover, the sand traps can be edged, their bottoms formed into nice bowl shapes that are smoothed and packed, drain tile lines exposed, checked, and regraveled, and then sand transported and spread by hand or rake (some contractors prefer to stockpile the sand in the bunker and edge and spread later). In those areas where the ground freezes hard enough to support large trucks, many contractors prefer to edge traps in late fall and install the sand over winter by having the trucks drive directly to the trap. In those climates where winter freezes will break unprotected waterlines, the contractor will drain the irrigation system and winterize all controllers and the pumping plant. In the spring the contractor is responsible for reactivating the irrigation system and repairing any damage or leaks that developed over winter.

Spring Start-Up

The following spring is also the time for installing shelter houses and drinking fountains. By delaying these projects until the following spring, the turf has been allowed to mature and to support construction equipment without wholesale damage. Tree and landscaping plantings are best done during spring as well. It gives the plants the greatest chance of survival and it permits selection of the exact location to achieve most fully the desired impact of the plant in its grassy surroundings.

Early spring is also a time to repair erosion that may have developed over the winter. Shallow, narrow erosions of 1 inch or less in depth and not more than 4 inches across can often be repaired by rolling or tramping the soft soil on either side of it and forcing soil and young plants together to fill the void. On wider erosions that are not more than an inch in depth, the best repair method is sod strips cut to match the erosion width and fitted into place. Wide gully erosions that are deep must be retopsoiled and sodded. Seeding eroded areas usually does not give satisfactory results, for spring rains often wash away the seed and soil. Where surface water moves with any velocity, the sod should be pinned in place with wire hoops, wood pegs, screens, or netting until the sod is fully rooted. When sheet erosion occurs and a wide area is eroded, it is most economical to replace the topsoil and reseed the area and then to expect to have to fix small rill or gully erosions that may develop later on. To reduce the risk of a second sheet erosion, the contractor may wish to establish a waterway to confine possible damage to a narrow area or simply to sod the slopes that erode.

As warm weather arrives, the maintenance procedures should ensure that greens are mowed every day. Other play areas are not allowed to grow more than an inch over the planned height or cut, and water and fertilizer are amply applied. With a normal spring the new golf course, in the Midwest at least, should be ready to open for play by the first of June. Grow-ins take great patience and understanding of the physiological and morphological phases in a plant's life—along with hard work and some luck. That is why some are successful and others fail (see figure 289).

Figure 289. Grow-ins take lots of patience, perseverance, and luck.

20

Improvement Plans and Renovation

For most of us, a concept like geologic time is difficult to fathom. We tend to measure all things in relationship to our human experience. So it is understandable that most people view the golf course as a static entity. But in fact, it is a dynamic, slowly evolving organic complex. The growth, spread, and decline of trees, the succession of grasses and other plants, the meandering of streams, the ebb and flow of the edges, shapes, and sizes of tees, greens, and bunkers all contribute to the natural processes by which golf courses undergo gradual but perceptible change.

Reasons for Improvement

There are human factors as well that cause a golf course to change and age—factors such as increased play, demand for higher maintenance levels, automatic irrigation, golf carts, the buildup of chemicals, and, sad to say, damage from vandalism (see figures 290 and 291).

Moreover, the game of golf has changed over the last century, and with breakneck speed the last fifty years (see figure 292). Golf equipment has shifted from wood-shafted clubs and crudely made balls to space-age materials and computer-generated dimple patterns in the search for "the longest ball." The pitch-and-run shot has been replaced by the wedge shot. Small wonder that the golfer of today wants fast, sure-playing surfaces (see figure 293). The golf course, in turn, must respond to these changes if it is to endure the demands placed on it and serve the golfers who pay for its existence. As the golf course grows old slowly, like all complex systems, it must be rejuvenated, and oftentimes renovated.

Unproductive Improvements

Once the members of a golf course become aware of its needs, a typical pattern seems to develop. Usually a green committee chairman or course supervisor takes it upon himself to alter, add, or delete golf features using golf course personnel or a local bulldozer operator. Decisions about such things as a bunker's size and placement, tee location and expansion, or fairway width and mowing patterns are frequently made on an ad hoc basis, with each item modified as a stand-alone unit instead of as part of a whole. Sometimes the work turns out acceptably, but more often it is a feeble attempt to improve existing features, basically because most of the people involved are inexperienced. All the while, the rest of the membership indulges these men's fancies while patiently paying higher dues or green fees. And every time a club appoints a new green chairperson, he or she invariably sets out on his own pet project. There is seldom a plan or a semblance of continuity.

Proper Improvement Planning

Clubs considering structural changes to the design of the golf course need an experienced golf course architect to give them a long-range plan. Yet to suggest turning to "an outside agent" is tantamount to club heresy and usually ignored at least until two or three hair-brained schemes fail or are aborted.

Once the decision is finally made to employ a professional designer, the best procedure for a club to follow is the formation of a long-range golf course improvement committee. It should consist of the golf pro, the course superintendent, the green chairperson, a member from the

Figure 290. Mowing equipment for golf courses has moved from horse-drawn mower (teens and early 1920s), to gasoline powered (mid-1920s), to today's array of diesel and electric power.

Figure 291. This 1915 ad for putting green irrigation shows why—until about 1950—greens were designed to retain water. As irrigation improved, more emphasis was placed on the drainage aspects of green rootzones. Thus putting modern irrigation on an old golf course may also require replacing the rootzone of greens.

Figure 292. This century-old picture of the British Ladies' Championship shows how much about golf has changed. In fact, very little has remained the same, as shown at EagleSticks, requiring golf courses to adapt to those changes to survive.

Figure 293. Modern golf courses are designed to cope with the stresses and demands placed upon them by today's golfers. The 14th hole of Cook's Creek is a good example.

Board of Directors, a representative from the women's golf committee, and someone from the seniors golf committee. This committee can be supplemented by as many others as practical, but it should always provide for input from these various constituents. The functions of this committee are: to select a golf architect to prepare a long-range study; provide the architect with thoughts, ideas, feelings, and opinions regarding specific improvements; and approve the prepared plan before it is presented to the Board of Directors or the general membership.

Selecting the Architect

The first job of this committee is to contact several design firms and invite them to an interview (see Appendix A for address of American Society of Golf Course Architects membership list). The best time to arrange for such interviews would be just after the first of the year, before the construction season begins. After arranging these interviews, the committee should prepare a list of general objectives in order of importance. It should also locate a recent aerial photograph of the course and an up-to-date contour map.

The interview of the golf architect should be as specific as possible and deal with his past work on improvement studies. It is not unreasonable to ask for specific locations of his work and names of contacts in order to arrange for an inspection of his work. The committee should ask to see plans or studies that were prepared for those projects and the cost of preparation. It should also determine how the work will be done and the function the architect will serve during the renovation. Of course, the committee should inquire about his fees and present his philosophy of design.

The committee may show each architect the most troublesome hole on the course and ask what he or she would do to improve it and at what cost. After similar interviews, the committee can then choose the firm that is best for them. Once the designer is selected, the committee should ask for a written proposal that would include starting and completion dates of the study, the total cost of the study, an estimate on the number of trips to the site the golf architect will make in preparation for the study, the procedure to be used to prepare the plans, and the construction cost estimates for each major element, section, or hole.

When the proposal is in hand and funds are approved to retain the golf architect, the club should arrange to sign a contract or return a letter to him or her acknowledging his proposal and authorizing him to proceed.

Improvement Committee

There are many approaches to preparing improvement studies. The one that follows is a personal method that I've found best satisfies the needs of my clients at the most reasonable initial cost. The goal of an improvement study is to provide sufficient detail and rationale for proposed improvements and to communicate the intent of the plan to even the most inexperienced or emotionally hostile parties. I have never done an improvement study without some vigorous opposition from selected members who oppose any change whatsoever. However, after explaining the procedure used to form the plan and the reasons for the proposed change, and paying respect to their objections, I have found only a small percentage of members will steadfastly cling to total opposition. Changing a golf course is an emotionally charged issue that must be handled with patience and understanding. For the process to succeed, politically as well as architecturally, the architect has to rely upon persuasion, and to listen.

Required Base Maps

The club is expected to supply maps including: a new, scale-verified, engineering-type aerial photograph (see figure 294); a topographic map with at least 5- to 10-foot contour lines (1- or 2-foot lines are preferred); a property line map; existing irrigation map; and a map of any underground utilities or rights-of-way. All maps should be of a scale of 1 inch = 100 feet.

I begin preparing an improvement study by taking the maps supplied by the club, overlaying them, and redrawing the existing golf course to show the location of each golf feature—cart paths, property lines, trees, contour lines, and other prominent features (see figure 295). Then I return to the course and physically check the drawing against the actual golf course to guarantee that I have included all major items and that no items have changed since the aerial photograph or contour maps were made.

Analyzing the Golf Course Features

Satisfied that the drawing is complete, a meeting of the improvement committee is arranged to walk the course. The committee and I start at the first tee and we discuss that tee for any maintenance problems, location, size, quality, alignment, traffic patterns, and so on. I encourage input from all committee members, especially the senior and ladies representatives. We discuss possible solutions for the perceived deficiencies, and alternate plans, and I offer my personal views. Then we walk down to the first impact area of the seniors or ladies. That impact area is analyzed for golfers of all abilities.

Finally, we reach the green and it is analyzed for maintenance factors, number of cupset areas available, internal and surface drainage, slope, size, integration of mounds or traps, and so forth. Then we consider the entire hole as a unit and discuss what can be done to parts of it to make the hole safer, fairer to poor players yet more challenging for the best players, more enjoyable for all golfers, and a better aesthetic experience.

During the walkaround I summarize most of the collective thoughts for the hole until we

Figure 294. Aerial photograph of Blacklick Woods Golf Course as it was at the time an improvement study was initiated. Notice how easy it is to clearly identify and locate all features of the golf course. An overlay drawing will be made of this photo, and together with property lines, contour lines, and rights-of-way, will become the "base map".

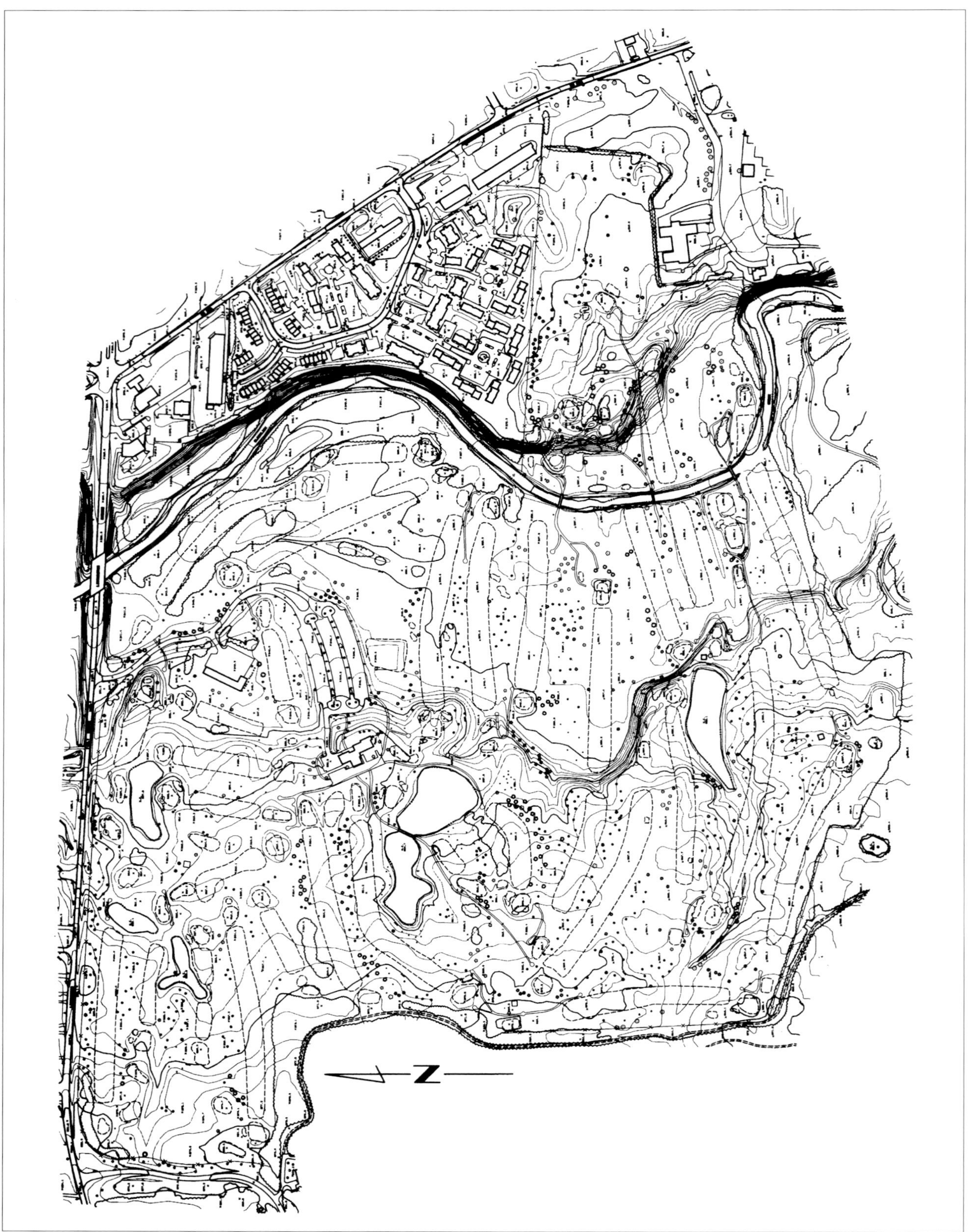

Figure 295. A base map for Blacklick Woods improvement study that combines lots of information onto one map.

have a general, if not complete, agreement on possible improvements. I then annotate my map accordingly. This procedure is followed for the other holes. To do so takes an entire day.

Summarizing Improvement Ideas

Having completed this analytical tour, I am then able to draw the proposed improvements onto a master map, which becomes the basis for the study. In addition, I write a few paragraphs on each hole, explaining the reasons for the proposed improvements. This is sent to the committee for its approval.

After reviewing the initial information we generated at the first walk-through of the course, the committee remarks are incorporated into a second incarnation of the plan, which is again returned for their review (see figure 296). The same procedure is used at another meeting to answer questions or clarify solutions to holes that still lack committee agreement. The committee provides insight into how it views each golf hole, and each group should be satisfied with the recommendations.

This method assumes that the delegate to the committee speaks for the entire group and does not simply give his or her personal opinion. This is especially true of better golfers, particularly the best woman player, who wants to make the course tougher at the expense of 95% of the other golfers. It has been my experience that sometimes the best players provide the most partisan information. The improvement committee is sometimes better served by average players, or by golfers who were very good 20 or 30 years earlier and now have a great deal of empathy for less skilled golfers.

Completing the Study

Having carefully and slowly examined the entire course, I am able to produce a plan that best suits the individual club's needs. By including a written rationale for the proposed changes, I permit any interested party to understand the problem and propose an alternative solution (see figure 297). This often helps the overall study gain majority approval. However, it is not enough simply to state the changes for all 18 holes, for the committee has no idea where to start. Therefore, I prioritize the holes according to need and I include an estimated cost. By listing the holes in order of need, and by generating an overall estimated cost, the long-range improvement committee can budget intelligently and phase the work out over a number of years.

With a completed study in hand and a phase and budget plan worked out, the committee is then ready to go to its board for approval. If the board approves the study and phase plan, then these should be presented to the general membership by the golf architect at a special meeting.

Explaining the Study

Without fail there will be many distortions and untruths about the study and plan, especially if word gets out and the media catch hold of the story. By having the special meeting and presenting the study and plan to the rank and file membership, anxiety is allayed, especially when it is explained that every group was represented and heard during the preparation phase. Once the study and plan are approved by the membership, it then becomes the basis for any and all improvements.

The cost of such a study depends upon the golf architectural firm, the scope of the study, and what the committee wants for a final plan. The study is not a set of working drawings, but rather a conceptual representation that only shows relative size and location. If working drawings are required, the cost would be five times higher than for the concept or feature plan. Since it is not known if all the improvements will be approved, it is better to wait until the actual work is to begin before creating detailed working documents.

Concept Versus Working Drawings

The kinds of detailed working documents that are needed to do the improvement can range from a verbal or written description of the work to grade stakes in the ground accompanied by detailed scaled drawings and voluminous specifications. The fewer drawings or descriptions

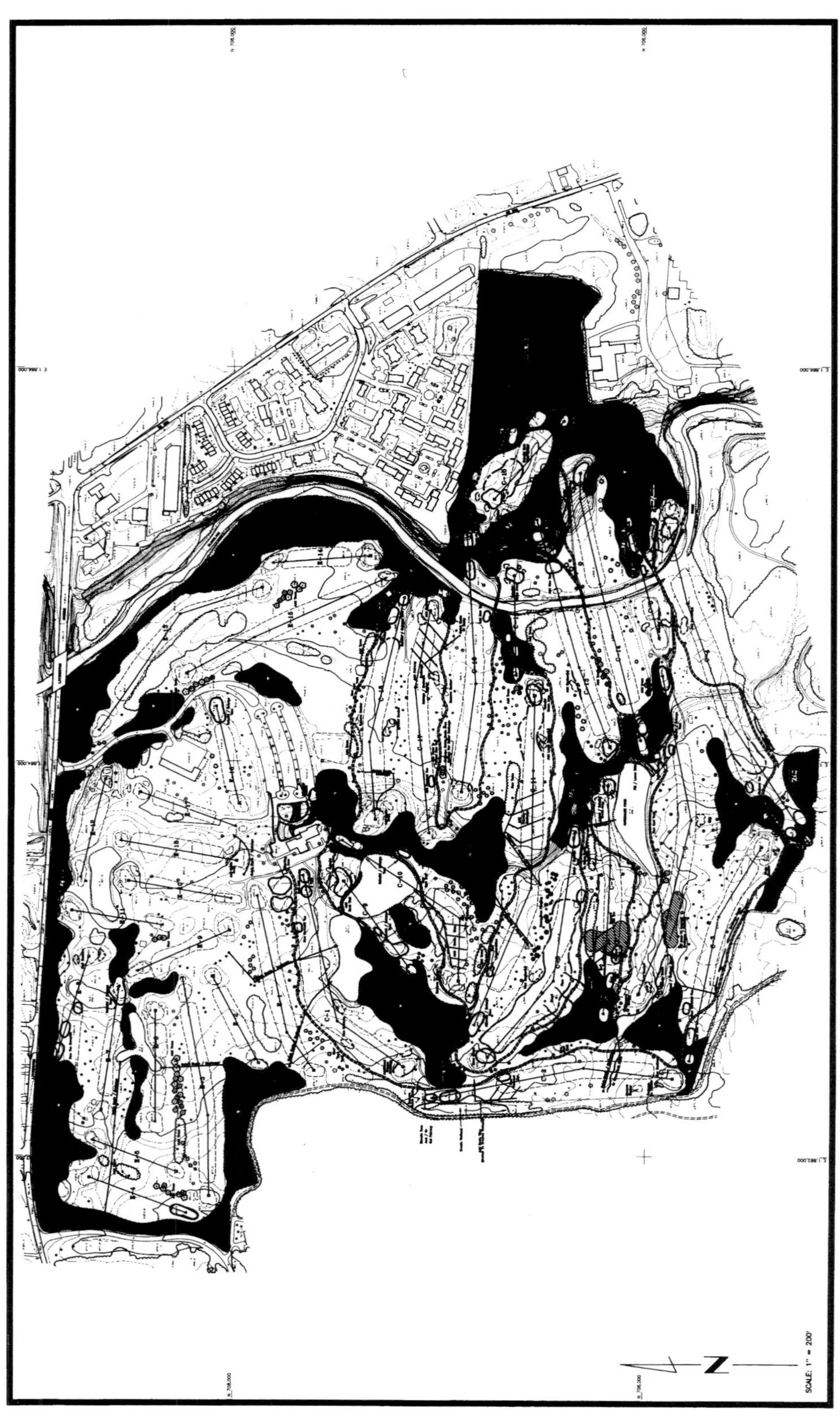

Figure 296. An overall concept plan of improvements to Blacklick Woods Golf Course, Columbus, Ohio.

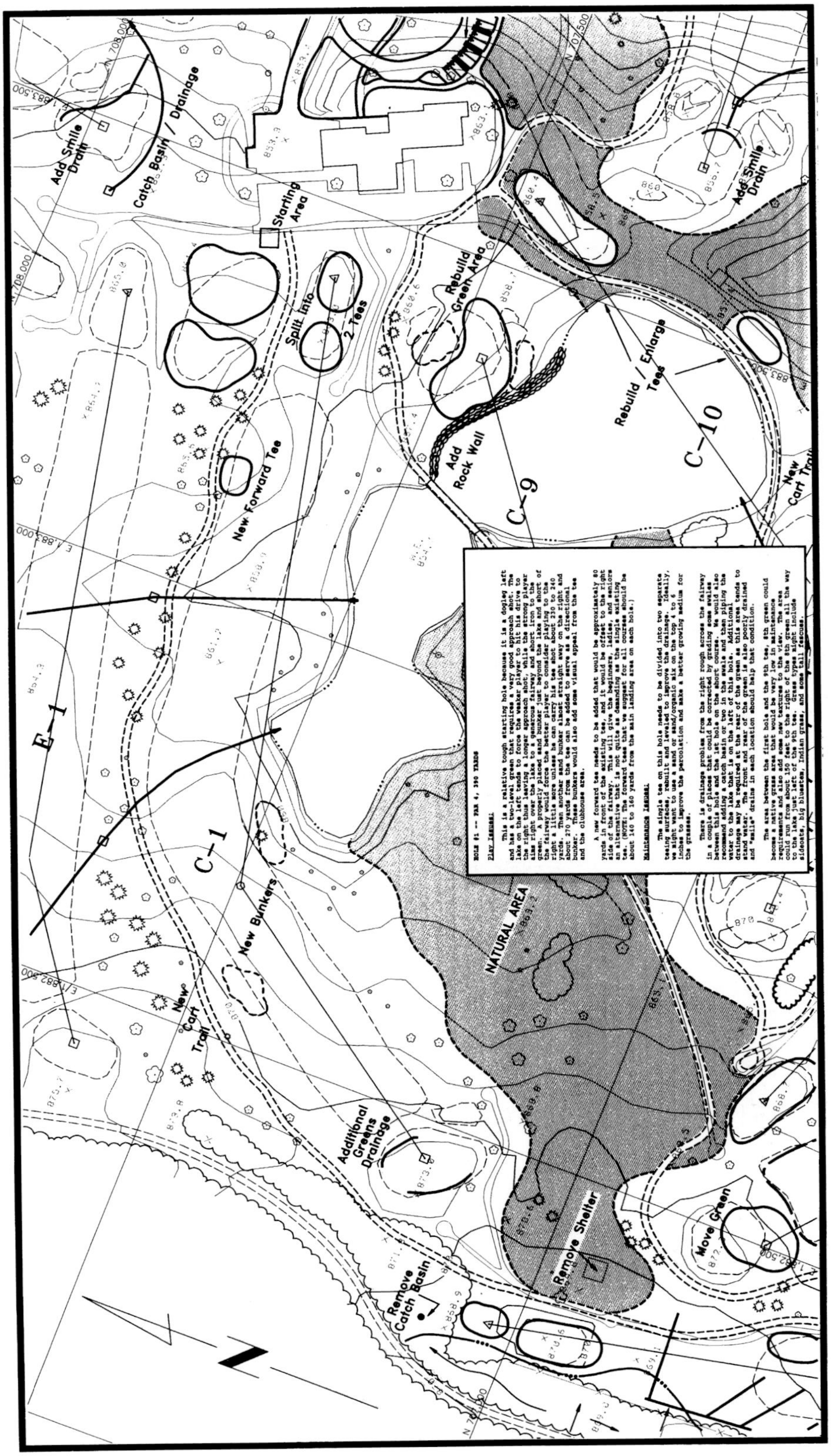

Figure 297. Detailed drawing showing proposed improvements to Blacklick Woods Golf Course, with written rationale.

used, the greater must be the club's trust in the golf architect and the contractor, for there is little basis for resolving misunderstandings of what the finished product is or how much it will cost. For simple improvements, such as reshaping a bunker, the club might wish to get bids from capable contractors to work by the hour, with the club buying all the materials. This way the club only pays for the labor and construction equipment, and not for overestimates of time and material. If the project is more complex, then the golf architect should be instructed to produce a written estimate of the total quantity of work involved and a description of acceptable standards of workmanship on which a contractor can bid and bond the work. If the improvement is extremely complex, such as on the sensitive issue of constructing new greens, then the club should pay the golf architect to make detailed drawings and specifications for the project that can be approved by the board before the contractors bid and bond the work.

Role of the Superintendent

Notice that no mention has been made of using golf course personnel to do any of the work. Although a course superintendent might believe he is capable of doing the work, he probably won't have the specialized equipment necessary, an efficient and trained construction crew, the necessary manpower, or the time. Some superintendents have done well with golf course construction work, but most are not properly trained or experienced to do the work quickly and efficiently. In addition, no matter how good the final result may be, the golf superintendent will rarely be thanked and will always be blamed for any mistake or disruption. If the superintendent and his crew are involved, it should be only on items with which they are experienced, such as irrigation installation, sodding, seeding, small backhoe work, and grading. Larger projects should always be given to a contractor.

Coordination and scheduling of the improvement work is a difficult task, one that falls to the long-range improvement committee. Among the crucial decisions to be made in this regard are whether the changes are to be phased in over several years so that play remains essentially undisturbed, or whether the changes will be implemented all at once. If construction can be confined to seasons when the golf course is not in play, all the better for the membership. But golfers may still be inconvenienced somewhat when it comes time for growing in any new turf that will be needed. In either case, effective communication is essential. Neither members nor owners enjoy the feeling that their club insignia has become a bulldozer. The only way to negotiate the difficult path of course renovation and improvement is by effective communication and openness, so that every party involved—the general membership, the green committee, the board of directors, the architect, the superintendent, and the construction contractor—all know exactly what the appropriate schedules are.

Restoration

There is always talk at the older clubs, especially ones done by a famous designer, about "restoring" the golf course back to the architect's original plans. Some contemporary golf course architects claim to specialize in restoration and are earning a good income from it. In fact, a couple of quasi social-golf organizations, like the Donald Ross Society, and the MacKenzie Society, have been formed to study the work of these past master designers, and advocate restorations of it. I am a member of the Ross Society and I applaud their work, while the MacKenzie group seems to be less organized and obscure at best. But I have some reservations about restoration.

As the reader must now know, I am a great fan of golf nostalgia, and I would venture to say that very few golfers living today have played more famous old courses with wood-shafted clubs than I have. In fact, I even played more than a few holes with real gutties (see figure 298). I do this so I can better understand the playing conditions of that period—how hazards were placed in relation to limitations of the older equipment—and thus better understand the underlying intent of the designer. As I play these courses I constantly ask why a particular

Figure 298. The author has played hundreds of rounds of golf on historical old courses to try to better understand the strategic placement of hazards in relationship to the performance limits of older golf equipment.

feature was designed that way, and what the philosophical judgment was that determined the exact size, shape, depth, scale, and proportion of what I see. On many golf courses, there is a discernable theme or message, and the genius of the architect is discoverable. Other times the designer's message is gibberish, meaning that somewhere along the line there was a poor translation, or the actual message made no sense. My point is that some "architect's original plans" are not worthy of restoration.

I have friends who do other kinds of restoration work, such as cars, boats, houses, etc., and they are fanatics for detail. One of them actually goes so far as to make "mistakes" like the factory did on things like paint overspray, mismatched parts, or misadjusted labels or stickers. Now *that* is restoration.

In golf course terms, restoration in the strictest sense means replicating the course down to the same level of detail. Some years ago one particularly famous top 100 club asked me to do a restoration plan for their golf course, designed by a famous architect. I diligently researched the course and found old plans, pictures, newspaper and magazine articles, and interviewed the oldest members and looked at photographs their parents had taken of the original golf course. In the end I could assure them that I could absolutely restore their golf course, but the membership almost unanimously rejected the plan. The reason was that from my research I suggested removing about 150 to 200 large oak trees that were planted years after the course opened, eliminating fairway irrigation, mowing greens at 1/4 inch, and getting rid of forward tees. These folks did not want to lose tree-lined fairways, green turf, fast greens, or an equitable golf course just to say they restored it (see figure 299).

I have often repeated this story to clubs interested in "restoration," and the usual response is that they really don't want a restoration either; instead they want to retain the flavor of their original course, only make it better. So now it becomes an improvement process, not a restoration one per se.

Perhaps the best example is the work I did at Shorehaven Club in East Norwalk, Connecticut, with the then superintendent Bob Phipps. The course was designed by Robert White in 1924, and was a precious example of old-time, damn good, message-rich golf architecture. But over the years too many trees were planted, the bunkers had lost character through power rakings, and tees and greens were too small for today's play. The membership approved an improvement study that would remove hundreds of storm brittle (white pine) trees, allowed bunker maintenance to return to hand labor, and permitted us to add forward and enlarged tees, expand greens through mowing and aeration, and contour fairways back to their original shapes.

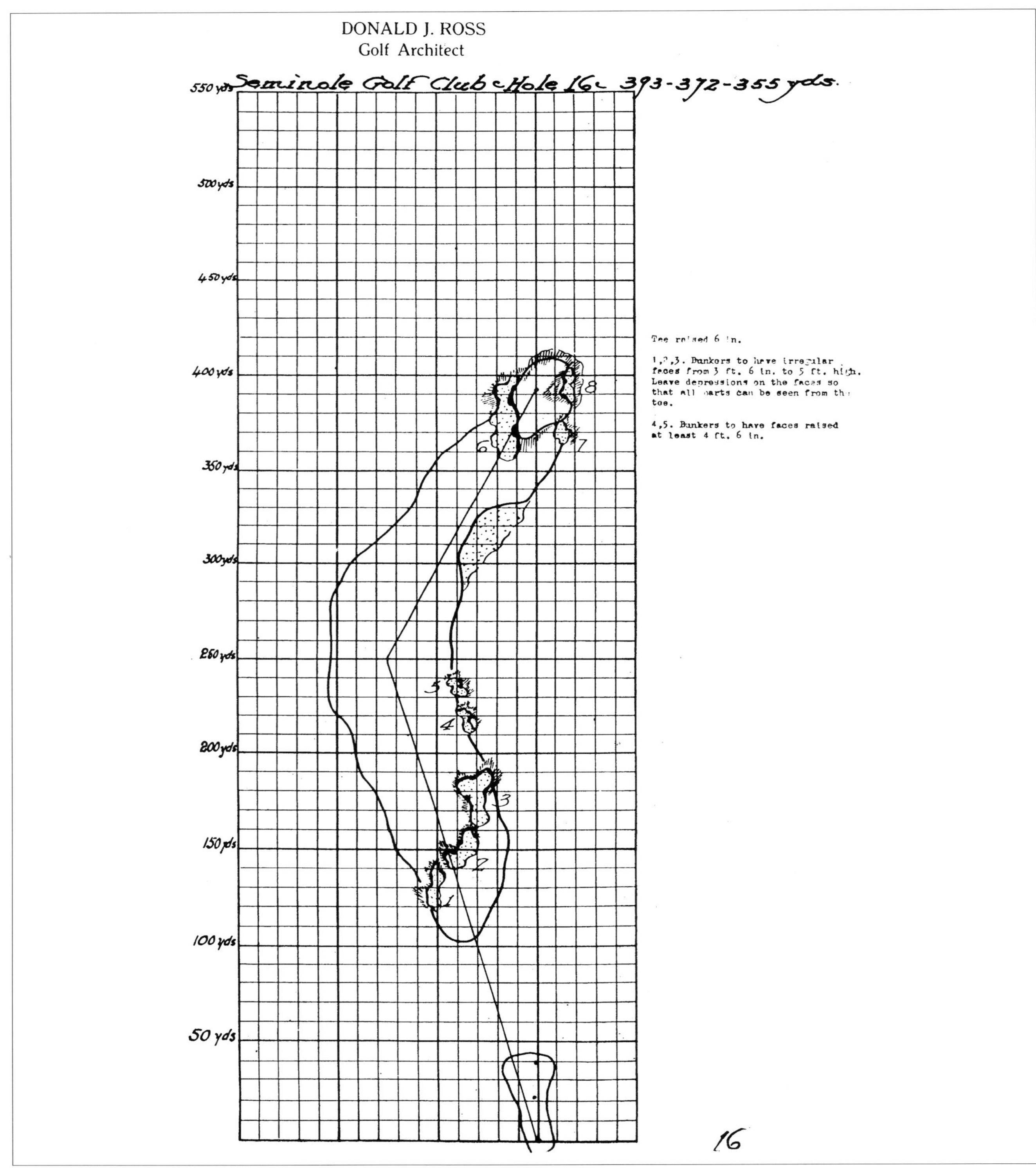

Figure 299. The original Donald Ross plan for the 16th hole at Seminole had penal cross bunkers for the tee shot, but none exist there now. One wonders if the members would really reinstall those bunkers in the name of pure restoration, or are they satisfied with the locations of the present bunkers.

Figure 300. One of the biggest improvements to some courses is to remove trees that were misguidedly planted by well-meaning green chairmen. Shorehaven in East Norwalk, Connecticut: removing trees reintroduced the wind and lovely offsite views that were so much of the original design's intent.

Bob and his crew did much of the tedious work, and today the golf course is markedly improved by every measure, and is closer to the original design than it ever had been for the past 60 years.

I don't consider that work to be restoration, except that we restored the influence of the wind off of the salt marsh, we restored breathtaking views of those salt marshes, we restored playing conditions back to their best ever, and we restored a unique look to an incredible initial design (see figure 300). I appreciate the trust and patience that the members of Shorehaven have given me, for without their support none of that would have been possible.

Many clubs have recently become interested in improving their greens by installing a new rootzone but retaining their original surface contours. This can be faithfully done using the method of Ed Connor described in Chapter 12, but only if form follows function for the green, as discussed in Chapter 4. When it does not, as was the case on the 17th green on MacKenzie's Scarlet Golf Course for the Ohio State University, which had too much slope for fair putting under today's maintenance conditions, it was rebuilt to look the same but with less slope (see again figure 49b.

Improvement Example

Sometimes this is not possible, as was the case at the Hugh Alison–designed Westwood Country Club course in Rocky River, Ohio. The green on the par 3 14th was simply too small to stand the amount of play it was receiving, drainage was poor, and trees planted years after the course opened were casting maintenance-causing shadows for most of the day (see figure 301). By midyear the *Poa annua* green had little or no grass on it, and the committee refused to let us remove any trees. The form of the green clearly did not follow the function, so a totally new look for the green complex was required. To avoid the shade and to expand the green, it was lowered 6 feet into the hill, pushed out away from the shade, and given superior surface and subsurface drainage and a new rootzone (see figure 302). In addition, the tees were made four times larger and given more flexibility in length. The form was designed to match the function, and today this is one of the members' favorite holes.

Figure 301. Years after the original Hugh Alison design for the 14th green at Westwood C.C. in Rocky River, Ohio was complete, trees were planted that have now grown to become major maintenance problems. They changed the microclimate of the green so much with shade and reduced air movement that only annual bluegrass could survive, and often it failed by midsummer. Rather than remove trees, the club decided to rebuild the green.

Figure 302. The par 3 14th hole at Westwood Country Club, with a rebuilt green where form follows function. The green is out of the shade, surface drains in four directions, and has lots of hole locations. As a result, members enjoy a great putting surface throughout the season. Also, notice all of the new tee space.

21

Golf and the Environment

Properly designed, built, and managed golf courses pose no threat to the environment; in fact, they can enhance it! (see figure 303)

There are those who oppose that view, but they do so based more on emotion and intuition than on fact and logic.

My Perspective

Allow me to digress for a moment and explain the basis of my attitudes and beliefs. I started working on golf courses in the mid 1950s when we sprayed chemicals like cadmium, chlordane, thiram, arsenicals, mercuries, DDT, 2,4,5-T, and 2,4-D out of a 55-gallon, open-top steel drum. I sprayed through a garden hose using my thumb for a dispersing nozzle and I wore only a tee shirt and shorts. This was not me being cavalier about pesticides, but just plain ignorant about their safety and effects.

In 1961, I entered Ohio State University in the first turfgrass management class, and I learned about Rachel Carson and her views, and this gave reason to reflect on the role and long-term unknown dangers of pesticides. In 1966, I was commissioned a lieutenant in the United States Army Chemical Corps because of my extensive schooling in chemistry. I was deferred from active military duty for graduate school for my Ph.D. in environmental plant physiology, and was then on orders to Vietnam with Operation Ranch Hand to spray jungles with 2,4,5-TP (Agent Orange, also known as Silvex®). Those operations were cancelled by President Nixon when, among other things, nerve gas was suspected of a massive sheep kill near Dugway proving grounds. I remained in the Chemical Corps until 1972, when I became a citizen soldier/golf course architect who went into the Special Forces Reserves and specialized in chemical warfare. I recently retired from the United States Army Reserve program as a colonel, and my last command was of the Army's only tactical Psychological Operations Group, with a worldwide mission of conducting psychological warfare. As

Figure 303. This poster communicates the concern of golf for the environment and the benefits it can bring.

a golf course architect I teach a GCSAA seminar on Design, Construction, and Renovation for Integrated Pest Management, and I teach a two-day class on Environmental Impact of Golf at the Harvard School of Design summer program. My point is that I have a fair amount of background on pesticides, chemicals, propaganda, and golf.

Environmental Due Process

Although in the United States the legal system is founded on "innocent until proven guilty," this is not always true in matters of income tax, child molestation or endangerment, or environmental impact. Instead of having your accuser prove your guilt in these matters, the current reality is that you must prove your innocence. Thus millions upon millions of dollars, untold thousands of man-hours, and unmeasured resources are misused or wasted disproving an assumption of guilt. For example, despite exhaustive research that has clearly established that properly selected and applied golf course fertilizers will not contaminate groundwater, nearly the first reason given in opposition to a golf course project is that applied fertilizer will pollute the groundwater—or runoff of chemicals will kill fish in nearby water bodies, or massive bird kills occur as a result of golf course pesticides. Hogwash—pure urban legend—with no routine basis in fact, as isolated and unusual as lightning strikes, but at every environmental hearing these accusations are made.

Inflammatory Rhetoric

Why people still believe these untruths is a result of well-meaning but poorly informed activists, who prey on the public's fear of the unknown—things that cannot be seen or measured, which might cause harm at any time. As a military propagandist, I know this is precisely the technique used to weaken the resolve of an enemy soldier, or to shake the confidence of citizens in their government. Propagandists do not need to lie, they simply reshape the truth. They lead the target audience to a point of obvious decision, applying circular logic or innuendo as necessary.

For example, I work with and help write golf course management plans all the time, and I am very familiar with the materials used and the active ingredients they contain. Likewise, my home is in the middle of a farm belt that grows corn, soybeans, hay, vegetable crops, and fruits, so I grew up with farmers and farm culture. Therefore I take serious issue with statements that say on a per-acre basis that golf courses use 4 to 7 times more pesticides than farms, as was stated in a 1991 report called "Toxic Fairways." The New York State Attorney General's office, which issued that report, most likely did one or more of the following:

1. did some very faulty research
2. took an isolated, worst-case scenario from one golf course
3. compared an intensively maintained golf green to an undermaintained farm
4. meant numbers of chemicals and not amounts of chemicals

I know that if golf course superintendents applied 4 to 7 times the amount of chemicals that farms use, you wouldn't have any concerns about golf courses, for the fairways and greens would all be dead from phytotoxicity to the applied chemicals. Further, turfgrasses prevent runoff of chemicals, while the farms in my area are identified as the primary cause of the nitrate and pesticides in drinking water each spring (see figure 304). Golf courses prevent soil erosion, and turfgrass culture actually makes rich topsoil, while the rivers of central Ohio run brown with erosion from farms and construction sites. Many chemicals restricted for golf courses are commonly available to farmers and homeowners, who are not required to be trained and registered to apply those chemicals. I live across the street from a 36-hole golf course, and I have more fear of my neighbors in search of the perfect lawn and prize-winning tomatoes than I do of the golf course.

As a propagandist, I too would seize on some abstract fact and use it to create an unfounded fear in the minds of my target audience. However, as a responsible educator, practitioner, and parent I would prefer to use sustaining research that has been through a peer review to support my view.

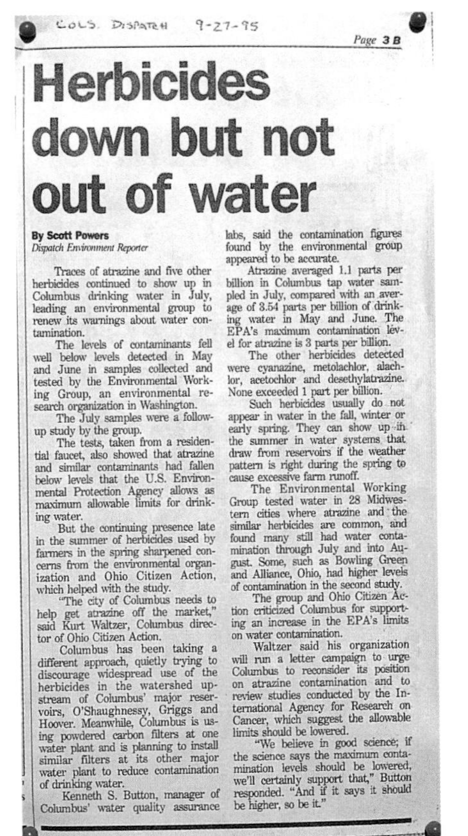

COLS. DISPATCH 9-27-95

Page 3B

Herbicides down but not out of water

By Scott Powers
Dispatch Environment Reporter

Traces of atrazine and five other herbicides continued to show up in Columbus drinking water in July, leading an environmental group to renew its warnings about water contamination.

The levels of contaminants fell well below levels detected in May and June in samples collected and tested by the Environmental Working Group, an environmental research organization in Washington.

The July samples were a follow-up study by the group.

The tests, taken from a residential faucet, also showed that atrazine and similar contaminants had fallen below levels that the U.S. Environmental Protection Agency allows as maximum allowable limits for drinking water.

But the continuing presence late in the summer of herbicides used by farmers in the spring sharpened concerns from the environmental organization and Ohio Citizen Action, which helped with the study.

"The city of Columbus needs to help get atrazine off the market," said Kurt Waltzer, Columbus director of Ohio Citizen Action.

Columbus has been taking a different approach, quietly trying to discourage widespread use of the herbicides in the watershed upstream of Columbus' major reservoirs, O'Shaughnessy, Griggs and Hoover. Meanwhile, Columbus is using powdered carbon filters at one water plant and is planning to install similar filters at its other major water plant to reduce contamination of drinking water.

Kenneth S. Button, manager of Columbus' water quality assurance labs, said the contamination figures found by the environmental group appeared to be accurate.

Atrazine averaged 1.1 parts per billion in Columbus tap water sampled in July, compared with an average of 3.54 parts per billion of drinking water in May and June. The EPA's maximum contamination level for atrazine is 3 parts per billion.

The other herbicides detected were cyanazine, metolachlor, alachlor, acetochlor and desethylatrazine. None exceeded 1 part per billion.

Such herbicides usually do not appear in water in the fall, winter or early spring. They can show up in the summer in water systems that draw from reservoirs if the weather pattern is right during the spring to cause excessive farm runoff.

The Environmental Working Group tested water in 28 Midwestern cities where atrazine and the similar herbicides are common, and found many still had water contamination through July and into August. Some, such as Bowling Green and Alliance, Ohio, had higher levels of contamination in the second study.

The group and Ohio Citizen Action criticized Columbus for supporting an increase in the EPA's limits on water contamination.

Waltzer said his organization will run a letter campaign to urge Columbus to reconsider its position on atrazine contamination and to review studies conducted by the International Agency for Research on Cancer, which suggest the allowable limits should be lowered.

"We believe in good science; if the science says the maximum contamination levels should be lowered, we'll certainly support that," Button responded. "And if it says it should be higher, so be it."

Figure 304. A newspaper clipping commonly seen in the farm belt of the U.S. The point of the article is the continued improvement shown by farming practices.

Scientific Fact

I would direct the serious reader's attention to the 1995, January–February issue of the *USGA Green Section Record,* which summarizes funded research from across the United States (see figure 305). Clearly these summaries and other independent results vindicate golf courses and proper turf management techniques (called Best Management Practices).

In addition, as part of permit approval processes in the late 1980s and early 1990s, many golf courses agreed to conduct environmental monitoring of their golf facilities as well as surrounding environmental resource areas. After years of such scrutiny, no negative effects have been measured that are attributable to the golf courses (see figure 306).

Continued Research and Innovation

Despite these positive findings of current turfgrass management practices and products, the industry itself is continuing to fund research and seek improvements that reduce potential impacts even further (see figure 307). Leading the way are the golf course superintendents who are committed to making the earth a better place to live, while providing golfers with the healthiest turf possible. Compared to even a decade ago, today's superintendents use less water, fertilizer, pesticides, and fossil fuel than their predecessors, but without a reduction in turf quality. They have become advocates of integrated pest management, or IPM for short (see figure 308). They conduct monitoring, scouting, and sampling of their courses, and only take corrective measures once turf damage exceeds a particular threshold. Pesticides are the last line of defense after all cultural remedies have failed, and even then they are only used for spot treatment of the affected area. Golf courses are not sources of pollution.

Irrigation systems are designed to conserve water and power by using smaller, low-volume, low-pressure sprinkler heads, closely spaced to deliver water where it is needed, which are controlled by a computer which enables precise programming. Often weather stations, soil moisture sensors, and rain switches are coupled to the central computer controller to make daily adjustments based upon that day's weather (see figure 309).

Plant breeders are rapidly developing new and improved turfgrasses that are more disease and insect resistant, more drought tolerant, require less fertility, and need less mowing (see figure 310). Discovery of a fungus that lives within the tissues of the grass plant, called endophyte, is being adapted to new grass types, that makes them more insect-resistant. Better grasses are being introduced and incorporated into golf courses almost every day.

Figure 305. The United States Golf Association has led the way in funding serious scientific research on golf and the environment. This peer reviewed research has provided volumes of factual data that vindicate golf.

Figure 306. Willowbend Golf Course in Mashpee, Cape Cod, Massachusetts is set among working cranberry bogs, thus proving golf and some agricultural interest are completely compatible. Harvest time adds another dimension to this exciting golf course.

Figure 307. Golf course superintendents are delivering excellent playing conditions while continuing to reduce environmental impacts.

Figure 308. Integrated pest management is such a big topic. The Environmental Protection Agency (EPA) has published helpful books on its use.

Figure 309. "Smart" irrigation design saves water and power, and produces healthier turfgrass. Golf course superintendents rely on weather data fed to their central irrigation controller to maximize irrigation efficiencies.

Figure 310. Plant breeders are developing and introducing superior turf cultivars through long-running testing and selection methods.

Innovations in maintenance equipment, such as lightweight mowers, deep tine and water aeration machines, as well as new diagnostic tools, are lowering the environmental impact of golf courses on their surroundings.

Fertigation, or microfertilization with soluble nutrients through the irrigation system, is becoming common. Similar systems are being fielded that apply biological controls for certain insects and diseases, including thatch decomposition. Beneficial organisms are being inoculated into the soil to fix nitrogen, build soil structure, and antagonize harmful organisms. Again, golf courses are driving the research and implementation of these "more natural treatments."

As golf course architects we are keenly aware of the importance of drainage in growing high-quality environmentally friendly turf, so golf courses are designed to drain well (see figure 311). Shaping directs surface water to catch basins, serviced by tile that connects to major underground drainage systems that often terminate at an irrigation pond. In this way, water is recycled. Well-drained turf is healthy turf.

Figure 311. Pete Dye should be recognized not only for his creative golf course design, but also his pioneering work at Old Marsh in Palm Beach, Florida in capturing and recycling drainage water. Pete is shown here explaining how the capture pit and pump system work at Brickyard Crossing.

Turf clippings and leaves are composted, sprayer rinsates are collected and often recycled, and petroleum-based wastes are properly disposed of. Workers are taught IPM principles, golf courses are used as learning laboratories for children, and golf courses have become part of an international cooperative sanctuary program aimed at improving the wildlife value of non-play areas (see figure 312). Bird and bat houses are common golf course fixtures, as are constructed wetlands, brush pile habitats, and no-mow areas for ground-dwelling creatures. Dead trees in out-of-play areas are left to rot and decompose while playing host to a large number of successive flora and fauna.

It has been estimated that only about 1% of the total turf area of the United States is attributable to golf courses, and it is being managed by college-trained, usually state-certified pesticide applicators, with a penchant to protect the environment. The other 99% is managed by less qualified and less trained individuals who are completely unregulated. Who poses the greater threat?

Golf courses have been successfully developed on numerous "fragile" sites, and exist in harmony with them, beginning with the great links courses of the United Kingdom, and continuing on to America's links on eastern Long Island and coastal islands, into forests, wetlands, mountains, prairies, farmland, deserts, and the California coastline (see figure 313). Not every site should have a golf course, for some are so rare as to require special protection by isolation from all human activity. In general, golf can become part of any environment and not materially affect it, and if proper planning, construction, and maintenance are done it can enhance the site.

Figure 312. A commonly seen sign in areas that seek first to identify and conserve environmental resource areas, but permit golf along their fringes.

Figure 313. Golf is at home on the fragile Headlands of the Cape Cod National Seashore. The 9-hole Highland Links Course is natural mixture of native grasses, predominantly fine fescue.

Golf Misidentified with Elitism

Why then is there such adamant opposition to golf courses by a small group hoping to incite the masses? The reasons are varied, but some common threads exist. First, golf is played by only 8 to 10% of the population, with most other people seeing golf as a silly, idle rich, white man's game. It has falsely been given an elitist brand that makes it easy to dislike. Golf has allowed itself to become identified as a country club pastime, not the healthy, public, outdoor, family recreation that it is. To 90% of our population, golf and country clubs are somewhat synonymous, and hence both are painted with the same brush of "snobbishness." How sad. Nonetheless, it is easy to arouse support against golf as a way of saying "no" to rich white folks who want to build themselves another private playground.

To say "no" requires foundation, and as a result many people willingly want to believe that golf courses pollute, destroy wildlife, and luxuriantly consume scarce resources. They are often afraid that a new golf course symbolizes a farewell to an old style of life with which they are now content. They believe that a golf course will attract people to their hidden paradise or neighborhood and destroy a comfortable numbness they enjoy. So they are predisposed to accept these environmental reasons for "no-growth" advocacy. They don't see the opportunity afforded their children or senior citizens to become exposed to one of the world's oldest and greatest games (see figure 314). They don't acknowledge the managed open space that a golf course provides, or entry level job opportunities, or the low demand it places on schools, police, and public services. However, most people privately approve of the additional tax income that golf might produce, the escalation of surrounding property values, and recognition and distinction it gives their community. So the reasons to deny approval to build a golf course must be quite emotive and overwhelmingly negative—and the "only dog that will hunt" is potential health risks. Thus golf courses must constantly prove their innocence.

So how can golf overcome this bum rap as a threat to the environment?

Public Education About Golf

The continuing research at colleges and universities, much of it funded by the USGA and other golf associations across North America, will help quantify possible impacts. They will identify areas for potential improvement and develop those solutions, as well as document the soundness of some current practices.

Secondly, the general public must be exposed or educated to *real* status of existing golf course

Figure 314. Investing in our children by providing them an opportunity to learn golf should be seen as another benefit to nature—human nature.

Figure 315. The Golf Course Superintendents Association of America (GCSAA) has become a key communications link to golfers and non-golfers about golf and environmental perspectives.

practices. The GCSAA TV program "Par for the Course," is an excellent tool (see figure 315). On a local level, superintendents must commit to personal campaigns to invite outside groups (scouts, senior citizens, school classes, wildlife organizations, etc.) to come to their golf courses and observe the natural systems in place there. Show off the strengths of your programs and don't be afraid to admit any weaknesses you are working on. Join local environmental organizations and participate as much as you can. Appear on local radio or TV shows to discuss how homeowners can apply IPM.

Devote space within the golf course for wildlife enhancement and seek to inform golfers of why these are there, what you hope to accomplish, and how they can help. If possible, photo document your successes and look for opportunities to show them or speak on them.

Be prepared to challenge environmental advocates against golf with logic and facts. Keep current on local environmental concerns and be ready to provide factual information to show how golf courses are responding to the concern. Sources of information include the USGA, GCSAA, ASGCA and NGF (see addresses in Appendix A). Attend any of 20 plus seminars of either one- or two-day duration, within the GCSAA Environmental Management program. Take classes or workshops in environmental subjects taught by local colleges or universities. Become a key communicator in environmental matters. These are specific ways to show the general public that there is nothing to fear from golf courses.

Golf is not at war with environmentalists; in fact most of the people I know in the turf industry are environmentalists, and likewise many staunch environmentalists are golfers. Unfortunately, some no-growth advocates try to use environmental issues as a means of blocking golf course development. Some of these issues are quantifiable, such as groundwater impacts, pesticide residuals, and water usage. These quantifiable objections to golf courses are easy to overcome with research, good planning, and monitoring. It is the issues like disruption to habitat that are more subjective and hence more difficult to answer. The complexity of an ecosystem requires an enormous investment of time and money to fully and completely understand impacts on it. Stories abound about projects that have been delayed for years while habitat issues are debated. Prominent among them was the reportedly almost extinct snail darter fish, which prevented construction of the TVA Tellico Dam. After millions and millions of dollars were spent on research and lawsuits, lo and behold, it was found that the "endangered" snail darter was found in many other locations. Although the dam was built, many environmentalists saw the delay they caused as a great victory. In this case, the TVA waited them out, but often golf course developers don't have the luxury of waiting and fighting, and will abandon the project. Time is on the side of the opposition.

Enhancement Through Biodiversity

Since major endangered indicator species are sometimes cited as reasons for protecting or isolating tracts of habitat, there is a counter argument that can be called "enhancement through diversity of species" (see figure 316). This is not to say that every effort should not be made to protect rare or endangered species when practical, but also a wider consideration or alternative should be considered. Instead of focusing on one selected species for preservation, it may make more sense to proliferate the number of other species by developing that site. The fundamental tenet in this argument is the rhetorical question "Which is more important, an earthworm or a monkey?" To choose one over the other is to act like God, for who is qualified to distinguish and determine intrinsic worth of a species? To use biological complexity as a guide would then pose the question of which is more important between a monkey or a man. Obviously there is no way to ascribe a higher value for one species over another, for all flora and fauna contribute to the web of life. But it can be argued that increasing the diversity of species on a site has merit.

It has been estimated that 70% of all species live in the soil. This includes worms, insects, fungi, bacteria, nematodes, some mammals and reptiles, even some birds, and most plants. The point is that the soil is rich in diversity, and hence managing soils is managing habitat. As a profession, today's golf course superintendents are perhaps the most competent of soil managers, employing cultural techniques such as aeration, fertilization, soil modification, drainage, irrigation, plant root development, topdressing, microclimate modulation, and soil preservation. In addition, the golf course superintendent often manages a wide variety of planted trees and grasses, water bodies and their aquatic vegetation, native plants, and a wide diversity of creatures. Overall, the superintendent has management responsibility for a very complex and integrated ecosystem called a golf course that rivals Mother Nature's best. A difference is that the superintendent must tend to the health of that ecosystem under everyday scrutiny.

Consider for a moment the ecological value of just constructing one pond or lake on a golf course site that had none (see figure 317). With good design and construction this pond can become a sustainable habitat for open water and shore-loving plants and animals, a resting place of migratory creatures, and a springboard for emerging or succeeding organisms. The golf course development established the need and the economic incentive to build the pond or lake, and skillful management of the golf course around it will sustain and protect it. Few natural sites are so complete as not to be made biologically complex and stable by the intelligent planning, construction, and management of a golf course. This fact may irritate preservationists or no-growth advocates, but one cannot deny the truth of it.

Besides being a good environment within itself, a golf course offers man an opportunity to not only share that open space with those natural systems in a non-threatening way, but it also satisfies his recreative imperative (see figure 318). Golf is a healthful, outdoor, family, or socially oriented activity that can be played from cradle to grave, that is rich in honor, sportsmanship, integrity, and other social virtues. Golf is usually a self-supporting or perhaps profit-producing facility that often contributes to the subsidization of other not-for-profit recreation. A golf course is an intensively used parcel of ground that is kept healthy by intelligent management for the recreation of people who will fund the facility.

Not all golf course ground is used for golf. There are normally unused or infrequently used parcels with any property that can be made into minihabitats. By practicing zonal management that matches the intensity of golf use, the golf course can establish natural areas by simply not mowing or chemically treating areas within the property. It is once again popular to erect bird or bat houses, as it was in the 1920s, leave out-of-play dead trees to slowly decay while supporting successive life-forms, or build brush pile shelters for ground animals. Animal corridors, food and water sources, and nesting or foraging areas are established. Only the most sterile of golf courses

Doug Ball

Figure 316. This great blue heron is happy to share the Devil's Pulpit Golf Course with other lovers of nature.

Doug Ball

Figure 317. Constructing water bodies on golf courses provides several of the essential elements of a good animal habitat—namely water, and perhaps food, shelter, or both. Adding permanent water where none previously existed increases the biodiversity of the entire site, such as here at Blackthorn.

Figure 318. A good environment should not exclude either man or animal, and one of the places this happens is on a golf course like Cypress Point.

Figure 319. Zonal maintenance has allowed the golf course superintendent to introduce habitat into the golf course, while reducing maintenance costs for those areas. Devil's Paintbrush is made special because of that concept.

Figure 320. In the late 1920s, the great golfer Robert Tyre (Bobby) Jones, along with the famous golf writer Grantland Rice, served on a committee for the National Association of Audubon Societies to write a book called "Golf Clubs as Bird Sanctuaries." Today the Audubon Society of New York State is co-sponsoring with the USGA a program called the Cooperative Sanctuary Program. Good ideas live forever.

Figure 321. This poster was the theme for a historic meeting between environmental and golf industry representatives, who came to the meeting with very different perspectives on golf course impact. Those three days of meetings have led to many subsequent efforts to further improve the environmental friendliness of golf courses.

cannot boast of more biodiversity than a farm or fallow field, a city park, or a woodlot. Adding the golfing activity of man to open space does not diminish the ecological value of that space; it only diversifies it, and often improves it if the total ecosystem is objectively looked at.

I think that with the current work in gene manipulation that is occurring throughout biological research and medicine, one must question whether extinction of another of God's creatures is of the same magnitude of importance now as it was when we relied on a gene pool for evolution. Granted, the movie *Jurassic Park* was a bit far-fetched, but scientists are isolating DNA from insects trapped in amber millions of years ago. Is this planet a poorer place without saber-toothed tigers, passenger pigeons, or some exotic orchid that must have existed in the past million years? I think my world would be poorer without golf.

It is easy to sympathize with the critics of modern society who see burgeoning world populations, moral and social decay, and rising demands for natural and developed resources. But to single out golf courses as a symbol of that plight, or to believe that stopping golf course developments will lessen those problems, is naive at best. Golf courses are instead laboratories for peaceful integration of men and nature, from which humans learn respect for nature, themselves, and fellow beings. However, as long as golf courses are falsely seen as elitist symbols, or unnatural nature, then they will be easy targets for emotional opposition by propagandists with hidden agendas. Every golfer or industry representative must be prepared to defend the value of the golf course, by being educated to the truth about its development and management, while constantly seeking to produce an even better and healthier product.

Environmental Demonstration Project

One such initiative that has been jointly endorsed by both environmental interests and golf representatives is a demonstration golf course—a golf course planned by the cooperative efforts, skills, and knowledge of environmentalists, whether they favor golf or not, with the goal of gaining more common knowledge to produce better golf courses for the future. An initiative by *Golf Digest* magazine, the National Wildlife Federation, and the Center for Resource Management, in January 1995 has brought substance to that dream by organizing an international meeting of the best minds on the subject. The first demonstration project was selected in March, 1995, and is located in the town of Scituate, Massachusetts, on Boston's south shore. This town of 18,000 had years before acquired a 120-acre, played-out sand and gravel pit within their borders. A sanitary landfill had been established on an adjacent property, while the other sides were bordered by housing and a seashore road known as the Driftway. The town had chosen to establish a water well in the middle of the property, but otherwise had found no permanent public use for a very exciting and dramatic piece of sand hill topography (see figure 322). Although a fairly large dredged out lake and several small vernal (seasonal) pools were found on the site, along with spring-fed wetlands and isolated lands subject to flooding, the site was biologically impoverished. Creditable year-long observations and investigations by local biologists confirmed that the site had enormous wildlife potential, but had very little current wildlife owing to the illegal dumping on the site, the activity of dirt bikes, and other deleterious activities (see figure 323). Here was a wonderful parcel of ground, nestled between the salt marshes of Cape Cod Bay and urban development of a lovely New England town, that in its present native state and use was a resource wasted, and a community eyesore. Any development or improvements to the site had to be financially self-supporting, create added value for the town, and provide public recreational value. Only golf courses do all of that.

In early 1993, the town manager, Rick Agnew, courageously but cautiously convinced sympathetic selectmen that the Driftway land might be perfect for a golf course, and that a modest amount of money should be approved to study that prospect. The selectmen agreed, and over the next year a professional golf course planning team was selected, and subsequently their results confirmed Agnew's intuitive sense. Soon a

Figure 322. The site for Widow's Walk, the first golf course/environmental demonstration project jointly planned by golf and environmental advocates, is a played out sand and gravel pit with a town well in the middle of it. Note how dirt bikers have fragmented the habitat, thus rendering it biologically impoverished. Notice the neighboring landfill.

Figure 323. Besides ending illegal dumping and uncontrolled abuse, environmentalists see an enormous potential for enhancing wildlife food, cover, and water access. Acres of wetlands, ponds, native plant revegetation, and habitat edge management is being integrated into the Widow's Walk site.

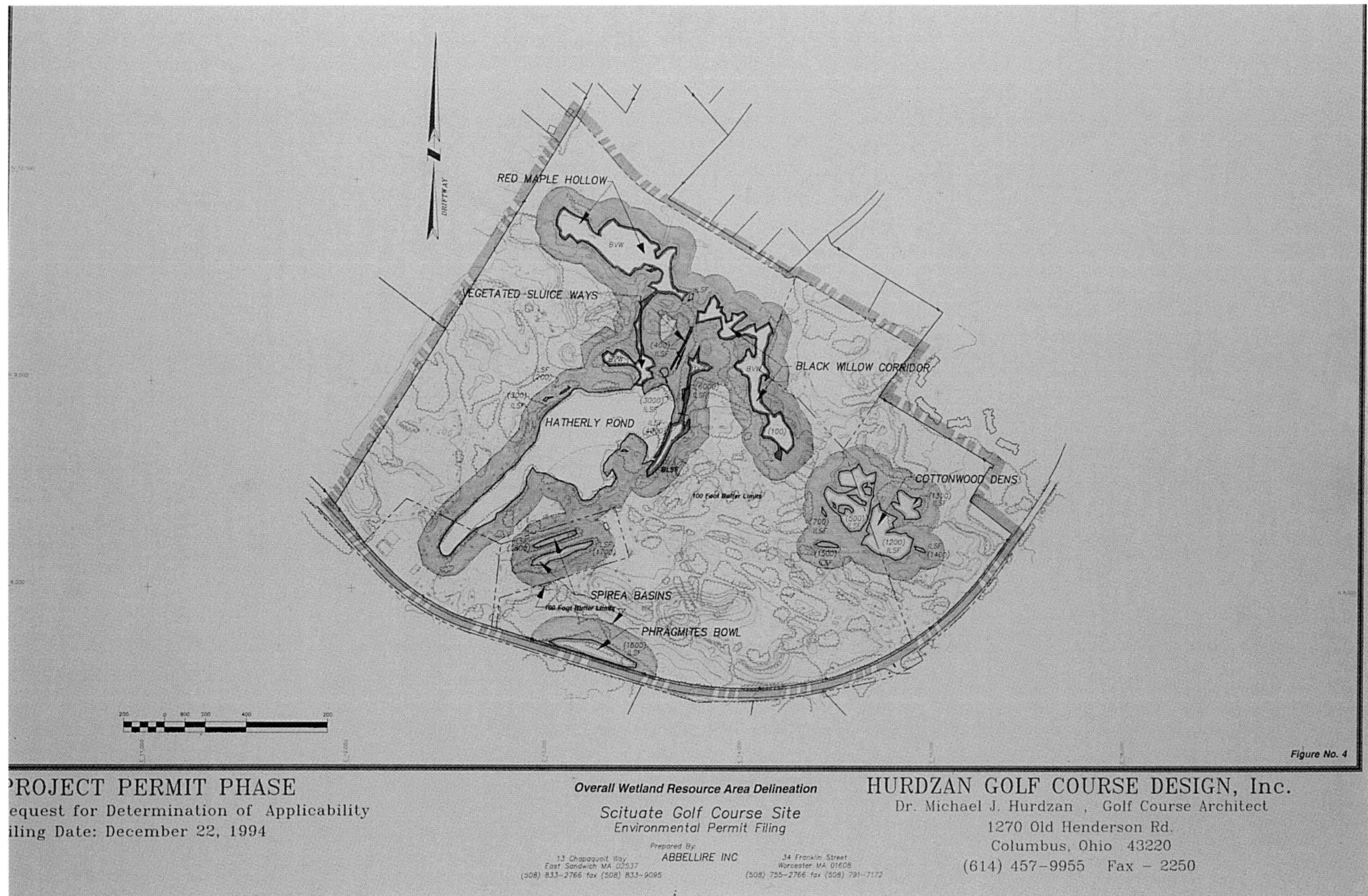

Figure 324. The first step on any site, especially Widow's Walk, is to accurately identify and map all environmental resource areas, and surrounding buffer zones marked in blue. Vegetation mapping demonstrated how fragmented the site was, and even in areas of consolidated foliage the site was classified as low-grade habitat.

Figure 325. The routing for Widow's Walk golf course artfully avoided the most important environmental resource areas of the site, and where mitigation had to be done it enriched those low-quality areas it impacted.

financial feasibility study was commissioned and completed which favorably supported the golf course idea, and at the most heavily attended town meeting in memory, the citizens of Scituate passed the golf course proposal by a vote of almost 20 to 1.

Getting environmental approvals for any project in Massachusetts is very difficult, especially one that is close to salt marshes, has a town well on it, and outwardly appears to be a productive natural area. Mapping and initial environmental resource area limits were started in the autumn of 1994 and completed by December, when the first submittal was made to the town's conservation commission (see figure 324). The planning team demonstrated why they believed the site was so biologically poor, and how development of a profit-producing golf course would enhance the wildlife value of the property. It was at this point that the project, now named "Widow's Walk" for the rooftop viewing platform found on old New England seacoast homes, was accepted as a national demonstration project by the *Golf Digest*–initiated conference. Widow's Walk now became the collaborative effort of golf course and environmental interests, with the objective of producing the least environmentally impacting golf course possible while enhancing wildlife potential (see figure 325).

Best management practices for Widow's Walk are rooted in century-old techniques, and are based upon successes and knowledge gained at contemporary golf courses like Devil's Paintbrush. The entire golf course, except for greens, will be planted to a fine fescue blend of grasses, as was done in the late 1800s, when little irrigation was used and low fertility rates were the norm. Using today's improved fine fescue

Figure 326. The greatest golf courses of the world have so many redeeming and timeless qualities that the maintenance standard is not to perpetuate lush green, but rather at times to allow healthy brown. Widow's Walk is prepared to sacrifice forced green grass for healthy brown to save water, fertilizer, pesticides, and fossil fuel used in maintenance.

grasses with bred-in endophyte to resist insects and disease, the turf on Widow's Walk will require about one-half the amount of water, fertilizer, pesticide, and fossil fuel for maintenance compared to the usual New England course. The turf will turn off-color or even brown during summer's heat and drought, but it will offer playing conditions normally associated with the great links courses of the world (see figure 326). Landscaping will be exclusively with native vegetation using experimental techniques that are hoped to improve percentages of transplanting success. Irrigation water will come from abandoned, nonpotable wells, with the thought of using the golf course turf as a biological filter to remove excess minerals and recharge the aquifer with potable water. Since little or no topsoil exists on the site, composted sewage sludge will be added to the pure sand to speed development of topsoil and establishment of vast populations of beneficial soil organisms.

In the pursuit of comparable and transferable pure knowledge, six greens will be built according to the USGA recommendations—six to the California concept, and six greens will be push-up or topsoil (loam). A water meter and leachate sampling pit installed at each green should permit a comparison of efficiencies and conservation practices of each type of green. Several tile drainage systems will be experimented with to see whether any practical differences are discernable. Recycling, composting, and reuse driven management practices will be implemented, with the aim of finding and sharing best management practices with others.

Corporate sponsors are being solicited to fund pure research and educational efforts within and as part of the Widow's Walk site. The goal of the corporate commitment is to produce meaningful, transferable information, technology, and practices for future developers and homeowners, as well as convincing golfers that lowering maintenance standards of lush green does not diminish the pleasure of golf.

No one involved with Widow's Walk expects it to be without problems or mistakes. The only expectation is that those mistakes will not be repeated, but successes will. This is a noble experiment that will hopefully dispel many myths about golf and the environment, and will expose the ridiculousness of anti-golf propagandists. Truth is the eternal child of the universe—for it never grows old. Other research efforts are being coordinated with local universities and schools, as well as other environmental interest groups.

Postscript

I have tried to communicate to you, my patient reader, about 40 years of experience and education on the design, construction, and maintenance of a golf course. Even after all that time and experience I still wonder at the process. It is both methodical and mystical—occasionally simultaneously. There is no right answer, but there are lots of wrong ones. What constitutes a great golf course is purely subjective, but amazingly some golf courses are hailed universally as being able to induce awe; I am still searching for a mathematical formula to describe that correctness. A mechanically correct golf course might be boring to play, a visually stimulating one might have poor shot values, and either kind might be impossible to maintain.

Golf course design is as changeable as clothing fashions, and what is considered good design by one generation may be abhorred by the next.

Figure 327. A great golf hole has physical and etherial qualities that make it both scary and serene simultaneously, like the 234- to 120-yard par 3 3rd hole at Westwood Plateau.

Figure 328. Complete golf courses have the power to ignite the senses, and intensify the pleasure beyond that of their individual elements. The beauty of the 7th hole at Glenmaura National is recognized instantly.

The only true test of greatness is not some rating or list, or the name of the person who designed or built it, or even what competitions were contested there. The true test is time.

If a golf course can persist through changes in fashion—or shifts in social values, or innovations in golf equipment and golf course maintenance—virtually unchanged because it is so satisfying to its users, and its form fits its function, then it is a damn good golf course. But to inspire awe, a golf course must possess not only timeless values, it must transcend simple pleasure and the landscape must communicate to the golfer and burn unforgettable images into his brain that when triggered produce intense pleasure.

A golf shot lasts for a few seconds, and a round for a few hours (if you're lucky), but the memory of that shot or round has the potential to last a lifetime.

Golf can transform physical exertion into ethereal bliss, and the golf course can just be the place this happens; or, it can add to the intensity. No golf course is truly bad if it permits even a small amount of this transformation. The magic of a golf course cannot be measured by slope rating, par, or yardage, but rather by the memories it produces for those who play it. Each of us has his or her own idea of what makes a perfect golf course, just as each of us has a different idea of our ideal spouse, lover, or parent. So every golf course is loved by someone. In fact, one of the sacred rules of etiquette a golf course architect should learn is: given a choice of saying something unkind about a person's golf course or spouse—always choose the spouse.

I sincerely hope that by reading my words and understanding my humble attempts at analyzing and explaining the golf course, I can move you one step closer to reaching the state of awe. My goal for this effort is not only to chronicle the state of golf course design in the 1990s for future historians, but also to help each golfer become a connoisseur. Understanding the complexities of even a seemingly simple golf course can increase your pleasure of it, and foster that love affair that develops between the golfer and his or her course.

Good luck, have fun, and may you experience, at least once, a state of awe.

Michael J. Hurdzan, Ph.D.
Golf Course Lover

APPENDIX A

Allied Associations of Golf

American Society of Golf Course Architects
221 N. LaSalle Street
Chicago, IL 60601
(312) 372-7090

Club Managers Association of America
1733 King Street
Alexandria, VA 22314
(703) 739-9500

Golf Course Builders of America
920 Airport Road, Suite 210
Chapel Hill, NC 29514
(919) 942-8922

Golf Course Superintendents Association of America
1421 Research Park Drive
Lawrence, KS 66049
(913) 841-2240

Ladies Professional Golf Association
2570 W. International Speedway Blvd.
Daytona Beach, FL 32114
(904) 254-8800

National Club Association
3050 K. Street N.W.
Suite 300
Washington, DC 20007
(202) 625-2080

National Golf Course Owners of America
19 Exchange Street
P.O. Box 1061
Charleston, SC 29402
(803) 577-5239

National Golf Foundation
1150 South U.S. Highway 1
Jupiter, FL 33477
(407) 744-6006

Professional Golf Association of America
100 Avenue of the Champions
P.O. Box 10961
Palm Beach Gardens, FL 33418
(407) 624-8400

PGA Tour
112 TPC Boulevard
Ponte Vedra, FL 32082
(904) 285-3700

United States Golf Association
Golf House
P.O. Box 708
Far Hills, NJ 07931
(908) 234-2300

INDEX

NAPLES NATIONAL
GOLF CLUB
NAPLES, FLORIDA
HURDZAN GOLF COURSE DESIGN, Inc.